TAKING SIDES

Clashing Views in

Life-Span Development

FOURTH EDITION

Selected, Edited, and with Introductions by

Andrew M. Guest
University of Portland

D1508973

Connect
Learn
Succeed™

TAKING SIDES: CLASHING VIEWS IN LIFE-SPAN DEVELOPMENT, FOURTH EDITION

1 2 3 4 5 6 7 8 9 0 DOC/DOC 1 0 9 8 7 6 5 4 3 2

MHID: 0-07-805029-4
ISBN: 978-0-07-805029-9
ISSN: 1559-2642 (print)

Managing Editor: *Larry Loeppke*
Developmental Editor: *Jade Benedict*
Permissions Coordinator: *Lenny J. Behnke*
Senior Marketing Communications Specialist: *Mary Klein*
Project Manager: *Erin Melloy*
Design Coordinator: *Brenda A. Rolwes*
Cover Graphics: *Rick D. Noel*
Buyer: *Nicole Baumgartner*
Media Project Manager: *Sridevi Palani*

Compositor: MPS Limited, a Macmillan Company
Cover Image: © Brand X Pictures/PunchStock RF

Editors/Academic Advisory Board

Members of the Academic Advisory Board are instrumental in the final selection of articles for each edition of TAKING SIDES. Their review of articles for content, level, and appropriateness provides critical direction to the editors and staff. We think that you will find their careful consideration well reflected in this volume.

TAKING SIDES: Clashing Views in LIFE-SPAN DEVELOPMENT

Fourth Edition

EDITOR

Andrew M. Guest
University of Portland

ACADEMIC ADVISORY BOARD MEMBERS

Editors/Academic Advisory Board continued

Preface

Everyone has opinions about what matters in lifespan development. Sometimes we blame it all on our parents—the good and the bad—but other times we think genes and evolution make for our destinies. Some of us fear for younger generations confronting so many new risks and challenges, while other long for the freedom and opportunities of contemporary childhood. We often define adult success by the tangible results of career and family life, yet we also idealize abstract qualities such as happiness and well-being. Most of us dread aging, even while envying the freedom and wisdom of older adults. These contrasting opinions suggest that the study of lifespan development is inherently controversial; the purpose of this book is to make that controversy useful. This book provides educated and intelligent perspectives on issues that are important to everyone's life, not to mention being important to academic study of the lifespan.

This fourth edition of *Taking Sides: Clashing Views on Controversial Issues in Lifespan Development* presents 19 issues that challenge students and scholars to think deeply about issues confronted through the ages and stages of our lives. Nine of these issues are entirely new to this edition, offering both recent controversies and updated perspectives on ongoing debates. In all cases, each issue is framed by a question about what, why, or how we develop, and each question is addressed from two distinct perspectives selected from previously published work. These 38 pieces of previously published writing represent the perspectives of a broad group of scholars and experts. Each of the 19 issues also has an introduction with an explanation of how and why it is important for the larger study of lifespan development, and a postscript providing challenge questions to elaborate on the issue along with suggestions for further reading.

The book presents the issues in an order that generally fits the chronology of the lifespan, but also balances topics addressing different domains of development including the physical, cognitive, and social. As such, the materials and ideas dealt with in this book derive from diverse fields of study including psychology, sociology, biology, cognitive science, neuroscience, education, gerontology, and pediatrics. In fact, one appealing aspect of studying lifespan development is that it is an interdisciplinary subject focused more on answering interesting questions than on exclusive theories or methods. Thus, while the materials provided with each issue allow an understanding of what experts in diverse subjects think, the challenge for readers is to use the evidence and opinions to answer the questions for themselves. The book explains, for example, why understanding how much our development depends upon our parents is important, but it is up to readers to take that explanation and the available evidence to establish their own educated position.

Although the perspectives presented in this book represent educated thinking on these issues, the reason the issues are controversial is because that thinking is still evolving. Researchers are always developing new techniques for studying lifespan development, individuals are always adapting to the different challenges faced at each stage of life, and societies are always changing the way they treat children, adults, and the elderly. Likewise, readers of this book, as experts in their own lifespan development, will have valuable experiences and perspectives that complement those discussed in the book. In the end, what is most important is to have a point of view on these issues that is educated and informed—sometimes that point of view will match previous opinions, other times it will represent a dramatic change. In all cases, however, the most valuable understandings derive from using controversy as an opportunity to think through the ongoing challenges of lifespan development.

A word to the instructor   An *Instructor's Resource Guide with Test Questions* (multiple-choice and essay) is available through the publisher for the instructor using Taking Sides in the classroom. A general guidebook, *Using Taking Sides in the Classroom,* which discusses methods and techniques for integrating the pro-con approach into any classroom setting, is also available. An online version of *Using Taking Sides in the Classroom* and a correspondence service for Taking Sides adopters can be found at http://www.mhhe/cls. *Taking Sides: Clashing Views in Life-Span Development* is only one title in the Taking Sides series. If you are interested in seeing the table of contents for any of the other titles, please visit the Taking Sides Web site at http://www.mhhe.com/cls.

Acknowledgments   As editor, I'd like to say thanks to my current students at the University of Portland (who allowed me the opportunity to draft material with an intelligent and critical audience), and to my former teachers and colleagues at the University of Chicago's Committee on Human Development (who gave me the foundation for thinking seriously about the lifespan). Thanks also to Sara and Zane Guest for kindly sharing a living laboratory.

Contents in Brief

Contents

UNIT 1   GENERAL ISSUES IN THE STUDY OF LIFESPAN DEVELOPMENT   1

Stanford University professors of biology Paul Ehrlich and Marcus Feldman argue that human behavior exhibits such complexity that genetic programs simply cannot explain the way people develop. Psychologist and researcher Gary Marcus asserts that research clearly demonstrates how a relatively small number of genes influence our environmental learning by "cascading" to determine the paths of our behavioral development.

Developmental psychology writer Judith Rich Harris presents a strong and provocative argument suggesting that parents do not influence child development to any significant degree, while peers and social groups have a primary influence. Harvard psychologist Howard Gardner reviews Harris's work and suggests her argument is overstated and misleading—parents do matter.

Yale law professor and self-proclaimed "Tiger Mother" Amy Chua argues that Chinese parenting is distinct from most Western parenting in its rigor, high expectations, and unwillingness to accept anything less than true excellence. Sociologist Markella B. Rutherford instead sees the "Tiger Mother" idea as just another example of the types of privileged parenting that ultimately prioritizes self-confidence, self-esteem, and perpetuates differences more dependent on class than on culture.

Michael Robb, who are scholars of children and the media, describe limitations on infant's ability to learn from electronic media and note concerns about the diminishing of direct infant to parent interactions.

Kelley King, Michael Gurian, and Kathy Stevens, all affiliated with an institute that advocates for accommodating gender differences in learning, identify developmental differences between boys and girls that are deep enough to merit distinct educational practices. Neuroscientist Lise Eliot offers a brain-based perspective to suggest that popular applications of findings on gender differences exaggerate innate tendencies. Instead, Eliot emphasizes that socialization practices are much more influential to the ways boys and girls learn.

The Child and Adolescent Bipolar Foundation offers an overview of how pediatric bipolar disorder is defined, identified, and studied to help parents and others understand this relatively new way of thinking about psychiatric problems among children. Child psychiatrist Stuart L. Kaplan thinks that the concept of pediatric bipolar disorder is too eagerly embraced considering its newness, and that there is insufficient evidence for labeling children with a serious psychiatric problem that historically only applied to adults.

Psychologist and researcher Craig A. Anderson finds that violent video game play consistently associates with aggression and problematic behavior, arguing that there is no good reason for making them available to children. Cheryl K. Olsen, Lawrence Kutner, and Eugene Beresin have all been affiliated with a Harvard Medical School center devoted to studying mental health and the media. In their work they recognize the potential risks of violent video games, but find that most children play video games in ways that pose little risk and offer some potential benefit.

Developmental psychologist Jeffrey Jensen Arnett has earned wide acclaim among scholars for defining an "emerging adulthood" as a distinctly modern stage of the life-span. Life-span research scholars Lew B. Hendry and Marion Kloep argue that defining emerging adulthood as a discrete stage provides a misleading account of the age period between the late teens and the mid- to late twenties.

Jean M. Twenge and Joshua D. Foster present evidence from surveys of college students that reinforces their claim of a "narcissism epidemic." Research psychologists M. Brent Donnellan, Kali H. Trzesniewski, and Richard W. Robins take the evidence used by Twenge and colleagues and draw different conclusions, arguing claims of an epidemic are greatly exaggerated.

Religion scholar Diane Winston describes interacting with students at her university and finding that the students have vibrant religious engagements despite eschewing traditional types of religiosity. Tim Clydesdale, a sociologist who studies young adults transitioning from high school, finds instead that most college students "stow" away their religious engagements and generally immerse themselves in other identity commitments.

Philosophers Janice E. Graham and Karen Ritchie raise concerns that rigidly defining Mild Cognitive Impairment (MCI) as a disorder associated with aging artificially creates the harmful impression that the conditions of old age are merely biomedical problems. Medical doctor and researcher Ronald C. Petersen has been a prominent proponent of defining MCI as an intermediate stage between normal aging and Alzheimer's disease. In this selection he counters Graham and Ritchie by emphasizing the usefulness of MCI as a diagnosis.

Michael J. Rae was lead author on an article presenting the position a group of prominent antiaging scholars. They promote more funding and support for what they consider promising research directions towards slowing or even curing aging. Molecular biologist Robin Holliday takes a skeptical view of antiaging science, coming away from his own work on cellular aging with a respect for the necessary inevitability of old age.

Correlation Guide

The *Taking Sides* series presents current issues in a debate-style format designed to stimulate student interest and develop critical thinking skills. Each issue is thoughtfully framed with an issue summary, an issue introduction, and challenge questions. The pro and con essays—selected for their liveliness and substance—represent the arguments of leading scholars and commentators in their fields.

Taking Sides: Clashing Views in Life-Span Development, 4/e is an easy-to-use reader that presents issues on important topics such as the *value of marriage, violent video games,* and the idea of a *narcissism epidemic.* For more information on *Taking Sides* and other *McGraw-Hill Contemporary Learning Series* titles, visit http://www.mhhe.com/cls.

This convenient guide matches the issues in **Taking Sides: Clashing Views in Life-Span Development, 4/e** with the corresponding chapters in three of our best-selling McGraw-Hill Human Development textbooks by Crandell et al., Santrock, and Papalia/Feldman.

Taking Sides: Life-Span Development, 4/e	Human Development, 10/e by Crandell	A Topical Approach to Life-Span Development, 6/e by Santrock	Experience Human Development, 12/e by Papalia/Feldman
Issue 1: Does the Cultural Environment Influence Lifespan Development More Than Our Genes?	**Chapter 2:** Theories of Development **Chapter 3:** Reproduction, Heredity, and Prenatal Development	**Chapter 3:** Physical Development and Biological Aging	**Chapter 2:** Theory and Research
Issue 2: Are Peers More Important Than Parents During the Process of Development?	**Chapter 8:** Early Childhood: Emotional and Social Development	**Chapter 11:** The Self, Identity, and Personality	**Chapter 8:** Psychosocial Development in Early Childhood
Issue 3: Is Chinese Parenting Culturally Distinct?	**Chapter 8:** Early Childhood: Emotional and Social Development **Chapter 10:** Middle Childhood: Emotional and Social Development	**Chapter 13:** Moral Development, Values and Religion	**Chapter 8:** Psychosocial Development in Early Childhood **Chapter 10:** Psychosocial Development in Middle Childhood
Issue 4: Is Drinking Alcohol While Pregnant an Unnecessary Risk to Prenatal Development?	**Chapter 3:** Reproduction, Heredity, and Prenatal Development	**Chapter 3:** Physical Development and Biological Aging	**Chapter 4:** Birth and Physical Development During the First Three Years
Issue 5: Is Breastfeeding Inevitably Best for Healthy Development?	**Chapter 4:** Birth and Physical Development: The First Two Years	**Chapter 3:** Physical Development and Biological Aging **Chapter 4:** Health	**Chapter 4:** Birth and Physical Development During the First Three Years

Taking Sides: Life-Span Development, 4/e	Human Development, 10/e by Crandell	A Topical Approach to Life-Span Development, 6/e by Santrock	Experience Human Development, 12/e by Papalia/Feldman
Issue 6: Are There Good Reasons to Allow Infants to Consume Electronic Media, Such as Television?	**Chapter 5:** Infancy: Cognitive and Language Development	**Chapter 6:** Cognitive Developmental Approaches **Chapter 7:** Information Processing	**Chapter 6:** Psychosocial Development During the First Three Years
Issue 7: Do Innate Gender Differences Influence How Children Learn?	**Chapter 7:** Early Childhood: Physical and Cognitive Development	**Chapter 11:** The Self, Identity, and Personality **Chapter 12:** Gender and Sexuality	**Chapter 7:** Physical and Cognitive Development in Early Childhood
Issue 8: Should Bipolar Disorder be Diagnosed and Treated in Children?	**Chapter 7:** Early Childhood: Physical and Cognitive Development	**Chapter 10:** Emotional Development	**Chapter 8:** Psychosocial Development in Early Childhood
Issue 9: Are Violent Video Games Necessarily Bad for Children?	**Chapter 10:** Middle Childhood: Emotional and Social Development **Chapter 12:** Adolescence: Emotional and Social Development	**Chapter 10:** Emotional Development	**Chapter 10:** Psychosocial Development in Middle Childhood **Chapter 12:** Psychosocial Development in Adolescence
Issue 10: Should Contemporary Adolescents Be Engaged in More Structured Activities?	**Chapter 12:** Adolescence: Emotional and Social Development	**Chapter 10:** Emotional Development **Chapter 15:** Peers and the Sociocultural World	**Chapter 11:** Physical and Cognitive Development in Adolescence **Chapter 12:** Psychosocial Development in Adolescence
Issue 11: Does the Adolescent Brain Make Risk Taking Inevitable?	**Chapter 12:** Adolescence: Emotional and Social Development	**Chapter 10:** Emotional Development **Chapter 11:** The Self, Identity, and Personality	**Chapter 12:** Psychosocial Development in Adolescence
Issue 12: Is There Such a Thing as "Emerging Adulthood"?	**Chapter 13:** Early Adulthood: Physical and Cognitive Development	**Chapter 11:** The Self, Identity, and Personality **Chapter 15:** Peers and the Sociocultural World	**Chapter 13:** Physical and Cognitive Development in Emerging and Young Adulthood **Chapter 14:** Psychosocial Development in Emerging and Young Adulthood
Issue 13: Is There a "Narcissism Epidemic" Among Contemporary Young Adults?	**Chapter 14:** Early Adulthood: Emotional and Social Development	**Chapter 11:** The Self, Identity, and Personality **Chapter 13:** Moral Development, Values, and Religion	**Chapter 14:** Psychosocial Development in Emerging and Young Adulthood

(Continued)

Taking Sides: Life-Span Development, 4/e	Human Development, 10/e by Crandell	A Topical Approach to Life-Span Development, 6/e by Santrock	Experience Human Development, 12/e by Papalia/Feldman
Issue 14: Are Today's College Students Interested in Engaging with Religion and Spirituality?	**Chapter 14:** Early Adulthood: Emotional and Social Development	**Chapter 13:** Moral Development, Values, and Religion	**Chapter 14:** Psychosocial Development in Emerging and Young Adulthood
Issue 15: Do Adults Need to Place More Value on Marriage?	**Chapter 14:** Early Adulthood: Emotional and Social Development **Chapter 16:** Middle Adulthood: Emotional and Social Development	**Chapter 13:** Moral Development, Values, and Religion	**Chapter 16:** Psychosocial Development in Middle Adulthood
Issue 16: Is Parenthood a Detriment to Well-Being?	**Chapter 14:** Early Adulthood: Emotional and Social Development	**Chapter 14:** Families, Lifestyles, and Parenting	**Chapter 16:** Psychosocial Development in Middle Adulthood
Issue 17: Is More Civic Engagement Among Older Adults Necessarily Better?	**Chapter 16:** Middle Adulthood: Emotional and Social Development **Chapter 18:** Late Adulthood: Emotional and Social Development	**Chapter 14:** Families, Lifestyles, and Parenting	**Chapter 16:** Psychosocial Development in Middle Adulthood **Chapter 18:** Psychosocial Development in Late Adulthood
Issue 18: Is "Mild Cognitive Impairment" Too Similar to Normal Aging to be a Relevant Concept?	**Chapter 17:** Late Adulthood: Physical and Cognitive Development	**Chapter 6:** Cognitive Developmental Approaches	**Chapter 17:** Physical and Cognitive Development in Late Adulthood
Issue 19: Should We Try to "Cure" Old Age?	**Chapter 17:** Late Adulthood: Physical and Cognitive Development	**Chapter 6:** Cognitive Developmental Approaches	**Chapter 18:** Psychosocial Development in Late Adulthood

Topic Guide

This topic guide suggests how the selections in this book relate to the subjects covered in your course. You may want to use the topics listed on these pages to search the Web more easily. They are arranged to reflect the units of this Taking Sides reader. You can link to these sites by going to http://www.mhhe.com/cls. All the articles that relate to each topic are listed below the bold-faced term.

Adolescence
10. Should Contemporary Adolescents Be Engaged in More Structured Activities?
11. Does the Adolescent Brain Make Risk Taking Inevitable?

Adulthood
13. Is There a "Narcissism Epidemic" Among Contemporary Young Adults?
15. Do Adults Need to Place More Value on Marriage?
17. Is More Civic Engagement Among Older Adults Necessarily Better?

Aggression
9. Are Violent Video Games Necessarily Bad for Children?

Aging
18. Is "Mild Cognitive Impairment" Too Similar to Normal Aging to be a Relevant Concept?
19. Should We Try to "Cure" Old Age?

Brain Development
6. Are There Good Reasons to Allow Infants to Consume Electronic Media, Such as Television?
7. Do Innate Gender Differences Influence How Children Learn?
11. Does the Adolescent Brain Make Risk Taking Inevitable?
12. Is There Such a Thing as "Emerging Adulthood"?
18. Is "Mild Cognitive Impairment" Too Similar to Normal Aging to be a Relevant Concept?

Children
8. Should Bipolar Disorder be Diagnosed and Treated in Children?

9. Are Violent Video Games Necessarily Bad for Children?

Cognition
6. Are There Good Reasons to Allow Infants to Consume Electronic Media, Such as Television?

Creativity
10. Should Contemporary Adolescents Be Engaged in More Structured Activities?

Culture
1. Does the Cultural Environment Influence Lifespan Development More Than Our Genes?
3. Is Chinese Parenting Culturally Distinct?
12. Is There Such a Thing as "Emerging Adulthood"?
13. Is There a "Narcissism Epidemic" Among Contemporary Young Adults?
14. Are Today's College Students Interested in Engaging with Religion and Spirituality?

Early Childhood
8. Should Bipolar Disorder be Diagnosed and Treated in Children?

Emotions
11. Does the Adolescent Brain Make Risk Taking Inevitable?

Ethics and Moral Choices
13. Is There a "Narcissism Epidemic" Among Contemporary Young Adults?
14. Are Today's College Students Interested in Engaging with Religion and Spirituality?
17. Is More Civic Engagement Among Older Adults Necessarily Better?

Introduction

Perspectives and Lifespan Development

One of the best things about studying lifespan development is that it matters to all of us. Whether you like it or not you have a vested interest in at least one lifespan: your own. What kinds of relationships do you value? What will be your life's work? Are you happy? Are you normal? Should you be? Whether your interest in those types of questions is something you reflect on carefully, try to ignore, or study systematically, lifespan development is relevant to everyone.

Ironically, however, that very relevance also means that one of the most difficult things about studying lifespan development is that it matters to all of us. Many of the issues that arise in the study of development, and many of the controversial issues in this book are ones that evoke strong personal opinions. What is the responsibility of parents? Do children need more structure or more freedom? Is old age something to fear? These types of questions are the object of much scholarly theorizing and many research studies, but academic perspectives are often less persuasive than how someone feels.

The challenge of studying lifespan development thus becomes to balance one's personal interest with the knowledge and methods accumulated through systematic study. The question of what kinds of relationships you value becomes a matter of looking at studies of how parents and peers influence our personality. Or the question of how to be happy becomes a matter of considering the statistical relationships between variables such as career success, parenthood, religious participation, and psychological well-being. The challenge becomes letting personal experiences and scholarly perspectives inform each other, even when they might initially seem contradictory.

I have recently had many reminders about the challenges of balancing personal and scholarly perspectives thanks to witnessing the start of what I consider a very important lifespan: the birth of my first child. When delving into the scholarly literature about questions such as whether drinking alcohol while pregnant is an unnecessary risk to prenatal development (Issue 4) or whether breastfeeding is necessarily best for babies (Issue 5) I cannot help but think about my experiences with my infant son. I think about the overwhelming joy I felt when he was born healthy, and I was able to count ten fingers and ten toes, not sure how much of that had to do with my wife's careful attention to her own health while pregnant. Or I think about occasional nights lying awake wondering about my son's crying, not sure if he is hungry or cold or uncomfortable or just not sure himself. And I find myself constantly confronted by big picture questions such as whether the things we have done as caregivers or the genes we passed along as parents have more influence on his seemingly boundless energy, the innocent intensity with which he stares into the eyes of everyone we meet, or the way he smiles in toothless wonder at the sight of fuzzy animals.

I have also found myself wondering whether having a child allows me to more intelligently analyze controversial issues in the study of lifespan development. It has certainly offered me a new perspective on many of the issues in this book. When I think about questions such as how electronic media influences the development of infants (Issue 6) or older children (Issue 9), I now think about how I hope to manage my own son's experiences with the ubiquitous presence of television, video games, social media, and other accoutrements of growing up in the modern world. Or when I think about education-related issues such as gender differences in learning (Issue 7) or the roots of adult expertise (Issue 17), I now wonder about what I can learn that might help me ensure my son has the best opportunities possible to fulfill his potential. But I am also aware that these personal investments constitute a new bias in my own ways of thinking about lifespan development: I don't think having a child makes me better able to analyze controversial issues in the study of lifespan development, but I do now think about those issues from another valuable perspective.

If nothing else, then, having a child has helped me further appreciate the ways that we all evaluate controversies related to lifespan development from our own particular perspectives, and the way we all benefit from being sure to allow for multiple perspectives. Being able to think about these controversies through the lens of parenting offers me new perspectives, but it also makes it important for me to recognize the value of perspectives from nonparents, or from scholars in other disciplines, or from scholars in other historical epochs. It reminds me that the most sophisticated understandings of lifespan development come from carefully considering a diverse variety of perspectives, and using those perspectives to formulate an educated understanding of my own. This process has long been how knowledge has advanced in the study of lifespan development, and it is worth considering how some of that history may relate to the contemporary controversies discussed in this book.

Historical Perspectives

The most basic controversy related to the study of lifespan development has seemingly always been the famous debate between nature and nurture. Parents, societies, philosophers, and scientists have long negotiated between an assumption that people have an inherent developmental destiny (i.e., the person my son will grow up to be is already programmed into his disproportionately large head), and the knowledge that what happens to people in the social world can alter that destiny (i.e., my son's future is mostly a matter of his ongoing experiences). Although these positions have an extensive history, in academic circles they are most commonly identified with seventeenth- and eighteenth-century European philosophers Jean-Jacques Rousseau and John Locke. Rousseau suggested that infants were "noble savages" born with an inherent nature that is only corrupted by society. Locke, in contrast, is known for the claim that people come into the world as a *tabula rasa,* or blank slate, to be shaped entirely by experience. This basic opposition, according to the book *Raising America* by Ann Hulbert, seems to consistently cycle through historical and contemporary debates between "experts" on development. In slightly varying forms, there are always some experts arguing that people are primarily the product of potent natural dispositions and some experts arguing that social experiences are what matters.

What has changed historically in debates about lifespan development is how we place questions of nature and nurture into the context of different ages and stages. In fact, the very idea of childhood as a distinct lifespan stage, rather than as just adulthood in miniature, may be a relatively recent invention. In a famous and controversial book titled *Centuries of Childhood*, French historian Philippe Aries argued Western societies only began treating children as different from adults in the fifteenth and sixteenth centuries, and such treatment did not become commonplace until the nineteenth and twentieth centuries. This theory generated strong reactions, with many scholars responding to say that childhood has always been associated with distinct characteristics, but imagine how different society would be if we dressed children like adults, talked to children like adults, and put children to work like adults.

Instead, people now often seem reluctant to ever fully embrace adulthood. Due to factors including higher educational expectations and less urgency to get married and start families, the transition to worlds of adulthood with work and responsibility happens later than ever. When I ask the traditional-age college students in my classes whether they are adults, they are usually not quite sure. In most legal senses they are adults at 18 years of age, but many 18-year-olds do not feel fully adult.

It turns out that although we now generally accept the concept of the lifespan as a series of stages, the parameters for those stages are not always clear. Where does "childhood" start and stop? What does it mean to be "middle-aged?" Who is "elderly?" These stages are often as much about social context, and about how people feel, as they are about chronological age. And some of that social context is set by famous stage theories of lifespan development.

Perhaps the most well-known stage theory was presented by Sigmund Freud over a century ago, who suggested that formative developmental experiences cohered around different foci at different ages: infants were concerned with oral gratification—being able to suck and bite, toddlers with anal functions and toilet training, young children with phallic organs—learning about gender roles, and teenagers with genital functions—experiencing puberty and a blossoming sexuality. Though few scholars take the details of Freud's theory very seriously anymore, due largely to a lack of convincing evidence to supplement Freud's clinical anecdotes, the broad idea that early experiences shape personality through life is now taken for granted.

Similarly, the Swiss psychologist Jean Piaget virtually founded modern developmental psychology in the early- to mid-twentieth century through his recognition that the manner of children's thought progresses in orderly patterns. In a way, Piaget provided enduring support for stage models, drawing on careful observations to suggest that children's cognitive development is not just less sophisticated than that of adults—it is qualitatively different. Thus, when children make assumptions about toy dolls being alive, or about objects only existing when they can see them, they are not making "errors" but instead are demonstrating patterns of thought that meaningfully represent their age.

A third important stage theory from the history of lifespan development was put forth by Erik Erikson—a one-time student of Freud. In the middle part of the twentieth century, Erikson took Freud's basic insights about personality, built on the increasing popularity of stage models for the lifespan, and outlined an influential framework for understanding lifespan development—a framework that helps to broadly organize this book. Erikson's model of the lifespan had two major advantages over previous models. First, in contrast to Freud, Erikson reduced the emphasis on sexuality, focusing on psychosocial challenges rather than psychosexual stages. Second, in contrast to both Freud and Piaget, Erikson asserted that developmental stages continue throughout life, rather than ending after adolescence.

Though this now seems somewhat obvious—of course adults continue to develop—for much of the twentieth-century scholars paid little attention to anything other than child development. The implicit assumption was that the lifespan included a period of rapid growth during childhood, a period of decline at the end of life, and was largely at stasis in the many years of adulthood. In recent decades, however, scholars have focused much more on patterned development and change during the long years of adulthood.

Erik Erikson was also influential because he recognized the "biopsychosocial" nature of lifespan development. Although biology, psychology, and society are often studied separately, biological factors (such as physical health, sexual maturation, and genetic predispositions) interact with psychological factors (such as personality, attitudes, and cognitive appraisals), which interact with social factors (such as schools, peer networks, the media, and cultural meaning systems) to craft our individual lives. Over time, scholars interested in lifespan development have become more sophisticated in their ability to study specific topics within each of these domains of development—particularly with technological advances such as brain scanning and gene sequencing—but the basic recognition of development as a biopsychosocial process persists.

The increasing sophistication of research in lifespan development also means that contemporary scholars often focus less on grand theories and more on specialized knowledge. There has been a proliferation of subdisciplines relevant to understanding the lifespan, which offer a rich diversity of perspectives. The issues in this book alone draw on academic disciplines including psychology, sociology, anthropology, education, social work, biology, neuroscience, history, cognitive science, geriatrics, and pediatrics. But all of this work is ultimately addressing questions that have long been at the core of the study of lifespan development: what are the patterns of thought, feeling, and behavior that characterize particular ages and stages, and how do those patterns change over time.

Perspectives in This Book

Building off the historical evolution of the study of lifespan development, this book is organized into seven parts that generally correspond with the stages most commonly delineated by scholars; the book, after an initial part addressing general issues that cross the stages, progresses through prenatal development and infancy, early childhood and middle childhood, adolescence, youth and emerging adulthood, middle adulthood, and later adulthood. As noted above, scholars sometimes debate the specific meaning of these stages (a debate evident in Issue 12 of this book questioning whether there is such a thing as "emerging adulthood") and there are other viable ways to orient the study of lifespan development. Most particularly, some prefer a topical approach to a chronological approach, often focusing on the pieces of the biopsychosocial model individually. The controversies included in this book were selected with a balance of those pieces in mind, such that a more topical biopsychosocial approach might group together issues as follows:

- Focusing on biological topics oriented more to physical health and development by combining Issue 1 (regarding the role of genes and culture in development), Issue 4 (regarding the consumption of alcohol during pregnancy), Issue 5 (regarding breastfeeding), Issue 11 (regarding the brain and adolescent risk taking), and Issue 18 (regarding attempts to "cure" the aging process)
- Focusing on psychological topics oriented more to mental health and cognitive development by combining Issue 2 (regarding the role of parents and peers in development), Issue 6 (regarding the influence of electronic media on infants), Issue 8 (regarding the diagnosis of bipolar disorder in children), Issue 9 (regarding violent video game play), Issue 13 (regarding a potential "narcissism epidemic" among emerging adults), and Issue 18 (regarding "mild cognitive impairment" in old age)
- Focusing on social topics oriented more to cultural issues and personality development by combining Issue 3 (regarding cultural differences and Chinese parenting styles), Issue 7 (regarding gender differences and children's learning), Issue 10 (regarding structured activity participation in adolescence), Issue 14 (regarding college student engagement with religion and spirituality), Issue 15 (regarding the way people value marriage), and Issue 17 (regarding civic engagement among older adults)

Whichever ways the issues in this book are organized, however, the underlying themes are ones that have long provoked controversy: nature or nurture, normal or abnormal, structure or freedom, change or continuity. Although the persistence of these themes can be occasionally confusing and frustrating to those who want to know the "right" answers about development, controversy is how our knowledge of the lifespan advances. Over time, controversies challenge us to explore beyond our personal beliefs, and force us to engage with rigorously gathered evidence. There are several intriguing historical examples of how this matters to lifespan development.

One comes from the very start of the lifespan: what do newborns need immediately after birth? Prior to advances in medical technology during the twentieth century, an extraordinarily high number of babies died before reaching their first birthday (sadly, this is still the case in many parts of the developing world—but that is a slightly different issue). When the germ theory of disease became prominent, doctors and scientists realized that inadequate hygiene and unnecessary exposure to germs caused many infant deaths. In a well-intentioned effort to keep babies safe and healthy, many hospitals started immediately placing newborn babies in sterile conditions separate from human contact—not even their mothers' waiting arms. Over time, such efforts were extended to children born to mothers who were considered deviant, such as those convicted of crimes. The logic in all these cases was that of contagion: Certain types of human contact were too risky for vulnerable infants.

Fortunately, this logic was controversial, and researchers studying the earliest stages of life began to challenge the changing practices. Studies found that children deprived of human contact struggled with physical, social, and psychological deficits: Love mattered as much as hygiene. Researchers began to hypothesize that something about caring interactions, and forming attachment bonds, was virtually essential to healthy human development. The issue was controversial for years, with one side suggesting that infants needed to be kept safely away from excessive contact and the other suggesting that human contact was exactly what made infants safe. Eventually the evidence became overwhelming in favor of the latter position; babies seem to have an innate need for attachment, contact, and simple touch.

In a more contemporary example of how controversy matters, recent decades have brought increasing attention to the role of self-esteem in lifespan development. Due to a confluence of historical and social conditions, the idea that feeling good about one's self is a foundation for healthy development became received wisdom in the 1970s and 1980s. Numerous social service agencies, schools, activity programs, and therapists made promoting self-esteem the centerpiece of efforts to facilitate healthy development. Although self-esteem is still extremely popular—as it is indeed nice to feel good about one's self—scholars have generated controversy by raising important questions about the evidence for self-esteem as a cure for social and personal ills. Despite massive research attention, the evidence suggests that high self-esteem is more a pleasant by-product of competence and achievement rather than a root cause. In some cases, emphasizing self-esteem may even encourage egotism and discourage motivation. Though an industry of self-esteem promoters has resisted the challenge, the controversy continues to have important implications for schools, counselors, parents, and programs. And for scholars the controversy has generated a much more nuanced and realistic perspective on how and why feeling good about one's self might matter.

In both of these examples, and in most of the issues discussed in this book, controversy proves most useful when it challenges us to put aside conventional wisdom and focus on tangible evidence. In the case of infant attachment and touch, both sides cared about healthy babies and both sides deeply believed their side was right. In the case of self-esteem and positive development, both sides care about reducing social ills and both sides believe in what they are doing. Ultimately, however, resolving these issues, and resolving other controversies in social science, requires intelligent interpretations of evidence that go beyond our personal beliefs and experiences.

Going beyond personal beliefs and experiences does not, of course, mean that the personal does not matter. Instead, it means that the personal takes its place alongside the acquired knowledge, methods, and evidence derived from the study of lifespan development. In fact, when I teach with these controversial issues I do not allow my students to make statements that start with "I believe . . ." or "in my opinion . . ." because I want them to make claims and arguments that they can back up with evidence. Students seem to find this hard—they are often more comfortable expressing what they believe than what they have found through their studies—but I tell them that just as in a court of law statements of opinion will be "inadmissible" since they are based on speculation. I do, of course, value the importance of students' beliefs and opinions. In fact, I hope discussing controversial issues allows them to further formulate the beliefs and opinions that matter to them the most. But the point of discussing controversial issues is to learn more than we already know and to reflect on the possibility of our own biases. The point is to recognize the value in understanding multiple viewpoints, and to use those understandings to develop one's own coherent perspective.

My own perspective on the lifespan is currently so overwhelmed by the constant needs and joy of an infant son that I suspect my students may soon turn the tables on me. They may have to start reminding me that speculation based on personal experience (as a father) is "inadmissible." If nothing else, it would be a way to get me to stop telling that particular type of kid story that only a father could love. But it would also be true to the nature of studying controversial issues in the study of lifespan development, and the reality that deep understandings require accounting for multiple perspectives and rigorous evidence. I would be doing a disservice to my students if I let my experiences as a parent crowd out the historical, theoretical, empirical, and nonparent perspectives on the lifespan that are represented in this book, just as we all do a disservice to ourselves when we do not consider issues from different sides. Whether you have recently had a child, or have simply thought about issues such as relationships, work, or happiness as they relate to your own life, keep in mind that the way lifespan development matters to all of us can simultaneously be its best and its most difficult quality.

Internet References . . .

Socialpsychology.org

This Web site provides academic resources and links related to developmental psychology.

http://www.socialpsychology.org/develop.htm

American Psychological Association

The American Psychological Association offers general information and resources for many of the issues most pertinent to developmental psychology and lifespan development.

http://www.apa.org/

Nature Versus Nurture

An overview of the debate on whether nature or nurture—culture or genes—is more influential in lifespan development.

http://en.wikipedia.org/wiki/Nature_versus_nurture

American Academy of Pediatrics

The American Academy of Pediatrics is a professional organization focused on the health of children. Their Web site and provides featured articles, books, and other reference materials on children's health topics.

http://www.aap.org/

judithrichharris.info

This Web site provides extensive links related to the controversial argument that parents do not matter as much in development as most people think.

http://judithrichharris.info/tna/index.html

Future of Children

Future of Children is a digital journal, providing an example of developmental research aimed at promoting effective policies and programs for families and children.

http://www.futureofchildren.org/

Society for Research on Child Development

The Society for Research on Child Development is an interdisciplinary scholarly group focused on studying development up to adulthood. The Web site offers many highly regarded publications and other reference material.

http://www.srcd.org/

General Issues in the Study of Lifespan Development

*A*lthough this book organizes development into a series of stages, several issues central to understanding the lifespan are not exclusive to one particular age. These issues relate to larger questions about the nature of development: what forces and characteristics shape us into the people we become? The issues in this section deal with this larger question, and provide a foundation for thinking about specific stages, by directly addressing the role of culture, genes, parents, and social class in shaping the thoughts, feelings, behaviors, and experiences that make us human.

- Does the Cultural Environment Influence Lifespan Development More Than Our Genes?

- Are Peers More Important Than Parents During the Process of Development?

- Is Chinese Parenting Culturally Distinct?

ISSUE 1

Does the Cultural Environment Influence Lifespan Development More Than Our Genes?

YES: Paul Ehrlich and Marcus Feldman, from "Genes and Cultures: What Creates Our Behavioral Phenome?" *Current Anthropology* (February 2003)

NO: Gary Marcus, from "Making the Mind: Why We've Misunderstood the Nature-Nurture Debate," *Boston Review* (December 2003/January 2004)

Learning Outcomes

As you read the issue, focus on the following points:

1. There are too few genes for any one to determine complex behavior by itself, but they may shape behavior through cascades and combinations.
2. Gender differences are an example of an area where seemingly innate differences vary significantly by cultural and historical context.
3. Focusing excessively on the genetic causes of behavior and development has led to horrible social policies such as those of the Nazis during World War II.
4. Our brains are remarkably "plastic" in the sense of changing through development, but those changes are often constrained by genetic limits.

ISSUE SUMMARY

YES: Stanford University professors of biology Paul Ehrlich and Marcus Feldman argue that human behavior exhibits such complexity that genetic programs simply cannot explain the way people develop.

NO: Psychologist and researcher Gary Marcus asserts that research clearly demonstrates how a relatively small number of genes influence our environmental learning by "cascading" to determine the paths of our behavioral development.

Perhaps the most central question in the study of lifespan development is whether nature or nurture exerts more influence on our developing thoughts, feelings, and behavior. Even in daily life, we regularly wonder about people—do they act that way because of things in their experience (nurture), or is it just the way they were born (nature)? This debate takes many different forms, and it underlies many of the important topics of study within lifespan development.

Most reasonable people agree that both nature and nurture, both genes and culture, shape development. Thus, the debate is mostly about the relative influence of each: does nature overwhelm nurture, or does nurture trump nature. Historically, the pendulum of popular opinion has tended to swing back and forth between trusting nature or emphasizing nurture.

In recent years, with advanced technology and research methods, the pendulum seems to have swung in favor of nature. With the ability to identify individual genes and image activity in the brain, scientists have made regular claims about how diverse aspects of behavior and development—everything from political affiliation to sexual behavior—are controlled by innate biology.

In the YES selection, however, renowned biologists Paul Ehrlich and Marcus Feldman argue that biological determinism, the idea that evolved predispositions determine behavior beyond the influence of the environment, does not make biological sense. Drawing from the recent mapping of the human genome, they claim there are simply too few genes and too much variation in human development. They take particular aim at claims that gender differences are biological, which has been an important part of this debate because gender differences often seem to persist despite diverse environments. Ehrlich and Feldman, however, claim that in looking at the grand scheme of history the clear variations in behavior patterns belie a biological explanation.

In contrast, in the NO selection, New York University professor of psychology Gary Marcus claims that the dominant influence of genes on development has only become more clear in recent research. Although acknowledging that genes and the environment always interact, Marcus draws on extensive research with animals demonstrating that small genetic manipulations have dramatic influences on behavior. He also responds to the claim that there are not enough genes to control complex behaviors by insisting that relationships between genes and behavior do not have to be one to one. Genes often interact, or "cascade," in various patterns that account for a massive number of developmental outcomes.

POINT

- There are simply too few genes to explain all of the complexity in human development.
- A gender differences are frequently cited as having a genetic base, there is actually significant historical variation in what is considered "normal" behavior for each gender.
- Focusing on the genetic causes of behavior and development has led to horrible social policies such as those of the Nazis during World War II.

COUNTERPOINT

- Genes do not influence behavior individually, but rather through nearly infinite combinations.
- Small genetic differences in animals create large differences in behavior patterns.

- Although our brains are "plastic" in the sense of changing through development, those changes are constrained by genetic limits.

YES

**Paul Ehrlich and
Marcus Feldman**

Genes and Cultures: What Creates Our Behavioral Phenome?

The recent publication of the first draft of the human genome has brought to public attention the relationship between two concepts, genotype and phenotype—a relationship that had previously been discussed largely by academics. The genotype of an organism is encoded in the DNA that is held in chromosomes and other structures inside its cells. The phenotype is what we are able to observe about that organism's biochemistry, physiology, morphology, and behaviors. We will use the term "phenome" to circumscribe a set of phenotypes whose properties and variability we wish to study. Our focus will be on that part of the human phenome that is defined by behaviors and especially on the behavioral phenome's connection with the human genome.

Our understanding of human behavioral traits has evolved; explanations of the control of those traits offered 50 years ago differ from those most common today. In prewar decades genetic determinism—the idea that genes are destiny—had enormous influence on public policy in many countries: on American immigration and racial policies, Swedish sterilization programs, and, of course, Nazi laws on racial purity. Much of this public policy was built on support from biological, medical, and social scientists, but after Hitler's genocidal policies it was no longer politically correct to focus on putative hereditary differences. The fading of genetic determinism was an understandable reaction to Nazism and related racial, sexual, and religious prejudices which had long been prevalent in the United States and elsewhere. Thus, after World War II, it became the norm in American academia to consider all of human behavior as originating in the environment—in the way people were raised and the social contexts in which they lived.

Gradually, though, beginning in the 1960s, books like Robert Ardrey's *Territorial Imperative* and Desmond Morris's *The Naked Ape* began proposing explanations for human behaviors that were biologically reductionist and essentially genetic. Their extreme hereditarian bias may have been stimulated by the rapid progress at that time in understanding of the role of DNA, which spurred interest in genetics in both scientists and the public. But perhaps no publication had broader effect in reestablishing genetic credibility in the behavioral sciences than Arthur Jensen's article "How Much Can We Boost IQ?" Although roundly criticized by quantitative geneticists and shown to be based on the fraudulent data of Sir Cyril Burt, Jensen's work established a tradition

From *Current Anthropology,* vol. 44, no. 1, February 2003, pp. 87–89, 92–95. Copyright © 2003 by University of Chicago Press via the Copyright Clearance Center. Reprinted by permission.

that attempts to allocate to genetics a considerable portion of the variation in such human behaviors as for whom we vote, how religious we are, how likely we are to take risks, and, of course, measured IQ and school performance. This tradition is alive and well today.

Within the normal range of human phenotypic variation, including commonly occurring diseases, the role of genetics remains a matter of controversy even as more is revealed about variation at the level of DNA. Here we would like to reexamine the issue of genetics and human behavior in light of the enormous interest in the Human Genome Project, the expansion of behavioral genetics as described above, and the recent proliferation of books emphasizing the genetic programming of every behavior from rape to the learning of grammar. The philosopher Helena Cronin and her coeditor, Oliver Curry, tell us in the introduction to Yale University Press's "Darwinism Today" series that "Darwinian ideas . . . are setting today's intellectual agenda." In the *New York Times*, Nicholas Wade has written that human genes contain the "behavioral instructions" for "instincts to slaughter or show mercy, the contexts for love and hatred, the taste for obedience or rebellion—they are the determinants of human nature."

Genes, Cultures, and Behavior

It is incontrovertible that human beings are a product of evolution, but with respect to behavior that evolutionary process involves chance, natural selection, and, especially in the case of human beings, transmission and alteration of a body of extragenetic information called "culture." Cultural evolution, a process very different from genetic evolution by natural selection, has played a central role in producing our behaviors.

This is not to say that genes are uninvolved in human behavior. *Every* aspect of a person's phenome is a product of interaction between genome and environment. An obvious example of genetic involvement in the behavioral phenome is the degree to which most people use vision to orient themselves—in doing everything from hitting a baseball to selecting new clothes for their children. This is because we have evolved genetically to be "sight animals"—our dominant perceptual system is vision, with hearing coming in second. Had we, like dogs, evolved more sophisticated chemical detection, we might behave very differently in response to the toxic chemicals in our environment. The information in our DNA required to produce the basic morphology and physiology that make sight so important to us has clearly been molded by natural selection. And the physical increase in human brain size, which certainly involved a response to natural selection (although the precise environmental factors causing this selection remain something of a mystery, has allowed us to evolve language, a high level of tool use, the ability to plan for the future, and a wide range of other behaviors not seen in other animals.

Thus at the very least, genetic evolution both biased our ability to perceive the world and gave us the capacity to develop a vast culture. But the long-running nature-versus-nurture debate is not about sight versus smell. It is about the degree to which differences in today's human behavioral patterns from person to person, group to group, and society to society are influenced by genetic differences, that is, are traceable to differences in human genetic endowments. Do men "naturally" want to mate with as many women as possible while women "naturally" want to be more cautious in choosing their copulatory partners? Is there a "gay gene"? Are human beings "innately" aggressive? Are differences in educational achievement or income "caused" by differences in genes? And are people of all groups genetically programmed to be selfish? A critical social issue to keep in mind throughout our discussion is what the response of our society would be if we knew the answer to these questions. Two related schools of thought take the view that genetic evolution explains much of the human behavioral phenome; they are known as evolutionary psychology and behavioral genetics.

Evolutionary Psychology

Evolutionary psychology claims that many human behaviors became universally fixed as a result of natural selection acting during the environment of evolutionary adaptation, essentially the Pleistocene. A shortcoming of this argument, as emphasized by the anthropologist Robert Foley (1995–96), lies in the nonexistence of such an environment. Our ancestors lived in a wide diversity of habitats, and the impacts of the many environmental changes (e.g., glaciations) over the past million years differed geographically among their varied surroundings. Evolutionary psychologists also postulate that natural selection produced modules ("complex structures that are functionally organized for processing information") in the brain that "tell" us such things as which individuals are likely to cheat, which mates are likely to give us the best or most offspring, and how to form the best coalitions. These brain "modules," which are assumed to be biological entities fixed in humans by evolution, also have other names often bestowed on them by the same writers, such as "computational machines," "decision-making algorithms," "specialized systems," "inference engines," and "reasoning mechanisms." The research claims of evolutionary psychology have been heavily criticized by, among others, colleagues in psychology.

Those critics are correct. There is a general tendency for evolutionary psychologists vastly to overestimate how much of human behavior is primarily traceable to biological universals that are reflected in our genes. One reason for this overestimation is the ease with which a little evolutionary story can be invented to explain almost any observed pattern of behavior. For example, it seems logical that natural selection would result in the coding of a fear of snakes and spiders into our DNA, as the evolutionary psychologist Steven Pinker thinks. But while Pinker may have genes that make him fear snakes, as the evolutionist Jared Diamond points out, such genes are clearly lacking in New Guinea natives. As Diamond says, "If there is any single place in the world where we might expect an innate fear of snakes among native peoples, it would be in New Guinea, where one-third or more of the snake species are poisonous, and certain non-poisonous constrictor snakes are sufficiently big to be dangerous." Yet there is no sign of innate fear of snakes or spiders among the indigenous people, and children regularly "capture large spiders, singe off the legs and hairs, and eat the bodies. The people there laugh at the idea of an inborn phobia about snakes, and account for the fear in Europeans as a result of their stupidity in being unable to distinguish which snakes might be dangerous." Furthermore, there is reason to believe that fear of snakes in other primates is largely learned as well.

Another example is the set of predictions advanced by Bruce Ellis about the mating behavior that would be found in a previously unknown culture. The first five characteristics that "the average woman in this culture will seek . . . in her ideal mate," he predicts, are:

1. He will be dependable, emotionally stable and mature, and kind/considerate toward her.
2. He will be generous. He may communicate a spirit of caring through a willingness to share time and whatever commodities are valued in this culture with the woman in question.
3. He will be ambitious and perceived by the woman in question as clever or intelligent.
4. He will be genuinely interested in the woman in question, and she in him. He may express his interest through displays of concern for her well-being.
5. He will have a strong social presence and be well liked and respected by others. He will possess a strong sense of efficacy, confidence, and self-respect.

Evolutionary theory does not support such predictions, even if an "average woman" could be defined. First of all, it would be no small developmental trick genetically to program detailed, different, and *independent* reproductive strategies into modules in male and female brains. Those brains, after all are minor variants of the same incredibly complex structures, and, furthermore, the degree to which they are organized into modules is far from clear. If the women in the unknown culture actually chose mates meeting Ellis's criteria, a quite sufficient alternative evolutionary explanation would be that women (simultaneously with men) have evolved big brains, are not stupid, and respond to the norms of their cultures. Scientifically, the notion that the detailed attributes of desirable mates must be engraved in our genetic makeup is without basis, especially in light of the enormous cultural differences in sexual preferences.

For any culture, Ellis's evolutionary arguments would require that in past populations of women there were DNA-based differences that made some more likely to choose in those ways and others more likely to seek mates with other characteristics. And those that chose as Ellis predicts would have to have borne and raised more children that survived to reproduce than those with other preferences. Might, for example, a woman who married a stingy male who kept her barefoot and pregnant out-reproduce the wife of a generous and considerate mate? That is the way genetic evolution changes the characteristics of populations over time: by some genetic variants' out-reproducing others. When that happens, we say that natural selection has occurred.

But, unfortunately, there are no data that speak to whether there is (or was) genetic variation in human mate preferences—variation in, say, ability to evaluate specifically whether a potential mate is "ambitious"—upon which selection could be based. And there are no data for any population showing that women who seek those characteristics in their sexual partners are more successful reproductively—are represented by more children in the subsequent generation—than women who seek husbands with other characteristics. Ellis is simply confusing the preferences of women he knows in his society with evolutionary fitness. . . .

What Does Determine the Behavioral Phenome?

Geneticists know that a large portion of the behavioral phenome must be programmed into the brain by factors in the environment, including the internal environment in which the fetus develops and, most important, the cultural environment in which human beings spend their entire lives. Behavioral scientists know, for instance, that many dramatic personality differences *must* be traced to environmental influences. Perhaps the most important reason to doubt that genetic variation accounts for a substantial portion of observed differences in human behavior is simply that we lack an extensive enough hereditary apparatus to do the job—that we have a "gene shortage." To what extent could genes control the production of these differences?

It is important to remember that behaviors are the results of charge changes that occur in our network of neurons, the specialized cells that make up our nervous system. Behaviors are ultimately under some degree of control in the brain. Neuron networks are the locus of the memories that are also important to our behavior. That genes can control some general patterns is unquestioned; they are obviously involved in the construction of our brains. They might therefore also build in the potential for experience to affect a large part of the details involved in the neural circuitry. But they cannot be controlling our individual behavioral choices.

Human beings have only three times as many genes as have fruit flies (many of those genes appear to be duplicates of those in the flies, and the biochemistry of fly nerve cells seems quite close to ours). But in addition to having sex and eating (what flies mostly do) we get married, establish charities, build hydrogen bombs, commit genocide, compose sonatas, and publish books on evolution. It is a little hard to credit all this to the determining action of those few additional genes. Those genes are, however, likely to have contributed to the increased brain size and complexity that support the vast cultural superstructure created by the interaction of our neurons and their environments. They may also contribute to the wonderful flexibility and plasticity of human behavior—the very attributes that make our behavior less rather than more genetically determined. But to understand the development of and variation in specific human behaviors such as creating charities and cheesecakes, we must invoke culture, its evolution, and its potential interaction with biology.

It might be argued that since a relative handful of genes can control our basic body plan—one's height depends on millions of the body's cells' being stacked precisely—a handful could also determine our behavioral phenome. Genes initiate a process of development that might be analogized with the way a mountain stream entering a floodplain can initiate the development of a complex delta. Why, then, couldn't just a few genes have evolved to program millions of our behaviors? In theory they might have, but in that case human behavior would be very stereotyped. Consider the problem of evolving human behavioral flexibility under such circumstances of genetic determination. Changing just one behavioral pattern—say, making women more desirous of mating with affluent men—would be somewhat analogous to changing the course of one distributary (branch in the delta) without altering the braided pattern of the rest of the delta. It would be difficult to do by just changing the flow of the mountain stream (equivalent to changing the genes) but easily accomplished by throwing big rocks in the distributary (changing the environment).

This partial analogy seems particularly apt in that it is apparently difficult for evolution to accomplish just one thing at a time. There are two principal reasons for this. The first is the complexity of interactions among alleles and phenotypic traits, especially pleiotropy and epistasis. Because there are relatively so few of them, most genes must be involved in more than one process (pleiotropy). Then if a mutation leads to better functioning of one process, it may not be selected for because the change might degrade the functioning of another process. And changes in one gene can modify the influence of another in very complex ways (epistasis). Second, because they are physically coupled to other genes on the same chromosome, the fates of genes are not independent. Selection that increases the frequency of one allele in a population will often, because of linkage, necessarily increase the frequency of another. Selection favoring a gene that made one prefer tall mates might also result in the increase of a nearby gene that produced greater susceptibility to a childhood cancer.

The Mysteries of Environmental Control

Behavioral scientists are still, unhappily, generally unable to determine the key environmental factors that influence the behavioral phenome. For instance, in the case of the Dionne quintuplets, quite subtle environmental differences—perhaps initiated by different positions in the womb or chance interactions among young quints, their parents, and their observers—clearly led to substantially different behavioral and health outcomes in five children with identical genomes. As their story shows, we really know very little about what environmental factors can modify behavior. For example, some virtually undetectable differences in environments may be greatly amplified as developing individuals change their own environments and those of their siblings. Equally, subtle and undetected environmental factors may put individuals with the same genetic endowments on similar life courses even if they are reared apart, perhaps explaining anecdotes about the similarities of some reunited identical twins.

We also know too little about the routes through which genes may influence behavior, where again changes may be behaviorally amplified. Suppose that a study shows that identical twins, separated at birth, nonetheless show a high correlation of personality type—both members of twin pairs tend to be either introverted or extraverted. This is interpreted as a high heritability of introversion and extraversion. What really is heavily influenced by genetics, however, could be height, and tall people in that society (as in many societies) may be better treated by their peers and thus more likely to become extraverted. Genes in this case will clearly be involved in personality type but by such an indirect route as to make talk of "genes for introversion or extraversion" essentially meaningless.

And, of course, scientists *do* know that what appears to be "genetic" is often simply a function of the environment. An example suggested by the philosopher Elliott Sober illustrates this. In England before the 18th century, evolutionary psychologists (had there been any) would have assumed that males had a genetic proclivity for knitting. The knitting gene would have been assumed to reside on the Y chromosome. But by the 19th century, evolutionary psychologists would have claimed that women had that genetic proclivity, with the knitting gene on the X chromosome. With historical perspective, we can see that the change was purely culture-driven, not due to a genetic change. As it did with knitting, the environment, especially the cultural environment, seems to do a good job of fine-tuning our behavior. A major challenge for science today is to elucidate how that fine-tuning occurs.

Would Selection Generally Favor Genetic Control of Behavior?

Would we be better off if we had more than enough genes to play a controlling role in every one of our choices and actions and those genes could operate independently? Probably not. One could imagine a Hobbesian battle in which genes would compete with each other to improve the performance of the reproducing individuals that possessed them—genes for caution being favored in one environment one day and genes for impulsiveness in another environment the next ("Look before you leap," "He who hesitates is lost"). It is difficult to imagine how *any* organism could make the grade evolutionarily if its behavior were completely genetically determined and interactions between its genes and its environments did not exist. Even single-celled organisms respond to changes in their surroundings. Without substantial environmental inputs, evolution would not occur and life could not exist.

Biological evolution has avoided that problem by allowing our behavior to be deeply influenced by the environments in which genes operate. In normal human environments, genes are heavily involved in creating a basic brain with an enormous capacity for learning—taking in information from the environment and incorporating that information into the brain's structure. It is learning that proceeds after birth as an infant's brain uses inputs such as patterns of light from the eyes to wire up the brain so that it can see, patterns of sound that wire up the brain so that it can speak one or more languages, and so on. As the brain scientist John Allman put it, "the brain is unique among the organs of the body in requiring a great deal of feedback from experience to develop its full capacities." And the situation is not so different for height. There aren't enough genes to control a child's growth rate from day to day— adding cells rapidly in favorable (e.g., food-rich) situations and slowly or not at all under starvation. And there aren't enough genes to govern the growth of each column of cells, some to regulate those in each column on the right side of the spine, some for each in the left. Instead, all growth patterns depend on environmental feedback. . . .

Conclusions

What the recent evidence from the Human Genome Project tells us is that the interaction between genes, between the separate components of genes, and between controlling elements of these separate components must be much more complex than we ever realized. Simple additive models of gene action or of the relationship between genes and environments must be revised. They have formed the basis for our interpretation of phenotype-genotype relation- ships for 84 years, ever since R. A. Fisher's famous paper that for the first time related Mendelian genes to measurable phenotypes. New models and para- digms are needed to go from the genome to the phenome in any quantitative way. The simplistic approach of behavioral genetics cannot do the job. We must dig deeper into the environmental and especially cultural factors that contribute to the phenome. The ascendancy of molecular biology has, unin- tentionally, militated against progress in studies of cultural evolution.

Theories of culture and its evolution in the 20th century, from Boas's insistence on the particularity of cultural identities to the debates between material and cultural determinism described by Sahlins, were proudly non- quantitative. Recent discussions on the ideational or symbolic nature of the subjects of cultural evolution, while critical of attempts to construct dynami- cal models of cultural evolution based on individual-to-individual cultural transmission, nevertheless acknowledge the centrality of cultural evolution to human behavioral analysis. Thus, although the quantitative paradigms used in behavioral genetics do not inform evolutionary analysis, this does not mean that we cannot or should not take an evolutionary approach to the under- standing and modification of human behavior. Genetically evolved features such as the dominance of our visual sense should always be kept in mind, but an evolutionary approach to changing behavior in our species must primarily focus on *cultural* evolution. In the last 40,000 years or so, the scale of that cultural evolution has produced a volume of information that dwarfs what is coded into our genes. Just consider what is now stored in human memories, libraries, photographs, films, video tapes, the Worldwide Web, blueprints, and computer data banks—in addition to what is inherent in other artifacts and human-made structures. Although there have been preliminary investigations by Cavalli-Sforza and Feldman and Boyd and Richerson, scientists have barely begun to investigate the basic processes by which that body of information changes (or remains constant for long periods)—a task that social scientists have been taking up piecemeal and largely qualitatively for a very long time.

Developing a unified quantitative theory of cultural change is one of the great challenges for evolutionary and social science in the 21st century.

Identifying the basic mechanisms by which our culture evolves will be difficult; the most recent attempts using a "meme" approach appear to be a dead end. Learning how to influence that evolution is likely to be more difficult still and fraught with pitfalls. No sensible geneticist envisions a eugenic future in which people are selected to show certain behavioral traits, and most thinking people are aware of the ethical (if not technical and social) problems of trying to change our behavior by altering our genetic endowments. Society has long been mucking around in cultural evolution, despite warnings of the potential abuses of doing so. Nazi eugenic policies and Soviet, Cambodian, Chinese, and other social engineering experiments stand as monuments to the ethical dangers that must be guarded against when trying systematically to alter either genetic or cultural evolution.

Nevertheless, we are today all involved in carrying out or (with our taxes) supporting experiments designed to change behavior. This is attested to by the advertising business, Head Start programs, and the existence of institutions such as Sing Sing Prison and Stanford University. The data used by evolutionary psychologists to infer the biological antecedents of human behavior, while not telling us anything about genetic evolution, may actually be helpful in improving our grasp of cultural evolution. What seems clear today, however, is that evolutionary psychology and behavioral genetics are promoting a vast overemphasis on the part played by genetic factors (and a serious underestimation of the role of cultural evolution) in shaping our behavioral phenomes.

Gary Marcus  **NO**

Making the Mind: Why We've Misunderstood the Nature-Nurture Debate

What do our minds owe to our nature, and what to our nurture? The question has long been vexed, in no small part because until recently we knew relatively little about the nature of nature—how genes work and what they bring to the biological structures that underlie the mind. But now, 50 years after the discovery of the molecular structure of DNA, we are for the first time in a position to understand directly DNA's contribution to the mind. And the story is vastly different from—and vastly more interesting than—anything we had anticipated.

The emerging picture of nature's role in the formation of the mind is at odds with a conventional view, recently summarized by Louis Menand. According to Menand, "every aspect of life has a biological foundation in exactly the same sense, which is that unless it was biologically possible it wouldn't exist. After that, it's up for grabs." More particularly, some scholars have taken recent research on genes and on the brain as suggesting a profoundly limited role for nature in the formation of the mind.

Their position rests on two arguments, what Stanford anthropologist Paul Ehrlich dubbed a "gene shortage" and widespread, well-documented findings of "brain plasticity." According to the gene shortage argument, genes can't be very important to the birth of the mind because the genome contains only about 30,000 genes, simply too few to account even for the brain's complexity—with its billions of cells and tens of billions of connections between neurons—much less the mind's. "Given that ratio," Ehrlich suggested, "it would be quite a trick for genes typically to control more than the most general aspects of human behavior."

According to the brain plasticity argument, genes can't be terribly important because the developing brain is so flexible. For instance, whereas adults who lose their left hemisphere are likely to lose permanently much of their ability to talk, a child who loses a left hemisphere may very well recover the ability to speak, even in the absence of a left hemisphere. Such flexibility is pervasive, down to the level of individual cells. Rather than being fixed in their fates the instant they are born, newly formed brain cells—neurons—can

From *Boston Review*, December 2003/January 2004. Copyright © 2003 by Gary Marcus. Reprinted by permission.

sometimes shift their function, depending on their context. A cell that would ordinarily help to give us a sense of touch can (in the right circumstances) be recruited into the visual system and accept signals from the eye. With that high level of brain plasticity, some imagine that genes are left on the sidelines, as scarcely relevant onlookers.

All of this is, I think, a mistake. It is certainly true that the number of genes is tiny in comparison to the number of neurons, and that the developing brain is highly plastic. Nevertheless, nature—in the form of genes—has an enormous impact on the developing brain and mind. The general outlines of how genes build the brain are finally becoming clear, and we are also starting to see how, in forming the brain, genes make room for the environment's essential role. While vast amounts of work remain to be done, it is becoming equally clear that understanding the coordination of nature and nurture will require letting go of some long-held beliefs.

How to Build a Brain

In the nine-month dash from conception to birth—the flurry of dividing, specializing, and migrating cells that scientists call embryogenesis—organs such as the heart and kidney unfold in a series of ever more mature stages. In contrast to a 17th century theory known as preformationism, the organs of the body cannot be found preformed in miniature in a fertilized egg; at the moment of conception there is neither a tiny heart nor a tiny brain. Instead, the fertilized egg contains information: the three billion nucleotides of DNA that make up the human genome. That information, copied into the nucleus of every newly formed cell, guides the gradual but powerful process of successive approximation that shapes each of the body's organs. The heart, for example, begins as a simple sheet of cell that gradually folds over to form a tube; the tube sprouts bulges, the bulges sprout further bulges, and every day the growing heart looks a bit more like an adult heart.

Even before the dawn of the modern genetic era, biologists understood that something similar was happening in the development of the brain—that the organ of thought and language was formed in much the same way as the rest of the body. The brain, too, develops in the first instance from a simple sheet of cells that gradually curls up into a tube that sprouts bulges, which over time differentiate into ever more complex shapes. Yet 2,000 years of thinking of the mind as independent from the body kept people from appreciating the significance of this seemingly obvious point.

The notion that the brain is drastically different from other physical systems has a long tradition; it can be seen as a modernized version of the ancient belief that the mind and body are wholly separate—but it is untenable. The brain is a physical system. Although the brain's function is different from that of other organs, the brain's capabilities, like those of other organs, emerge from its physical properties. We now know that strokes and gunshot wounds can interfere with language by destroying parts of the brain, and that Prozac and Ritalin can influence mood by altering the flow of neurotransmitters. The fundamental components of the brain—the neurons and the synapses that connect them—can be understood as physical systems, with chemical and electrical properties that follow from their composition.

Yet even as late as the 1990s, latter-day dualists might have thought that the brain developed by different principles. There were, of course, many hints that genes must be important for the brain: identical twins resemble each other more than nonidentical twins in personality as well as in physique; mental disorders such as schizophrenia and depression run in families and are shared even by twins reared apart; and animal breeders know that shaping the bodies of animals often leads to correlated changes in behavior. All of these observations provided clues of genetic effects on the brain.

But such clues are achingly indirect, and it was easy enough to pay them little heed. Even in the mid-1990s, despite all the discoveries that had been made in molecular biology, hardly anything specific was known about how the brain formed. By the end of that decade, however, revolutions in the methodology of molecular biology—techniques for studying and manipulating genes—were beginning to enter the study of the brain. Now, just a few years later, it has become clear that to an enormous extent the brain really is sculpted by the same processes as the rest of the body, not just at the macroscopic level (i.e., as a product of successive approximation) but also at the microscopic level, in terms of the mechanics of how genes are switched on and off, and even in terms of which genes are involved; a huge number of the genes that participate in the development of the brain play important (and often closely related) roles in the rest of the body. . . .

The . . . power of genes holds even for the most unusual yet most characteristic parts of neurons: the long axons that carry signals away from the cell, the tree-like dendrites that allow neurons to receive signals from other nerve cells, and the trillions of synapses that serve as connections between them. What your brain does is largely a function of how those synaptic connections are set up—alter those connections, and you alter the mind—and how they are set up is no small part a function of the genome. In the laboratory, mutant flies and mice with aberrant brain wiring have trouble with everything from motor control (one mutant mouse is named "reeler" for its almost drunken gait) to vision. And in humans, faulty brain wiring contributes to disorders such as schizophrenia and autism.

Proper neural wiring depends on the behavior of individual axons and dendrites. And this behavior once again depends on the content of the genome. For example, much of what axons do is governed by special wiggly, almost hand-like protuberances at the end of each axon known as growth cones. Growth cones (and the axonal wiring they trail behind them) are like little animals that swerve back and forth, maneuvering around obstacles, extending and retracting feelers known as filopodia (the "fingers" of a growth cone) as the cone hunts around in search of its destination—say in the auditory cortex. Rather than simply being launched like projectiles that blindly and helplessly follow whatever route they first set out on, growth cones constantly compensate and adjust, taking in new information as they find their way to their targets.

Growth cones don't just head in a particular direction and hope for the best. They "know" what they are looking for and can make new plans even if experimentally induced obstacles get in their way. In their efforts to find their destinations, growth cones use every trick they can, from "short-range" cues emanating from the surface of nearby cells to long-distance cues that broadcast their signals from millimeters away—miles and miles in the geography of an axon. For example, some proteins appear to serve as "radio beacons" that can diffuse across great distances and serve as guides to distant growth cones—provided that they are tuned to the right station. Which stations a growth cone picks up—and whether it finds a particular signal attractive or repellent—depends on the protein receptors it has on its surface, in turn a function of which genes are expressed within.

Researchers are now in a position where they can begin to understand and even manipulate those genes. In 2000, a team of researchers at the Salk Institute in San Diego took a group of thoracic (chest) motor neurons that normally extend their axons into several different places, such as axial muscles (midline muscles that play a role in posture), intercostal muscles (the muscles between the ribs), and sympathetic neurons (which, among other things, participate in the fast energy mobilization for fight-or-flight responses), and by changing their genetic labels persuaded virtually the entire group of thoracic neurons to abandon their usual targets in favor of the axial muscles. (The few exceptions were a tiny number that apparently couldn't fit into the newly crowded axial destinations and had to find other targets.)

What this all boils down to, from the perspective of psychology, is an astonishingly powerful system for wiring the mind. Instead of vaguely telling axons and dendrites to send and accept signals from their neighbors, thereby leaving all of the burden of mind development to experience, nature in effect lays down the cable: it supplies the brain's wires—axons and dendrites—with elaborate tools for finding their way on their own. Rather than waiting for experience, brains can use the complex menagerie of genes and proteins to create a rich, intricate starting point for the brain and mind.

The sheer overlap between the cellular and molecular processes by which the brain is built and the processes by which the rest of the body is built has meant that new techniques designed for the study of the one can often be readily imported into the study of the other. New techniques in staining, for instance, by which biologists trace the movements and fates of individual cells, can often be brought to bear on the study of the brain as soon as they are developed; even more important, new techniques for altering the genomes of experimental animals can often be almost immediately applied to studies of brain development. Our collective understanding of biology is growing by leaps and bounds because sauce for the goose is so often sauce for the gander.

Nature and Nurture Redux

This seemingly simple idea—that what's good enough for the body is good enough for the brain—has important implications for how we understand the roles of nature and nurture in the development of the mind and brain.

Beyond the Blueprint

Since the early 1960s biologists have realized that genes are neither blue-prints nor dictators; instead, as I will explain in a moment, genes are better seen as *providers of opportunity*. Yet because the brain has for so long been treated as separate from the body, the notion of genes as sources of options rather than purveyors of commands has yet to really enter into our understanding of the origins of human psychology.

Biologists have long understood that all genes have two functions. First, they serve as templates for building particular proteins. The insulin gene provides a template for insulin, the hemoglobin genes give templates for building hemoglobin, and so forth. Second, each gene contains what is called a regulatory sequence, a set of conditions that guide whether or not that gene's template gets converted into protein. Although every cell contains a complete copy of the genome, most of the genes in any given cell are silent. Your lung cells, for example, contain the recipe for insulin but they don't produce any, because in those cells the insulin gene is switched off (or "repressed"); each protein is produced only in the cells in which the relevant gene is switched on. So individual genes are like lines in a computer program. Each gene has an IF and a THEN, a precondition (IF) and an action (THEN). And here is one of the most important places where the environment can enter: the IFs of genes are responsive to the environment of the cells in which they are contained. Rather than being static entities that decide the fate of each cell in advance, genes—because of the regulatory sequence—are dynamic and can guide a cell in different ways at different times, depending on the balance of molecules in their environment.

This basic logic—which was worked out in the early 1960s by two French biologists, Fran ois Jacob and Jacques Monod, in a series of painstaking studies of the diet of a simple bacterium—applies as much to humans as to bacteria, and as much for the brain as for any other part of the body. Monod and Jacob aimed to understand how *E. coli* bacteria could switch almost instantaneously from a diet of glucose (its favorite) to a diet of lactose (an emergency backup food). What they found was that this abrupt change in diet was accomplished by a process that switched genes on and off. To metabolize lactose, the bacterium needed to build a certain set of protein-based enzymes that for simplicity I'll refer to collectively as lactase, the product of a cluster of lactase genes. Every *E. coli* had those lactase genes lying in wait, but they were only expressed—switched on—when a bit of lactose could bind (attach to) a certain spot of DNA that lay near them, and this in turn could happen only if there was no glucose around to get in the way. In essence, the simple bacterium had an IF-THEN—if lactose and not glucose, then build lactase—that is very much of a piece with the billions of IF-THENs that run the world's computer software.

The essential point is that genes are IFs rather than MUSTs. So even a single environmental cue can radically reshape the course of development. In the African butterfly *Bicyclus anynana*, for example, high temperature during development (associated with the rainy season in its native tropical climate) leads the butterfly to become brightly colored; low temperature (associated with a dry fall) leads the butterfly to become a dull brown. The growing butterfly doesn't learn (in the course of its development) how to blend in better—it will do the same thing in a lab where the temperature varies and the foliage is constant; instead it is genetically programmed to develop in two different ways in two different environments.

The lesson of the last five years of research in developmental neuroscience is that IF-THENs are as crucial and omnipresent in brain development as they are elsewhere. To take one recently worked out example: rats, mice, and other rodents devote a particular region of the cerebral cortex known as barrel fields to the problem of analyzing the stimulation of their whiskers. The exact placement of those barrel fields appears to be driven by a gene or set of genes whose IF region is responsive to the quantity of a particular molecule, Fibroblast Growth Factor 8 (FGF8). By altering the distribution of that molecule, researchers were able to alter barrel development: increasing the concentration of FGF8 led to mice with barrel fields that were unusually far forward, while decreasing the concentration led to mice with barrel fields that were unusually far back. In essence, the quantity of FGF8 serves as a beacon, guiding growing cells to their fate by driving the regulatory IFs of the many genes that are presumably involved in barrel-field formation.

Other IF-THENs contribute to the function of the brain throughout life, e.g., supervising the control of neurotransmitters and participating . . . in the process of laying down memory traces. Because each gene has an IF, every aspect of the brain's development is in principle linked to some aspect of the environment; chemicals such as alcohol that are ingested during pregnancy have such enormous effects because they fool the IFs that regulate genes that guide cells into dividing too much or too little, into moving too far or not far enough, and so forth. The brain is the product of the actions of its component cells, and those actions are the products of the genes they contain within, each cell guided by 30,000 IFs paired with 30,000 THENs—as many possibilities as there are genes. (More, really, because many genes have multiple IFs, and genes can and often do work in combination.)

From Genes to Behavior

Whether we speak of the brain or other parts of the body, changes in even a single gene—leading to either a new IF or a new THEN—can have great consequences. Just as a single alteration to the hemoglobin gene can lead to a predisposition for sickle-cell anemia, a single change to the genes involved in the brain can lead to a language impairment or mental retardation.

And at least in animals, small differences within genomes can lead to significant differences in behavior. A Toronto team, for example, recently used genetic techniques to investigate—and ultimately modify—the foraging habits of *C. elegans* worms. Some *elegans* prefer to forage in groups, others are loners, and the Toronto group was able to tie these behavioral differences to differences in a single amino acid in the protein template (THEN) region of a particular gene known as npr-1; worms with the amino acid valine in the critical spot are "social" whereas worms with phenylalanine are loners. Armed with that knowledge and modern genetic engineering techniques, the team was able to switch a strain of loner *C. elegans* worms into social worms by altering that one gene.

Another team of researchers, at Emory University, has shown that changing the regulatory IF region of a single gene can also have a significant effect on social behavior. Building on an observation that differences in sociability in different species of voles correlated with how many vasopressin receptors they had, they transferred the regulatory IF region of sociable prairie voles' vasopressin receptor genes into the genome of a less sociable species, the mouse— and in so doing created mutant mice, more social than normal, with more vasopressin receptors. With other small genetic modifications, researchers have created strains of anxious, fearful mice, mice that progressively increase alcohol consumption under stress, mice that lack the nurturing instinct, and even mice that groom themselves constantly, pulling and tugging on their own hair to the point of baldness. Each of those studies demonstrates how behavior can be significantly changed when even a single gene is altered.

Still, complex biological structures—whether we speak of hearts or kidneys or brains—are the product of the concerted actions and interactions of many genes, not just one. A mutation in a single gene known as FOXP2 can interfere with the ability of a child to learn language; an alteration in the vasopressin gene can alter a rodent's sociability—but this doesn't mean that FOXP2 is solely responsible for language or that vasopressin is the only gene a rat needs in order to be sociable. Although individual genes can have powerful effects, no trait is the consequence of any single gene. There can no more be a single gene for language, or for the propensity for talking about the weather, than there can be for the left ventricle of a human heart. Even a single brain cell—or a single heart cell—is the product of many genes working together.

The mapping between genes and behavior is made even more complex by the fact that few if any neural circuits operate entirely autonomously. Except perhaps in the case of reflexes, most behaviors are the product of multiple interacting systems. In a complex animal like a mammal or a bird, virtually every action depends on a coming together of systems for perception, attention, motivation, and so forth. Whether or not a pigeon pecks a lever to get a pellet depends on whether it is hungry, whether it is tired, whether there is anything else more interesting around, and so forth. Furthermore, even within a single system, genes rarely participate directly "on-line," in part because they are just too slow. Genes do seem to play an active, major role in "off-line" processing, such as consolidation of long-term memory—which can even happen during sleep—but when it comes to rapid on-line decision-making, genes, which work on a time scale of seconds or minutes, turn over the reins to neurons, which act on a scale of hundredths of a second. The chief contribution of genes comes in advance, in laying down and adjusting neural circuitry, not in the moment-by-moment running of the nervous system. Genes build neural structures—not behavior.

In the assembly of the brain, as in the assembly of other organs, one of the most important ideas is that of a cascade, one gene influencing another, which influences another, which influences another, and so on. Rather than acting in absolute isolation, most genes act as parts of elaborate networks in which the expression of one gene is a precondition for the expression of the next. The THEN of one gene can satisfy the IF of another and thus induce it to turn on. Regulatory proteins are proteins (themselves the product of genes) that control the expression of other genes and thus tie the whole genetic system together. A single regulatory gene at the top of a complex network can indirectly launch a cascade of hundreds or thousands of other genes leading to, for example, the development of an eye or a limb.

In the words of Swiss biologist Walter Gehring, such genes can serve as "master control genes" and exert enormous power on a growing system. PAX6, for example, is a regulatory protein that plays a role in eye development, and Gehring has shown that artificially activating it in the right spot on a fruit fly's antenna can lead to an extra eye, right there on the antenna—thus, a simple regulatory gene leads directly and indirectly to the expression of approximately 2,500 other genes. What is true for the fly's eye is also true for its brain—and also for the human brain: by compounding and coordinating their effects, genes can exert enormous influence on biological structure.

From a Tiny Number of Genes to a Complex Brain

The cascades in turn help us to make sense of the alleged gene shortage, the idea that the discrepancy between the number of genes and the number of neurons might somehow minimize the importance of genes when it comes to constructing brain or behavior.

Reflection on the relation between brain and body immediately vitiates the gene shortage argument: if 30,000 genes weren't enough to have significant influence on the 20 billion cells in the brain, they surely wouldn't have much impact on the trillions that are found in the body as a whole. The confusion, once again, can be traced to the mistaken idea of genome as blueprint, to the misguided expectation of a one-to-one mapping from individual genes to individual neurons; in reality, genomes describe processes for building things rather than pictures of finished products: better to think of the genome as a compression scheme than a blueprint.

Computer scientists use compression schemes when they want to store and transmit information efficiently. All compression schemes rely in one way or another on ferreting out redundancy. For instance, programs that use the GIF format look for patterns of repeated pixels (the colored dots of which digital images are made). If a whole series of pixels are of exactly the same color, the software that creates GIF files will assign a code that represents the color of those pixels, followed by a number to indicate how many pixels in a row are of the same color. Instead of having to list every blue pixel individually, the GIF format saves space by storing only two numbers: the code for blue and the number of repeated blue pixels. When you "open" a GIF file, the computer converts those codes back into the appropriate strings of identical bits; in the meantime, the computer has saved a considerable amount of memory. Computer scientists have devised dozens of different compression schemes, from JPEGs for photographs to MP3s for music, each designed to exploit a different kind of redundancy. The general procedure is always the same: some end product is converted into a compact description of how to reconstruct that end product; a "decompressor" reconstructs the desired end product from that compact description.

Biology doesn't know in advance what the end product will be; there's no StuffIt Compressor to convert a human being into a genome. But the genome is very much akin to a compression scheme, a terrifically efficient description of how to build something of great complexity—perhaps more efficient than anything yet developed in the labs of computer scientists (never mind the complexities of the brain—there are trillions of cells in the rest of the body, and they are all supervised by the same 30,000-gene genome). And although nature has no counterpart to a program that stuffs a picture into a compressed encoding, it does offer a counterpart to the program that performs decompression: the cell. Genome in, organism out. Through the logic of gene expression, cells are self-regulating factories that translate genomes into biological structure.

Cascades are at the heart of this process of decompression, because the regulatory proteins that are at the top of genetic cascades serve as shorthand that can be used over and over again, like the subroutine of a software engineer. For example, the genome of a centipede probably doesn't specify separate sets of hundreds or thousands of genes for each of the centipede's legs; instead, it appears that the leg-building "subroutine"—a cascade of perhaps hundreds or thousands of genes—gets invoked many times, once for each new pair of legs. Something similar lies behind the construction of a vertebrate's ribs. And within the last few years it has become clear that the embryonic brain relies on the same sort of genetic recycling, using the same repeated motifs—such as sets of parallel connections known as topographic maps—over and over again, to supervise the development of thousands or even millions of neurons with each use of a given genetic subroutine. There's no gene shortage, because every cascade represents the shorthand for a different reuseable subroutine, a different way of creating more from less.

From Prewiring to Rewiring

In the final analysis, I think the most important question about the biological roots of the mind may not be the question that has preoccupied my colleagues and myself for a number of years—the extent to which genes prewire the brain—but a different question that until recently had never been seriously raised: the extent to which (and ways in which) genes make it possible for experience to *rewire* the brain. Efforts to address the nature-nurture question typically falter because of the false assumption that the two—prewiring and rewiring—are competing ideas. "Anti-nativists"—critics of the view that we might be born with significant mental structure prior to experience—often attempt to downplay the significance of genes by making what I earlier called "the argument from plasticity": they point to the brain's resilience to damage and its ability to modify itself in response to experience. Nativists sometimes seem to think that their position rests on downplaying (or demonstrating limits on) plasticity.

In reality, plasticity and innateness are almost logically separate. Innateness is about the extent to which the brain is prewired, plasticity about the extent to which it can be rewired. Some organisms may be good at one but not the other: chimpanzees, for example, may have intricate innate wiring yet, in comparison to humans, relatively few mechanisms for rewiring their brains. Other organisms may be lousy at both: *C. elegans* worms have limited initial structure, and relatively little in the way of techniques for rewiring their nervous system on the basis of experience. And some organisms, such as humans, are well-endowed in both respects, with enormously intricate initial architecture and fantastically powerful and flexible means for rewiring in the face of experience. . . .

CHALLENGE QUESTIONS

Does the Cultural Environment Influence Lifespan Development More Than Our Genes?

1. Does it make sense that the human brain would be programmed in different ways for men and women, who do, on average, show clear developmental differences?
2. Do studies that show identical twins to be more alike than fraternal (nonidentical) twins provide convincing evidence of genetic dominance? Why or why not?
3. Applying Darwinian principles to explain psychological aspects of behavior and development has become increasingly popular in recent years, often phrased as "evolutionary psychology." Does that popularity suggest the applications are correct, or could there be other reasons for the popularity of this approach?
4. Marcus suggests that understanding genetic influences on development requires appreciating the complexity of how genes work. Is it possible that that complexity will make it too difficult to analyze?
5. Much of the evidence for this debate comes from nonhuman animal research. How much can we learn about the nature and nurture of human development from experiments on other species?

Is There Common Ground?

Though it has become common practice to talk about the "nature or nurture" debate, virtually no one believes that our development is an either/or proposition. It is clear that genes matter, and it is clear that socialization through the cultural environment matters. The question here is really about the relative degree of influence of nature and nurture in different domains of development, and the processes through which genes and experience interact. In fact, in their own ways both of the above selections are emphasizing the importance of not over-simplifying human development. If we put too much stock in genes and evolutionary psychology we risk implying that people have little influence over their own destinies and implying that social roles are fixed by nature. But if we put too much stock in culture and socialization we risk ignoring the natural constraints on our behavior and assuming that attitude is all that matters. So what is the right balance, and how does that balance happen during the lived experience of lifespan development?

Suggested Readings

S. Ceci and W. Williams, *The Nature-Nurture Debate: The Essential Readings* (Blackwell Publishers, 1999)

S. Johnson, "Sociobiology and You," *The Nation* (November 18, 2002)

G. Marcus, *The Birth of the Mind: How a Tiny Number of Genes Creates the Complexity of Human Thought* (Basic Books, 2004)

L. Menand, "What Comes Naturally," *The New Yorker* (November 25, 2002)

S. Pinker, *The Blank Slate* (Viking Adult, 2002)

S. Pinker, "Why Nature and Nurture Won't Go Away," *Daedalus* (Fall 2004)

M. Ridley, *Nature via Nurture* (Harper Collins, 2003)

ISSUE 2

Are Peers More Important Than Parents During the Process of Development?

YES: Judith Rich Harris, from "How to Succeed in Childhood," *Wilson Quarterly* (Winter 1991)

NO: Howard Gardner, from "Do Parents Count?" *New York Times Book Review* (November 5, 1998)

Learning Outcomes

As you read the issue, focus on the following points:

1. The statistical correlation between parenting behaviors and developmental outcomes is surprisingly modest in much research on child development.
2. It may be that our assumptions about the importance of parents is part of a powerful cultural myth, though it is also worth noting that diverse cultures vary not only in parenting but also in a variety of values and practices that interact to shape development.
3. Though holding parents responsible for child development serves a valuable social function, children often intentionally try to differentiate themselves from their parents to fit in with peers.
4. Because parents and children usually share both genetics and environment, it can be hard for researchers to tease out the influence of parenting from the influence of shared genes—though behavioral geneticists doing twin studies have offered some provocative data addressing this question.

ISSUE SUMMARY

YES: Developmental psychology writer Judith Rich Harris presents a strong and provocative argument suggesting that parents do not influence child development to any significant degree, while peers and social groups have a primary influence.

NO: Harvard psychologist Howard Gardner reviews Harris's work and suggests her argument is overstated and misleading—parents do matter.

If you ask people about their personal development—why did you turn out the way you have—most will tell you about their parents. In contrast, when you ask researchers and scholars about the role of parents in personal development their answer tends to be a little more complicated. Many years of research have focused on estimating and understanding the influence of parenting, but the results have not been as clear as you might expect.

In fact, many scholars now feel the influence of parental "socialization" (the forming of behavior and personality by parenting behaviors) may be much less than most people think. It may be that parents are simply an easy target for child-rearing "experts" because most parents want to make sure they are doing the best for their children. Instead of only focusing on parents, however, researchers are devoting significant attention to at least two alternative explanations for what influences lifespan development. One explanation is based on increased attention to biological and genetic influences on behavior, finding high levels of significance for our inherited predispositions. The other explanation is based on the role of culture and society, beyond individual parents, that shapes norms and expectations for children.

That being the case, perhaps it was inevitable that someone would turn the tables on all of the parenting experts by drawing on developmental research to suggest that parents may not really matter much at all. That person turned out to be Judith Rich Harris, who had been writing textbooks about developmental psychology for years before realizing that there was very little evidence for all of the emphasis on the influence of parents in development. She eventually turned this realization into a provocative and award-winning article for psychologists and a controversial book for a popular audience. Her basic argument, stated simply as "parents don't matter nearly as much as we think, and peers matter a lot more," went against both popular wisdom and academic trends. Harris's work instigated a flurry of debate.

One of the prominent psychologists to respond was Howard Gardner, most well known for his influential theory of multiple intelligences. Although appreciating Harris's ability to challenge conventional wisdom, Gardner asserts that she significantly overstates her case by massaging data. Gardner is relatively certain that parents do matter, and that the problem with research is simply that personality and character are too difficult to measure. He suggests that the lack of evidence for parents' direct influence derives from an over-reliance on crude surveys, which creates an impression of development that is not true to its complex nature.

POINT

- Most research finds a very modest correlation between parenting behaviors and developmental outcomes.

- The idea that parents matter is really a cultural myth based on invalid aspects of Freudian theory.

- Children do not want to be like their parents and other adults; children want to be like other children.

- Much of what we assume to be parenting effects is actually based on parents sharing genetic material with their children.

COUNTERPOINT

- Harris is selective in what evidence she attends to; there is more evidence than she acknowledges suggesting that parents do matter.

- Although Harris claims that our ideas about how parents matter is a cultural myth, she assumes that what happens to children in American society is a true representation of development everywhere.

- It is a disservice to children to assume that they do not take direction from parents, who do most of the explicit care-giving for children.

- Most research on the influence of parents relies on methods that are too crude and general to pick up the nuances of personality development.

YES

Judith Rich Harris

How to Succeed in Childhood

Every day, tell your children that you love them. Hug them at least once every 24 hours. Never hit them. If they do something wrong, don't say, "You're bad!" Say, "What you did was bad." No, wait—even that might be too harsh. Say, instead, "What you did made me unhappy."

The people who are in the business of giving out this sort of advice are very angry at me, and with good reason. I'm the author of *The Nurture Assumption*—the book that allegedly claims that "parents don't matter." Though that's not what the book actually says, the advice givers are nonetheless justified in their anger. I don't pull punches, and I'm not impressed by their air of benevolent omniscience. Their advice is based not on scientific evidence but on prevailing cultural myths.

The advice isn't wrong; it's just ineffective. Whether parents do or don't follow it has no measurable effect on how their children turn out. There is a great deal of evidence that the differences in how parents rear their children are not responsible for the differences among the children. I've reviewed this evidence in my book; I will not do it again here.

Let me, however, bring one thing to your attention: the advice given to parents in the early part of this century was almost the mirror image of the advice that is given today. In the early part of this century, parents were not warned against damaging their children's self-esteem; they were warned against "spoiling" them. Too much attention and affection were thought to be bad for kids. In those days, spanking was considered not just the parents' right but their duty.

Partly as a result of the major retoolings in the advice industry, child-rearing styles have changed drastically over the course of this century. Although abusive parents have always existed, run-of-the-mill parents—the large majority of the population—administer more hugs and fewer spankings than they used to.

Now ask yourself this: Are children turning out better? Are they happier and better adjusted than they were in the earlier part of the century? Less aggressive? Less anxious? Nicer?

❧

It was Sigmund Freud who gave us the idea that parents are the be-all and end-all of the child's world. According to Freudian theory, children learn right

From *Wilson Quarterly*, Winter 1991, pp. 30–37. Copyright © 1991 by Judith Rich Harris. Reprinted by permission.

from wrong—that is, they learn to behave in ways their parents and their society deem acceptable—by identifying with their parents. In the calm after the storm of the oedipal crisis, or the reduced-for-quick-sale female version of the oedipal crisis, the child supposedly identifies with the parent of the same sex.

Freud's name is no longer heard much in academic departments of psychology, but the theory that children learn how to behave by identifying with their parents is still accepted. Every textbook in developmental psychology (including, I confess, the one I co-authored) has its obligatory photo of a father shaving and a little boy pretending to shave. Little boys imitate their fathers, little girls imitate their mothers, and, according to the theory, that's how children learn to be grownups. It takes them a while, of course, to perfect the act.

It's a theory that could have been thought up only by a grownup. From the child's point of view, it makes no sense at all. What happens when children try to behave like grownups is that, more often than not, it gets them into trouble. Consider this story, told by Selma Fraiberg, a child psychologist whose book. *The Magic Years* was popular in the 1960s:

> Thirty-month-old Julia finds herself alone in the kitchen while her mother is on the telephone. A bowl of eggs is on the table. An urge is experienced by Julia to make scrambled eggs. . . . When Julia's mother returns to the kitchen, she finds her daughter cheerfully plopping eggs on the linoleum and scolding herself sharply for each plop, "NoNoNo. Mustn't dood it! NoNoNo. Mustn't dood it!"

Fraiberg attributed Julia's lapse to the fact that she had not yet acquired a superego, presumably because she had not yet identified with her mother. But look at what was Julia doing when her mother came back and caught her egg-handed: she was imitating her mother! And yet Mother was not pleased.

Children cannot learn how to behave appropriately by imitating their parents. Parents do all sorts of things that children are not allowed to do—I don't have to list them, do I?—and many of them look like fun to people who are not allowed to do them. Such prohibitions are found not only in our own society but everywhere, and involve not only activities such as making scrambled eggs but patterns of social behavior as well. Around the world, children who behave too much like grownups are considered impertinent.

Sure, children sometimes pretend to be adults. They also pretend to be horses and monsters and babies, but that doesn't mean they aspire to be horses or monsters or babies. Freud jumped to the wrong conclusions, and so did several generations of developmental psychologists. A child's goal is not to become an adult; a child's goal is to be a successful child.

What does it take to be a successful child? The child's first job is to learn how to get along with her parents and siblings and to do the things that are expected of her at home. This is a very important job—no question about it. But it is only the first of the child's jobs, and in the long run it is overshadowed in importance by the child's second job: to learn how to get along with the members of her own generation and to do the things that are expected of her outside the home.

Almost every psychologist, Freudian or not, believes that what the child learns (or doesn't learn) in job 1 helps her to succeed (or fail) in job 2. But this belief is based on an obsolete idea of how the child's mind works, and there is good evidence that it is wrong.

Consider the experiments of developmental psychologist Carolyn Rovee-Collier. A young baby lies on its back in a crib. A mobile with dangling doodads hangs overhead. A ribbon runs from the baby's right ankle to the mobile in such a way that whenever the baby kicks its right leg, the doodads jiggle. Babies are delighted to discover that they can make something happen; they quickly learn how to make the mobile move. Two weeks later, if you show them the mobile again, they will immediately start kicking that right leg.

But only if you haven't changed anything. If the doodads hanging from the mobile are blue instead of red, or if the liner surrounding the crib has a pattern of squares instead of circles, or if the crib is placed in a different room, they will gape at the mobile cluelessly, as if they've never seen such a thing in their lives.

It's not that they're stupid. Babies enter the world with a mind designed for learning and they start using it right away. But the learning device comes with a warning label: what you learn in one situation might not work in another. Babies do not assume that what they learned about the mobile with the red doodads will work for the mobile with the blue doodads. They do not assume that what worked in the bedroom will work in the den. And they do not assume that what worked with their mother will work with their father or the babysitter or their jealous big sister or the kids at the daycare center.

Fortunately, the child's mind is equipped with plenty of storage capacity. As the cognitive scientist Steven Pinker put it in his foreword to my book, "Relationships with parents, with siblings, with peers, and with strangers could not be more different, and the trillion-synapse human brain is hardly short of the computational power it would take to keep each one in a separate mental account."

That's exactly what the child does: keeps each one in a separate mental account. Studies have shown that a baby with a depressed mother behaves in a subdued fashion in the presence of its mother, but behaves normally with a caregiver who is not depressed. A toddler taught by his mother to play elaborate fantasy games does not play these games when he's with his playmates—he and his playmates devise their own games. A preschooler who has perfected the delicate art of getting along with a bossy older sibling is no more likely than a first-born to allow her peers in nursery school to dominate her. A school-age child who says she hates her younger brother—they fight like cats and dogs, their mother complains—is as likely as any other child to have warm and serene peer relationships. Most telling, the child who follows the rules at home, even when no one is watching, may lie or cheat in the schoolroom or on the playground, and vice versa.

Children learn separately how to behave at home and how to behave outside the home, and parents can influence only the way they behave at home. Children behave differently in different social settings because different behaviors are required. Displays of emotion that are acceptable at home are not acceptable outside the home. A clever remark that would be rewarded with a laugh at home will land a child in the principal's office at school. Parents are often surprised to discover that the child they see at home is not the child the teacher sees. I imagine teachers get tired of hearing parents exclaim, "Really? Are you sure you're talking about *my* child?"

The compartmentalized world of childhood is vividly illustrated by the child of immigrant parents. When immigrants settle in a neighborhood of native-born Americans, their children become bicultural, at least for a while. At home they practice their parents' culture and language, outside the home they adopt the culture and language of their peers. But though their two worlds are separate, they are not equal. Little by little, the outside world takes precedence: the children adopt the language and culture of their peers and bring that language and culture home. Their parents go on addressing them in Russian or Korean or Portuguese, but the children reply in English. What the children of immigrants end up with is not a compromise, not a blend. They end up, pure and simple, with the language and culture of their peers. The only aspects of their parents' culture they retain are things that are carried out at home, such as cooking.

⋘◉⋙

Late-20th-century native-born Americans of European descent are as ethnocentric as the members of any other culture. They think there is only one way to raise children—the way they do it. But that is not the way children are reared in the kinds of cultures studied by anthropologists and ethologists. The German ethologist Irenäus Eibl-Eibesfeldt has described what childhood is like in the hunter-gatherer and tribal societies he spent many years observing.

In traditional cultures, the baby is coddled for two or three years—carried about by its mother and nursed whenever it whimpers. Then, when the next baby comes along, the child is sent off to play in the local play group, usually in the care of an older sibling. In his 1989 book *Human Ethology,* Eibl-Eibesfeldt describes how children are socialized in these societies:

> Three-year-old children are able to join in a play group, and it is in such play groups that children are truly raised. The older ones explain the rules of play and will admonish those who do not adhere to them, such as by taking something away from another or otherwise being aggressive. Thus the child's socialization occurs mainly within the play group. . . . By playing together in the children's group the members learn what aggravates others and which rules they must obey. This occurs in most cultures in which people live in small communities.

Once their tenure in their mothers' arms has ended, children in traditional cultures become members of a group. This is the way human children were designed to be reared. They were designed by evolution to become members of a group, because that's the way our ancestors lived for millions of years. Throughout the evolution of our species, the individual's survival depended upon the survival of his or her group, and the one who became a valued member of that group had an edge over the one who was merely tolerated.

❧

Human groups started out small: in a hunter-gatherer band, everyone knows everyone else and most are blood relatives. But once agriculture began to provide our ancestors with a more or less dependable supply of food, groups got bigger. Eventually they became large enough that not everyone in them knew everyone else. As long ago as 1500 B.C. they were sometimes that large. There is a story in the Old Testament about a conversation Joshua had with a stranger, shortly before the Battle of Jericho. They met outside the walls of the beleaguered town, and Joshua's first question to the stranger was, "Are you for us or for our adversaries?"

Are you one of *us* or one of *them*? The group had become an idea, a concept, and the concept was defined as much by what you weren't as by what you were. And the answer to the question could be a matter of life or death. When the walls came tumbling down, Joshua and his troops killed every man, woman, and child in Jericho. Even in Joshua's time, genocide was not a novelty: fighting between groups, and wholesale slaughter of the losers, had been going on for ages. According to the evolutionary biologist Jared Diamond, it is "part of our human and prehuman heritage."

Are you one of *us* or one of *them*? It was the question African Americans asked of Colin Powell. It was the question deaf people asked of a Miss America who couldn't hear very well but who preferred to communicate in a spoken language. I once saw a six-year-old go up to a 14-year-old and ask him, "Are you a kid or a grownup?"

The human mind likes to categorize. It is not deterred by the fact that nature often fails to arrange things in convenient clumps but instead provides a continuum. We have no difficulty splitting up continua. Night and day are as different as, well, night and day, even though you can't tell where one leaves off and the other begins. The mind constructs categories for people—male or female, kid or grownup, white or black, deaf or hearing—and does not hesitate to draw the lines, even if it's sometimes hard to decide whether a particular individual goes on one side or the other.

Babies only a few months old can categorize. By the time they reach their first birthday, they are capable of dividing up the members of their social world into categories based on age and sex: they distinguish between men and women, between adults and children. A preference for the members of their own social category also shows up early. One-year-olds are wary of strange adults but are attracted to other children, even ones they've never met before. By the age of two, children are beginning to show a preference for members of their own sex. This preference grows steadily stronger over the next few years. School-age girls and boys will play together in places where there aren't many children, but when they have a choice of playmates, they tend to form all-girl and all-boy groups. This is true the world around.

•❦•

The brain we won in the evolutionary lottery gave us the ability to categorize, and we use that skill on people as well as things. Our long evolutionary history of fighting with other groups predisposes us to identify with one social category, to like our own category best, and to feel wary of (or hostile toward) members of other categories. The emotions and motivations that were originally applied to real physical groups are now applied to groups that are only concepts: "Americans" or "Democrats" or "the class of 2001." You don't have to like the other members of your group in order to consider yourself one of them; you don't even have to know who they are. The British social psychologist Henri Tajfel asked his subjects—a bunch of Bristol schoolboys—to estimate the number of dots flashed on a screen. Then half the boys were privately told that they were "overestimators," the others that they were "underestimators." That was all it took to make them favor their own group. They didn't even know which of their schoolmates were in their group and which were in the other.

•❦•

The most famous experiment in social psychology is the Robber's Cave study. Muzafer Sherif and his colleagues started with 22 eleven-year-old boys, carefully selected to be as alike as possible, and divided them into two equal groups. The groups—the "Rattlers" and the "Eagles"—were separately transported to the Robber's Cave summer camp in a wilderness area of Oklahoma. For a while, neither group knew of the other's existence. But the first time the Rattlers heard the Eagles playing in the distance, they reacted with hostility. They wanted to "run them off." When the boys were brought together in games arranged by researchers disguised as camp counselors, push quickly came to shove. Before long, the two groups were raiding each other's cabins and filling socks with stones in preparation for retaliatory raids.

When people are divided (or divide themselves) into two groups, hostility is one common result. The other, which happens more reliably though it is less well known, is called the "group contrast effect." The mere division into two groups tends to make each group see the other as different from itself in an unfavorable way, and that makes its members *want* to be different from the other group. The result is that any pre-existing differences between the groups tend to widen, and if there aren't any differences to begin with, the members create them. Groups develop contrasting norms, contrasting images of themselves.

In the Robber's Cave study, it happened very quickly. Within a few days of their first encounter, the Eagles had decided that the Rattlers used too many "cuss-words" and resolved to give up cussing; they began to say a prayer before every game. The Rattlers, who saw themselves as tough and manly, continued to favor scatology over eschatology. If an Eagle turned an ankle or skinned a knee, it was all right for him to cry. A Rattler who sustained a similar injury might cuss a bit, but he would bear up stoically.

⊷◈⊶

The idea for group socialization theory came to me while I was reading an article on juvenile delinquency. The article reported that breaking the law is highly common among adolescents, even among those who were well behaved as children and who are destined to turn into law-abiding adults. This unendearing foible was attributed to the frustration teenagers experience at not being adults: they are longing for the power and privilege of adulthood.

"Wait a minute," I thought. "That's not right. If teenagers really wanted to be adults, they wouldn't be spraying graffiti on overpasses or swiping nail polish from drugstores. If they really wanted to emulate adults they would be doing boring adult things, like sorting the laundry or figuring out their taxes. Teenagers aren't trying to be like adults; they are trying to *contrast* themselves with adults! They are showing their loyalty to their own group and their disdain for adults' rules!"

I don't know what put the idea into my head; at the time, I didn't know beans about social psychology. It took eight months of reading to fill the gaps in my education. What I learned in those eight months was that there is a lot of good evidence to back up my hunch, and that it applies not only to teenagers but to young children as well.

Sociologist William Corsaro has spent many years observing nursery school children in the United States and Italy. Here is his description of four-year-olds in an Italian *scuola materna*, a government-sponsored nursery school:

> In the process of resisting adult rules, the children develop a sense of community and a group identity. [I would have put it the other way around: I think group identity leads to the resistance.] The children's resistance to adult rules can be seen as a routine because it is a daily occurrence in the nursery school and is produced in a style that is easily recognizable to members of the peer culture. Such activity is often highly exaggerated (for instance, making faces behind the teacher's back or running around) or is prefaced by "calls for the attention" of other children (such as, "look what I got" in reference to possession of a forbidden object, or "look what I'm doing" to call attention to a restricted activity).

Group contrast effects show up most clearly when "groupness"—Henri Tajfel's term—is salient. Children see adults as serious and sedentary, so when the social categories *kids* and *grownups* are salient—as they might be, for instance, when the teacher is being particularly bossy—the children become sillier and more active. They demonstrate their fealty to their own age group by making faces and running around.

This has nothing to do with whether they like their teachers personally. You can like people even if they're members of a different group and even if you don't much like that group—a conflict of interests summed up in the saying, "Some of my best friends are Jews." When groupness is salient, even young children contrast themselves with adults and collude with each other in defying them. And yet some of their best friends are grownups.

◆

Learning how to behave properly is complicated, because proper behavior depends on which social category you're in. In every society, the rules of behavior depend on whether you're a grownup or a kid, a female or a male, a prince or a peon. Children first have to figure out the social categories that are relevant in their society, decide which category they belong in, and then tailor their behavior to the other members of their category.

That brief description seems to imply that socialization makes children more alike, and so it does, in some ways. But groups also work to create or exaggerate differences among their members—differences in personality. Even identical twins reared in the same home do not have identical personalities. When groupness is not salient—when there is no other group around to serve as a foil—a group tends to fall apart into individuals, and differences among them emerge or increase. In boys' groups, for example, there is usually a dominance hierarchy, or "pecking order." I have found evidence that dominant boys develop different personalities from those at the bottom of the ladder.

Groups also typecast their members, pinning labels on them—joker, nerd, brain—that can have lifelong repercussions. And children find out about themselves by comparing themselves with their group mates. They come to think well or poorly of themselves by judging how they compare with the other members of their own group. It doesn't matter if they don't measure up to the standards of another group. A third-grade boy can think of himself as smart if he knows more than most of his fellow third-graders. He doesn't have to know more than a fourth-grader.

◆

According to my theory, the culture acts upon children not through their parents but through the peer group. Children's groups have their own cultures, loosely based on the adult culture. They can pick and choose from the adult culture, and it's impossible to predict what they'll include. Anything that's common to the majority of the kids in the group may be incorporated into the children's culture, whether they learned it from their parents or from the television set. If most of the children learned to say "please" and "thank you" at home, they will probably continue to do so when they're with their peers. The child whose parents failed to teach her that custom will pick it up from the other children: it will be transmitted to her, via the peer group, from the parents of her peers. Similarly, if most of the children watch a particular TV show, the behaviors and attitudes depicted in the show may be incorporated into the norms of their group. The child whose parents do not permit him to watch that show will nonetheless be exposed to those behaviors and attitudes. They are transmitted to him via the peer group.

Thus, even though individual parents may have no lasting effects on their children's behavior, the larger culture does have an effect. Child-rearing practices common to most of the people in a culture, such as teaching children to say "please" and "thank you," can have an effect. And the media can have an effect.

In the hunter-gatherer or tribal society, there was no privacy: everybody knew what everybody else was doing. Nowadays children can't ordinarily watch their neighbors making love, having babies, fighting, and dying, but they can watch these things happening on the television screen. Television has become their window on society, their village square. They take what they see on the screen to be an indication of what life is like—what life is supposed to be—and they incorporate it into their children's cultures.

One of my goals in writing *The Nurture Assumption* was to lighten some of the burdens of modern parenthood. Back in the 1940s, when I was young, the parents of a troublesome child—my parents, for instance—got sympathy, not blame. Nowadays parents are likely to be held culpable for anything that goes wrong with their child, even if they've done their best. The evidence I've assembled in my book indicates that there is a limit to what parents can do: how their child turns out is largely out of their hands. Their major contribution occurs at the moment of conception. This doesn't mean it's mostly genetic; it means that the environment that shapes the child's personality and social behavior is outside the home.

I am not advocating irresponsibility. Parents are in charge of how their children behave at home. They can decide where their children will grow up and, at least in the early years, who their peers will be. They are the chief determiners of whether their children's life at home will be happy or miserable, and they have a moral obligation to keep it from being miserable. My theory does not grant people the license to treat children in a cruel or negligent way.

Although individual parents have little power to influence the culture of children's peer groups, larger numbers of parents acting together have a great deal of power, and so does the society as a whole. Through the prevailing methods of child rearing it fosters, and through influences—especially the media—that act directly on peer-group norms and values, a society shapes the adults of the future. Are we shaping them the way we ought to?

Do Parents Count?

1.

We all want to know how and why we got to be who we are. Parents have a special interest in answering the "how" and "why" questions with respect to their own children. In addressing the mysteries of human growth, traditional societies have invoked God, the gods, the fates, with luck sometimes thrown in. Shakespeare called our attention to the struggle between "nature and nurture."

In our own time the natural sciences and the social sciences have been supplying a bewildering variety of answers. Those with biological leanings look to heredity—the gene complexes of each parent and the ways in which their melded sets of genes express themselves in the offspring. The traits and capacities of the biological parents are seen as in large part determining the characteristics of offspring. Those with a psychological or sociological perspective point to the factors beyond the child's physiology. Psychoanalysts emphasize the pivotal role of parents, and especially the young child's relationship to his or her mother. Behaviorists look at the contingencies of reward and punishment in the child's experience; the character of the child depends on the qualities that are "reinforced," with those in control of reinforcement in early life having an especially significant influence.

Recently, three new candidates have been proposed to explain "socialization"—i.e., how children grow up within a society and absorb its norms. Impressed and alarmed by the powers of new means of communication, particularly television, students of culture like Marie Winn and Neil Postman have described a generation raised by the electronic media. The historian of science Frank Sulloway has brought new attention to the once discounted factor of "birth order": on his account, first-borns embrace the status quo, while later-borns are far more likely to support scientific, political, or religious revolutions. And now, in a much publicized new work, Judith Rich Harris suggests that all of these authorities have got it wrong. On her account, the most potent "socializers" are the child's peers, with parents having little or no effect.

Harris's work has many things going for it. For a start, she has an arresting hypothesis, one that should strike especially responsive chords in adults who feel they are inadequately involved in the formation of the post-baby boom Generation X and the generations to come. She has an appealing personal story. Kicked out of graduate school in psychology in the early 1960s and a victim of a lupus-like disease, she has hitherto led the life of a semi-invalid, making her living coauthoring textbooks in psychology. One day in 1994, after reading a scholarly article about juvenile delinquency, she was struck by the idea that the role of peers in socialization had largely been ignored while the influence of parents had been much overestimated. She succeeded in publishing a theoretical statement of her view in *Psychological Review*, the most prestigious journal of psychological theory. She soon gained recognition among scholars and, in a delicious irony, won a prestigious award named after George Miller, the very professor who had signed her letter of expulsion from Harvard almost four decades ago. Harris's book is well-written, toughly argued, filled with telling anecdotes and biting wit. It has endorsements from some of the most prestigious names in the field. Already it has been widely—and mostly favorably—reported on and reviewed in the popular press.

However, in my view, Harris's thesis is overstated, misleading, and potentially harmful. Overstated in the sense that she highlights evidence consistent with her thesis and understates evidence that undermines it. Misleading because she treats as "natural" and "universal" what, in my view, is really a characterization of contemporary American culture (and those societies influenced by America). Potentially harmful in that it may, if inadvertently, discourage parents from promoting their own beliefs and values, and from becoming models of behavior, at a time when such values and models should be clearly and continually conveyed to children.

2.

Harris begins by outlining familiar positions in psychology. On her account, Freud's view of the Oedipal period is quaint and unsupported, while the behaviorists have been widely discredited, both by the cognitivists (who put the mind back into psychology) and the biologists (who reminded us that we are as much a product of our genes as of our experiences). She then turns her keen critical skills to an attack on the branch of empirical psychology that attempts to document important contributions of parents to their children's personality and character. (Harris uses both terms.)

For over half a century, psychologists and anthropologists have observed parents and children in different settings; they have filled out checklists in which they record predominant kinds of behavior and action, and they have administered questionnaires to the parents and children themselves. These researchers, according to Harris, began with the "nurture assumption"; they presupposed that the most important force in the child's environment is the child's parents and then collected evidence to support that assumption. Moreover, while scholars themselves are often guarded in their conclusions, some "pop" psychologists have no inhibitions whatever. They stress the role of parents over all other forces, thus making parents feel guilty if they fail (according to their own criteria), and full of pride when they succeed.

As Harris shrewdly points out, there are two problems with the nurture assumption. First, when viewed with a critical eye, the empirical evidence about parental influences on their children is weak, and often equivocal. After hundreds of studies, many with individually suggestive findings, it is still difficult to pinpoint the strong effects that parents have on their children. Even the effects of the most extreme experiences—divorce, adoption, and abuse— prove elusive to capture. Harris cites Eleanor Maccoby, one of the leading researchers in the field, who concluded that "in a study of nearly four hundred families, few connections were found between parental child-rearing practices (as reported by parents in detailed interviews) and independent assessments of children's personality characteristics—so few, indeed, that virtually nothing was published relating the two sets of data.

The second problem with the nurture assumption is potentially more devastating. Harris draws heavily on recent results from behavioral genetics to argue that, even in those cases where children resemble their parents, the presence and actions of parents have little to do with that resemblance. The argument she makes from behavioral genetics runs as follows. Studies of siblings, fraternal twins, identical twins reared together, and identical twins reared apart all point to the same conclusion: about half of one's intellect and personality results from one's genes. That is, in any group of people drawn from a particular "population" (e.g., middle-class white youngsters living in the United States), about one half of the variations in an observed trait (for instance, IQ or aggressiveness) is owing to one's parents' genetic contribution. The other half is, of course, the result of one's environment.

For those who assume that the behavior of parents and the models they offer make up a major part of the child's environment, the results of studies in behavioral genetics are surprising. According to those studies, when we examine any population of children and try to account for the nongenetic variations among them, we find that remarkably few variations can be attributed to their "shared environment"—i.e., when parents treat all of their children the same way, for example, being equally punitive to each child.

In fact, according to the behavioral geneticists, nearly all of the variation is due to what is called the "nonshared environment"—i.e., the variety of other influences, including instances where children are treated differently by the parents (e.g., a brother is punished more than his sister, or differently). In the case of any particular child, we simply do not know with any accuracy what makes up the nonshared environment. We can guess that it consists of siblings, printed matter, radio and television, other adults, school, luck, accident, the different (as opposed to the common or "shared") ways in which each parent responds to each child, and—if Judith Rich Harris is correct—most especially, a child's peers.

So much for Harris's demolition of the importance of parents—except genetically—to the behavior and psyche of the child. Harris adduces evidence from a wide variety of sources, moreover, to stress the important contribution of peers. She goes back to the studies of nonhuman primates to indicate the importance of peer groups in child-rearing—pointing out that monkeys can be successfully reared by peers alone but not by their mothers alone. (It's not known whether this would be true in "higher" primates.) She cites observations of children in different cultures who play together as much and as early as possible, and routinely gang up on the adults (teachers, parents, masters). She searches in the experimental literature for cases where peers exert an appreciable influence upon one another—for example, adolescents who have the same friends turn out to resemble one another. And she places great emphasis on the human tendency to form groups—and particularly "in-groups" with which one strongly identifies.

Harris also provides many telling anecdotes from her own experiences, and from the press and television, about how adults are ignored and peers admired. British boys who rarely see their parents successfully absorb social values at boarding school. Secretary of Labor Robert Reich quit the Cabinet to be with his sons in Cambridge and found that they would rather hang out "in the Square." Touchingly she indicates how she and her husband tried to deal with their wayward adopted daughter but finally realized that the peers had more influence. No such problems existed with their biological daughter, who simply followed her biological destiny; the model provided by her parents was no more than an unnecessary bonus.

Harris describes recurrent situations where youngsters overlook the evident models of their parents in favor of those provided by peers. Deaf children of speaking parents ignore their parents' attempts to teach them to read lips and instead begin to invent gestural signs to communicate with other deaf children and seek opportunities to learn formal signing. The hearing children of deaf parents, Harris points out, learn to speak normally in the absence of a parental model. Analogously, children raised by parents with foreign accents soon begin to speak like their peers, without an accent; like the deaf children, they ignore the models at home and turn, as if magnetized, to the most available set of peers. Arguments like these convince Harris, and apparently many readers (both lay and professional), that young human beings are wired to attend to people of similar age, rather than to those large and obvious authority figures who give them birth and early shelter.

3.

Harris has collected an impressive set of examples and findings to fortify a position that is indeed novel in empirical investigations of "human socialization." I have sought to do justice to her arguments, though I cannot convey her passion, her missionary sense of having seen the light. Yet I do not find her "peer hypothesis" convincing, partly because I read the literature on the subject differently. My deeper reservations come from my belief that Harris has misconstrued the problem of socialization and, in doing so, has put forth a position that harbors its own dangers.

When we consider the empirical part of Harris's argument, we find it is indeed true that the research on parent-child socialization is not what we would hope for. However, this says less about parents and children and more about the state of psychological research, particularly with reference to "softer variables" such as affection and ambition. While psychologists have made genuine progress in the study of visual perception and measurable progress in the study of cognition, we do not really know what to look for or how to measure human personality traits, individual emotions, and motivations, let alone character.

Consider, as an example, the categories that the respondents must use when they describe themselves or others on the Personal Attributes Questionnaire, a test used to obtain data about a person's self-esteem and gender-linked traits. Drawing on a list reminiscent of the Boy Scout oath, those who answer the questionnaire are asked whether they would describe themselves as Gentle, Helpful, Active, Competitive, and Worldly. These terms are not easy to define and people are certainly prone to apply them favorably to their own case. Or consider the list of acts from which observers can choose to characterize children from different cultures—Offers Help, Acts Sociably, Assaults Sociably, Seeks Dominance. Even if we could agree on what kinds of physical behavior merit these labels, we don't know with any confidence what these acts mean to children, adolescents, and adults in diverse cultures—let alone to the observers from a distant university. What does a raised fist or a frown mean to a three-year-old or to the thirty-year-old who observes it? The same question could be asked about a wink or an imitated curtsy. We are not measuring chemical bonds or electrical voltage in such cases. We are seeking to quantify the most subtle human characteristics—the sentiments described so finely by Henry James. And therefore it is not surprising when studies—whether by empirical psychologists or behavioral geneticists—do not yield strong results.

I do not want to elevate psychoanalytic theory or practice over other kinds of inquiry, but at least the Freudians were grappling with the deeper aspects of human character and personality—our urgent longings, our innermost fears and anxieties, our wrenching conflicts. We might perhaps find evidence for these complex feelings—and their putative causes—through long narratives, or projective testing (where the subjects respond to ambiguous photographs or inkblots), or by analyzing a series of sessions on the couch. We won't reach them through questionnaires or checklists; yet Harris relies on many studies that use them.

As social scientists we have been frustrated by our own clumsy efforts to understand personality and character, and even relatively measurable skills, like intelligence or the capacity for problem-solving. And perhaps that is why so many talented psychologists—including the ones quoted on the jacket of *The Nurture Assumption*—have become drawn to evolutionary psychology and behavioral genetics. Here, at last, is the chance to put psychology and social science (and even squishy inquiries into personality, temperament, and character) on what seems a "real" scientific footing. Physics envy has been replaced by biological bias.

But things are not as clear-cut in the biobehavioral world as outsiders may imagine. Because of the possibility of controlled experiments, sociobiology has made genuine progress in explaining the social life of insects; but its account of human behavior remains controversial. The speculations of evolutionary psychology are just that; as commentators such as Stephen Jay Gould and Steve Jones have pointed out . . . , it is difficult to know how to disprove a hypothesis in evolutionary psychology. (For example, what evidence can help us decide whether genes, or humans, are really selfish, or really altruistic, or really both?—in which case we are back where we started.)

⋯◉⋯

And what of behavioral genetics? Certainly the opportunity to study twins who have been separated early in life gives us an additional advantage in understanding the heritability of various traits. And Judith Harris rightly calls attention to two enigmas: the fact that identical twins reared apart are almost as alike as those that are reared together; and the fact that identical twins still turn out to be quite different from one another.

But this subject is also dogged by difficulties. We cannot really do experiments in human behavioral genetics; we have to wait until events happen (as when twins are separated early in life) and then study the effects retrospectively. But this approach leaves too many puzzles unaddressed. First of all, for at least nine crucial months, the twins share the same environment—the womb of the birth mother—and we still know very little about the shared chemical and other effects of gestation on their neurological systems. Then, too, they may or may not have been separated right at birth. (And under what extraordinary circumstances does such separation occur?) They may or may not have been raised for a while by family members. The children are not randomly placed; in nearly all cases, they are raised within the same culture and very often in the same community, with similar social settings. Also, infants who look the same and behave the same are likely to elicit similar responses from adults, while those who are raised in the same house may try all the harder to distinguish themselves from one another. Or they may not.

When you add together the uncertainties (and I have only suggested a few of them here) of human behavioral genetics, and the imprecision of the measures used to describe personality and character, it is no wonder that we find little reliable evidence of parental influence. It would be reassuring if we did—but it is not surprising that we do not.

Which brings me to the alternative picture that Harris attempts to construct. She argues that "peers" are the real instrument of socialization. She may be right; but she does not have the evidence to show this. Her assertions depend almost entirely on what she thinks could one day be shown. Indeed, I find it extremely telling that she relies very heavily on the arguments about language—language-learning among the deaf, and the loss of foreign accents. Neither of these has to do with personality, character, or temperament, her supposed topics. In the case of accents, I assume that we are dealing with an unconscious (and presumably innate) process in which the growing child generalizes from his encounters with many of the adults and children he meets outside the home and through television, the movies, and other media. In the case of deafness, the enormous difference between child and parents forces youngsters to make use of resources outside the home—ranging from adult teachers to television and other visual media.

Indeed, despite some imaginative suggestions by Harris, it is very difficult to envision how one could test her hypothesis. For, after all, who are peers? Do they include siblings? Are they the children in the neighborhood? The children in class? The children in after-school activities or in Sunday school? The children on television? In the movies? At some remote spot on the Internet? Who decides? What happens when peers change because the family moves, or one child switches schools, or leaves (or is kicked out of) one group and then enters another? Most important, who selects peers? At least with parents, we researchers stand on fairly firm ground; and with siblings as well. But for all Ms. Harris's anecdotes, when it comes to peers, we're afloat.

Undoubtedly, psychological researchers inspired by Harris's book will seek evidence bearing on her thesis. We will learn from these studies; and some of us who have taken skeptical positions in this debate may have to acknowledge influences we hadn't sufficiently recognized. Meanwhile, I want to suggest an entirely different approach to the problem, one that might be called "the culture assumption."

4.

What is socialization about? It is about becoming a certain kind of person— gaining specific knowledge, skills, manners, attitudes, and habits. Animals have little culture; human beings revel in it. Yet what is striking in Harris's book is that the words "disciplines," "civilization," and "culture" (in the sense of civilization) are largely absent from the text and from her thinking. Socialization is reduced to having, or not having, certain personality traits—traits that are measured by rather coarsely conceived and applied tests.

The work of the much-maligned Freud remains the best point of departure for a treatment of these issues. In his *Civilization and Its Discontents*, Freud defined culture: "the sum of the achievements and institutions which differentiate our lives from those of our animal forebears, namely that of protecting humanity against nature and of regulating the relations of human beings among themselves." He concentrates particularly on "the one feature of culture which characterizes it better than any other, and that is the value that it sets upon the higher mental activities—intellectual, scientific, and aesthetic achievement." And he speculates that culture (or civilization) rests upon the human superego—the sense of guilt—which develops (or fails to develop) during the child's early interactions with his parents. Guilt keeps us from murdering our fellow citizens; guilt prompts us to delay gratification, to sublimate our primordial passions in favor of loftier pursuits.

Whether one examines the least developed preliterate culture or the most advanced technological society, the question remains the same: What structures and practices will enable children to assume their places in that culture and ultimately aid in transmitting it to the generations to come?

Children will have some say in this process, and it is to Harris's credit (and that of the authorities whom she cites) that she has called attention to this fact. But children are not born just into a family or into a peer group. They are born into an entire culture, whose assumptions begin when the parents say, happily or with a twinge of regret, "It's a girl," and continues to exert its influence in nearly every interaction and experience until the funerary rites, burial, cremation, or ascent to heaven takes place.

Earlier, I referred to Eleanor Maccoby's pessimistic conclusions about documenting parental influence, and I mentioned some of the studies of it that both Maccoby and Harris seem to have had in mind. But let me reconsider the most ambitious of these studies in a different light. In the 1950s and 1960s, John Whiting, Beatrice Whiting, and their colleagues studied childrearing in six cultures, ranging from a small New England town to agricultural settings in Kenya, India, Mexico, the Philippines, and Okinawa. What emerges from that study is that childrearing practices are distinctly different around the globe: different in treatment of infants, in parental sleeping patterns, in how children do chores, in their helping or not helping in rearing younger siblings, in initiation rites, in ways of handling aggression, and in dozens of other variables. So differently are children reared in these cultures that no one would confuse an adult New Englander with an adult Gusii of Kenya or an adult Taira of Okinawa—whether in their knowledge, skills, manners, habits, personality, or temperament.

For the social scientist, the analytic problem is to find the source of these differences. Parents behave differently in these cultures, but so do siblings, peers, other adults, and even visiting anthropologists. And of course the adult roles, natural resources, technology, and means of communication (primitive or modern) differ as well. In all probability, each of these factors makes its contribution to the child's "personality and character." But how to tell them apart? Harris chooses to minimize these other factors and zooms in on the peers, but her confident choice is not justified.

5.

Harris takes little note of a crucial fact: all but a few of the studies that she reviews, including several of the most influential behavioral genetic ones, were carried out in the United States. The United States is not a country without culture; it has many subcultures and a more general "national" culture as well. Harris and most of the authorities that she cites are not studying child-rearing in general; indeed, they are studying child-rearing largely in the white, middle-class United States during the last half-century.

From the time of Alexis de Tocqueville's visit to the United States in the early 1830s, observers have noted the relative importance in this country of peers, friends, or fellow workers of the same age, the members of one's own community. Tocqueville commented, "In America the family, in the Roman and aristocratic signification of the word, does not exist. All that remains are a few vestiges in the first years of childhood. . . ." As a sociologist might put it, America is a more horizontal, "peer-oriented" society than most others, and particularly more so than most traditional societies.

When empirical social science began in this country, these unusual cultural patterns were noted as well. Studying the America of the 1940s, the sociologist David Riesman and his coauthors called attention to the decline of tradition-centered and "inner-directed" families, where the parental models were powerful; and to the concomitant rise of the "other-directed families" that made up "the Lonely Crowd." In this increasingly common family constellation, much socialization occurred at the behest of the peer group, whether for adults or for children. Riesman wrote, "The American peer group, too, cannot be matched for power throughout the middle-class world."

Examining the America of the 1950s and 1960s, the psychologist Urie Bronfenbrenner noted that children spend more time with peers than with parents and reached the same conclusion: "Whether in comparison to other contemporary cultures, or to itself over time, American society emerges as one that gives decreasing prominence to the family as a socializing agency. . . . We are coming to live in a society that is exaggerated not only by race and class, but also by age." Thus not only has the peer group had an important part in American society from the first; but in recent decades this trend has accelerated.

But there are many possible peer groups. To which ones are children drawn and why? Here I believe (and Harris concedes this) that parents have a decisive role—by the friendships they encourage or discourage, by the schools they select or avoid, by the after-school activities they encourage and summer camps they approve of, parents contribute substantially to the choice of possible peer groups. I would go one step further. Children themselves select—and are selected for—various peer groups according to parental predilections. The work of the social psychologist Mihaly Csikszentmihalyi on "talented teens" strongly suggests that the values exhibited at home—integrity vs. dishonesty, hard work vs. laziness, artistic interests vs. philistinism—imprint themselves on children and in turn serve as major determinants of the peer groups to which children are attracted and, not incidentally, the ones where they are welcomed or spurned.

6.

It seems that in every passing decade—perhaps in every passing selection of fall books—we are told of a new approach to bringing up children or of a new, villainous influence on family life. Certainly, we do not have the feeling of a steady scientific march toward truth. It is more as if we are on a roller-coaster, with each new hypothesis tending to invalidate the previous one.

Still, it would be defeatist simply to embrace the opposite perspective, to declare that each of the various factors—mother, father, grandparents, same-sex siblings, different-sex peers, television, etc.—is important and be done with it. As a scientific community, we can do better than this. To do so, we should be undertaking two activities.

First, even as we welcome the clarifications provided by evolution and genetics, we cannot lose sight of the different cultural settings in which research is carried out and the different meanings attached to seemingly similar traits and actions. Parents and peers have different meanings in Japan, Brazil, and the United States; what we learn from the Whitings, and from much other sociological and anthropological research, is that these "independent variables" cannot simply be equated in designing research or in interpreting findings. In fact, a father may be treated more like a sibling in one society, and an older sibling more like a father in another; parents may encourage children to associate with peers in one culture and to steer clear of them in another and, in yet another, to combat their influence in every way they can.

Second, even as we discover genes or gene clusters that appear to influence important social or psychological variables, we must not assume that we have "solved" the problem of socialization. We still don't know the physical mechanisms by which genes actually affect the brain and cause people to make one choice or another. What triggers (or fails to trigger) genes will vary across cultural settings; and how their expression is understood will also vary. Young men, for example, may have a proclivity to imitate other young men of similar size and power, but that proclivity can be manipulated, depending upon whom the child is exposed to and which rewards and punishments are contingent upon imitation or non-imitation.

Each of the numerous influences on a child's personality I have mentioned can surely have an effect, but the effect will vary among different children, families, and cultures. As science progresses, we may someday be able to predict the relative importance of each across these different factors. My reading of the research suggests that, on the average, parents and peers will turn out to have complementary roles: parents are more important when it comes to education, discipline, responsibility, orderliness, charitableness, and ways of interacting with authority figures. Peers are more important for learning cooperation, for finding the road to popularity, for inventing styles of interaction among people of the same age. Youngsters may find their peers more interesting, but they will look to their parents when contemplating their own futures.

Parental attitudes and efforts will determine to a significant extent how a child resolves the conflicting messages of the home and the wider community as well as the kind of parent the child one day becomes. I would give much weight to the hundreds of studies pointing toward parental influence and to the folk wisdom accumulated by hundreds of societies over thousands of years. And I would, accordingly, be skeptical of a perspective, such as Ms. Harris's, that relies too heavily on heritability statistics and manages to reanalyze numerous studies and practices so that they all somehow point to the peer group.

To gain attention, an author often states a finding or hypothesis very strongly. (I've been guilty of this myself.) In Harris's case, this has led to a belittling of the roles of parents in childrearing and to a stronger endorsement of the role of peers than the current data allow. I do not question Harris's motives but I do question her judgment, which might have been better guided by the old medical oath "first, do no harm."

It is all to the good if parents do not become crushed with anxiety when they have problems with their children or when their children turn out differently than they would like. Guilt is not always productive. But to suggest, with little foundation, that parents are not important in socialization borders on the irresponsible. Perhaps, on the average, those of us who are parents are not particularly successful in encouraging the personality traits we would hope to see in our children, whether because we do not know how to get their attention, or because they are "primed" to pay attention to their peers and we are not aware of how long and how hard we must work to counter these proclivities.

But children would not—could not—grow to be members of a civilized culture if they were simply left to the examples of their peers. Indeed, parents are especially important when children's peers set strong and destructive examples. In the absence of credible parents and other adults, most children will not be able to deal effectively with life. A social science—or a layman's guide—that largely left out parents after birth would be absurd. So would a society.

Whether on the scene, or behind the scenes, parents have jointly created the institutions that train and inspire children: apprenticeships, schools, works of art and literature, religious classes, playing fields, and even forms of resistance and rebellion. These institutions, and the adults who run them, sustain civilization and provide the disciplines—however fragile they may seem—that keep our societies from reverting to barbarism.

Sad to say, these most important parts of life—which make life satisfying and fascinating—are largely absent from *The Nurture Assumption*. They are absent as well from most of the work emanating from the biotropic pole of contemporary social science. Until their importance is realized, and the biological and cultural perspectives are somehow deeply integrated with one another, scientific claims about children and family life are bound to remain barren.

CHALLENGE QUESTIONS

Are Peers More Important Than Parents During the Process of Development?

1. Although most people automatically assume parents are the most significant influence on lifespan development, what is the tangible evidence?
2. Harris never finished her PhD in developmental psychology, causing some scholars to criticize her for lacking proper academic credentials. Should that matter for her argument?
3. Gardner claims that current research methods do not really give a full picture of how complex people are. Will psychology ever be able to fully describe personality and the outcomes of development in ways that are true to who we become?
4. Most people concerned with lifespan development would acknowledge that many factors influence how we turn out—parents, genes, peers, the media, schools, and more. Why is it worth the effort to try and understand which of those influences matter the most and in what ways?

Is There Common Ground?

The flurry of attention Judith Rich Harris garnered with her theory that parents do not matter as much as we think has now mostly passed. But the issue is still worth discussing because it highlights the importance of challenging conventional wisdom and looking carefully at research evidence when thinking about lifespan development. Although Howard Gardner does not agree with Harris's theory, you may have noticed that some of his critique involves reconsidering the research methods we use to study children. In a certain way, Gardner agrees with Harris that we need to be constantly thinking about the ways our research and our theories are embedded in questionable assumptions. There is little question that parents matter to development, but recognizing that they may not matter as much as most people think allows us a chance to question other assumptions about development. What else, beyond what Harris calls "the nurture assumption," should we not take for granted in thinking about the lifespan?

Suggested Readings

N. Barber, *Why Parents Matter: Parental Investment and Child Outcomes* (Greenwood Publishing Group, 2000)

W. A. Collins, E. E. Maccoby, L. Steinberg, E. M. Hetherington, and M. H. Bornstein, "Contemporary Research on Parenting: The Case for Nature and Nurture," *American Psychologist* (February 2002)

J. Rich Harris, *The Nurture Assumption: Why Children Turn Out the Way They Do* (The Free Press, 1998)

J. Rich Harris, *No Two Alike: Human Nature and Human Individuality* (W. W. Norton, 2006)

J. Rich Harris and J. Kagan, "Slate Dialogues: E-mail Debates of Newsworthy Topics—The Nature of Nurture: Parents or Peers?" available at http://slate .msn.com/id/5853/ (November 1998)

M. Spett, "Is It True That Parenting Has No Influence on Children's Adult Personalities?" *NJ-ACT Newsletter* (March 1999)

D. L. Vandell and J. R. Harris, "Genes, Parents, and Peers: An Invited Exchange of Views," *Developmental Psychology* (November 2000)

W. Williams, "Do Parents Matter? Scholars Need to Explain What Research Really Shows," *The Chronicle of Higher Education* (December 11, 1998)

ISSUE 3

Is Chinese Parenting Culturally Distinct?

YES: **Amy Chua,** from "Why Chinese Mothers Are Superior," *Wall Street Journal—The Saturday Essay* (January 8, 2011)

NO: **Markella B. Rutherford,** from "The Social Value of Self-Esteem," *Society* (September 2011, vol 48, no. 5)

Learning Outcomes

As you read the issue, focus on the following points:

1. What is considered an optimal parenting style, and an optimal model of lifespan development, varies significantly across by both culture and social class.
2. Putting an emphasis on self-esteem as a key foundation of lifespan development is historically and culturally unusual, but underlies much of contemporary Western parenting.
3. Globalization and the global economy influence the way people think about the nature of successful development.

ISSUE SUMMARY

YES: Yale law professor and self-proclaimed "Tiger Mother" Amy Chua argues that Chinese parenting is distinct from most Western parenting in its rigor, high expectations, and unwillingness to accept anything less than true excellence.

NO: Sociologist Markella B. Rutherford instead sees the "Tiger Mother" idea as just another example of the types of privileged parenting that ultimately prioritizes self-confidence, self-esteem, and perpetuates differences more dependent on class than on culture.

In an increasingly competitive and globalized world, what does it take for an individual to become a success? For many the support of parents is the starting point, and most parents certainly want their children to succeed.

But what does that mean in practice? For modern Western parents that often means emphasizing unconditional love and boosting self-esteem: We tend to believe that if we give our children enough attention and encouragement they will develop into successful adults. Although that may not seem terribly controversial, there are some interesting questions as to whether attention and encouragement is enough. Particularly with the growing global prominence of non-Western nations such as China, some are raising the question of whether Western parents set their expectations too low.

The optimal parenting style has long been a question of interest to scholars of lifespan development. One well-known scheme, developed by psychologist Diana Baumrind in the 1960s, identified three primary parenting styles: authoritarian parenting with strict rules and unquestioned authority, authoritative parenting with a combination of some rules and some more democratic responsiveness, and permissive parenting with few demands and many indulgences. Most developmentalists have promoted authoritative parenting, though striking an effective balance between setting rules and being responsive is a persistent challenge. When does mother or father know best, and when should the child be in charge?

The question of optimal parenting style is further complicated by a growing recognition that cultural contexts can change the definition of "optimal." Some scholars have suggested, for example, that the American emphasis on self-esteem as the top priority for children is a curious cultural construction not considered essential in many cultural contexts. Or, as another example, there is some research evidence suggesting that when raising children in crowded or dangerous communities, using an authoritarian parenting style can be more effective than an authoritative style. Further complicating matters is the fact that culture itself is neither static nor clearly defined: The values, norms, and beliefs that shape what we consider optimal parenting and ideal development vary considerably both within and between communities.

Perhaps because defining optimal parenting is such a complicated task, people are often intrigued when experts claim to have figured it out. When such a claim also includes a provocative challenge to familiar cultural beliefs it can be all the more intriguing. This confluence was exactly what propelled Amy Chua's parenting memoir into national prominence in early 2011. Chua's essay claiming that "Chinese mothers are superior" in the pages of the *Wall Street Journal* drew broad attention, curiosity, and some outrage. Her claim that most "Western" parents are too easy on their children, and that the hard-driving style she identified as Chinese is better for ensuring children's success, led many to respond with a mix of defensiveness and recognition. The response implied that Western parents feel a close attachment to a developmental ideal based on affection and self-esteem while simultaneously recognizing that success in modern society requires discipline, effort, and competitive excellence.

Much of the critical reaction to Chua's essay focused on the perceived harshness of her description of Chinese parenting. As an example, one *Wall Street Journal* columnist proudly contrasted himself with the "Tiger Mother" by proclaiming himself a "Panda Dad" and extolling the virtues of allowing children the freedom to have fun and be creative. But Chua's daughters came to her defense, with one writing an essay of her own titled "Why I love my strict Chinese mom." It turns out Chua's parenting style mostly worked.

The scholarly reaction to the concept of the "Tiger Mother" has, however, been more considered. Many scholars have observed that Chua's perspective triggered broader global economic fears in the West that Chinese ways are the future, and consider the controversy to be as much about modern society as it is about individual parenting style. From that standpoint, Markella B. Rutherford's perspective as a sociologist interested in how child-rearing norms contribute to social inequalities brings together several lines of critique. In fact, Rutherford argues that at root the "Tiger Mother" style is less a cultural model of development and more another way privileged parents can give their children a head start in the global economy. As she notes in her essay, "The claims of cultural differences between so-called Chinese and American approaches are, in fact, red herrings; the 'tiger' and 'panda' approaches are different means for achieving the same goal— children with a strong sense of accomplishment and self-confidence."

Ultimately, then, this controversy invokes a variety of questions relevant to lifespan development. It starts as a consideration of the classic question of whether parents should be strict or lenient, proceeds to consider whether self-esteem matters and how it can be produced, and ends up raising issues about how social inequalities get reproduced. Whether it is culture, social class, or self-esteem, it all comes down to a question of what makes for successful lifespan development.

YES

Amy Chua

Why Chinese Mothers Are Superior

A lot of people wonder how Chinese parents raise such stereotypically successful kids. They wonder what these parents do to produce so many math whizzes and music prodigies, what it's like inside the family, and whether they could do it too. Well, I can tell them, because I've done it. Here are some things my daughters, Sophia and Louisa, were never allowed to do:

- attend a sleepover
- have a playdate
- be in a school play
- complain about not being in a school play
- watch TV or play computer games
- choose their own extracurricular activities
- get any grade less than an A
- not be the No. 1 student in every subject except gym and drama
- play any instrument other than the piano or violin
- not play the piano or violin.

I'm using the term "Chinese mother" loosely. I know some Korean, Indian, Jamaican, Irish and Ghanaian parents who qualify too. Conversely, I know some mothers of Chinese heritage, almost always born in the West, who are not Chinese mothers, by choice or otherwise. I'm also using the term "Western parents" loosely. Western parents come in all varieties.

All the same, even when Western parents think they're being strict, they usually don't come close to being Chinese mothers. For example, my Western friends who consider themselves strict make their children practice their instruments 30 minutes every day. An hour at most. For a Chinese mother, the first hour is the easy part. It's hours two and three that get tough.

Despite our squeamishness about cultural stereotypes, there are tons of studies out there showing marked and quantifiable differences between Chinese and Westerners when it comes to parenting. In one study of 50 Western American mothers and 48 Chinese immigrant mothers, almost 70% of the Western mothers said either that "stressing academic success is not good for children" or that "parents need to foster the idea that learning is fun." By contrast, roughly 0% of the Chinese mothers felt the same way. Instead, the vast majority of the Chinese mothers said that they believe their children can be "the best" students, that "academic achievement reflects successful parenting," and that if children did not excel at school then there was "a problem" and parents "were not doing their job." Other studies indicate that compared to Western parents, Chinese parents spend approximately 10 times as long every day drilling academic activities with their children. By contrast, Western kids are more likely to participate in sports teams.

What Chinese parents understand is that nothing is fun until you're good at it. To get good at anything you have to work, and children on their own never want to work, which is why it is crucial to override their preferences. This often requires fortitude on the part of the parents because the child will resist; things are always hardest at the beginning, which is where Western parents tend to give up. But if done properly, the Chinese strategy produces a virtuous circle. Tenacious practice, practice, practice is crucial for excellence; rote repetition is underrated in America. Once a child starts to excel at something—whether it's math, piano, pitching or ballet—he or she gets praise, admiration and satisfaction. This builds confidence and makes the once not-fun activity fun. This in turn makes it easier for the parent to get the child to work even more.

Chinese parents can get away with things that Western parents can't. Once when I was young—maybe more than once—when I was extremely disrespectful to my mother, my father angrily called me "garbage" in our native Hokkien dialect. It worked really well. I felt terrible and deeply ashamed of what I had done. But it didn't damage my self-esteem or anything like that. I knew exactly how highly he thought of me. I didn't actually think I was worthless or feel like a piece of garbage.

As an adult, I once did the same thing to Sophia, calling her garbage in English when she acted extremely disrespectfully toward me. When I mentioned that I had done this at a dinner party, I was immediately ostracized. One guest named Marcy got so upset she broke down in tears and had to leave early. My friend Susan, the host, tried to rehabilitate me with the remaining guests.

The fact is that Chinese parents can do things that would seem unimaginable—even legally actionable—to Westerners. Chinese mothers can say to their daughters, "Hey fatty—lose some weight." By contrast, Western parents have to tiptoe around the issue, talking in terms of "health" and never ever mentioning the f-word, and their kids still end up in therapy for eating disorders and negative self-image. (I also once heard a Western father toast his adult daughter by calling her "beautiful and incredibly competent." She later told me that made her feel like garbage.)

Chinese parents can order their kids to get straight As. Western parents can only ask their kids to try their best. Chinese parents can say, "You're lazy. All your classmates are getting ahead of you." By contrast, Western parents have to struggle with their own conflicted feelings about achievement, and try to persuade themselves that they're not disappointed about how their kids turned out.

I've thought long and hard about how Chinese parents can get away with what they do. I think there are three big differences between the Chinese and Western parental mind-sets.

First, I've noticed that Western parents are extremely anxious about their children's self-esteem. They worry about how their children will feel if they fail at something, and they constantly try to reassure their children about how good they are notwithstanding a mediocre performance on a test or at a recital. In other words, Western parents are concerned about their children's psyches. Chinese parents aren't. They assume strength, not fragility, and as a result they behave very differently.

For example, if a child comes home with an A-minus on a test, a Western parent will most likely praise the child. The Chinese mother will gasp in horror and ask what went wrong. If the child comes home with a B on the test, some Western parents will still praise the child. Other Western parents will sit their child down and express disapproval, but they will be careful not to make their child feel inadequate or insecure, and they will not call their child "stupid," "worthless" or "a disgrace." Privately, the Western parents may worry that their child does not test well or have aptitude in the subject or that there is something wrong with the curriculum and possibly the whole school. If the child's grades do not improve, they may eventually schedule a meeting with the school principal to challenge the way the subject is being taught or to call into question the teacher's credentials.

If a Chinese child gets a B—which would never happen—there would first be a screaming, hair-tearing explosion. The devastated Chinese mother would then get dozens, maybe hundreds of practice tests and work through them with her child for as long as it takes to get the grade up to an A.

Chinese parents demand perfect grades because they believe that their child can get them. If their child doesn't get them, the Chinese parent assumes it's because the child didn't work hard enough. That's why the solution to substandard performance is always to excoriate, punish and shame the child. The Chinese parent believes that their child will be strong enough to take the shaming and to improve from it. (And when Chinese kids do excel, there is plenty of ego-inflating parental praise lavished in the privacy of the home.)

Second, Chinese parents believe that their kids owe them everything. The reason for this is a little unclear, but it's probably a combination of Confucian filial piety and the fact that the parents have sacrificed and done so much for their children. (And it's true that Chinese mothers get in the trenches, putting in long grueling hours personally tutoring, training, interrogating and spying on their kids.) Anyway, the understanding is that Chinese children must spend their lives repaying their parents by obeying them and making them proud.

By contrast, I don't think most Westerners have the same view of children being permanently indebted to their parents. My husband, Jed, actually has the opposite view. "Children don't choose their parents," he once said to me. "They don't even choose to be born. It's parents who foist life on their kids, so it's the parents' responsibility to provide for them. Kids don't owe their parents anything. Their duty will be to their own kids." This strikes me as a terrible deal for the Western parent.

Third, Chinese parents believe that they know what is best for their children and therefore override all of their children's own desires and preferences. That's why Chinese daughters can't have boyfriends in high school and why Chinese kids can't go to sleepaway camp. It's also why no Chinese kid would ever dare say to their mother, "I got a part in the school play! I'm Villager

Number Six. I'll have to stay after school for rehearsal every day from 3:00 to 7:00, and I'll also need a ride on weekends." God help any Chinese kid who tried that one.

Don't get me wrong: It's not that Chinese parents don't care about their children. Just the opposite. They would give up anything for their children. It's just an entirely different parenting model.

Here's a story in favor of coercion, Chinese-style. Lulu was about 7, still playing two instruments, and working on a piano piece called "The Little White Donkey" by the French composer Jacques Ibert. The piece is really cute—you can just imagine a little donkey ambling along a country road with its master—but it's also incredibly difficult for young players because the two hands have to keep schizophrenically different rhythms.

Lulu couldn't do it. We worked on it nonstop for a week, drilling each of her hands separately, over and over. But whenever we tried putting the hands together, one always morphed into the other, and everything fell apart. Finally, the day before her lesson, Lulu announced in exasperation that she was giving up and stomped off.

"Get back to the piano now," I ordered.

"You can't make me."

"Oh yes, I can."

Back at the piano, Lulu made me pay. She punched, thrashed and kicked. She grabbed the music score and tore it to shreds. I taped the score back together and encased it in a plastic shield so that it could never be destroyed again. Then I hauled Lulu's dollhouse to the car and told her I'd donate it to the Salvation Army piece by piece if she didn't have "The Little White Donkey" perfect by the next day. When Lulu said, "I thought you were going to the Salvation Army, why are you still here?" I threatened her with no lunch, no dinner, no Christmas or Hanukkah presents, no birthday parties for two, three, four years. When she still kept playing it wrong, I told her she was purposely working herself into a frenzy because she was secretly afraid she couldn't do it. I told her to stop being lazy, cowardly, self-indulgent and pathetic.

Jed took me aside. He told me to stop insulting Lulu—which I wasn't even doing, I was just motivating her—and that he didn't think threatening Lulu was helpful. Also, he said, maybe Lulu really just couldn't do the technique—perhaps she didn't have the coordination yet—had I considered that possibility?

"You just don't believe in her," I accused.

"That's ridiculous," Jed said scornfully. "Of course I do."

"Sophia could play the piece when she was this age."

"But Lulu and Sophia are different people," Jed pointed out.

"Oh no, not this," I said, rolling my eyes. "Everyone is special in their special own way," I mimicked sarcastically. "Even losers are special in their own special way. Well don't worry, you don't have to lift a finger. I'm willing to put in as long as it takes, and I'm happy to be the one hated. And you can be the one they adore because you make them pancakes and take them to Yankees games."

I rolled up my sleeves and went back to Lulu. I used every weapon and tactic I could think of. We worked right through dinner into the night, and

I wouldn't let Lulu get up, not for water, not even to go to the bathroom. The house became a war zone, and I lost my voice yelling, but still there seemed to be only negative progress, and even I began to have doubts.

Then, out of the blue, Lulu did it. Her hands suddenly came together—her right and left hands each doing their own imperturbable thing—just like that.

Lulu realized it the same time I did. I held my breath. She tried it tentatively again. Then she played it more confidently and faster, and still the rhythm held. A moment later, she was beaming.

"Mommy, look—it's easy!" After that, she wanted to play the piece over and over and wouldn't leave the piano. That night, she came to sleep in my bed, and we snuggled and hugged, cracking each other up. When she performed "The Little White Donkey" at a recital a few weeks later, parents came up to me and said, "What a perfect piece for Lulu—it's so spunky and so *her*."

Even Jed gave me credit for that one. Western parents worry a lot about their children's self-esteem. But as a parent, one of the worst things you can do for your child's self-esteem is to let them give up. On the flip side, there's nothing better for building confidence than learning you can do something you thought you couldn't.

There are all these new books out there portraying Asian mothers as scheming, callous, overdriven people indifferent to their kids' true interests. For their part, many Chinese secretly believe that they care more about their children and are willing to sacrifice much more for them than Westerners, who seem perfectly content to let their children turn out badly. I think it's a misunderstanding on both sides. All decent parents want to do what's best for their children. The Chinese just have a totally different idea of how to do that.

Western parents try to respect their children's individuality, encouraging them to pursue their true passions, supporting their choices, and providing positive reinforcement and a nurturing environment. By contrast, the Chinese believe that the best way to protect their children is by preparing them for the future, letting them see what they're capable of, and arming them with skills, work habits and inner confidence that no one can ever take away.

Markella B. Rutherford  **NO**

The Social Value of Self-Esteem

A number of cultural skirmishes over the parenting practices of Americans have recently played out in the popular media and blogosphere. Often invoking inventive and colorfully descriptive labels, these rhetorical battles have pitted "Helicopter Parents" against "Free-Range Kids" and "Tiger Mothers" against "Panda Dads." Some parents insist that they should hover over their children, being immediately accessible and responsive at all times; others counter that we must encourage independent development and problem-solving by ensuring that children have opportunities to be on their own, unguarded. Some parents attempt to ensure children's future successes by providing a regimented round of enrichment activities; critics argue that children are over-scheduled and that we must protect children's down time for free play. A varied mixture of "confessionals" published by relatively privileged parents has intermingled with a wide array of diatribes against the contemporary parenting styles of affluent parents.

Of course, moral panics about proper parenting are not new. Before popular concerns about the "over-parenting" of the new professional elites, there were the "mommy wars" of the 1980s and 90s. Before that, there were misgivings about the seemingly relaxed morals of the 60s and 70s, which were themselves a kind of backlash against the conformist tendencies of the post-WWII era. Like critiques of previous generations' parenting practices, this latest round of debates still sometimes places mothers, specifically, in the cross-hairs of public disapproval; however, these contemporary debates are less about social control over adults' gender roles and more about a widespread sense of anxiety over whether parents can ensure their children's future success in an era that is increasingly characterized by risk and uncertainty.

The intense anxieties felt by Americans about parenting in the early-twenty-first century are grounded in the uncertainties of work in a post-industrial and global economy. They also point toward the individualized responsibility that has come to shape parenting in contemporary America, where cultural and community-level support for parenting are generally quite weak. This individualization of responsibility affects all parents, across the socioeconomic spectrum, but has led most intensely to a sense of isolation and status anxiety among the highly-educated and highly-credentialed professionals who make up the so-called "knowledge class" or "new elites." It is these parents, in particular, who are often the focus of discussion when

From *Society*, September 2011, pp. 407–412. Copyright © 2011 by Springer Science and Business Media. Reprinted by permission via Rightslink.

contemporary parenting practices come under critique in the media. Unlike the uniform disapproval expressed whenever the parenting of less-affluent parents enters public discourse, there is a great deal of ambivalence about the practices of today's more elite professionals.

Although a relatively privileged group of parents are at the center of contemporary controversies about over-parenting, questions about how parents can ensure their children's success extend far beyond the relatively privileged bloggers and writers who provide easy targets for equally-privileged critics. Hot-button concerns about how much parenting is enough intersect with much more widespread public concerns about both the quality of public education and the limits of meritocracy. Are American kids "Waiting for Superman" and "Rac[ing] to Nowhere," as the titles of two recent documentary films assert? If the system of public education is failing our children, how should parents respond? Should they advocate for higher educational standards or for less homework? Should they insist on greater state investment in education (and the bureaucratic oversight that accompanies it) or should they focus their attention on local investments of targeted solutions and community volunteers? Uncertain about which investments will "pay off" for children in the future, contemporary parents are increasingly placing their trust in the talisman of children's self esteem; this central focus on self-esteem has led to many of the unique parenting practices of our time and is consistent with the divergent styles that engender such passionate debates in the media.

The "Magic" of Self-Esteem

Despite the exaggerated claims of difference in popular representations of the parenting wars, a common theme of building children's self-esteem is evident as a cornerstone of contemporary American parenting practices. Whether through a heavy-handed strategy or a more hands-off approach, the relatively privileged parents who write child-rearing confessionals profess a strikingly similar end: to build and enhance their children's self-concept, confidence, and emotional competence. Advocates of "free range kids" (see FreeRangeKids .wordpress.com) believe that allowing children ample independence and opportunities to make mistakes are key to developing self-confidence. Defenders of "helicopter parenting" believe that the best way to protect children's self-esteem is to be present and intervene liberally. Despite different strategies, both groups agree that their goal is to raise confident children.

Yale University Law Professor Amy Chua caused a media storm earlier this year with her book, *Battle Hymn of the Tiger Mother* (2011, Penguin Press), in which she asserted, among other things, that Western parents worry too much about their children's self-esteem. Nonetheless, her own measure of successful parenting takes self-confidence as its yardstick: "As a parent, one of the worst things you can do for your child's self-esteem is to let them give up. On the flip side, there's nothing better for building confidence than learning you can do something you thought you couldn't." One of Chua's critics was *Wall Street Journal* columnist Alan Paul, who called himself the "Panda Dad" in opposition. Paul advocates a "cuddlier" strategy of "controlled chaos," explaining his aversion to "Tiger" parenting specifically because he believes it conflicts with his parenting goals "to raise independent, competent, confident adults." According to Paul, his parenting strategy means that his kids are "constantly learning to take responsibility for their own homework, play time and everything else. Doing so allows them to take genuine pride in their accomplishments. They need to succeed for their own benefit . . ." The claims of cultural differences between so-called Chinese and American approaches are, in fact, red herrings; the "tiger" and "panda" approaches are different means for achieving the same goal—children with a strong sense of accomplishment and self-confidence.

Self-esteem has not always been the primary measure of good parenting. This new cultural development represents a particular context and set of conditions that are unique to a particular class position in a global, knowledge economy. Professional-class parents who are anxious about their own prospects for continued success in a risky economy turn toward emotional capital as a necessary supplement to educational end extra-curricular success to ensure generational reproduction of class advantages. Whether through a strictly-directed or laissez-faire approach, they explicitly seek to help their children discover and cultivate their passions and build their self-esteem through personalized successes.

In the myth of meritocracy, we believe that success depends upon talent and hard work. In reality, however, "achieved" statuses depend much more heavily upon received advantages than upon individual merit. Even if children's future successes do not depend wholly upon how good they are, the centrality of self-esteem in current parenting practices indicates that success may be influenced by how good children *believe* they are. Parents who make up the new professional knowledge class recognize that self-confidence and self-promotion are necessary, even if not sufficient, components of success. Thus, though it is certainly not the only form of cultural capital that matters in the reproduction of class advantages, self-esteem is an important kind of emotional capital that forms part of the *habitus* of today's elites.

Working- and lower-middle class parents also care about their children's self-esteem. In particular, those who are keen to foster upward mobility for their children seize upon the idea of self-esteem as a secret ingredient in the elusive recipe for success. Nonetheless, though these less-privileged parents care about their children's self-feelings, one rarely sees them engaging in debates over which strategy is best for cultivating self-esteem. Indeed, they may see positive self-esteem more as a feeling that develops in response to positive circumstances and that parents should support and encourage whenever possible. They do not engage in public philosophical debates about which elaborate strategies are best for the careful cultivation of self-confident children. Therefore, the kind of self-esteem targeted by more elite parents can be regarded a key form of contemporary cultural capital.

There is compelling sociological evidence that we should be paying more attention today to emotions as a form of cultural capital. In charting the emotional terrain of social class, self-esteem offers a particularly useful emotion to begin with. Self-esteem is a critical part of the sense of entitlement that

Annette Lareau documents in *Unequal Childhoods* as emerging from the "concerted cultivation" childrearing approach of the middle class. (In contrast, Lareau argues that the result of the strategy of "accomplishment of natural growth," preferred by working-class parents, is an emerging sense of constraint.) In *Parenting Out of Control*, Margaret Nelson has recently documented, through her nuanced understanding of the interdependence of parenting practices and new technologies, that the sense of entitlement gained by privileged children begins from birth. Nelson documents that an elite parenting strategy of intensive responsiveness and availability is enacted through the use of baby monitors. This practical, technological choice is crucial to establishing, as one respondent told Nelson: "Part of the whole realm of invisible assumptions they have about life . . . if they cry someone will come, if they need help someone will help . . . knowing that someone will always respond." (Nelson 2010, 116) In my own work, I have documented that the approach to building self-esteem in current parenting advice literature hinges on teaching children emotional competency to recognize and express their feelings and the sense children develop that "my feelings matter."

Class Reproduction Among the New Elites

In order to see how a focus on emotional competency and self-esteem have become key components of the childrearing philosophies of today's elites, we must consider the ways that their parenting strategies grow out of the anxieties that upper-middle-class professionals feel about their ability to reproduce their class advantages. For quite some time, we sociologists have insisted that class-based childrearing practices reflect differences in working conditions. We accept that working class parents who are subject to considerable authority and hierarchy at work emphasize obedience in their childrearing, whereas middle-class parents who enjoy considerable autonomy at work emphasize independence and creativity. If we are to understand the foundations of the self-esteem-driven parenting style common today among the elite professional class, we must ask how this style both reflects the demands of professional working conditions and serves to reproduce that class position. If these parents are seeking to pass on their class advantages to their children, we should question: what, exactly is the nature of the advantage they are attempting to reproduce? How does this form of advantage require these strategies? Finally, what do parenting strategies reveal about the changing nature of social class and class reproduction in our time?

The new elites of today, composed of a class of professional, highly-credentialed knowledge workers, earn high incomes and enjoy a great deal of prestige. However, when compared with elites of previous eras, they have relatively low levels of wealth. This means that the reproduction of class advantage among these elites has to happen through a ricky set of mechanisms that is not as easily institutionalized as other historical forms of elite reproduction. In particular, the key source of these elites' status and earning potential—their degrees, credentials, and knowledge—are not (directly) heritable, making these advantages fundamentally different than strictly economic wealth. Because it depends so heavily upon educational credentials, the rise of these new elites signals an intensely individualized form of capital production and has been heralded as the rise of a "new meritocracy." Their class advantage stems not just from *private* property; indeed, it is a highly *personalized* property. The shift from physical and economic capital to the post-industrial capital of degrees and credentials requires new mechanisms for embodying cultural capital. Increasingly, emotional capital is an important element of class reproduction, with self-esteem playing a key role as one of its mechanisms.

Let us look closer at the working conditions of these privileged parents in order to understand why the habit of emphasizing self-esteem makes sense as a parenting strategy for reproducing their class advantages, as well as how the emphasis on self-esteem can unite the seemingly divergent styles through which it is enacted.

Professional Control

In her analysis of diverging class cultures of parenting and how parents make use of various surveillance technologies, Margaret Nelson draws on a Foucaultian framework to distinguish between parenting through discipline and parenting through control. Discipline, a la Foucault, means that hierarchical authority is exercised in such a way that it induces inmates to self-discipline. Children subject to discipline develop an inner compulsion to "do the right thing," thus becoming "docile bodies." In *Parenting Out of Control*, Nelson argues that while previous generations parented from discipline, today's upper-middle-class professionals parent from a strategy of control, which "relies less on enclosure and confinement than on constant communication, less on clear rules than on shifting possibilities, less on hierarchy than on intimacy, less on acknowledged surveillance than on the denial that it is necessary (because of trust), and less on the finished product that on the ongoing processes of shaping 'inmates.' Indeed in this model, there is no 'finished product' or launch into self-discipline" (Nelson 2010, 12). Nelson's analysis examines how these features influence parents' use of various technologies—baby monitors, cell phones, child locator devices, home drug testing—for surveillance and control. Here, I wish to use these features of control to examine the conditions of contemporary capitalism as experienced in the occupational lives of professional, middle-class parents and to better understand why an emphasis on emotional capital and self-esteem are key aspects of these parents' attempts to reproduce class advantage.

Constant Communication and Shifting Possibilities

Nelson points out that elite parents today rely on constant communication and a set of shifting possibilities rather than either confinement or pre-established rules when dealing with their children. For example, parents stay in touch with kids by cell phone rather than establishing a curfew, making many decisions about what is allowable on a case-by-case basis as part of this steady stream of communication. In many ways these parenting strategies mirror the occupational lives of parents. Many elite professionals enjoy relatively flexible work hours and locations but remain in nearly-constant contact with their employers, colleagues, and clients through email and cell phones. Furthermore, a set of shifting possibilities rather than clear rules are necessary in professions that reward creative problem-solving abilities and encourage workers to find ways to recreate existing guidelines and overcome obstacles. Therefore, children growing up in families with fewer clearly-established boundaries and a considerable sense of latitude are being socialized into the kind of working conditions experienced by their professional parents.

Intimacy and Trust

The oft-criticized parenting philosophies of today's elite parents place great importance on intimacy and trust. These emotional elements of elite parenting undergird the concrete practices of latitude and constant communication described above. However, these are not free-floating parenting philosophies: intimacy and trust are also reflective of the emotional demands of a growing number of professional occupations. Increasingly, corporate capitalism has downplayed the appearance of strict hierarchy and come to favor instead a form of "soft power" that requires that managers and others placed in positions of relative power exhibit high levels of emotional competency and use strategies of therapeutic communication such as active listening (Illouz 2007). For corporate managers and for elite professionals, the ability to manage one's own emotions and respond subtly to the emotionality of others is increasingly a necessary skill for occupational success. Recent trends of building kids' emotional intelligence through therapeutic communication and parent–child intimacy therefore serve to reproduce an emotional skill set that is needed for success in many upper-middle-class occupations under the contemporary conditions of capitalism.

Parents who emphasize emotional intimacy with their children are also likely to employ trust as a preferred disciplinary strategy. Nelson found that parents who eschewed certain technologies—such as automobile tracking devices, key stroke recorders, and home drug-testing kits—claimed it was because they value trust and that until trust was clearly broken they saw no need to use such blatant forms of surveillance. To these parents, this trust provided a foundation for the flexible discipline they offered through discussion, negotiation, and constant communication with their children.

Here, too, we can trace clear parallels to the working conditions of many contemporary professionals, who are subject to relatively low levels of short-term accountability at work. These are high prestige occupations in part because of the autonomy they offer. Most professionals are not subjected to the kinds of surveillance that other workers endure—time clocks, nanny cams, customer comment cards, tracking of computer use or online activities are the realm of a different class of workers. Such panoptic disciplinary measures are often unnecessary precisely because of the very high stakes for overall productivity in professional careers. Employer "trust" based on the metric of productivity is brittle and not easily restored once it is broken. Trust is therefore an effective strategy of control because elite workers know that if they do not produce desired results they will be fired, down-sized, or denied tenure. This precariousness of institutional trust creates some of the anxiety that contemporary professionals feel about both maintaining their own status and ensuring that they can pass on their status advantages to their children.

The intimacy and trust that are cornerstones of elites' parenting philosophies replicate their working conditions. These philosophies not only ensure that children will internalize parents' norms and values, they also socialize children into the emotional capital and self-concept that parents hope will help them be successful twenty-first-century professionals. Like the privileges and demands of professional autonomy, intimacy and trust offer children considerable disciplinary latitude while making heavy emotional demands. Children who grow up negotiating the emotional terrain of intimate communication with parents and trust-based, flexible discipline must test out for themselves the boundaries of their parents' latitude and of their own potential. Parents following this philosophy want their children to develop a particular kind of self-confidence that will serve as a basis for the creative risk-taking that is often required for professional success in contemporary capitalism. They presume that this philosophy will lead their children to develop the resilience that Richard Sennett claims is a necessary feature for workers in the unpredictable conditions of the "new capitalism."

An Ongoing Process With No Finished Product

Finally, strategies of control (as opposed to discipline) emphasize ongoing processes rather than finished products. The contemporary professional middle-class experiences anxiety for many reasons, not least of which are the current precarious economic conditions. However, anxiety is also built into the structure of elite jobs in contemporary capitalism. These highly accomplished new elites work under conditions in which the limits are not clearly spelled out and the bar always seems to be changing. Their jobs are structured to make them feel that they have never accomplished enough. Professional socialization into these high-status professions emphasizes that constant productivity matters more than the finished product. The "product," once it is produced, fades in importance, because ultimately what these elites are producing are their own careers, which are ongoing and never complete. Furthermore, because career paths are increasingly flexible and illegible, rather than linear and logical, the *real* product is the *self* that is being shaped and marketed in the package of a career.

Parents subject to this ongoing process of career control tend to favor parenting strategies that also revolve around the ongoing process of shaping children's selves. Because the child's self is an ongoing and unfinished project, self-esteem becomes a convenient gauge of how the project is going. Occasionally warning flags are raised about the intense anxieties of kids who are coping with a never-ending process of ever-increasing educational requirements: in primary and secondary schools, children learn that education is more targeted to standardized tests than the joy of discovery; kids are told that higher and higher levels of education are required as "tickets" to middle-class jobs; sports and extra-curricular activities are seen as resume-builders for college; college, too matters not just for its educational value, but as a prerequisite to a graduate or professional degree, or perhaps to an unpaid internship; and so on.

Despite the psychological toll that the extended gauntlet of adolescence and emerging adulthood exacts, parents and children are largely powerless to reshape the system both because this is how post-industrial capitalism operates and because the heavy emphasis on credentialing produces distinct economic and social benefits for elites. It is more complicated to pass on "achieved" class advantages than heritable wealth. These extended sifting mechanisms severely limit upward mobility and are therefore the price that the new elite pays to reproduce its class advantage. In the absence of systemic strategies to reshape the current game of post-industrial capitalism, then, parents rely upon the individualized task of building children's self-esteem in the hopes that it will see them through the ever-increasing years of education and credentialing, followed by career-building. Self-esteem becomes a critical form of cultural capital when this level of emotional endurance is called for.

The Future of Emotional Styles

Despite claims of difference about which strategies are most effective in producing self-confident children, today's parents agree that children's self-esteem is a vital measure of good parenting. The professional, upper-middle-class parents who have come under scrutiny in the past few years are not inventing a new pattern of childrearing so much as—just like parents in other social locations—they're adapting a pattern of occupational requirements and constraints to the task of childhood and adolescent socialization. Emotional competence and self-confidence are critical to success in contemporary professional spheres; therefore, these same characteristics have become the "gold standard" of good parenting. Though tactics may vary, the cultural goal of elite parenting styles is remarkably similar.

Based upon their experiences as upwardly mobile professionals and their understanding of what it takes to be successful as the new elite knowledge class, elite parents cultivate the same qualities through their childrearing strategies, whether these strategies are criticized as too strict or too lenient. Their distinctive parenting approaches are neither simply passing fads nor a mere generation gap. Instead, social and economic changes in the shift to a new capitalism have meant that the upwardly-mobile parents who make up the new elite have found themselves playing a game that operates by different rules than the ones their parents taught them. Control, much more than discipline, is a fundamental feature of the working conditions in the new elite professions. In their occupational lives, they are rewarded not for staying within clearly-defined limits, but for problem solving, overcoming obstacles, and "thinking outside the box." Because the institutions they work for have sought to flatten hierarchies, their work success requires emotional competence both in managing their own and others' feelings.

Because self-esteem forms a crucial part of the cultural capital that allows elite parents to reproduce their class advantages, it is no passing fad. By considering the structural experience of control in elite parents' occupational lives, we can see why professionals tend to prefer childrearing philosophies that hinge on communication, flexibility, intimacy, and trust. Furthermore, we can see in their working conditions the experiences that have caused them to focus in especially on the project of self in childrearing, making self-esteem both a desirable personal trait as well as cornerstone of class reproduction. In fact, the correspondence between professional control and parental control should cause us to question whether the popular ambivalence often expressed about the particular practices of contemporary parents might not mask a deeper anxiety about the conditions of elite status and its reproduction in contemporary capitalism. A new group of social elites requires new mechanisms for passing on status advantages to their offspring. The current group of professional elites is developing mechanisms of status reproduction that depend upon particular emotional styles. Further study should elucidate additional elements of these emotional styles in order to better understand the current workings of social inequality and the possibilities for social mobility.

CHALLENGE QUESTIONS

Is Chinese Parenting Culturally Distinct?

1. How much does parenting, and by extension ideals about development, really vary by cultural context? What seem to be the points of potential difference and points of potential similarity?
2. There is a classic and persistent tension in parenting debates between being too strict and being too lenient. Why is that dimension in particular so difficult to negotiate?
3. Though Amy Chua's description of her parenting style can seem harsh, her own children seem to have appreciated her efforts with one personally defending Chua against popular criticism. Why? What about the "Tiger Mother" style might actually appeal to a child?
4. How does parenting differ by social class? Why does Markella B. Rutherford think privileged parents are able to subtly give advantages to their children despite the particular parenting style they adopt.
5. Does parenting really determine whether or not people develop into successful adults? What are the things that parents do and do not influence that relate to people's success in society?

Is There Common Ground?

Different models of parenting, whether across cultures or across social class lines, are crucial to understand beyond the issue of how individual parents influence individual children. Models of parenting represent the very ideals we hold about lifespan development. When Amy Chua argues for the superiority of the "Chinese mother," she is implicitly advocating for the importance of discipline and achievement above fun and comfort. When Markella B. Rutherford highlights the way privileged parents confer subtle advantages to their children, she is pointing out the importance of how people are positioned to compete in the global economy. Both Chua and Rutherford thus see parenting as meaningful beyond the actual act of interacting with a child, and it is worth thinking about how and why those meanings come into being.

Suggested Readings

A. Chua, *Battle Hymn of the Tiger Mother* (Penguin Press 2011)

S. Chua-Rubenfeld, "Why I Love My Strict Chinese Mom," *New York Post* (January 18, 2011)

D. Johnson, "Finish That Homework!" *The New York Review of Books* (August 18, 2011)

F. Furedi, "Western Parents Need to Chill Out About Their Kids," *Spiked-Online* (June 9, 2011)

A. Lareau, *Unequal Childhoods: Class, Race, and Family Life* (Second Edition, University of California Press 2011)

M. Nelson, *Parenting Out of Control: Anxious Parents in Uncertain Times,* (NYU Press, 2010)

A. Paul, "Tiger Mom . . . Meet Panda Dad," *Wall Street Journal Ideas Market* (March 29, 2011: http://blogs.wsj.com/ideas-market/2011/03/29/tiger-mom-meet-panda-dad/)

S.T. Russell, L.J. Crockett, and R.K. Chao (Eds.), *Asian American Parenting and Parent-Adolescent Relationships* (Springer 2010)

K. Seal, "Do Asian-American Parents Push Their Kids?" *Miller-McCune* (January 2011)

Internet References . . .

Safe Fetus

This Web site is an extensive reference for checking the influence of various substances on a fetus during pregnancy.

http://www.safefetus.com

The Mayo Clinic

The Mayo Clinic is a well-respected medical institution that offers a variety of articles and resources related to infant health and development.

http://www.mayoclinic.com/health/infant-and-toddler-health/MY00362

The Centers for Disease Control and Prevention

The Centers for Disease Control and Prevention is a government agency offering information about health at all ages, including information specific to infants.

http://www.cdc.gov/ncbddd/child/infants.htm

Jean Piaget and Cognitive Development

This site provides a good overview of the work of Jean Piaget, who started the discussion of infant symbolic representation.

http://www.ship.edu/~cgboeree/genpsypiaget.html

Zero to Three

Zero to Three is a non-profit organization working to facilitate healthy development, and their Web site contains information and resources focused on infants and their families.

http://www.zerotothree.org/

The American Pregnancy Association

The American Pregnancy Association is a non-profit organization offering educational resources related to healthy pregnancies.

http://www.americanpregnancy.org/

March of Dimes

The March of Dimes is a non-profit organization devoted to healthy pregnancies and children, and offer related information at their Web site.

http://www.marchofdimes.com/

La Leche League

The La Leche League is a group promoting and support breastfeeding.

http://www.llli.org

Prenatal Development and Infancy

*O*ur most rapid and astonishing physical changes occur during approximately nine months prior to birth and during the first years of postnatal life. These are unique years in development because of our complete dependence on others. Being without language, a concept of self, and other complex capacities, it is easy to imagine these initial stages as a simple matter of accommodating needs and wants. There is, however, an increasing awareness that there is more to our earliest development than initially meets the eye. This section considers three issues dealing with ways that our experiences during prenatal development and infancy provide a foundation for all the complexity that follows.

- Is Drinking Alcohol While Pregnant an Unnecessary Risk to Prenatal Development?
- Is Breastfeeding Inevitably Best for Healthy Development?
- Are There Good Reasons to Allow Infants to Consume Electronic Media, Such as Television?

ISSUE 4

Is Drinking Alcohol While Pregnant an Unnecessary Risk to Prenatal Development?

YES: Phyllida Brown, from "Drinking for Two," *New Scientist* (July 1, 2006)

NO: Julia Moskin, from "The Weighty Responsibility of Drinking for Two," *The New York Times* (November 29, 2006)

Learning Outcomes

As you read the issue, focus on the following points:

1. Many governments and researchers have become more stringent in recommending that pregnant women should not consume any alcohol, often making no distinction between heavy drinking and light drinking.
2. The recognition of fetal alcohol syndrome is relatively recent (only since the early 1970s), and while it causes a wide variety of problems with physical and mental health it does not affect all children whose mothers drank during pregnancy.
3. Magnetic resonance imaging studies find some changes in the brain structure of children whose mother drank during pregnancy, while animal studies suggest that exposure to alcohol during critical periods of brain development can cause neuronal cell death.
4. Anxiety around maintaining perfect health behaviors may also have some negative effects during pregnancy, and some feel that society should be more trusting of women's ability to make intelligent choices.

ISSUE SUMMARY

YES: Science writer Phyllida Brown reviews contemporary research about the effects of alcohol exposure during prenatal development and concludes that total abstinence from drinking is the smart option during pregnancy.

NO: Journalist Julia Moskin finds the evidence against light drinking lacking, and argues that women should be allowed to decide for themselves if an occasional alcoholic beverage is harmful.

Drinking alcohol while pregnant carries a powerful negative stigma. Public health campaigns and government warnings have effectively conveyed the message that alcohol, along with other drugs, can harm prenatal development. Most people are now familiar with fetal alcohol syndrome (FAS), its symptoms, and its effects. Given that familiarity, however, it is interesting to note that FAS was only "discovered" in 1973. For generations women had drank alcohol during pregnancy. Although there were certainly some negative consequences, there had significantly fewer judgments about women's choices. Has society simply become more enlightened, or have we gone too far?

Scientific research on this issue tends to devote less attention to stigma and more attention to the physical effects of prenatal exposure to alcohol and other teratogens. A teratogen is any external agent that causes malformation of organs and tissue during prenatal development. Fetal exposure to external agents, most often through the mother, is not a process of direct transmission: there are widely varying degrees of detrimental influence on prenatal development.

Further complicating matters, the relationship between teratogens and prenatal development does not necessarily correspond to popular perceptions of danger. In fact, according to ratings by the federal Food and Drug Administration, a drug such as aspirin has more established negative biological effects on a fetus than a drug such as cocaine. These biological effects, however, are often complicated by social context.

Understanding the relationship between exposure to alcohol and prenatal development is also complicated by the fact that many babies born to women who drank during pregnancy do not seem to suffer ill effects. Science writer Phyllida Brown, in arguing that it is safest to avoid all alcohol while pregnant, even acknowledges that "not all babies born to alcolohic women have FAS." So the relationship between a pregnant mother's alcohol consumption and prenatal development is imperfect and requires negotiating uncertain odds. The question then becomes about what sort of odds make drinking while pregnant worth the risk. From Brown's perspective knowing that there is some chance alcohol can harm prenatal development means the only reasonable choice is complete abstinence.

Journalist Julia Moskin argues that a pregnant women can reasonably choose to drink lightly at certain points in a pregnancy. Moskin points out that while much research has been done comparing the effects of heavy drinking during pregnancy with the effects of no drinking during pregnancy, significantly less research has considered the effects of light drinking. As such, when pressed, some doctors will acknowledge that light drinking at later points in pregnancy is not likely to have long-term effects on prenatal development. Moskin's underlying point is relevant to much of what we know about pregnancy: prenatal development is often too complicated a process to allow for simple certainties about what will or won't ensure the healthy children all parents desire.

POINT

- Many governments and researchers are becoming more stringent in recommending pregnant women should not consume any alcohol.
- Government restrictions are being overly cautious by making no distinction between heavy drinking and occasional light drinking during pregnancy.
- Fetal alcohol spectrum disorders can cause children to have a wide range of problems with both physical and mental health during later development.
- The recognition of FAS is relatively recent, and generations of women had healthy children despite drinking during pregnancy.
- Worrying about every potential minor risk to prenatal development can have a negative effect on mental health; in many world cultures, it has historically been considered normal for women to drink lightly during pregnancy.

COUNTERPOINT

- Magnetic resonance imaging studies find some changes in the brain structure of children whose mother drank during pregnancy, while animal studies suggest that exposure to alcohol during critical periods of brain development can cause neuronal cell death.
- Though the science is not yet entirely definitive, the best policy is to take no chances.

- Much of the public reaction against women drinking during pregnancy is really about not trusting women to make intelligent decisions on their own.

YES

Drinking for Two

AT FIRST, Susie's teachers thought she was a bright child. Her adoptive mother knew different. Give Susie a set of instructions and only a few seconds later she would have forgotten them. She was talkative, with a large vocabulary, but could not seem to form lasting friendships. Then, one day, Susie's adoptive mother heard a lecture that described fetal alcohol syndrome—a condition which affects some children born to heavy drinkers. "Bells went off in my head," she says. "The lecturer described eight traits, and my daughter had seven of them."

Children like Susie could well be just the tip of the iceberg. Fetal alcohol syndrome was once thought to affect only the children of heavy drinkers, such as Susie's biological mother, but a mounting body of research suggests that even a small amount of alcohol can damage a developing fetus—a single binge during pregnancy or a moderate seven small glasses of wine per week.

The new research has already prompted some governments to tighten up their advice on drinking during pregnancy. Others, however, say there is no convincing evidence that modest alcohol intake is dangerous for the fetus. With advice varying wildly from one country to another, the message for pregnant women has never been so confusing.

Last year the U.S. Surgeon General revised official advice warning pregnant women to limit their alcohol intake. Now they are told "simply not to drink" alcohol—not only in pregnancy, but as soon as they plan to try for a baby. France also advises abstinence, as does Canada. The UK's Department of Health says that pregnant women should avoid more than "one to two units, once or twice a week", but is finalising a review of the latest evidence, which it will publish within weeks. In Australia, women are advised to "consider" abstinence, but if choosing to drink should limit their intake to less than seven standard Australian drinks a week, with no more than two standard drinks on any one day.

Whichever guidelines women choose to follow, some level of drinking during pregnancy is common in many countries. The last time pregnant women in the UK were asked, in 2002, 61 percent admitted to drinking some alcohol. Even in the U.S., where abstinence is expected, and where pregnant women in some states have been arrested for drinking, 13 percent still admit to doing it.

From *New Scientist Magazine*, July 1, 2006, pp. 46–49. Copyright © 2006 by Reed Business Information, Ltd. Reprinted by permission of Tribune Media Services.

Children with fetal alcohol syndrome (FAS) are generally smaller than average and have a range of developmental and behavioural problems such as an inability to relate to others and a tendency to be impulsive. They also have distinctive facial features such as a thin upper lip, an extra fold of skin in the inner corners of the eyes and a flattening of the groove between the nose and upper lip.

In recent years researchers investigating the effects of alcohol in pregnancy have begun to widen their definition of antenatal alcohol damage beyond the diagnosis of FAS. They now talk of fetal alcohol spectrum disorders, or FASD, an umbrella term that covers a range of physical, mental and behavioural effects which can occur without the facial features of FAS. Like children with FAS, those with FASD may have problems with arithmetic, paying attention, working memory and the planning of tasks. They may be impulsive, find it difficult to judge social situations correctly and relate badly to others, or be labelled as aggressive or defiant. In adulthood they may find it difficult to lead independent lives, be diagnosed with mental illnesses, or get into trouble with the law. Some have damage to the heart, ears or eyes.

While some children with FASD have been exposed to as much alcohol before birth as those with FAS, others may be damaged by lower levels, says Helen Barr, a statistician at the University of Washington, Seattle. Barr has spent 30 years tracking children exposed to alcohol before birth and comparing them with non-exposed children. The less alcohol, in general, says Barr, the milder the effects, such as more subtle attention problems or memory difficulties. Other factors that can affect the type of damage include the fetus's stage of development when exposed to alcohol and the mother's genetic make-up.

Although FASD is not yet an official medical diagnosis, some researchers estimate that it could be very common indeed. While FAS is thought to account for 1 in 500 live births, Ann Streissguth and her colleagues at the University of Washington believe that as many as 1 in every 100 babies born in the U.S. are affected by FASD. Others put the figure at about 1 in 300. Whichever figure is more accurate, it would still make the condition far more common than, say, Downs syndrome, which affects 1 in 800 babies born in the U.S.

Streissguth was among the first to study the long-term effects of moderate drinking in pregnancy. In 1993 she reported that a group of 7-year-olds whose mothers had drunk 7 to 14 standard drinks per week in pregnancy tended to have specific problems with arithmetic and attention. Compared with children of similar IQ whose mothers had abstained during pregnancy, they struggled to remember strings of digits or the details of stories read to them, and were unable to discriminate between two rhythmic sound patterns.

When Streissguth's team followed the alcohol-exposed children through adolescence and into their early twenties they found them significantly more likely than other individuals of similar IQ and social background to be labelled as aggressive by their teachers. According to their parents, these children were unable to consider the effects of their actions on others, and unable to take hints or understand social cues. As young adults, they were more likely to drink heavily and use drugs than their peers.

These findings were borne out by similar studies later in the 1990s by Sandra Jacobson and Joseph Jacobson, both psychologists at Wayne State University in Detroit, Michigan. To try and work out what dose of alcohol might be harmful, the Jacobsons ran a study of children born to 480 women in Detroit. In it, they compared the children born to women who, at their first antenatal appointment, said they drank seven or more standard U.S. drinks a week with the babies of women who drank less than seven, and with those whose mothers abstained altogether. The psychologists then tested the children's mental function in infancy and again at 7 years old. In the children whose mothers had seven drinks or more, the pair found significant deficits in their children's mental function in infancy, and again at age 7, mainly in arithmetic, working memory and attention (*Alcoholism: Clinical and Experimental Research*, vol 28, p. 1732). Where the mother drank less than that they found no effect.

Spread it Out

Seven drinks a week may be more than many pregnant women manage, but according to the Jacobsons, what's important is when you are drinking them, whether you have eaten, and how quickly your body metabolises alcohol. In their study, only one woman of the 480 drank daily; most of the others restricted their drinking to a couple of weekend evenings. If a woman is drinking seven standard drinks on average across the week, but having them all on two nights, she must be reaching four drinks on one night. That constitutes a binge. "Women don't realise that if they save up their alcohol 'allowance' to the end of the week, they are concentrating their drinking in a way that is potentially harmful," she says. This means that even women who have fewer than seven glasses per week could potentially be putting their babies at risk if they drink them all on one night.

There is also some evidence that fewer than seven drinks a week could have measurable effects on an unborn baby. Peter Hepper at Queen's University, Belfast, UK, examined the movements of fetuses scanned on ultrasound in response to a noise stimulus. Having asked women about their drinking habits, they compared the responses of fetuses exposed to low levels of alcohol—between 1 and 6 British units per week, each containing 10 millilitres of alcohol—and those exposed to none. When tested between 20 and 35 weeks, the fetuses exposed to alcohol tended to show a "startle response" usually found only in the earlier stages of pregnancy, when the nervous system is less developed. Five months after birth, the same babies showed different responses to visual stimuli from the babies whose mothers had abstained. Hepper interprets these findings as evidence that a low dose of alcohol has some as yet unexplained effect on the developing nervous system. Whether or not these differences will translate into behaviour problems in later life is as yet unknown.

When Ed Riley and colleagues at San Diego State University in California looked at children's brains using magnetic resonance imaging, they found obvious changes in the brain structure of children whose mothers drank very heavily, but also some changes in children born to moderate drinkers. For example, there were abnormalities in the corpus callosum, the tract of fibres connecting the right and left hemispheres of the brain. The greater the abnormality, the worse the children performed on a verbal learning task.

Despite these recent studies, the link between alcohol and fetal development is far from clear. Not all babies born to alcoholic women have FAS, yet other babies appear to be damaged by their mothers indulging in just a single binge. And if 61 percent of British women drink while pregnant, how come there are not hundreds of thousands of British children with FASD? Wouldn't we notice if 1 in 100 children being born were affected?

Hepper argues that few teachers would raise an eyebrow if they had two or three children in a class of 30 with marked behaviour difficulties, and several more with milder, manageable problems. He therefore thinks it is plausible to suggest that 1 in 100 children could have alcohol-related problems of some sort.

Hepper's research is widely quoted by anti-drinking campaigners such as FAS Aware, an international organisation which advertises in the women's bathrooms of bars to encourage pregnant women not to drink. The posters warn that "drinking in pregnancy could leave you with a hangover for life" and that "everything you drink goes to your baby's head."

Critics of these tactics point out that trying to scare women into abstinence is not helpful. There are reports in North America of women rushing off for an abortion because they had one drink before they knew they were pregnant or being racked with guilt about past drinking if they have a child with a mild disability.

Researchers like the Jacobsons acknowledge that it is hard to be certain about how alcohol affects a developing fetus on the basis of epidemiological studies, especially when they measure the notoriously messy subject of human behaviour. Any effect on the developing brain would vary depending on exactly when the fetus was exposed, and since some behavioural effects may not become apparent until several years after birth, it is difficult to pin down specific disabilities to specific antenatal exposure to alcohol.

To try and get around the epidemiological problem, John Olney, a neuroscientist at Washington University in St Louis, Missouri, has examined the impact of alcohol on developing rodent brains as a model for what happens in humans. Six years ago Olney and others showed that alcohol causes neurons in the developing rat brain to undergo programmed cell death, or apoptosis (*Science,* vol 287, p 1056).

Olney found that alcohol does the most serious damage if exposure happens during synaptogenesis, a critical time in development when neurons are rapidly forming connections. In rats, this happens just after birth, but in humans it begins in the second half of pregnancy and continues for two or more years. In the *Science* study, the team found that exposure to alcohol for baby rats during this developmental stage, at levels equivalent to a binge lasting several hours, could trigger the suicide of millions of neurons, damaging the structure of the animals' forebrains. The alcohol seems to interfere with the action of receptors for two chemical signals or neurotransmitters, glutamate and GABA (gamma amino butyric acid), that must function normally for connections to form.

Lost Neurons

The changes to brain development in rodents, Olney believes, could explain some of the behavioural problems seen in children with FASD, including attention deficit, learning and memory problems. For example, in the rat study, large numbers of neurons were lost in the brain regions that comprise the extended hippocampal circuit, which is disrupted in other disorders of learning and memory (*Addiction Biology,* vol 9, p 137). Loss of cells in the thalamus, which is thought to play a role in "filtering" irrelevant stimuli, may partly explain why FASD children are easily distracted.

The timing of alcohol exposure during pregnancy dictates what type of damage will occur, Olney says: if it is early on, when facial structures are forming, the facial characteristics of FAS may be obvious. Later, when synapses are forming, mental function may be affected. This runs counter to the popular view that the fetus is only vulnerable in the first trimester; in fact, different stages may be vulnerable in different ways.

Olney has recently tried to find out exactly how much alcohol is enough to trigger apoptosis. This year he reported that, in infant mice whose brains are at the equivalent stage of development to a third-trimester fetus, some 20,000 neurons are deleted when they are exposed to only mildly raised blood alcohol levels, for periods as short as 45 minutes. In humans, he says, this is equivalent to deleting 20 million neurons with a 45-minute exposure to blood alcohol levels of just 50 milligrams per 100 millilitres of blood—which is well below the legal limit for driving, and easily achieved in "normal social" drinking (*Neurobiology of Disease,* DOI: 10.1016/j.nbd.2005.12.015). At blood alcohol levels below this, the team found no apoptosis.

Olney is quick to stress that, alarming as 20 million neurons sounds, it is "a very small amount of brain damage" in the context of the human brain, which is estimated to have trillions of neurons. He has no evidence that such small-scale damage would translate into any detectable effects on a child's cognitive abilities. "But if a mother is advised that one or two glasses of wine with dinner is OK, and if she then has two glasses with dinner three times a week, this is exposing the fetus to a little bit of damage three times a week," he says.

The bottom line is that, as yet, it's impossible to translate these findings into blanket advice for women about how many drinks they can or can't have when pregnant. A drink before food will raise blood alcohol concentrations faster than a drink with a meal; two drinks downed quickly will raise it more sharply than two drinks spread over 3 hours. Because of this uncertainty, some researchers—and some authorities—would rather take no chances. "The best possible advice I can give mothers is to totally abstain from alcohol the moment they know they are pregnant," Olney says.

Julia Moskin  **NO**

The Weighty Responsibility of Drinking for Two

IT happens at coffee bars. It happens at cheese counters. But most of all, it happens at bars and restaurants. Pregnant women are slow-moving targets for strangers who judge what we eat—and, especially, drink.

"Nothing makes people more uncomfortable than a pregnant woman sitting at the bar," said Brianna Walker, a bartender in Los Angeles. "The other customers can't take their eyes off her."

Drinking during *pregnancy* quickly became taboo in the United States after 1981, when the Surgeon General began warning women about the dangers of alcohol. The warnings came after researchers at the *University of Washington* identified Fetal Alcohol Syndrome, a group of physical and mental birth defects caused by alcohol consumption, in 1973. In its recommendations, the government does not distinguish between heavy drinking and the occasional beer: all alcohol poses an unacceptable risk, it says.

So those of us who drink, even occasionally, during pregnancy face unanswerable questions, like why would anyone risk the health of a child for a passing pleasure like a beer?

"It comes down to this: I just don't buy it," said Holly Masur, a mother of two in Deerfield, Ill., who often had half a glass of wine with dinner during her pregnancies, based on advice from both her mother and her obstetrician. "How can a few sips of wine be dangerous when women used to drink martinis and smoke all through their pregnancies?"

Many American obstetricians, skeptical about the need for total abstinence, quietly tell their patients that an occasional beer or glass of wine—no hard liquor—is fine.

"If a patient tells me that she's drinking two or three glasses of wine a week, I am personally comfortable with that after the first trimester," said Dr. Austin Chen, an obstetrician in TriBeCa. "But technically I am sticking my neck out by saying so."

Americans' complicated relationship with food and drink—in which everything desirable is also potentially dangerous—only becomes magnified in pregnancy.

When I was pregnant with my first child in 2001 there was so much conflicting information that doubt became a reflexive response. Why was tea allowed but not coffee? How could all "soft cheeses" be forbidden if cream cheese was recommended? What were the real risks of having a glass of wine on my birthday?

Pregnant women are told that danger lurks everywhere: listeria in soft cheese, mercury in canned tuna, *salmonella* in fresh-squeezed orange juice. Our responsibility for minimizing risk through perfect behavior feels vast.

Eventually, instead of automatically following every rule, I began looking for proof.

Proof, it turns out, is hard to come by when it comes to "moderate" or "occasional" drinking during pregnancy. Standard definitions, clinical trials and long-range studies simply do not exist.

"Clinically speaking, there is no such thing as moderate drinking in pregnancy" said Dr. Ernest L. Abel, a professor at Wayne State University Medical School in Detroit, who has led many studies on pregnancy and alcohol. "The studies address only heavy drinking"—defined by the *National Institutes of Health* as five drinks or more per day—"or no drinking."

Most pregnant women in America say in surveys that they do not drink at all—although they may not be reporting with total accuracy. But others make a conscious choice not to rule out drinking altogether.

For me, the desire to drink turned out to be all tied up with the ritual of the table—sitting down in a restaurant, reading the menu, taking that first bite of bread and butter. That was the only time, I found, that sparkling water or nonalcoholic beer didn't quite do it. And so, after examining my conscience and the research available, I concluded that one drink with dinner was an acceptable risk.

My husband, frankly, is uncomfortable with it. But he recognizes that there is no way for him to put himself in my position, or to know what he would do under the same circumstances.

While occasional drinking is not a decision I take lightly, it is also a decision in which I am not (quite) alone. Lisa Felter McKenney, a teacher in Chicago whose first child is due in January, said she feels comfortable at her current level of three drinks a week, having been grudgingly cleared by her obstetrician. "Being able to look forward to a beer with my husband at the end of the day really helps me deal with the horrible parts of being pregnant," she said. "It makes me feel like myself: not the alcohol, but the ritual. Usually I just take a few sips and that's enough."

Ana Sortun, a chef in Cambridge, Mass., who gave birth last year, said that she (and the nurse practitioner who delivered her baby) both drank wine during their pregnancies. "I didn't do it every day, but I did it often," she said. "Ultimately I trusted my own instincts, and my doctor's, more than anything else. Plus, I really believe all that stuff about the European tradition."

Many women who choose to drink have pointed to the habits of European women who legendarily drink wine, eat raw-milk cheese and quaff Guinness to improve breast milk production, as justification for their own choices in pregnancy.

Of course, those countries have their own taboos. "Just try to buy unpasteurized cheese in England, or to eat salad in France when you're pregnant," wrote a friend living in York, England. (Many French obstetricians warn patients that raw vegetables are risky.) However, she said, a drink a day is taken for granted. In those cultures, wine and beer are considered akin to food, part of daily life; in ours, they are treated more like drugs.

But more European countries are adopting the American stance of abstinence. . . .

If pregnant Frenchwomen are giving up wine completely (although whether that will happen is debatable—the effects of warning labels are far from proven), where does that leave the rest of us?

"I never thought it would happen," said Jancis Robinson, a prominent wine critic in Britain, one of the few countries with government guidelines that still allow pregnant women any alcohol—one to two drinks per week. Ms. Robinson, who spent three days tasting wine for her Masters of Wine qualification in 1990 while pregnant with her second child, said that she studied the research then available and while she was inclined to be cautious, she didn't see proof that total abstinence was the only safe course.

One thing is certain: drinking is a confusing and controversial choice for pregnant women, and among the hardest areas in which to interpret the research.

Numerous long-term studies, including the original one at the University of Washington at Seattle, have established beyond doubt that heavy drinkers are taking tremendous risks with their children's health.

But for women who want to apply that research to the question of whether they must refuse a single glass of champagne on New Year's Eve or a serving of rum-soaked Christmas pudding, there is almost no information at all.

My own decision came down to a stubborn conviction that feels like common sense: a single drink—sipped slowly, with food to slow the absorption—is unlikely to have much effect.

Some clinicians agree with that instinct. Others claim that the threat at any level is real.

"Blood alcohol level is the key," said Dr. Abel, whose view, after 30 years of research, is that brain damage and other alcohol-related problems most likely result from the spikes in blood alcohol concentration that come from binge drinking—another difficult definition, since according to Dr. Abel a binge can be as few as two drinks, drunk in rapid succession, or as many as 14, depending on a woman's physiology.

Because of ethical considerations, virtually no clinical trials can be performed on pregnant women.

"Part of the research problem is that we have mostly animal studies to work with," Dr. Abel said. "And who knows what is two drinks, for a mouse?"

Little attention has been paid to pregnant women at the low end of the consumption spectrum because there isn't a clear threat to public health there, according to Janet Golden, a history professor at Rutgers who has written about Americans' changing attitudes toward drinking in pregnancy.

The research—and the public health concern—is focused on getting pregnant women who don't regulate their intake to stop completely.

And the public seems to seriously doubt whether pregnant women can be trusted to make responsible decisions on their own.

"Strangers, and courts, will intervene with a pregnant woman when they would never dream of touching anyone else," Ms. Golden said.

Ms. Walker, the bartender, agreed. "I've had customers ask me to tell them what the pregnant woman is drinking," she said. "But I don't tell them. Like with all customers, unless someone is drunk and difficult it's no one else's business—or mine."

CHALLENGE QUESTIONS

Is Drinking Alcohol While Pregnant an Unnecessary Risk to Prenatal Development?

1. If science was able to offer odds as to the likelihood of drinking during pregnancy causing developmental problems, what odds would be too great to risk? Is any risk at all too much, or does the potential comfort and familiarity of light drinking matter for mothers?
2. Why would government agencies be getting more conservative with their recommendations regarding drinking during pregnancy? Should mothers have the right to make informed decisions on their own, or is this really a public issue?
3. How likely does it seem that a good postnatal environment could make up for significant exposure to teratogens, such as alcohol, during prenatal development?
4. What would be the various advantages and disadvantages to labeling children exposed to alcohol during prenatal development as susceptible to fetal alcohol "disorders"? Is it possible such labels could themselves be a problem during development?
5. What are the particular challenges of researching prenatal development, and how might those challenges complicate efforts to understand the effects of alcohol on prenatal development?

Is There Common Ground?

Both Phyllida Brown and Julia Moskin would likely agree that the "discovery" of fetal alcohol syndrome in the early 1970s was a good thing. Both would also likely agree that research into fetal alcohol syndrome has provided valuable information related to prenatal development. Where they differ most is in what to do with that information. Because we have learned that alcohol can cause problems during prenatal development, even though we do not know the exact circumstances that produce those problems, is it fair to prohibit all drinking during pregnancy? When do we err on the side of caution, and when do we err on the side of trusting pregnant women to make good decisions? And if we do get more nuanced research findings of the sort that both Brown and Moskin would likely appreciate, when do we have enough to make definitive judgments about the risks of drinking during pregnancy?

Suggested Readings

R. Gray, R.A.S. Mukherjee, and M. Rutter, "Alcohol Consumption During Pregnancy and its Effects on Neurodevelopment: What Is Known and What Remains Uncertain," *Addiction* (August 2009)

E. Abel, "Fetal Alcohol Syndrome: Same Old, Same Old," *Addiction* (August 2009)

C.M. O'Leary and C. Bower, "Measurement and Clarification of Prenatal Alcohol Exposure and Child Outcomes: Time for Improvement," *Addiction* (August 2009)

C. Gavaghan, "'You Can't *Handle* the Truth'; Medical Paternalism and Prenatal Alcohol Use," *Journal of Medical Ethics*, (May 2009)

V. Nathanson, N. Jayesinghe, and G. Roycroft, "Is it All Right for Women to Drink Small Amounts of Alcohol in Pregnancy? No," *British Medical Journal* (October 2007)

P. O'Brien, "Is it All Right for Women to Drink Small Amounts of Alcohol in Pregnancy? Yes," *British Medical Journal* (October 2007)

J. Golden, *Message in a Bottle: The Making of Fetal Alcohol Syndrome*, (Harvard University Press 2006)

ISSUE 5

Is Breastfeeding Inevitably Best for Healthy Development?

YES: U.S. Department of Health and Human Services, from *The Surgeon General's Call to Action to Support Breastfeeding* (Office of the Surgeon General, 2011)

NO: Julie E. Artis, from "Breastfeed at Your Own Risk," *Contexts* (vol. 8, no. 4, Fall 2009)

Learning Outcomes

As you read the issue, focus on the following points:

1. Research suggests that the breastfeeding of infants can have positive health effects, psychosocial effects, economic effects, and environmental effects, but it is not a simple issue to research.

2. The decision to breastfeed is not entirely the responsibility of individual mothers; the health care system, workplaces, family members, communities, and many other circumstances play both obvious and subtle roles in shaping breastfeeding rates.

3. Historical shifts and demographic differences in breastfeeding rates have depended upon cultural values that shape attitudes towards the "natural" and technology as part of healthy development.

4. Breastfeeding may be an example of a broader ideology of "intensive mothering" where mothers feel obliged to sacrifice their own independence to take total responsibility for their children.

ISSUE SUMMARY

YES: As part of a broad mandate to advocate for public health, the U.S. Surgeon General cites numerous benefits of breastfeeding as part of "call to action" oriented toward increasing the practice among new mothers.

NO: Sociologist Julie E. Artis argues that the broad promotion of breastfeeding has the potential to unfairly stigmatize women who do not breastfeed while overstating the benefits.

"**B**reast is best." It is a catchy, alliterative, simple slogan that inundates new parents trying to figure out how to ensure their children get off to the best possible developmental start. And most mothers do start their children on breast milk: according to the U.S. Surgeon General, 75 percent of American newborns are breastfed. The Surgeon General also notes, however, that those rates quickly decline: "only 13 percent of babies are exclusively breastfed at the end of six months." With the easy availability of formula as an alternative to breastfeeding, the challenges mothers face in needing to be constantly available to their infants, the physical limitations some mothers confront in producing breast milk, and numerous other barriers to exclusive breastfeeding, many parents use alternative means of feeding their babies despite hearing "breast is best." It turns out that for many parents breastfeeding may not be so simple after all.

One major complication related to breastfeeding is the mixed messages sent throughout our society. On the one hand, major public health campaigns (such as that originating in the U.S. Surgeon General's office through the U.S. Department of Health and Human Services) heavily promote breastfeeding. Those campaigns are then complemented by the messaging of many health care providers and by advocacy groups such as the La Leche League. On the other hand, companies promoting baby food and formula produce extensive marketing suggesting their products can be similarly nutritious, while many workplaces and public spaces implicitly discourage breastfeeding through a lack of time or privacy. Those discouragements are then enhanced by confusing attitudes about public decency and the display of a breast.

The mixed messages around breastfeeding can become overwhelming to already anxious parents. In fact, sociologist Julie E. Artis argues that confusing messages about breastfeeding are one specific manifestation of a general anxiety that tends to characterize modern childrearing. Mothers in particular often feel as though they are responsible for every detail of infant development, and we are taught that infancy is a critical foundation for all later development. There are "right" ways to stimulate infants, to rest infants, to transport infants, to interact with infants, and perhaps nothing feels more important to get right than feeding. Artis is therefore concerned that women who are unable to breastfeed will end up feeling unnecessarily stressed and guilty.

Artis also offers an intriguing historical overview of generational changes in attitudes toward breastfeeding, noting that as recently as 1971 only 24 percent of American mothers breastfed newborns. She ties this to "technological advancements" that led many in the mid to late twentieth century to think "a scientifically developed substance [infant formula] was at least equivalent to, and possibly better than, breastmilk." This shift is part of an interesting general tension in lifespan development between relying on new technology and relying on "natural" tools and old ways that have worked for generations. It is worth remembering that infants have thrived for the whole of human history on a diet consisting primarily of breastmilk. But it is similarly noteworthy that the 76 percent of American babies born in 1971 who were not breastfed have mostly turned out fine (think about the 40-somethings you know).

Another challenge around both the importance of breastfeeding and the idealization of "natural" ways to facilitate infant development is to interpret the available science. The U.S. Surgeon General cites significant evidence suggesting that breastfed babies do better on measures ranging from physical health to IQ. But Artis points out that those findings may not be as definitive as they seem—research in this area often contrasts children of mothers who choose to breastfeed with children of mothers who choose not to breastfed, and there may be systematic differences between those groups. In support of that possibility, both the U.S. Surgeon General and Artis note that there are wide variations in breastfeeding rates between demographic groups differing by ethnicity, education, and so forth.

Most scholars and public health officials ultimately agree that breastfeeding seems to have general advantages for infant development. Mother's milk is remarkably well suited to fulfill the needs of a newborn child, the process of breastfeeding can provide intensely valuable bonding experiences, and the whole endeavor offers and awe-inspiring example of the integral nature of lifespan development. But saying that breastfeeding has general advantages is not the same as assuming the breast is always best—campaigns to promote breastfeeding may do as much to promote a particular version of "intensive mothering" as to promote healthy infant development.

YES

U.S. Department of Health and Human Services

The Surgeon General's Call to Action to Support Breastfeeding

Foreword from the Surgeon General, U.S. Department of Health and Human Services

For nearly all infants, breastfeeding is the best source of infant nutrition and immunologic protection, and it provides remarkable health benefits to mothers as well. Babies who are breastfed are less likely to become overweight and obese. Many mothers in the United States want to breastfeed, and most try. And yet within only three months after giving birth, more than two-thirds of breastfeeding mothers have already begun using formula. By six months postpartum, more than half of mothers have given up on breastfeeding, and mothers who breastfeed one-year-olds or toddlers are a rarity in our society.

October 2010 marked the 10th anniversary of the release of the *HHS Blueprint for Action on Breastfeeding*, in which former Surgeon General David Satcher, M.D., Ph.D., reiterated the commitment of previous Surgeons General to support breastfeeding as a public health goal. This was the first comprehensive framework for national action on breastfeeding. It was created through collaboration among representatives from medical, business, women's health, and advocacy groups as well as academic communities. The *Blueprint* provided specific action steps for the health care system, researchers, employers, and communities to better protect, promote, and support breastfeeding.

I have issued this *Call to Action* because the time has come to set forth the important roles and responsibilities of clinicians, employers, communities, researchers, and government leaders and to urge us all to take on a commitment to enable mothers to meet their personal goals for breastfeeding. Mothers are acutely aware of and devoted to their responsibilities when it comes to feeding their children, but the responsibilities of others must be identified so that all mothers can obtain the information, help, and support they deserve when they breastfeed their infants. Identifying the support systems that are needed to help mothers meet their personal breastfeeding goals will allow them to stop feeling guilty and alone when problems with breastfeeding arise. All too often, mothers who wish to breastfeed encounter daunting challenges in moving through the health care system. Furthermore, there is often an incompatibility between employment and breastfeeding, but with help this is not impossible to overcome. Even so, because the barriers can seem insurmountable at times, many mothers stop breastfeeding. In addition, families

U.S. Department of Health and Human Services, 2011.

are often unable to find the support they need in their communities to make breastfeeding work for them. From a societal perspective, many research questions related to breastfeeding remain unanswered, and for too long, breastfeeding has received insufficient national attention as a public health issue.

This *Call to Action* describes in detail how different people and organizations can contribute to the health of mothers and their children. Rarely are we given the chance to make such a profound and lasting difference in the lives of so many. I am confident that this *Call to Action* will spark countless imaginative, effective, and mutually supportive endeavors that improve support for breastfeeding mothers and children in our nation.

Regina M. Benjamin, M.D., M.B.A.
Vice Admiral, U.S. Public Health Service
Surgeon General

The Importance of Breastfeeding

Health Effects

The health effects of breastfeeding are well recognized and apply to mothers and children in developed nations such as the United States as well as to those in developing countries. Breast milk is uniquely suited to the human infant's nutritional needs and is a live substance with unparalleled immunological and anti-inflammatory properties that protect against a host of illnesses and diseases for both mothers and children.

In 2007, the Agency for Healthcare Research and Quality (AHRQ) published a summary of systematic reviews and meta-analyses on breastfeeding and maternal and infant health outcomes in developed countries. The AHRQ report reaffirmed the health risks associated with formula feeding and early weaning from breastfeeding. With regard to short-term risks, formula feeding is associated with increases in common childhood infections, such as diarrhea and ear infections. The risk of acute ear infection, also called acute otitis media, is 100 percent higher among exclusively formula-fed infants than in those who are exclusively breastfed during the first six months (see Table 1).

The risk associated with some relatively rare but serious infections and diseases, such as severe lower respiratory infections and leukemia are also higher for formula-fed infants. The risk of hospitalization for lower respiratory tract disease in the first year of life is more than 250 percent higher among babies who are formula fed than in those who are exclusively breastfed at least four months. Furthermore, the risk of sudden infant death syndrome is 56 percent higher among infants who are never breastfed. For vulnerable premature infants, formula feeding is associated with higher rates of necrotizing enterocolitis (NEC). The AHRQ report also concludes that formula feeding is associated with higher risks for major chronic diseases and conditions, such as type 2 diabetes, asthma, and childhood obesity, all three of which have increased among U.S. children over time.

As shown in Table 1, compared with mothers who breastfeed, those who do not breastfeed also experience increased risks for certain poor health

Table 1

Excess Health Risks Associated with Not Breastfeeding

Outcome	Excess Risk* (%)
Among full-term infants	
Acute ear infection (otitis media)	100
Eczema (atopic dermatitis)	47
Diarrhea and vomiting (gastrointestinal infection)	178
Hospitalization for lower respiratory tract diseases in the first year	257
Asthma, with family history	67
Asthma, no family history	35
Childhood obesity	32
Type 2 diabetes mellitus	64
Acute lymphocytic leukemia	23
Acute myelogenous leukemia	18
Sudden infant death syndrome	56
Among preterm infants	
Necrotizing enterocolitis	138
Among mothers	
Breast cancer	4
Ovarian cancer	27

* The excess risk is approximated by using the odds ratios reported in the referenced studies.

outcomes. For example, several studies have found the risk of breast cancer to be higher for women who have never breastfed. Similarly, the risk of ovarian cancer was found to be 27 percent higher for women who had never breastfed than for those who had breastfed for some period of time. In general, exclusive breastfeeding and longer durations of breastfeeding are associated with better maternal health outcomes.

The AHRQ report cautioned that, although a history of breastfeeding is associated with a reduced risk of many diseases in infants and mothers, almost all the data in the AHRQ review were gathered from observational studies. Therefore, the associations described in the report do not necessarily represent causality. Another limitation of the systematic review was the wide variation in quality among the body of evidence across health outcomes.

As stated by the U.S. Preventive Services Task Force (USPSTF) evidence review, human milk is the natural source of nutrition for all infants. The value of breastfeeding and human milk for infant nutrition and growth has been long recognized, and the health outcomes of nutrition and growth were not covered by the AHRQ review.

Psychosocial Effects

Although the typical woman may cite the health advantages for herself and her child as major reasons that she breastfeeds, another important factor is the desire to experience a sense of bonding or closeness with her newborn. Indeed, some women indicate that the psychological benefit of breastfeeding, including bonding more closely with their babies, is the most important influence on their decision to breastfeed. Even women who exclusively formula feed have reported feeling that breastfeeding is more likely than formula feeding to create a close bond between mother and child.

In addition, although the literature is not conclusive on this matter, breastfeeding may help to lower the risk of postpartum depression, a serious condition that almost 13 percent of mothers experience. This disorder poses risks not only to the mother's health but also to the health of her child, particularly when she is unable to fully care for her infant. Research findings in this area are mixed, but some studies have found that women who have breastfed and women with longer durations of breastfeeding have a lower risk of postpartum depression. Whether postpartum depression affects breastfeeding or vice versa, however, is not well understood.

Economic Effects

In addition to the health advantages of breastfeeding for mothers and their children, there are economic benefits associated with breastfeeding that can be realized by families, employers, private and government insurers, and the nation as a whole. For example, a study conducted more than a decade ago estimated that families who followed optimal breastfeeding practices could save more than $1,200–$1,500 in expenditures for infant formula in the first year alone. In addition, better infant health means fewer health insurance claims, less employee time off to care for sick children, and higher productivity, all of which concern employers.

Increasing rates of breastfeeding can help reduce the prevalence of various illnesses and health conditions, which in turn results in lower health care costs. A study conducted in 2001 on the economic impact of breastfeeding for three illnesses—otitis media, gastroenteritis, and NEG—found that increasing the proportion of children who were breastfed in 2000 to the targets established in *Healthy People 2010* would have saved an estimated $3.6 billion annually. These savings were based on direct costs (e.g., costs for formula as well as physician, hospital, clinic, laboratory, and procedural fees) and indirect costs (e.g., wages parents lose while caring for an ill child), as well as the estimated cost of premature death. A more recent study that used costs adjusted to 2007 dollars and evaluated costs associated with additional illnesses and diseases (sudden infant death syndrome, hospitalization for lower respiratory tract infection in infancy, atopic dermatitis, childhood leukemia, childhood obesity, childhood asthma, and type 1 diabetes mellitus) found that if 90 percent of U.S. families followed guidelines to breastfeed exclusively for six months, the United States would save $13 billion annually from reduced direct medical and indirect costs and the cost of premature death. If 80 percent of U.S. families complied, $10.5 billion per year would be saved.

Environmental Effects

Breastfeeding also confers global environmental benefits; human milk is a natural, renewable food that acts as a complete source of babies' nutrition for about the first six months of life. Furthermore, there are no packages involved, as opposed to infant formulas and other substitutes for human milk that require packaging that ultimately may be deposited in landfills. For every one million formula-fed babies, 150 million containers of formula are consumed; while some of those containers could be recycled, many end up in landfills. In addition, infant formulas must be transported from their place of manufacture to retail locations, such as grocery stores, so that they can be purchased by families. Although breastfeeding requires mothers to consume a small amount of additional calories, it generally requires no containers, no paper, no fuel to prepare, and no transportation to deliver, and it reduces the carbon footprint by saving precious global resources and energy.

Endorsement of Breastfeeding as the Best Nutrition for Infants

Because breastfeeding confers many important health and other benefits, including psychosocial, economic, and environmental benefits, it is not surprising that breastfeeding has been recommended by several prominent organizations of health professionals, among them the American Academy of Pediatrics (AAP), American Academy of Family Physicians, American College of Obstetricians and Gynecologists, American College of Nurse-Midwives, American Dietetic Association, and American Public Health Association, all of which recommend that most infants in the United States be breastfed for at least 12 months. These organizations also recommend that for about the first six months, infants be exclusively breastfed, meaning they should not be given any foods or liquids other than breast milk, not even water.

Regarding nutrient composition, the American Dietetic Association stated, "Human milk is uniquely tailored to meet the nutrition needs of human infants. It has the appropriate balance of nutrients provided in easily digestible and bioavailable forms." The AAP stated, "Human milk is species-specific, and all substitute feeding preparations differ markedly from it, making human milk uniquely superior for infant feeding. Exclusive breastfeeding is the reference or normative model against which all alternative feeding methods must be measured with regard to growth, health, development, and all other short- and long-term outcomes."

While breastfeeding is recommended for most infants, it is also recognized that a small number of women cannot or should not breastfeed. For example, AAP states that breastfeeding is contraindicated for mothers with HIV, human T-cell lymphotropic virus type 1 or type 2, active untreated tuberculosis, or herpes simplex lesions on the breast. Infants with galactosemia should not be breastfed. Additionally, the maternal use of certain drugs or treatments, including illicit drugs, antimetabolites, chemotherapeutic agents, and radioactive isotope therapies, is cause for not breastfeeding.

Federal Policy on Breastfeeding

Over the last 25 years, the Surgeons General of the United States have worked to protect, promote, and support breastfeeding. In 1984, Surgeon General C. Everett Koop convened the first Surgeon General's Workshop on Breastfeeding, which drew together professional and lay experts to outline key actions needed to improve breastfeeding rates. Participants developed recommendations in six distinct areas: 1) the world of work, 2) public education, 3) professional education, 4) health care system, 5) support services, and 6) research. Follow-up reports in 1985 and 1991 documented progress in implementing the original recommendations.

In 1990, the United States signed onto the *Innocenti Declaration on the Protection, Promotion and Support of Breastfeeding,* which was adopted by the World Health Organization (WHO) and the United Nations Children's Fund (UNICEF). This declaration called upon all governments to nationally coordinate breastfeeding activities, ensure optimal practices in support of breastfeeding through maternity services, take action on the *International Code of Marketing of Breast-milk Substitutes* (the Code), and enact legislation to protect breastfeeding among working women.

In 1999, Surgeon General David Satcher requested that a departmental policy on breastfeeding be developed, with particular emphasis on reducing racial and ethnic disparities in breastfeeding. The following year, the Secretary of the U.S. Department of Health and Human Services (HHS), under the leadership of the department's Office on Women's Health (OWH), released the *HHS Blueprint for Action on Breastfeeding.* This document, which has received widespread attention in the years since its release, declared breastfeeding to be a key public health issue in the United States.

Rates of Breastfeeding

Over the last few decades, rates of breastfeeding have improved, but in recent years, rates generally have climbed more slowly. Figure 1 presents data from 1970 through 2007 from two sources. Data before 1999 are from the Ross Mothers Survey. Data for 1999 through 2007 are from the Centers for Disease Control and Prevention's (CDC) annual National Immunization Survey (NIS), which includes a series of questions regarding breastfeeding practices.

National objectives for *Healthy People 2010,* in addition to calling for 75 percent of mothers to initiate breastfeeding, called for 50 percent to continue breastfeeding for six months and 25 percent to continue breastfeeding for one year. *Healthy People 2010* also included objectives for exclusive breastfeeding: targets were for 40 percent of women to breastfeed exclusively for three months and for 17 percent to do so for six months.

The most recent NIS data shown in Figure 1 indicate that, while the rate of breastfeeding initiation has met the 2010 target, rates of duration and

Figure 1

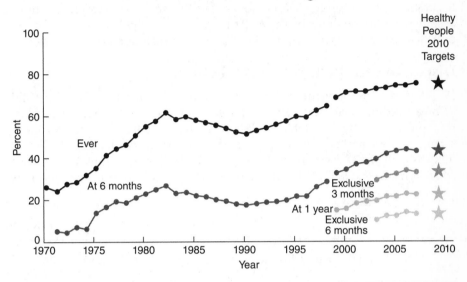

National Trends in Breastfeeding Rates

Note: Data from before 1999 are from a different source, as indicated by the line break.

Sources: 1970–1998, Ross Mothers Survey; 1999–2007, Centers for Disease Control and Prevention, National Immunization Survey.

exclusivity still fall short of *Healthy People 2010* objectives. Among children born in 2007, 75 percent of mothers initiated breastfeeding, 43 percent were breastfeeding at six months, and 22 percent were breastfeeding at 12 months (see Figure 1). Although human milk is the only nutrition most babies need for about the first six months, many women discontinue breastfeeding or add other foods or liquids to their baby's diet well before the child reaches six months of age. Among breastfed infants born in 2007, an estimated 33 percent were exclusively breastfed through age three months, and only 13 percent were exclusively breastfed for six months.

Although much is known about rates of breastfeeding in the population, mothers' breastfeeding practices have not been well understood until recently. The Infant Feeding Practices Study II, conducted during 2005–2007 by the U.S. Food and Drug Administration (FDA) in collaboration with CDC, was designed to fill in some of the gaps. For this longitudinal study of women followed from late pregnancy through their infants' first year of life, participants were selected from across the United States. On average, members of the study group had higher levels of education, were older, were more likely to be white, were more likely to have a middle-level income, and were more likely to be employed than the overall U.S. female population.

Some of the findings from this study were discouraging; for instance, almost half of breastfed newborns were supplemented with infant formula while they were still in the hospital after birth. Most healthy, full-term, breastfed newborns have no medical need to receive supplemental infant formula, and supplementing with infant formula can be detrimental to breastfeeding. In addition, more than 40 percent of infants in the Infant Feeding Practices Study II sample were consuming solid foods within the first four months after birth despite recommendations by the AAP that no infant, whether breastfed or formula fed, should be given any solid foods until at least the age of four months.

Disparities in Breastfeeding Practices

Despite overall improvements in breastfeeding rates, unacceptable disparities in breastfeeding have persisted by race/ethnicity, socioeconomic characteristics, and geography (see Table 2). For example, breastfeeding rates for black infants are about 50 percent lower than those for white infants at birth, age six months, and age 12 months, even when controlling for the family's income or educational level. On the other hand, the gap between white and black mothers

Table 2

Provisional Breastfeeding Rates Among Children Born in 2007*

Sociodemographic Factor	Ever Breastfed (%)	Breastfeeding at 6 Months (%)	Breastfeeding at 12 Months (%)
United States	75.0	43.0	22.4
Race/ethnicity			
American Indian or Alaska Native	73.8	42.4	20.7
Asian or Pacific Islander	83.0	56.4	32.8
Hispanic or Latino	80.6	46.0	24.7
Non-Hispanic Black or African American	58.1	27.5	12.5
Non-Hispanic White	76.2	44.7	23.3
Receiving WIC[†]			
Yes	67.5	33.7	17.5
No, but eligible	77.5	48.2	30.7
Ineligible	84.6	54.2	27.6
Maternal education			
Not a high school graduate	67.0	37.0	21.9
High school graduate	66.1	31.4	15.1
Some college	76.5	41.0	20.5
College graduate	88.3	59.9	31.1

* Survey limited to children aged 19–35 months at the time of data collection. The lag between birth and collection of data allows for tracking of breastfeeding initiation as well as calculating the duration of breastfeeding.
† WIC = Special Supplemental Nutrition Program for Women, Infants, and Children; U.S. Department of Agriculture.
Source: Centers for Disease Control and Prevention, National Immunization Survey.

in initiation of breastfeeding has diminished over time, from 35 percentage points in 1990 to 18 percentage points in 2007. Yet, the gap in rates of breast-feeding continuation at six months has remained around 15 percentage points throughout this period.

The reasons for the persistently lower rates of breastfeeding among African American women are not well understood, but employment may play a role. African American women tend to return to work earlier after childbirth than white women, and they are more likely to work in environments that do not support breastfeeding. Although research has shown that returning to work is associated with early discontinuation of breastfeeding, a supportive work environment may make a difference in whether mothers are able to con-tinue breastfeeding.

With regard to socioeconomic characteristics, many studies have found income to be positively associated with breastfeeding. For example, a study that included children participating in the U.S. Department of Agriculture's (USDA) Special Supplemental Nutrition Program for Women, Infants, and Children (WIC), which uses income to determine eligibility, found they were less likely to be breastfed than children in middle- and upper-income families. Educa-tional status is also associated with breastfeeding; women with less than a high school education are far less likely to breastfeed than women who have earned a college degree. Geographic disparities are also evident; women living in the southeastern United States are less likely to initiate and continue breastfeeding than women in other areas of the country and women living in rural areas are less likely to breastfeed than women in urban areas. Understanding the reasons for these disparities is crucial for identifying, developing, and implementing strategies to overcome the barriers to breastfeeding that women and families experience throughout our country. Research suggests that 1) race and ethnic-ity are associated with breastfeeding regardless of income, and 2) income is associated with breastfeeding regardless of race or ethnicity. Other possible contributors to the disparities in breastfeeding include the media, which has often cited more difficulties with breastfeeding than positive stories, hospital policies and practices, the recommendations of WIC counselors, marketing of infant formula, policies on work and parental leave, legislation, social and cultural norms, and advice from family and friends.

Barriers to Breastfeeding in the United states

Even though a variety of evidence indicates that breastfeeding reduces many different health risks for mothers and children, numerous barriers to breast-feeding remain—and action is needed to overcome these barriers. . . .

Julie E. Artis  **NO**

Breastfeed at Your Own Risk

For nearly two years, the U.S. Department of Health and Human Services spent $2 million on an ad campaign to promote breastfeeding by educating mothers about the risks of not doing so. Those risks were often communicated in provocative ways. One television ad, for example, showed a pregnant African American woman riding a mechanical bull, and then the message appears on the screen, "You wouldn't take risks before your baby is born. Why start after?"

This campaign was the culmination of three decades of increasing consensus among medical and public health professionals that, as the saying goes, "breast is best"—that there is no better nutrition for the first year of an infant's life than breastmilk. The endorsement of the medical establishment is echoed in advice books and parenting magazines that overwhelmingly recommend breastfeeding over formula. Communities have passed laws to support breastfeeding mothers in the workplace and to ensure public breastfeeding isn't legally categorized as indecency.

And rates of breastfeeding in the United States have increased dramatically—nearly 75 percent of mothers now breastfeed newborns, up from 24 percent in 1971. Rates of breastfeeding are even higher among middle-class, educated mothers. For these mothers, breastfeeding has become less of a choice and more of an imperative—a way to protect their infant's health and boost their IQ. Breastfeeding is a way to achieve so-called good mothering, the idealized notion of mothers as selfless and child-centered.

Taking a sociological look at the cultural imperative to breastfeed illustrates how mothering is shaped by discussions among scientists, doctors, and other experts, as well as policy recommendations that grow out of scientific findings. It also reveals that breastfeeding and infant feeding practices differ by culture, race, class, and ethnicity, and that the "breast is best" conventional wisdom doesn't take these differences into account. Thus, this campaign leaves many mothers feeling inadequate—and perhaps unnecessarily so because the scientific evidence about the benefits of breastfeeding are less clear-cut than mothers have been led to believe.

Historical Trends in Breastfeeding

Cultural ideas about motherhood and family in the United States have changed significantly over time, thanks in part to science and technology.

Religious authorities, midwives, and physicians encouraged mothers in the 17th and 18th centuries to breastfeed their infants. The practice through the mid-1800s, in a primarily farm-based society, was to nurse infants through their "second summer" to avoid unrefrigerated and possibly spoiled food and milk.

Wet nursing—breastfeeding a child who is not a woman's own—became necessary when a mother was severely ill or died during childbirth. Breast-milk was widely thought superior to "hand-feeding"—providing milk, tea, or "pap" (a mixture of flour, sugar, water, and milk)—in promoting infant health, but even so, according to historian Janet Golden in her study *A Social History of Wet Nursing,* families worried about having a wet nurse of "questionable" moral fitness, and these fears were exacerbated by race and class divisions. In the north, wet nurses were typically poor immigrant mothers; in the south, they tended to be African Americans, and it was common for female slaves to be wet nurses in the antebellum south. However, by the turn of the 20th century, the use of wet nurses had declined, in part because pasteurization made bottle-feeding a safe alternative to breastmilk. This was also the era in which children came to be seen as priceless, in need of protection, and worth extraordinary investment, sociologist Viviana Zelizer explained in *Pricing the Priceless Child.*

Technological advancements led to the development of mass-marketed infant formula in the 1950s. Doctors then began to recommend formula, say-ing a scientifically developed substance was at least equivalent to, and possibly better than, breastmilk. By the early 1970s, breastfeeding rates in hospitals were at a low of approximately 24 percent, with only 5 percent of mothers nursing for several months following birth.

It was in this era that some feminist women's health groups and Chris-tian women's groups such as La Leche League began challenging the medical model by promoting "natural" childbirth and breastfeeding. These groups pro-moted the benefits of breastfeeding and also raised public awareness about the activities of formula companies.

For example, some feminist health groups helped organize a boycott of Nestle in the late 1970s for promoting formula in developing countries. These groups claimed that Nestle's formula marketing tactics in Africa had led to 1 million infant deaths (from mixing powered formula with contaminated water, or feeding infants diluted formula because of the expense). The success of these small groups in challenging the corporate marketing of formula led to increasing consensus that breastfeeding was better than bottlefeeding. Soon, the medical establishment was embracing breastfeeding, based on scientific studies that confirmed the benefits La Leche League and other feminist health groups had been talking about for years. In 1978, the American Academy of Pediatricians (AAP) recommended breastfeeding over formula, marking the beginning of the shift in mainstream medical advice to mothers. Since then, scientific evidence and the medical establishment have continued to reaffirm the benefits of breastmilk.

Trends over the last 40 years gathered from a survey of mothers show how experts' recommendations and public discussions about breastfeeding have

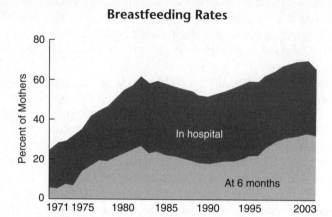

Breastfeeding Rates

Source: Mothers Survey, Ross Products Division of Abbott

influenced breastfeeding rates. The graph above shows the sharp increase in breastfeeding in the 1970s. In the 1980s, there is a slight decrease and plateau in breastfeeding initiation rates, and then, in the 1990s, the rate steadily rises to nearly 70 percent. The rates of breastfeeding until six months of age follow a very similar pattern, although overall the rates are quite lower than breastfeeding initiation; currently, only about one-third of mothers report breastfeeding at six months. This recent rise in breastfeeding rates can be explained, at least in part, by the ideology of intensive mothering.

Breastfeeding as Intensive Mothering

Childrearing advice books, pediatricians, parenting magazines, and even formula companies themselves now universally recommend breastmilk over formula. The consensus that "breast is best" is embedded in cultural ideals of motherhood.

In her book *The Cultural Contradictions of Motherhood*, sociologist Sharon Hays identifies an ideology of intensive mothering and describes how it's at work in the United States: Mothers—not fathers—serve as the primary caregivers of children; mothering practices are time-intensive, expensive, supported by expert advice, child-centered, and emotionally absorbing; and children are viewed as priceless, and the work that must be done to raise them can't be compared to paid work because it's infinitely more important.

The ideology of intensive mothering helps explain why we hear so much playground chatter and read so many magazine articles about getting children into the "best" school, the idea that natural childbirth is better than one assisted by medication or other medical interventions, and the recent discussion of "opt-out" mothers who leave high-powered jobs to stay home with their children. Hays contends the strength of the intensive mothering ideology is the result of an "ambivalence about a society based solely on the competitive pursuit of self-interest."

This may be one reason, for example, journalist Judith Warner, in her book *Perfect Madness: Motherhood in the Age of Anxiety*, felt such a difference when she was mothering in France compared to when she returned with her children to the United States. In France the state offers practical support to mothers, including subsidized childcare, universal healthcare, and excellent public education beginning at age 3. Furthermore, Warner explained that, as a new mother there, she found herself in the middle of an extensive and sympathetic support network that attended to her needs as a mother as much as they attended to the needs of her child. "It was a bad thing [for mothers] to go it alone," she wrote. In contrast, upon her return to the United States Warner felt isolated and anxious. She linked this directly to what she called the "American culture of rugged individualism." Mothers in the United States were under extraordinary pressure to be a "good mother"—otherwise, who else would protect their child from an individualistic, self-interested society?

The cultural imperative to breastfeed is part of the ideology of intensive mothering—it requires the mother be the central caregiver, because only she produces milk; breastfeeding is in line with expert advice and takes a great deal of time and commitment; and finally, the act of breastfeeding is a way to demonstrate that the child is priceless, and that whatever the cost, be it a loss of productivity at work or staying at home, children come first.

Since Hays links the intensive motherhood ideology to American individualistic sensibilities, it would seem to suggest that breastfeeding rates in the United States would be higher than other countries. To return to the example of France, only 50 percent of French mothers breastfeed their newborns, compared to 75 percent of American mothers. However, upon closer examination of statistics compiled by Le Leche League International, U.S. breastfeeding rates lag far behind many other countries, including European countries other than France (Germany, Italy, Spain, and the Scandinavian countries all have breastfeeding initiation rates around 90 percent). Most countries in Asia, Africa, and South America report breastfeeding initiation rates higher than the United States, as do New Zealand and Australia.

Clearly the cultural imperative to breastfeed in the United States has met some resistance. This resistance may be reflected in public debates about breastfeeding, which quickly dissolve into mud-slinging, judgmental arguments that pit mothers against mothers. Not "the mommy wars" in the traditional sense—working moms versus stay-at-home moms—but instead bottlefeeding versus breastfeeding moms.

Breastfeeding mothers, and a subset of those mothers who are deeply committed to breastfeeding promotion (sometimes referred to as "lactivists"), point to a continuing undercurrent of resistance to breastfeeding. Despite the fact that scientists and doctors recommend breastfeeding, and that these recommendations have been disseminated through a public health ad campaign and parenting magazines, breastfeeding remains controversial. While society wants mothers to breastfeed to protect and promote infant health, it wants them to do so behind closed doors. Indeed mothers are often asked to cover themselves while nursing in restaurants.

For example, in 2007 a nursing mother was asked by an Applebee's employee to cover herself while nursing or leave the restaurant. After repeated calls by enraged nursing mothers to the corporate headquarters, executives there insisted it was reasonable to ask the nursing mother to leave, despite a state law that extended mothers the right to nurse in public spaces. This incident resulted in "nurse-ins" at Applebee's locations all over the United States in protest. The social networking site Facebook found itself in a similar firestorm of controversy at the beginning of 2009 when it removed photos of breastfeeding mothers because they violated the site's decency standards. The resistance to nursing-in-public arises from the link between breasts and sexuality, including the idea that breasts are indecent.

Note that these public debates about breastfeeding and mothering in the United States emerge primarily from discussions by and about middle class mothers. The ideal of intensive mothering is much easier for these women to achieve. Even so, studies have explored the extensive labor middle class mothers must engage in just to meet current breastfeeding recommendations.

Sociologist Orit Avishai demonstrates through interviews of white, middle class mothers that they treat breastfeeding not as a natural, pleasurable, connective act with their infant but instead as a disembodied project to be researched and managed. They take classes about breastfeeding, have home visits from lactation consultants post-partum, and view their bodies as feeding machines. When returning to work, they set up elaborate systems to pump breastmilk and store it. These middle-class women were accustomed to setting goals and achieving them—so when they decided to breastfeed for the one year the AAP recommends, they set out to do just that despite the physical and mental drawbacks. Although it's easier for middle class mothers to meet the recommended breastfeeding standards than it is for less privileged mothers, they're at the same time controlled by a culture that equates good mothering with breastfeeding.

Variations in Class and Culture

In *At the Breast*, sociologist Linda Blum examined how mothers of different classes aspired to or rejected the intensive mothering ideology and mainstream cultural imperative to breastfeed. Through interviews with white middle-class mothers who were members of La Leche League, as well as with a sample of both white and black working-class mothers, Blum's study was the first (and is also the most extensive) to expose how the meaning of breastfeeding varies by class and race.

Her interviews with the La Leche mothers revealed the organization's emphasis on an intimate, relational bond between mother and child created through breastfeeding. They rejected medical, scheduled, and mechanized infant feeding and emphasized how important it is for mothers to read their babies' cues and be near them all the time. As such, a mother's care is seen as irreplaceable. One mother told Blum, "Only a mother can give what a child

Breastfeeding Rates by Race/Ethnicity

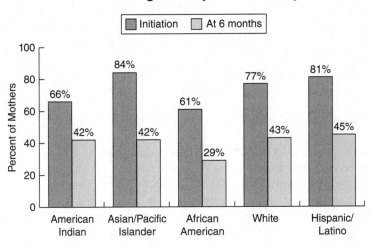

Source: National Immunization Survey, CDC 2005

needs, nobody else can, not even a father. A father can give almost as close, but only a mother can give what they really need." Some of these mothers were also very critical of working mothers. "I'm pretty negative to people who just want to dump their kids off and go to work eight hours a day," one said. Ultimately, Blum contends La Leche League is a self-help group largely created by and for white, middle-class women.

In contrast, interviews with white working-class mothers revealed they understood the health benefits of breastfeeding and embraced the ideal of intensive mothering, but that they often didn't breastfeed because of constraints with jobs, lack of social support, inadequate nutrition, and limited access to medical advice. Working-class mothers were less likely to have jobs that allowed time and privacy to pump breastmilk and were less likely to have access to (paid or unpaid) maternity leave. Some felt it was embarrassing or restrictive. Yet, they still aspired to the middle class ideal of intensive mothering, so they were left feeling guilty and inadequate. Many reported feeling like their bodies had failed them. One mother, for example, said, "At first [breast-feeding] was great. I can't explain the feeling, but at first it was really great. [But then,] I felt . . . useless, if I couldn't nurse my baby, I was a flop as a mother."

Ethnic and racial differences were even more unique and revealing. Black working-class mothers in Blum's study were similar to white working-class mothers in understanding the health benefits of breastmilk. However, their discussions about not breastfeeding were, for the most part, remarkably free of guilt. In short, black mothers rejected the dominant cultural ideal of intensive mothering, and had a more broadly construed definition of what it meant to be a good mother. Many African American women, for example, talked about the importance of involving older children and extended family in caring for the child, and insisted one way this could be accomplished was through bottlefeeding. Some black mothers reacted negatively to breastfeeding because they believed it reinforced long-standing racist stereotypes about the black female body as threatening or even animalistic. By rejecting medical advice about breastfeeding, black mothers asserted some control over their own bodies. "The doctors said that breastmilk was the best, but I told them I didn't want to. They tried to talk me into it, but they couldn't," one interviewee told Blum.

These cultural differences in the meaning of breastfeeding to white and African American mothers are reflected in breastfeeding initiation statistics. White, Asian, and Hispanic mothers have roughly similar rates of breastfeeding initiation, while African American and American Indian mothers have lower rates (above).

The importance of cultural differences and how they play out in breastfeeding practices has also been explored in studies of immigration. A study by public policy professor Christina Gibson-Davis and Jeanne Brooks-Gunn, co-director of the Columbia University Institute on Child and Family Policy, found that breastfeeding rates among Hispanics were related to the mother's country of birth. If the mother was born outside the United States and immigrated, she was more likely to breastfeed. Furthermore, for each additional year the mother had lived in the United States, her odds of breastfeeding decreased by 4 percent. These patterns suggest that the more acculturated the mother is in U.S. society, the less likely she is to breastfeed.

However, another study examining Vietnamese immigrant mothers in Quebec contradicts that model. Medical anthropologist Danielle Groleau and colleagues interviewed 19 Vietnamese mothers who immigrated to Quebec. They argue that geography and culture combine to create a context in which mothers decide not to breastfeed. In the Vietnamese traditional understanding of post-partum medicine and breastfeeding, women are said to suffer from excessive cold, which leads to fatigue, and the production of breastmilk that isn't fresh. In Vietnam, new mothers are cared for by extended family for several months post-partum in order to balance their health and allow them to produce "fresh" breastmilk. However, Vietnamese immigrants in Quebec had low rates of breastfeeding primarily because the lack of social support and caregiving that would have been offered in Vietnam wasn't available in Canada. They saw bottlefeeding as optimal for their babies because their breastmilk wasn't fresh. These mothers weren't adopting the dominant Canadian cultural model and had retained their own cultural ideals about breastfeeding.

Problematic Science

The understanding that "breast is best" is based on scientific studies linking breastfeeding to a variety of health benefits. The breastfeeding recommendations issued by AAP, the World Health Organization, and other public health organizations state that breastfeeding increases IQ and lowers the likelihood of ear infections, diabetes, respiratory and gastrointestinal illnesses, and obesity. These benefits are transmitted to the public as unambiguous scientific findings. But upon closer examination, the science behind these claims is problematic.

Political scientist Joan Wolf, in the *Journal of Health Politics, Policy, and Law*, argues that the benefits of breastfeeding have been vastly overstated. Perhaps the largest problem is that it's impossible to conduct a controlled experiment—by asking some mothers to breastfeed and others to formula-feed—so all studies are observational. In other words, researchers have to tease out the characteristics of those who decide to breastfeed from the benefits of breastmilk itself. Mothers who choose to breastfeed may also promote a host of other health-protective and IQ-promoting behaviors in their children that go unmeasured in observational studies. The problem becomes even more pronounced when trying to examine the long-term health benefits of breast-feeding because there are even more potential unmeasured factors between infancy and adolescence that contribute to overall health.

Some researchers have attempted to control for potential unmeasured factors by studying the health of siblings who were fed differently as infants. Although these studies can't discern why the mother breastfed one child but not the other, they do control for parenting factors that go unmeasured in other studies. For example, a recent sibling study by economists Eirik Even-house and Siobhan Reilly, based on data from the National Longitudinal Study of Adolescent Health, suggests correlations between breastfeeding and a variety health benefits, including diabetes, asthma, allergies, and obesity, disappear when studying siblings within families. Only one outcome remains significant—that the breastfed sibling had a slightly higher IQ score (siblings who were ever breastfed scored 1.68 percentile points higher than siblings who were never breastfed).

Most of these studies can be critiqued for exaggerating the importance of small and weak associations; however, although these correlations are weak, they are consistently found. Furthermore, despite weak correlations, biomedical researchers have in some cases been able to identify the biologi-cal mechanisms that offer infants health protection. For example, one very consistent finding seems to be that breastmilk lowers the incidence, length, and severity of gastrointestinal illness because gut-protective antibodies, including IgA and lactoferrin, are passed from mother to child through breastmilk.

To be sure, not all biomedical research on breastmilk identifies beneficial biological mechanisms. Medical researchers have found breastmilk to contain HIV, alcohol, drugs, and environmental toxins. How these findings are used by public health officials varies. To take the case of HIV, in parts of the world with high rates of infection, public health officials debate whether to recom-mend breastfeeding or not. Even if the mother is HIV positive, some argue the infant may gain other protective health benefits from breastmilk, espe-cially in resource-poor countries plagued by inadequate water supply, limited refrigeration, and poor sanitary conditions. In the United States, however, mothers are now routinely advised to bottlefeed if they have HIV. Mothers in the United States are also advised to stop nursing if, for medical reasons, they have to take medication that passes through breastmilk and may be harmful to the baby. Nevertheless, the overwhelming public health message continues to be "breast is best."

Breastfeeding for Public Health

The "Babies Were Born to be Breastfed" public health ad campaign was designed to educate the public about the benefits of breastfeeding and the risks of not doing so. The campaign hoped to achieve goals established by the Department of Health and Human Services "Blueprint for Action on Breastfeeding"—75 percent of mothers initiating breastfeeding and 50 percent breastfeeding their babies until five months by 2010.

But the campaign, along with doctors' advice and parenting publications, treat the decision to breastfeed as an individual choice without attending to the social and cultural situations in which this choice is made. The decision to breastfeed is shaped by a variety of social and cultural factors, including doctor-patient interaction, social support networks, labor force participation, child care arrangements, race and ethnicity, class, income, and education. Treating breastfeeding and other parenting practices as individual, decontextualized choices holds mothers solely responsible for their children's health.

In an analysis of discussions about mothering, bioethics professor Rebecca Kukla argues that we hold mothers accountable for all kinds of childhood health problems, including obesity, malnutrition, birth defects, and behavioral disorders. The fact that many of these health problems are disproportionately overrepresented among the lower class further demonizes poor, working-class mothers. Furthermore, by focusing on mothers' individual responsibility for child health and well-being, we aren't attending to other, more egregious societal issues that negatively affect children, such as pollution or lack of adequate health care.

Scientific research on infant health is incredibly important. However, as these findings are reported to the public, shaped into recommendations, and developed into public policy, it's important to view them with a critical eye. We need to consider the unintended consequences of breastfeeding promotion and other recommended parenting practices. These recommendations and policy based upon this science may inspire stress and guilt in mothers, especially poor and non-white mothers, when they don't measure up.

CHALLENGE QUESTIONS

Is Breastfeeding Inevitably Best for Healthy Development?

1. What research findings offer the most compelling support for the developmental importance of breastfeeding? What can researchers do to deal with the challenges of studying breastfeeding when those who choose to breastfeed often comprise distinct demographic groups?
2. Breastfeeding is one of several issues related to lifespan development that depends upon a contrast between doing what is "natural" and relying on "artificial" technology. What are the contexts in which "natural" ways of facilitating healthy infant development are best, and what are the ways that modern advances such as nutritious infant formula can have distinct advantages?
3. The U.S. Surgeon General notes that "a mother should not be made to feel guilty if she cannot or chooses not to breastfeed," but often that is easier said than felt. What are ways to promote breastfeeding when possible without implicitly criticizing those who do not or cannot breastfeed?
4. Artis critiques the ideology of "intensive mothering," but is it necessarily bad? What are the potential advantages and disadvantages of intensive mothering?

Is There Common Ground?

What would happen if we replaced the slogan "breast is best" with something like "breast is pretty good if there are no mitigating circumstances to prevent it"? Certainly not as catchy, but perhaps something the U.S. Surgeon General and Julie E. Artis could agree upon. In fact, both would likely agree that public messages about breastfeeding, whether from infant formula marketers or the La Leche League, help shape the decisions mothers make. That also means infant development is shaped as much by the meanings we attach to breastfeeding as by the actual breastmilk consumed. In fact, no one here is arguing that the actual act of an infant consuming breasmilk is a bad thing; the difference comes in conveying its relative value in a fair way that does not negatively stigmatize mothers. Or, at least in this case, perhaps stigma is an inevitable consequence of an honest effort to promote healthy development?

Suggested Readings

O. Avishai, "Managing the Lactating Body: The Breast-Feeding Project and Privileged Motherhood," *Qualitative Sociology* (June 2007)

E. Evenhouse and S. Reilly, "Improved Estimates of the Benefits of Breastfeeding Using Sibling Comparisons to Reduce Selection Bias," *Health Sciences Research* (December 2005)

M. McCaughey, "Got Milk? Breastfeeding as an 'Incurably Informed' Feminist STS Scholar," *Science as Culture* (March 2010)

Pediatrics: Official Journal of the American Academy of Pediatrics October 2008, volume 122, issue supplement articles on breastfeeding

P.A. Schulze and S.A. Carlisle, "What Research Does and Doesn't Say About Breastfeeding: A Critical Review," *Early Child Development and Care* (July 2010)

J. Warner, *Perfect Madness: Motherhood in the Age of Anxiety* (Riverhead Books 2005)

J.B. Wolf. "Is Breast Really Best? Risk and Total Motherhood in the National Breastfeeding Awareness Campaign," *Journal of Health Politics, Policy, and Law* (August 2007)

ISSUE 6

Are There Good Reasons to Allow Infants to Consume Electronic Media, Such as Television?

YES: **Victoria Rideout, Elizabeth Hamel, and the Kaiser Family Foundation,** from "The Media Family: Electronic Media in the Lives of Infants, Toddlers, Preschoolers and Their Parents" A Report from the Kaiser Family Foundation (May 2006)

NO: **Ellen Wartella and Michael Robb,** from "Young Children, New Media" *Journal of Children and Media* (Issue 1, 2007)

Learning Outcomes

As you read the issue, focus on the following points:

1. Exposing infants to electronic media is a relatively new phenomenon, but it is increasingly common largely because of its convenience to busy parents.
2. The American Academy of Pediatrics recommends against children under two years of age watching any screen media.
3. The marketplace for infant media tends to move faster than the science, such that many companies make claims about the value of media that are not supported by research.
4. Although some forms of video media may facilitate learning in older children, there is a concern that early exposure to screen media may actually detract from human interaction and impair the development of attention.

ISSUE SUMMARY

YES: Victoria Rideout, Elizabeth Hamel, and the Kaiser Family Foundation find that television and electronic media allow families to cope with busy schedules and are of value to parents of infants.

NO: Ellen Wartella and Michael Robb, who are scholars of children and the media, describe limitations on infant's ability to learn from electronic media and note concerns about the diminishing of direct infant to parent interactions.

In this technology age most people at all stages of the life-span consume massive amounts of electronic media, including television, computer media, music, and video games. For better or worse, the media and market forces tend to move faster than scientific efforts to understand the impact of that consumption. This fact is particularly evident in the contemporary controversy regarding electronic media and infancy. Despite a 1999 policy statement from the American Academy of Pediatricians recommending against any exposure to electronic screens during infancy, there is a growing market for DVDs, television shows, and electronic games specifically targeting very young children. The "Baby Einstein" products may be the best known, but even the Sesame Street Workshop has entered the fray with videos specifically targeting infants.

So what is the impact of this media on infants and the young mind during this developmental stage? The short answer is that no one is entirely sure. Parents and media companies hope that the impact might be positive—it seems logically possible that well-designed media could be a positive and educational influence on a developing mind. Some would argue that electronic media could not do any harm. However, many scholars are concerned that exposure to electronic media at very young ages may in fact have a negative impact on developing capacities for language, attention, and other crucial cognitive skills. Groups such as the *Campaign for a Commercial Free Childhood* have been vociferous in their opposition to electronic media marketed towards infants. At the heart of both sides is the core question for infant development: what constitutes a healthy environment for the young mind?

As Victoria Rideout, Elizabeth Hamel, and the Kaiser Family Foundation explain in their effort to understand the role of electronic media in contemporary families, many parents rely on electronic media to help create a safe environment. In surveys and interviews with diverse groups of parents, it becomes clear that parents are aware that certain types of electronic media can be problematic for infants but that there may be a thoughtful and healthy way to use other media formats to manage the challenges of raising children in contemporary society. They suggest that exposing children to electronic media is simply a realty of modern life, and that is not necessarily a bad thing.

Scholars Ellen Wartella and Michael Robb, on the other hand, focus their attention specifically on the capacity of a young mind to learn and develop in appropriate ways. They review evidence suggesting that during infancy, cognition may not allow for children to effectively learn from video, and any hopes invested in videos may actually take away from the ways that infants do learn. They are wary of the increasing amount of screen media directed toward infants, including a new cable channel named BabyFirstTV specifically targeting children younger than 3. Wartella and Robb also note that more research is needed to learn about this complex issue—with infants who have not yet acquired language, it is always a challenge to know exactly what is getting through.

POINT

- Electronic media is an important way that parents can manage the household in the face of increasing demands on their time, and many parents are very enthusiastic about electronic media.
- The educational value of media for infants and young children has improved.

- The research is not very up to date—the marketplace for infant media has moved faster than the science.

- Children can take messages from TV and interpret them—they may pick up things they would otherwise not be exposed to (such as different languages and types of people).

COUNTER POINT

- The American Academy of Pediatrics recommends against children under 2 years of age watching any screen media.

- While some forms of video media may facilitate learning in older children, there is very little evidence for similar processes during infancy.
- Research suggests that it is difficult for infants to learn from screen media because they are usually more attuned to physical realities and do not yet have the cognitive ability for elaborate symbolic representations.
- Early exposure to screen media may actually distract infants to the point where it diminishes human interaction and impairs the development of attention.

YES  Victoria Rideout, Elizabeth Hamel, and Kaiser Family Foundation

The Media Family

Introduction

Today's parents live in a world where media are an ever-changing but increasingly important part of their family's lives, including even their very youngest children. Baby videos designed for one-month-olds, computer games for 9-month-olds, and TV shows for one-year-olds are becoming commonplace. An increasing number of TV shows, videos, websites, software programs, video games, and interactive TV toys are designed specifically for babies, toddlers, and preschoolers.

One thing that hasn't changed is that parents have a tough job—in fact, maybe tougher, often with both husband and wife working and juggling complex schedules, and with a growing number of single parents. In this environment, parents often turn to media as an important tool to help them manage their household and keep their kids entertained.

And for many parents, media are much more than entertainment: from teaching children letters and numbers, to introducing them to foreign languages or how to work with computers, many parents find the educational value of media incredibly helpful.

> "My daughter is learning a lot from the different shows she watches. She's so into it. I think it's important."
>
> [Mother of a 1–3 year-old, Irvine, California]

At the same time, there is growing controversy about media use among very young children, with pediatricians recommending no screen media for babies under two, and limited screen time after that. Most child development experts believe that the stimuli children receive and the activities they engage in during the first few years of life are critical not only for their physical well-being but also for their social, emotional, and cognitive development.

But scientific research about the impact of media use on babies and toddlers has not kept pace with the marketplace. As a result, very little is known for sure about what is good and bad when it comes to media exposure in early childhood.

On the positive side of the ledger, research does indicate that well-designed educational programs, such as *Sesame Street,* can help 4- and 5-year-olds read and count and that children that age also benefit from pro-social messages on TV that teach them about kindness and sharing. On the other hand, studies have also found that exposure to television violence can increase the risk of children behaving aggressively and that media use in early childhood may be related to attentional problems later in life. And while the producers of early childhood media believe their products can help children learn even at the earliest ages, other experts worry that time spent with media may detract from time children spend interacting with their parents, engaging in physical activity, using their imaginations, or exploring the world around them.

One thing this study makes clear is that for many families, media use has become part of the fabric of daily life. Parents use TV or DVDs as a "safe" activity their kids can enjoy while the grownups get dressed for work, make a meal, or do the household chores. Working parents who worry that they don't have enough time to teach their kids the basics feel relieved that educational TV shows, videos, and computer games are helping their kids count and learn the alphabet and even say a word or two in Spanish. When children are grouchy, or hyper, or fighting with their siblings, moms and dads use TV as a tool to help change their mood, calm them down, or separate squabbling brothers and sisters. Media are also used in enforcing discipline, with a TV in the bedroom or a handheld video game player offered as a powerful reward or enticement for good behavior. Everyday activities, such as eating a meal or going to sleep, are often done with television as a companion. And media are used to facilitate moments of transition in daily life: waking up slowly while groggily watching a couple of cartoons on mom and dad's bed, or calming down to a favorite video before bedtime.

> "Media makes my life easier. We're all happier. He isn't throwing tantrums. I can get some work done."
>
> [Mother of a 4–6 year-old, Irvine, California]

Many parents of young children are quite enthusiastic about the role media plays in their lives and the impact it has on their kids. They are grateful for what they see as higher quality, more educational choices than when they were young, and for the wider variety of options they now have available. They see their children learning from TV and imitating the positive behaviors modeled on many shows. But it appears that the primary reason many parents choose to bring media into their children's lives is not because of the educational benefits it offers kids, but because of the practical benefits it offers parents: uninterrupted time for chores, some peace and quiet, or even just an opportunity to watch their own favorite shows.

At the same time, many parents feel an underlying guilt about their children's media use: primarily a sense that they should be spending more time with their kids and that they shouldn't be feeling so relieved at not having to be responsible for teaching their children their ABCs. Some express a suspicion that they may have set in motion something they soon won't be able to control: that today's good-natured educational shows will lead to tomorrow's sassy cartoons, and to next year's violent video games. And others also bemoan the fundamental changes they see from their own childhoods when they were more likely to play outside or to use their imaginations to make up their own play activities indoors.

> "It makes life easier now, but in the long run, when they're older and starting to run into all these problems, I think I'll wish I wouldn't have let them do it when they were five."
>
> [Mother of a 4–6 year-old in Columbus, Ohio]

Parents' beliefs about media—and their own media habits—are strongly related to how much time their children spend with media, the patterns of their children's use, and the types of content their children are exposed to. Two- and four-year-olds watching *CSI* and *ER* with their moms don't seem to be as rare as one might think. Parents who are big TV fans and hate the interruptions from their little ones are more likely to get a TV for their child's bedroom. Dads who play a lot of video games use that activity as a way to bond with their sons. And parents who think TV mostly hurts children's learning are more likely to limit their children's viewing and less likely to leave the TV on during the day. In short, children's media use is as much or more about parents as it is about children.

This report presents the results of a national study to document how much time infants, toddlers, and preschoolers are spending with media, what types of media they're using, and what role media are playing in their environments. The study has two parts: a nationally representative telephone survey of parents about their children's media use; and a series of focus groups with parents, for a more in-depth discussion of issues raised in the survey. All statistical findings in this report are from the national survey; all quotes are from the focus groups.

The study concerns children ages 6 months to 6 years old. It focuses primarily on the role of electronic screen media in young people's lives, including television, videos or DVDs, computers, and video games. Occasional references to "children 6 years and under" or "children six and under" are made as shorthand and refer to children ages 6 months to 6 years old. References to children "under two" refer to children 6–23 months old. . . .

One thing this study makes clear is that even the youngest children in our society have a substantial amount of experience with electronic media. Perhaps not surprisingly, almost all children ages 6 months to 6 years old have watched television (94%) and videos or DVDs (87%). But use of "new" media among this age group also abounds. More than four in ten (43%) have used a computer, about three in ten (29%) have played console video games, and just under one in five (18%) have played handheld video games.

Figure 1

In a Typical Day, Percent of Children 6 and Under Who . . .

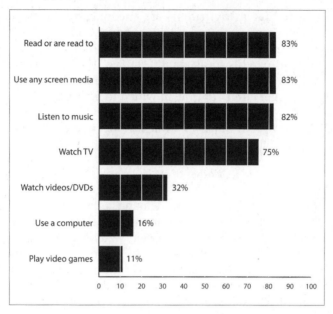

Note: Screen media includes TV, videos/DVDs, video games, or computers.

In a typical day, 83% of children ages 6 months to 6 years use some form of screen media, including 75% who watch television, 32% who watch videos or DVDs[1], 16% who use a computer, and 11% who play either console or handheld video games. The percent of children who watch TV in a typical day is somewhat smaller than the share who spend any time reading or being read to (83%) and listening to music (82%).

Kids who watch television and those who watch videos or DVDs spend an average of about one and a quarter hours on each (1:19 for TV and 1:18 for videos/DVDs), while those who play video games and use computers spend an average of just under an hour on each (0:55 for video games and 0:50 for computers). On the whole, the 83% of children who use screen media in a typical day spend an average of just under 2 hours (1:57) doing so. . . .

> "For our little guy, TV time is all of us on the couch together. The cat comes and sits with us. We'll talk about what's going on. If it's *Blues Clues,* we'll answer back. We only do 20 minutes a night."

> [Mother of a 1–3 year-old, Irvine, California]

Parents' Attitudes about Children's Media Use

Why Parents Want Their Kids to Use Media

Focus groups indicate that many parents are encouraging their children to spend time with media because they think it's good for their kids, and because it gives them a chance to get things done without their children underfoot. Indeed, in focus groups parents speak about "getting" their kids to watch certain videos or TV shows, or about DVDs being better than TV because they're longer and afford a longer chunk of time in which to get things done.

> "They wake up and get to watch TV while I shower and get dressed. It keeps them in my sight line."
>
> [Mother of a 4–6 year-old, Denver, Colorado]

Many parents speak of the numerous demands on their time and of their strong need to keep their kids occupied while they get chores done. As a mom from Denver said about her 1–3 year-old, "If he is watching TV, I can get other things done. I don't have to constantly watch him." Some parents spoke about the fact that they simply can't let their kids play outdoors unsupervised. Others pointed out how much trouble their children could cause inside the house if they are left unmonitored: "If the TV isn't on, he's putting the 'Orange Glo' all over my daughter's bedspread. That makes more work for me."

> "He's a good little boy. He won't bother anything. He won't get into stuff. He's glued to the TV."
>
> [Mother of a 4–6 year-old from Columbus, Ohio]

Many parents also talked about how important it is for them to have "me" time, which often means getting their kids set up with a TV show or a DVD. The mother of a 4–6 year-old from the Denver area pointed out that: "Being an adult is hard. There are times when my interacting with my children is best served by me having an opportunity to allow them to do something alone so I can regroup. When I got laid off a couple of weeks ago, I didn't know it was coming. I got blindsided. I couldn't have interacted with my children that night. I couldn't have done it. 'Let's watch *Finding Nemo,* kids. Here are some chicken strips, here are sippy cups—I'll see you in about an hour and a half'."

The Educational Value of Television

In the national survey, parents are fairly evenly split on whether, in general, TV mostly helps (38%) or mostly hurts (31%) children's learning (22% say it doesn't have much effect either way). But in focus groups, many parents cited "learning" as one of the positive things about television, and indicated that they thought their children were learning from TV. Several mothers mentioned being surprised by their children saying a word in Spanish or being able to count. The mother of a 4–6 year-old from Denver said, "My daughter started saying something to me in Spanish—I don't know a word of Spanish. [TV is] definitely educational." Another Denver-area mom said, "My 2-year-old can count to 10. I haven't really practiced that much with her. She did it. Where else would she have possibly learned it?"

> "Out of the blue one day my son counted to five in Spanish. I knew immediately that he got that from *Dora*."
>
> [Mother of a 1–3 year-old, Columbus, Ohio]

Mothers are also enthusiastic about the different experiences children are exposed to through television and videos. "[My son] has developed a passion about the ocean and angler fish because of Nemo," said one Denver mom. "He fell in love with that character. That door wouldn't have even been open if it wasn't for *Finding Nemo*." Another Denver mother said her 4–6 year-old son was "always telling me what is right and wrong from the things he sees on TV. It has opened doors in being able to talk to him." Several mothers mentioned the "diversity" TV brings their young children. As one mom from Columbus said, "I think they are exposed to a little bit more diversity. I think that it's good for them to be comfortable with that. . . . to know that it's okay for everyone to be different."

> "My daughter knows . . . her letters from *Sesame Street*. I haven't had to work with her on them at all."
>
> [Mother of a 1–3 year-old, Columbus, Ohio]

> "It shows them a world that they aren't familiar with. We live in the suburbs. She watches *Dora* and learns a little bit of Spanish."
>
> [Mother of a 4–6 year-old, Columbus, Ohio]

Some parents feel they need media to help them with their child's education. As one mother from Irvine, California, said, "I think they (media) are in a way necessary. So much more is expected of kids these days. . . . When you go to kindergarten now, you can't just go and play with toys. You have to know how to write your name and spell. It's all about what you know." Most parents seemed to think their children would learn what they needed to know just fine without media, but they would be under a lot more pressure to do the teaching themselves. As the mother of a 1–3 year-old from Denver said, "I don't think it's important to use it as a learning tool, but for me to use it to keep them occupied."

The national survey indicates that there is a relationship between parents' attitudes about the educational value of television and how much time their children spend watching TV. Children whose parents think TV mostly

Table 1

Relationship of Parental Attitudes to Children's Media Use

Child's Media Use	Parent Attitude Towards TV		
	Mostly helps	No effect	Mostly hurts
Percent who watch TV on typical day	84%‡~	75%~	64%
Mean hours watching TV for kids who watched	1:27~	1:16	1:12
Mean hours watching TV for all kids	1:12‡~	0:57~	0:45
Percent who watch TV daily	76%~	71%~	48%

‡Significantly higher than "No effect"; ~Significantly higher than "Mostly hurts."

hurts learning are *less likely* to watch than those whose parents say it mostly helps or doesn't have much effect one way or the other. For example, 48% of children whose parents say TV mostly hurts learning watch every day, compared to 76% of those whose parents believe TV mostly helps children's learning. Likewise, children whose parents say TV mostly hurts learning spend an average of 27 minutes less per day watching than children whose parents think TV mostly helps.

It is not possible to tell from this survey whether parents who think TV hurts learning are more likely to restrict their children's viewing, or whether parents whose children spend more time watching TV develop a higher opinion of television's role in learning, or whether some other factor is influencing this relationship.

> "I just don't have time to sit on the computer with him to try and teach him all this other stuff. . . . I'm not going to put him on it if I have to teach him how to use the mouse or something else. . . . I am like—play it at your dad's and break *his* computer."
>
> [Mother of a 1–3 year-old, Denver, Colorado]

Educational Value of Computers

When it comes to using computers, most parents think this activity helps rather than hurts learning (69% vs. 8%, with 15% saying it doesn't have much effect).

Many parents feel that since their children are going to have to use computers later in life, getting familiar with them at an early age is a benefit in and of itself, regardless of what they're doing on the computer. One mother from Irvine said, "Anything they are doing on the computer I think is learning." Another mom from Columbus said, "I think they get more skills from the computer. Our world is so computer-oriented. I certainly didn't know how to use a computer when I was 3. . . . If I had a choice of the computer or TV, I would definitely choose the computer."

> "They'll survive without the video games and TV. . . . I don't think they'll survive without the computer. When they're older, they aren't going to have a cashier to check them out at Kroger."
>
> [Mother of a 4–6 year-old, Columbus, Ohio]

Other focus group mothers pointed to certain features of the computer that they found beneficial, such as interactivity or the parent being able to control the content through specific software. The mother of a young child from Irvine said, "The computer is far more interactive than TV. His mind is more active when he is using the computer. It's more of an analysis and figuring things out." A Denver-area mom (of a 4–6 year-old) said, "I think you have more control over the computer. If they're watching TV, you don't know what the lesson is going to be. With the computer you can put in specific software or go to a specific website."

> "I don't spend nearly as much time with my son as I need to. He has learned huge amounts through the video and computer games that we have. . . . I'm very grateful for the computer games. My kid learned his colors and letters from the computer. It's been very beneficial to us."
>
> [Mother of a 1–3 year-old, Irvine, California]

Another mother from Denver (of a 1–3 year-old) described one of the CD-ROMs she and her daughter enjoy using: "They have a 5-a-day vegetable game. My daughter doesn't like to eat, so we show her all the different foods that are good for her. We make things on the computer, and then we will go downstairs and make them to eat. She seems to eat better after we play the food game."

Despite the advantages some focus group mothers pointed to, many others expressed a lot of concerns about having their kids use the family computer. There was a sense that most of what children can learn from a computer they can also learn from TV or videos—without as much parental oversight and without as much risk to expensive equipment. As one mom from Irvine said, "If they're on the Internet, I have to be right there with them. That can be annoying because I don't always have the time to sit there while my 3- and 6-year-old go on the Internet. It isn't that fun for me to watch the same *Dora* clip 20,000 times. I would rather do other things." Some pointed to the safety of the Nickelodeon TV channel over the Nick Jr. website: one mom said, "If I leave my son on Nick Jr. for just a minute, he will click on every possible ad or whatever, and there will be a thousand things open," while another noted, "If they're watching Nickelodeon, you know they aren't going to have any porn sites popping up."

Educational Value of Video Games

According to the national survey, most parents think playing video games hurts rather than helps learning (49% vs. 17%, with 22% saying not much effect). In the focus groups, parents didn't indicate having as much experience using educational video games as they did with TV, computers, or videos and DVDs. One mother of a 4–6 year-old from Columbus did have experience with an educational video game: "My daughter and I played a Mickey Mouse (video) game where you had to . . . move the cursor around to find different things. If you find the remote, you can go back to the TV, and it will show a clip. It's like thinking."

Focus group parents also felt that video games tended to be more violent, especially those for the older kids. Some worried about the types of games young children see their older siblings play: "My older kids play . . . a lot of the violent stuff. They let [my younger son] play one time, and the poor child was traumatized. . . . He couldn't even sleep that night. He kept telling us about it all night."

Many parents noted that their younger children tried to mimic either their dads or their older siblings by playing with game controllers, but just got frustrated because they couldn't do it properly.

Figure 2

Percent of Parents Who Say Each Medium Mostly Helps or Hurts Children's Learning:

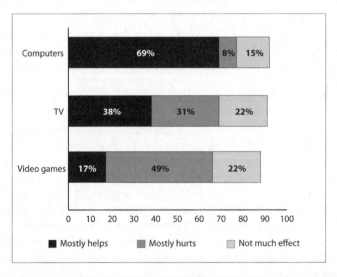

Conversations with Pediatricians

Relatively few parents (15%) say that their pediatrician has ever discussed their child's media use with them. Parents with higher income and more formal education are more likely to say their pediatrician has discussed this with them (for example, 22% of college graduates, vs. 11% of those with a high school education or less). There is no indication from these data that children whose parents have discussed media use with their pediatrician are less likely to watch TV or that the household media environment is different for these children than for those whose parents haven't had those discussions. Even the youngest children are growing up in homes where media are an integral part of the environment—with multiple TVs, VCRs, computers, and video game players in the home; TVs left on much of the time (many with large screens and surround sound), whether anyone is watching or not; TVs in children's bedrooms; and portable DVD players and handheld video game players ready for children on the go.

Television

Nearly all children ages 6 months to 6 years (99%) live in a home with at least one television. Eighty-four percent live in a home with two or more televisions, and nearly a quarter (24%) live in homes with four or more TVs.

A large majority (80%) of these children live in homes that have cable or satellite TV, and about half (53%) live in homes where the largest TV is 30 inches or larger (25% have TVs 40 inches or larger). Four in ten (40%) have a television with surround sound, and two in ten (20%) have TiVo or some other type of digital video recorder. The presence of TiVo in the home was not related to either the amount or type of shows children watched.

VCRs and DVD Players

Nearly all (93%) children ages 6 months to 6 years have a VCR or DVD player in the home, and a third (33%) have a portable DVD player. In addition, nearly one in five (18%) have a television or DVD player in their car.

> "While my daughter has her princess movie in, my son can be upstairs playing his *Blues Clues* CD-ROM. . . . It gives them their own space and their own quality time to be apart."
>
> [Mother of a 1–3 year-old, Denver, Colorado]

Video Games

Half (50%) of children 6 years and under have a console video game player in the home, and nearly three in ten (28%) have a handheld video game player. Children ages 4–6 are more likely than children ages 0–3 to live in homes with a console video game player (54% vs. 46%), and with a handheld video game player (34% vs. 22%).

"I told my kids we weren't going to get an Xbox. . . . because we have the computer. To me it's just one more thing that I would have to fight over with them. I'm big on entertaining yourself—go play. Don't just sit here vegetating."

[Mother of a 1–3 year-old, Columbus, Ohio]

Computers

More than three-quarters (78%) of children 6 years and under live in a household with a computer, and about three in ten (29%) live in a household with two or more computers. Nearly seven in ten (69%) have Internet access in the household, including 42% who have high-speed Internet access (26% have dial-up access). . . .

Calming Children Down or Pumping Them Up

Just over half (53%) of parents say that TV tends to calm their child down, while only about one in six (17%) say that TV gets their child excited. The rest of parents either say: TV calms and excites their child equally (9%); it depends on what the child is watching (8%) or on the child's mood or time of day (3%);

Figure 3

Percent of Children Age 6 and Under Who Live in a Home with . . .

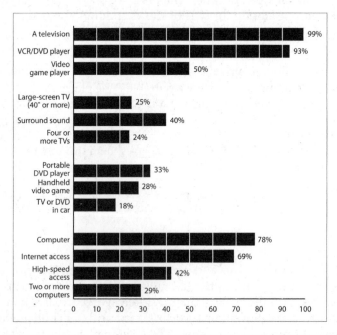

or they don't know (10%). Television's effect on children does not vary reliably with the child's age or gender. Children who watch mostly entertainment shows are more likely to be calmed by TV than are those who watch mostly educational shows (72% vs. 50%).

> "When he watched the *Buzz Lightyear of Star Command* video from the library, he was a monster child. The very next week I got *Teletubbies,* and it was completely opposite. He was very mellow."
>
> [Mother of a 1–3 year-old, Columbus, Ohio]

In focus groups, parents describe a range of responses their children have to TV. A number of parents talked about how TV can calm their children down. The mother of a 4–6 year-old from Irvine said, "My son is really hyper. That's a time when I can get him to actually calm down and watch a little TV. . . . He will slow down and that helps change his mood. . . . It's much better for him and for me."

> "She plays along with what she's watching most of the time. She's dancing. She's not being a couch potato . . ."
>
> [Mother of a 4–6 year-old, Columbus, Ohio]

But another mother, from Columbus, said, "My 2-year-old is so rambunctious you cannot turn your back for a second. With TV I notice that his temperament changes. He gets more wild and hyper when he is watching the stuff that he likes." Many parents pointed to a positive energy their kids get from watching TV as well as dancing and responding to the screen. "My kids will stand in front of the TV and hop and clap," a mother of a 1–3 year-old from Columbus said. Others describe kids who "zone out"or appear hypnotized by the TV. "The TV kind of turns their brain off, that's what I don't like," said one Denver mother.

> "I think [TV] builds confidence and self-esteem. My daughter was very introverted until she was about three and a half. She was very shy. . . . By her acting out with her imaginary friends on the TV or *Dora,* it just really brought her out. It really opened her up in preschool and she is really doing well."
>
> [Mother of a 4–6 year-old, Irvine, California]

Imitating Behavior from TV

Nearly seven in ten parents (68%) say they have seen their child imitate some type of behavior from TV. Far more parents say their child imitates positive behavior, such as sharing or helping (66%), than say their child imitates aggressive behavior, like hitting or kicking (23%). Parents of children ages 4–6 years

(83%) and of children ages 2–3 years (77%) are more likely than parents of children under 2 years (27%) to say their child imitates any type of behavior.

> "She was going around kissing everyone with her mouth open. She wanted to be like Ariel and Eric."(From Disney's *The Little Mermaid*.)
>
> [Mother of a 1–3 year-old, Columbus, Ohio]

Boys in both age ranges (2–3 and 4–6) are more likely than girls to imitate aggressive behavior (nearly half—45%—of parents of boys ages 4–6 say their child imitates aggressive behavior). Children who primarily watch kids' educational programming are more likely than those who primarily watch kids' entertainment shows to imitate positive behavior (76% vs. 59%).

> "My daughter just sits in the beanbag chair watching TV. If it's something that she's really into, she just sits there with her mouth hanging open."
>
> [Mother of a 4–6 year-old, Columbus, Ohio]

Response to Commercials

In focus groups, when asked to list the positives and negatives of TV for their children, many parents mentioned commercials as a negative. But when asked how many commercials their children were exposed to in a typical day, most parents seemed at a loss to guess, and estimates ranged from 5 to 100. Many parents indicated that their children liked commercials and were influenced by them. "She pays attention to the commercials more than the shows," said the mother of one 1–3 year-old from Columbus. "That's what gets her attention." Several talked about their children memorizing things from commercials. A

Table 2

Imitating Positive or Aggressive Behavior from TV

	Ages			Ages		
	2–3 Years			4–6 Years		
Percent whose parents say they . . .	All	Boys	Girls	All	Boys	Girls
Imitate positive behavior	75%	75%	75%	80%	79%	82%
Imitate aggressive behavior	24%	31%†	17%	33%*	45% †	21%
Imitate neither	23%^	20%	25%	17%	17%	17%

*Significantly higher than ages 2–3, ^Significantly higher than ages 4–6; †Significantly higher than girls in this age range.

Denver mom (of a 4–6 year-old) said, "My kids are—'I want that, I want that, I want that'. They commit things to memory for months." But one mother said she thought the commercials just went right past her kids: "I don't think they watch them. . . . I don't think they're paying attention."

> "I want this, I want that, I want chocolate cereal."
>
> [Mother of a 1–3 year-old, Denver, Colorado]

At the same time, a couple of parents mentioned that ads give them gift ideas, and they're grateful for them. The mother of one 1–3 year-old girl from Columbus said, "My daughter's birthday is next week. She saw a commercial for a Strawberry Shortcake doll toy. She said she wanted it for her birthday. If she hadn't seen the commercial, she wouldn't have known about it. I was glad that I was in the room and she could tell me that."

> "I would be at a total loss if it wasn't for commercials at Christmas time. I wouldn't know what to get my kids. They know what they like when they see it on TV."
>
> [Mother of a 4–6 year-old, Denver, Colorado]

Among parents whose children watch TV at least several times a month, the vast majority (83%) say their child watches mostly shows specifically for

Figure 4

Percent of Children Who Watch . . .

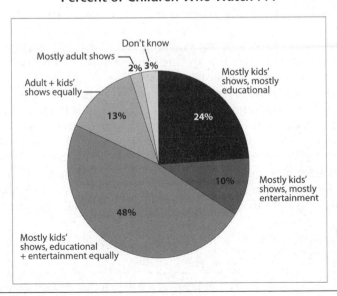

Note: Among those who watch TV at least several times a month.

kids around his or her age (2% say the child watches mostly shows for all ages, including adults; and 13% say the child watches both types of shows about equally). More parents say their child watches mostly educational shows (24%) than say their child watches mostly entertainment shows (10%), but a plurality (48%) say their child watches both types of shows about equally.

> "A show can seem fine one minute, and in the next minute Tom pulls a gun on Jerry."
>
> [Mother of a 4–6 year-old, Denver, Colorado]

In focus groups, a number of parents indicated that their young children watch mature content and that both the child and the parent seem fine with that. For example, the mother of one 4-year-old from Denver said, "*The Punisher,* my son loves that movie. He's more mature." Another said she "goes by her child's personality" in deciding what he can or can't watch. "Not a lot of people would be comfortable with a 4-year-old watching medical shows where they show people coming in and bleeding and crying," she said. "Obviously it is a tragedy. But he really loves the human body." Another mom from Irvine said, "I try not to really shelter my daughter. . . . She's two. She wants to watch *Jurassic Park*. . . . There's a dinosaur [that] ate a guy—that's what dinosaurs do—they eat people and animals. She understands that. She doesn't getfreaked about it. She even watched *Chuckie* the other day. She thought it was funny."

> "I've found that my kids are usually about a year ahead of what the games or movies say. My son is two so I look at ones for 3–4 year-olds. I always pick one that is above their level to help them learn."
>
> [Mother of a 1–3 year-old, Denver, Colorado]

Many parents in focus groups say they are guided by brands in choosing what their kids can or can't watch. One Denver mom said that children's TV shows are "all pretty much educational now. They help teach the kids how to help each other and how to love one another. Everything on Nick is like that." Another had a similar feeling about PBS: "I like my kids to watch PBS because it's more of a learning thing instead of the cartoons. I have no problem with them watching PBS for two hours straight. They have all those good learning shows." But one mother of a 4–6 year-old from Columbus said she made a mistake thinking she could go by the brand alone: "I thought you could trust Cartoon Network because of the name. I just recently paid attention to what he was watching and saw it. I said, 'What the *heck!*' I couldn't believe it."

> "Because of the rules that I have set forth he doesn't ask to watch things that he can't watch."
>
> [Mother of a 4–6 year-old, Denver, Colorado]

A number of parents in focus groups talked about the influence of their older siblings on what their younger kids see on TV or videos. The mother of one 1–3 year-old from Denver told about a time when her young son watched the movie *Alien vs. Predator:* "He liked it. . . . When I saw it I couldn't believe my older son let him watch it. I thought he would be up all night, but it didn't bother him at all." . . .

Children Under Age Two

Many experts consider the first two years of life especially critical for children's development and are particularly interested in monitoring media use patterns during this period. For example, the American Academy of Pediatrics has recommended no screen media use at all for children under two.

In fact, this study indicates that children under age 2 have quite different media habits than children 2 years and older, although it also indicates that they live media-rich lives. Almost all babies 6–23 months old have listened to music (98%), or been read to (94%). Nearly eight in ten (79%) have watched TV, and two-thirds (65%) have watched videos or DVDs. Only a very few have ever used a computer (5%) or played any kind of video game (3%).

More than four in ten (43%) children this age watch TV *every* day, while another 17% watch several times a week. Nearly one in five (18%) watch videos or DVDs every day, while another 26% watch at least several times a week. In a typical day, 61% of children this age watch TV, a video, or a DVD, for an average of one hour and nineteen minutes. Most parents say they are in the same room with their child while they're watching TV either all or most of the time (88% of those whose children this age watch TV in a typical day).

Around four in ten children under two can turn on the TV by themselves (38%) and change channels with the remote (40%). Almost one in five (19%) have a TV in their bedroom. A quarter (26%) of parents report that their children this age have already imitated a positive behavior from a TV show, like sharing or helping. Among the 63% of children this age who watch at least several times a month or more, 35% watch mostly kids' educational shows, 40% watch a mix of kids' educational and entertainment shows, and 19% watch a mix of programming for both children and adults.

In addition to watching their own shows, babies this age are also exposed to "background" television. A third (33%) live in homes where the TV is on most or all of the time, whether anyone is watching or not. Seventy percent of parents with children under two say they watch their own TV shows in a typical day, for an average of an hour and forty-three minutes, including 32% who say their child was in the room with them all or most of the time, 17% who say half or less of the time, and 20% who say none of the time.

More than half (58%) of children under two are read to every day, with another 25% being read to several times a week. In any given day, 77% are read to, for an average of 44 minutes. . . .

Figure 5

Percent of Children Under Age Two Who Watch TV . . .

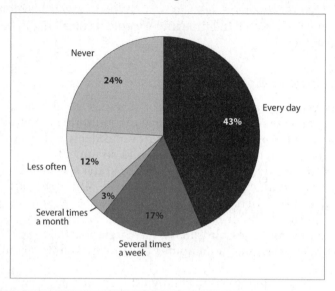

Summary and Conclusions

The Role of Parents

In the public debate about children and media, people on all sides of the issue often end up pointing to the role of parents in monitoring their children's media use, encouraging them to push the "off" button. This study provides important documentation of just how powerful a role parents have in shaping their children's media habits. A third of children live in homes where parents simply leave the TV on most of the day, whether anyone is watching or not—and, not surprisingly, those children end up watching significantly more than other kids do. Many parents spend a fair amount of time watching TV or on the computer themselves, and again, children of those parents also spend more time watching a screen each day. And a third of children 6 years and under have been allowed to have a TV in their bedroom—mostly to avoid conflicts with parents'or other family members' viewing—and again, those children spend more time watching TV.

Why Parents Are Drawn to Media

Many parents find media a tremendous benefit in parenting and can't imagine how they'd get through the day without it (especially TV, videos, and DVDs). Media allow parents a chance to get their chores done, quiet their kids down, or just have some "me" time, knowing that their kids are "safe"—not playing outside, and less likely to be making trouble around the house. Multiple

TV sets, DVD players, and computers help solve sibling quarrels and also let parents get their own screen time uninterrupted. While fewer than four in ten (38%) parents say they think TV mostly helps children's learning, parents are relieved that they can make use of media in these ways with less guilt, because of what they see as real advances in the educational quality of media content.

The Educational Value of Children's Television

While parents in the survey seem pretty evenly split on whether TV in general is mostly helpful (38%) or harmful (31%) to children's learning, in the focus groups almost all parents pointed to "learning" as one of the big positives of TV for their kids, and many made comments about observing their children learning things from TV shows. In general, parents in the focus groups seemed well satisfied with the quality of programming available to their kids. Most felt their children would learn just as well *without* TV, but didn't want the extra burden that that would place on them as parents. The reigning sentiment seemed to be that there is simply no way they can live their lives and get everything done without TV and videos, and that the educational content and positive lessons in much of the programming lessens their guilt at not spending more time with their kids. And while parents in the survey indicate that they think the computer is more educational than is TV, the focus groups revealed that many parents greatly prefer TV or videos because they require less supervision (and because they're worried about their kids hurting the computer).

A Big Role for Media

Media, especially television, are clearly playing a key role in children's lives, starting at an early age. In a typical day, more than eight in ten (83%) children ages 6 months to 6 years old use screen media, averaging about two hours each (1:57). As mentioned above, a third live in homes where the TV is left on most or all of the time, whether anyone is watching or not, and a similar proportion (30%) have the TV on during most or all of their meals. Homes with multiple TV sets and portable media allow kids to watch in the privacy of their rooms, or when they're on the go—a third (33%) have a portable DVD player, and a third (33%) have a TV in their bedroom. About one in eight (12%) are put to bed with the TV on at least half the time.

Less Time with TV and DVDs

While there haven't been any major changes in children's daily media habits since a similar survey was conducted in 2003—they aren't more likely to use computers or video games, or less likely to watch TV—when children *do* watch TV or videos, they are spending less time doing so (10 minutes less watching TV, and 7 minutes less watching videos or DVDs). It's possible that this change follows on the slight—but statistically significant—drop in the proportion of parents nationally who say they leave the TV on all or most of time (from 37% to 32%) or who say they usually eat meals in front of the TV (from 35% to

30%). It is also possible that the shift comes from a greater number of parents thinking TV mostly *hurts* children's learning (up from 27% to 31%). However, it is also possible that it is an artifact of a shift in the time of year the survey was conducted, from April and May to September, October, and November. Slight decreases in time spent with computers and playing video games were not statistically significant. We will continue to track these data over time.

American Academy of Pediatrics Recommendations

A substantial number of children are using media in excess of the amounts recommended by the American Academy of Pediatrics (AAP). In a typical day, nearly two-thirds (61%) of babies under two years old use screen media, and 43% of children this age watch TV *every* day (the AAP recommends no screen time for babies under two). And while the AAP recommends no more than 1–2 hours per day of screen media for children two and older, in a typical day 41% of 2–3 year-olds and 43% of 4–6 year-olds use screen media for 2 hours or more. Few parents report having spoken with their doctor about their child's media use. . . .

Electronic media have clearly become a central focus of many young children's lives, a key component in family routines such as working up, eating, relaxing, and falling asleep. Not only do children—starting when they are just babies—spend hours a day using media, but they are also learning to use the media by themselves, often watching their own TVs, DVD players or hand-held devices, many times in the privacy of their own rooms. As much as media have become a part of the fabric of family life, they are often consumed separately, used as much or more to keep the peace than to bring family members together.

It is hoped that the data in this report will be used to help families assess their own media habits; to spur the development of media products that are beneficial to children and families; to inform policy debates about public broadcasting, digital media, and children's commercial exposure; and to provide the data to help inform future research about the impact of various media on young children. To date, there has been very little research about the impact of media on the youngest children, especially those 2 years and under. Given how much a part of children's lives these media are, it seems important to explore in greater depth the impact media may be having on their development.

Note

1. The percent of parents who report that their children watched videos or DVDs may be an underestimate due to the way the question was worded. The question read "Did your child spend any time watching videos or DVDs, including while riding in the car?" In a previous survey, the question was asked without the phrase "including while riding in a car," and a far greater proportion of parents reported that their children had watched videos or DVDs (46%, compared to 32% in the current survey). Many respondents in the current survey may have misunderstood the question and answered "yes" *only* if their child watched videos or DVDs while riding in the car.

Ellen Wartella and
Michael Robb

 **NO**

Young Children, New Media

In May 2006 a new cable channel entered American television; BabyFirstTV became the first 24 hour cable and satellite network to offer programming aimed at viewers between 6 months and 3 years old. Earlier in the spring, Sesame Workshop released a DVD series, "Sesame Beginnings," designed for children 6 months to 2 years old to compete with the well known "Baby Einstein" series of infant videos. These media directed at the very young are only the latest of a trend to both program for and attract very young children to audio-visual media. In addition to cable networks and DVDs, interactive toys, cell phones, websites, and other content are now directed at the very young child as well. . . . Data from two Kaiser Family Foundation surveys of the parents of children 6 months to 6 years over the past 4 years . . . provide evidence that electronic media are an increasingly important part of the lives of the very young. This paper will examine the use of electronic media by children under three and will examine what impact such early viewing might have on children's development.

The past decade in American media life has demonstrated the presence of screen media—television, videos, DVDs, computers, videogames—in the lives of very young children. Both the 2003 and 2006 national surveys of media use by children under six conducted by the Kaiser Family Foundation have provided evidence that American children are more likely today to spend time with screen media than print media or free play. All of this is occurring at a time when media directed at young children is facing criticism: for instance, since 1999 the American Academy of Pediatrics recommends discouraging children under two from watching any screen media and limiting older children to 2 hours or less per day. . . . There are questions regarding the impact of such early media use on children's cognitive and social development, including questions regarding just how and when children do learn from screen media. . . . Moreover, more than 35 years of experience with preschoolers using *Sesame Street* has demonstrated that 4- to 6-year-olds can learn important skills such as their numbers and letters, as well as pre-reading skills that can have a positive effect on them as they enter elementary school . . . ; however, the impact of these educational shows on younger children is less clear. . . . There is no clear cut evidence regarding young children's learning from screen media. In fact, what is most surprising is the dearth of studies on the very young (those under three) including examination of the likely consequences of their early screen media on development.

From *Journal of Children and Media*, vol. 1, no. 1, 2007. Copyright © 2007 by Taylor & Francis Journals. Reprinted by permission.

Young Children's Media Use

The Kaiser Family Foundation has conducted two national studies in the US on very young children's media use: the Zero to Six study . . . and The Media Family. . . . In addition, a January 2005 issue of the *American Behavioral Scientist* reported on several subsequent analyses of the Kaiser Family Foundation . . . data set. The two national surveys are consistent on the large role of electronic media in the lives of very young children, those from 6 months to 3 years. According to the 2006 study (based on a representative sample of parents of children ages 0–6, $N = 1051$), American children under six almost universally live in homes with television (98.4 percent), with a vast majority having computers as well (80 percent) and nearly half having videogame consoles. A fairly large proportion of these very young children have television sets in their bedrooms (18 percent of those 0–2 years old, 39 percent of 3–4 year olds, and 37 percent of 4–6 year olds). These data are comparable to data collected on a similar national sample of parents of young children 0–6 conducted in 2003. . . .

As Anderson and Pempek note . . . , when compared to data from the 1980s and 1990s, data from Kaiser's studies show a dramatic increase in the number of very young children now attending to TV on an average day. Anderson and Pempek compared Kaiser data from 2003 to data analyzed by Certain and Kahn . . . from studies conducted in the early to mid-1990s and note that non-viewers of television on a typical day dropped between the 1990s and early 2000s such that for children younger than 1 year of age, the non-viewers dropped from 83 percent to 43 percent 10 years later; for 1-year-olds the non-viewers dropped from 52 to 40 percent. As Anderson and Pempek remark, it is the very young children who are now likely to watch television and videos and this is different from earlier years. . . .

What is clear from these surveys is that the very young child in the US is now exposed to unprecedented levels of screen media. Screen media use is a dominant activity of childhood. Such use is occurring against the backdrop of public concern about the consequences of such early exposure. This appears to be a trend that has arisen in the past decade of American life. It would appear that the majority of American parents of children under two are not following the AAP guidelines recommending no screen time for children under two. And considering that young children under two spend much of a 24 hour period sleeping—typically 12 or more hours a day—then media use is occupying a large part of their waking hours. In the next section we will discuss potential consequences of such early screen media use.

Consequences of Screen Viewing by Young Children

It is worth noting that over the course of the past several years there has been a heightened emphasis among child development specialists on the importance of the very early years of life, especially the first three years, on children's development. In particular the publication in 2000 of *From Neurons to Neighborhoods* by the National Research Council and Institute of Medicine . . . in the US signaled a major summary statement of the research literature on the importance of developmental growth in the first 3 years of life. How media use might influence such early development is increasingly the subject of academic speculation and public policy concerns.

There are several questions that need to be addressed regarding the very young child's use of screen media: first, can children three and younger learn from screen media? If so, how well can they learn from screen media? Finally, are there any benefits and/or risks to children's development from early screen media use? Each of these questions will be considered in turn.

Can Children Under Three Learn from Screen Media?

The success of baby videos is clearly based on parental observations of babies watching and apparently enjoying such videos; of course, almost all of this is based on anecdotal evidence. At least two studies have examined infants' attention to these specially designed baby videos: Rachel Barr and her colleagues . . . observed infants from 12 to 15 months watching baby videos in their home and found that the infant's attention varied from 48 to 74 percent of the time watching the screen with greater attention to familiar videos. Anderson and Pempek . . . report "high levels" of looking at *Teletubbies*—a program designed for 1-year-olds—when infants are placed on their parents laps in front of a screen in a laboratory setting and have a table of toys to play with in front of them. These studies would appear to confirm the anecdotal reports of parents of the success of baby videos and television programs in eliciting infants' attention to screen programming. Furthermore, Anderson and Pempek review a few studies that suggest that children as young as 18 months show more attention to televised content created especially for them, such as *Teletubbies*, than to adult content and show a sensitivity to the comprehensibility of the program (as indicated by distorting shot sequences or language distortion), both of which suggests that by 18 months children's attention to television is more than a primitive orienting response to visual and auditory elements on the screen (the formal features of the content) and may be guided by higher level cognitive skills such as the comprehensibility of the program. This would suggest that when a program is designed especially for infants they might be able to learn from that program. Indeed, this is the claim of the marketers of infant videos.

What evidence do we have that young infants can and do learn from screen images? What are the cognitive developmental skills necessary for babies to learn from screen media? What we might expect is that the ability of infants to make sense of screen images should follow the developmental achievement of infants' ability to learn to internally represent their environment, mentally encoding information across a wide spectrum of experience. . . . In doing so, they become able to use their representations to make sense of the world and more fully interact with it—from a Piagetian theoretical perspective such symbolic functioning occurs during the last stage of the sensorimotor period or somewhere between 18 and 24 months of age. Until this point, children are thought to not be able to represent information mentally or internally, but only through physical actions. For example, when faced with a problem, such as putting a toy block through a hole, an infant younger than 18 months would be unable to solve the problem internally through a mental representation, but rather would use physical action such as trying out different blocks until finding the right block that fits in the hole. By 24 months, development has proceeded so that children mentally represent objects (through language, symbolic play, and mental imagery) so that they can solve such problems without having to physically manipulate the object.

Media representations may be particularly difficult for infants to make sense of because they are more demanding than physical reality, offering images that manipulate time and space. Infants who already have difficulty understanding some of the basic properties of reality, such as the solid nature of objects and the continuity of objects over time (i.e., that objects cannot just disappear), may be even more confused when faced with object manipulations on television. In short, basic developmental achievements, such as understanding object permanence, may be necessary before infants learn much, if anything at all, from television or screen images.

What Evidence Do We Have That Children Can Learn from a Screen Image—and at What Age?

There is some evidence that infants under two may be more competent than Piaget suggests. Two sorts of studies are relevant here: studies that demonstrate deferred imitation of a televised model, or the ability to observe a model, mentally represent the observed behavior and then reproduce that behavior at a later time; and studies that demonstrate dual representation, or the ability to simultaneously represent an object as the object itself and as a representation of something else.

With respect to the first question, at what age do we have evidence that children can model what they see on television at some later time? There are a few, somewhat contradictory experimental studies of infant learning from televised models. Meltzoff . . . demonstrated deferred imitation from a video presentation in infants as young as 14 months. Meltzoff showed infants 14–24 months' old a simple task of pulling apart a dumbbell-shaped object on video; a control condition saw an experimenter place the dumbbell on a table, but not perform the designated action. Results showed that when children were allowed to play with the object after a 24 hour delay, the infants who had seen the target act were more likely to produce the action than the control group and that the 24-month-old infants were more successful than 14-month-old infants, although there was some evidence of imitation of this very simple action by the 14-month-olds.

However, when infants' ability to imitate a video action is compared to imitation of a live model, infants perform less well in the video condition—leading to a video deficit hypothesis. . . . For instance, Barr and Hayne . . . found that infants at 12, 15, and 18 months could imitate a behavior live, but that there were significant age-related and task-related differences in their abilities to demonstrate a behavior from a video. As in the Melztoff . . . experiment, infants were tested after a 24 hour delay but the behavior involved multiple steps. Infants observed an experimenter holding a puppet, removing a mitten from the puppet's hand, shaking a bell inside the mitten, and then putting the mitten back on the puppet's hand. In order for a child to successfully imitate this behavior, the behavior had to be mentally represented, encoded and expressed after a delay. The children had difficulty performing this behavior. Even in a second experiment eliminating the delay between the observed behavior and the imitation tests, the 12- and 15-month-olds generally did not imitate the video demonstration. The task appeared to strain the cognitive abilities of these young children.

However, in another study designed in a manner more similar to the research of Meltzoff, Barr and Hayne . . . found that when the task was made very simple (in this case demonstrating taking a mitten off) and children were tested immediately following the demonstration, even 15-month-old infants performed equally well in live and video demonstration conditions. Subsequent research also tested whether multiple exposures to a video task improved imitation. Muentener, Price, Garcia, and Barr . . . found that it took six repetitions of the more complex task to yield imitation effects as strong as one real life presentation for infants as young as 6 months and as old as 30 months. Under some conditions, infants younger than two can be shown to imitate a video as well as a live model. There is also some evidence for the potential of television for early learning from observational studies of babies in their home environment, including deferred imitation of behaviors . . . and language learning. . . .

A subsequent question is whether and when infants understand that a video of an object is not the same thing as an object, that it is a representation of that object. To perform this task, children must have acquired the cognitive ability of dual representation, the ability to represent an object simultaneously as the object itself and as a representation of something else. . . . This cognitive ability is thought to develop around 2½ years, or the late sensori-motor period. Again, screen presentations of objects may confuse even children who have acquired the ability of dual representation since most of what children see on television is distinctly different from reality. Not only do children deal with the two dimensionality of the presentation, but they are also viewing things that have been scaled down in size to fit inside the television monitor.

In a study by Pierroutsakos and Troseth . . . , the researchers examined infants' manual investigation of a video screen. On video, the experimenters displayed a toy, tapped it on a table to get the child's attention, and then left the frame, leaving the toy on the table. They observed 9-month-olds' evidencing behavior that suggested they did not understand the dual nature of the image and tried to manipulate the objects they were seeing on video. Over the presentation of ten toys, the 9-month-olds displayed on average 1.4 manual behaviors per toy trying to grasp, hit, or rub the toys observed. By 19 months, the infants appeared to grasp the distinction between the video representation and a real object. Further support for this distinction comes from an observational study by Lemish . . . in which very young children were observed to "pet" animals on the television screen. This behavior disappeared during the second year of life, suggesting children had acquired the ability to distinguish between television and reality, a hallmark of dual representation.

Aside from the ability to distinguish between an object and its representation, can young children use a video representation to guide their own behavior? In several studies, researchers have presented children with an object retrieval task in a video or live action condition to see whether children can find a hidden object. This task typically involves showing children a toy being hidden in a room while watching the event on television or while looking through a window at a live presentation. The children are then sent into the same room as seen in the video or through the window and asked to find the toy. Troseth and DeLoache . . . hypothesized that if the children in the video condition could find the hidden object, this would be evidence that they understood the representational nature of television. They found that 2½-year-olds were able to successfully find the toy almost 80 percent of the time, whereas 2-year-olds only found it 44 percent of the time, supporting the achievement of dual representation (and learning from video) for older but not the younger infants. By contrast when the children watched the toy being hidden live through a window of the same size, both the 2- and 2½-year-olds were able to find it.

Schmitt and Anderson . . . conducted a related experiment testing 2- to 3-year-olds' ability to use video to guide their behavior. Utilizing an object retrieval task similar to Troseth and DeLoache . . ., their findings were quite consistent with the earlier study: 2-year-olds did poorly on the object retrieval test in the video condition, completing the task only 23 percent of the time, compared to 2½-year-olds who were successful 56 percent of the time in the video condition and the 3-year-olds who performed equally well in the televised and live model conditions.

A reasonable hypothesis might be that the 2-year-old children need the perceptually richer 3-D representation of real world space in order to complete the task. . . . Television only allows for a 2-D representation, which might impair their ability to use it to guide their behavior. This possibility was tested by Troseth and DeLoache . . . using the same hidden object test but placing the television set behind a window and obscuring the body of the monitor, thus making it appear as though the children were looking through a window into the room and not at a television. They hypothesized that if the degraded 2-D quality of the video image hampered children's ability to complete the task, then children still would not be able to find the hidden toy when they entered the room themselves. However, if they believed they were seeing the actual room rather than a television image of the room, then they would be able to find the toy as accurately as they did in the real window condition. This is in fact what occurred, indicating that perceptual factors were not the reason for their failure in the hidden toy task. Since the television image was no longer a symbol of reality, but rather reality itself (or so it seemed), dual representation was not necessary.

Taken together these studies suggest that until about 2½ years of age, children's learning from video presentations may be limited. While 9-month-olds show little evidence of grasping the representational nature of very simple video images, there is some evidence that children as young as 14 months can imitate simple actions from a televised model . . .; however, learning more complex actions tends to occur around 2½ to 3 years of age. Up until this age, television is inferior to learning in live interactive situations, especially when the behavior being taught is complex. It has been shown to take up to six repetitions for children younger than two to complete a toy finding task that children of the same age can complete after one exposure to a live model.

Secondly, there is evidence of a developmental shift between 24 and 30 months, close to what Piaget calls the last sub-stage of sensori-motor development and the acquisition of mental representation of cognitive tasks. This developmental achievement is evidenced in learning from televised images. Schmitt and Anderson . . . theorize that part of the problem may also lie with information processing difficulties, such that connecting television's smaller images with real world objects may pose cognitive demands on young children that interfere with successful encoding of the televised objects. By 2½ to 3 years, maturational development has improved infants' limited cognitive capacity, allowing them to deal simultaneously with the perceptual differences and the dual nature of the video images. . . . Thus, a confluence of symbolic and representational limitations coupled with processing difficulties may preclude infants from understanding the nature of television and video and without this understanding learning from the medium proves extremely difficult for children younger than 30 months. This is consistent with evidence of a video deficit in children's ability to learn from video versus live models before this age.

What Are the Potential Benefits and/or Risks to Early Screen Viewing?

In any discussion of the potential benefits or potential risks from early screen viewing, it is easy for academics to stress the risks over the benefits and for television and video producers to do the opposite. It is quite clear that baby targeted videos with titles like "Baby Galileo" and "Baby Mozart" in the *Baby Einstein* series are all intended to give the impression that educational media that engages infants can make them smarter or at least give them early and successful preparation for schooling. Data from the Kaiser Family Foundation . . . surveys of parents of 6-month- to 6-year-olds suggests that parents believe that educational television can teach their child language, pre-reading, and other skills that will help them have a step up once they start school. Moreover, the research evidence of *Sesame Street* and other planned educational programs' positive impact on 4- and 5-year-olds' learning of the televised curriculum and even performance in elementary school . . . is more widely known today by American parents of young children. As well, there may be other benefits of early media use such as increased visual and spatial ability or earlier academic achievement or an increased ability to multitask in a world demanding such abilities. We can only speculate in the absence of empirical evidence and longer-term studies.

There is additional speculation and concern about the likely risks such early screen use might engender. It has now become well known that when the American Academy of Pediatrics in 1999 recommended that children under two not use screen media and that even older children should be limited to only 2 hours a day of screen media use, they did so in the absence of research evidence on the impact of early screen media use, but with an understanding that for healthy development children need caring adults and creative environments with objects that allow for engaged interaction.

DeLoache . . . has observed that there are several risks that might be associated with infants use of screen media such as (1) interference with the acquisition of crucial developmental skills that are engendered by playing with toys and enriching objects; (2) deprivation of social interaction with caring adults; and (3) interference with learning about real objects and reality per se, such as the fact of object permanence. Others, such as Christakis . . . have speculated on whether such early television use may be related to attention deficit disorder or other impaired brain development.

While these are all speculations, there is some empirical evidence that television as background to daily life may impair infants' ability to concentrate on tasks and consequently impact their development. Anderson and Pempek . . . are engaged in research examining how the presence of adult television programming (especially in heavy television households) as a background to the daily life of infants and toddlers might influence children's play activities and their ability to engage in sustained and concentrated attention to an object. They have argued that children's play is a necessary aspect of cognitive development in infancy and that the complexity of children's play is increased with parental involvement. However, such involvement may be diminished when parents and infants share a living room or other space while parents are watching television. Anderson and his colleagues have conducted research in a laboratory setting observing 12-, 24-, and 36-month-old children's toy play with and without an adult television program playing in the background . . . and noted that such background television reduces both the length of infants' play episodes and their apparent concentration during play. This seeming interference in children's concentration during play is coupled with decreased interaction between parents and children in the presence of background television—the parents are attending to the television and not their infants. Thus, Anderson argues that one risk of the presence of adult television (and not specially designed baby videos) on infants' development is that the presence of background television can interfere directly with children's play concentration at a time when play is important for their cognitive development and may also indirectly diminish parent–child interaction important for infant development.

Conclusions

Very young children's media use has increased steadily over the last few decades. While research in infant DVDs and television programs is still sparse, the evidence thus far suggests a developmental framework is needed to understand potential impact. While questions should certainly be asked about the appropriateness of screen media for children this age and potential outcomes, research should also be asking developmental questions about infants' cognitive abilities in relation to their exposure to screen media. Although it appears that infants can mentally represent and imitate very simple behaviors from video, there is strong evidence of a significant learning deficit when compared to live infant-adult interaction. The research thus far suggests that there may be too many representational and perceptual limitations on children under two for television and videos/DVDs to be of substantial educational or instructional value, although this eases somewhat between 30 and 36 months. Additionally, early screen media use may come at the cost of critical parent–child interaction time, as well as interfering with infants' play at a time when play is important to normal cognitive development. . . .

CHALLENGE QUESTIONS

Are There Good Reasons to Allow Infants to Consume Electronic Media, Such as Television?

1. Both sides in this controversy agree that more research needs to be done to fully understand the impact of electronic media on infants. What types of research would be most convincing to you? What are the key questions that we really need to understand?
2. If you were talking to the parents of an infant, what would you say? Do the potential benefits of electronic media outweigh the potential risks?
3. Rideout, Hamel, and the Kaiser Family Foundation rely entirely on parents' perspectives, without contrasting those to what research finds. Is this a case of parents know best, or do parents' perspectives need to be contrasted with scientific research?
4. Wartella and Robb do not consider the usefulness of electronic media in allowing parents to manage family life. Does that matter? Is it possible that by making parenting a more manageable task, electronic media may actually create a more healthy general environment for infants even if causing some immediate cognitive deficits?

Is There Common Ground?

Because the extensive presence of electronic media in the lives of infants is a relatively new phenomenon, there is much to still learn about developmental effects. Both the YES and NO readings acknowledge that electronic media has an appeal to parents because of its convenience and potential. But both would likely also agree that fulfilling that potential requires much more research and careful consideration of the issue. Does the convenience outweigh the risk? Does the intuitive appeal of "learning" from electronic media mask the risks of taking development off its natural course? Both sides of this issue would likely agree that human interaction is preferable to electronic media—but the process of lifespan development is often a matter of negotiating between the ideal and the real.

Suggested Readings

American Academy of Pediatrics, "Media Education," *Pediatrics*, (August 1999)

D. Anderson and M. Evans, "Peril and Potential of Media for Infants and Toddlers," *Zero to Three* (2001)

J. Golin, "Breaking Free from Baby TV," *Mothering.com* (July 2006)

D. Christakis, F. Zimmerman, D. DiGiuseppe, and C. McCarty, "Early Television Exposure and Subsequent Attentional Problems in Children," *Pediatrics* (April 2004)

S. Fisch and R. Truglio, (Eds.) *"G" is for "growing": Thirty years of research on children and Sesame Street* (Lawrence Erlbaum 2001)

A. Poussaint, S. Linn, and J. Golin, "Zero to Three and Sesame Beginnings: The Consequences of Selling Out Babies." *CommonDreams* (April 19, 2006)

Zero to Three, "Statement from ZERO TO THREE on Partnership with Sesame Workshop on *Sesame Beginnings* DVDs,". . .

E. Wartella, A. Caplovitz, and J. Lee "From Baby Einstein to Leapfrog, From Doom to Sims, From Instant Messaging to Internet Chat Rooms: Public Interest in the Role of Interactive Media in Children's Lives." *Society for Research in Child Development Social Policy Report* (2004)

M.L. Courage and A. Setliff, "Debating the Impact of Television and Video Material on Very Young Children: Attention, Learning, and the Developing Brain." *Child Development Perspectives* (2009)

D.R. Anderson and T.A. Pempek, "Television and Very Young Children." *The American Behavioral Scientist* (2005)

Internet References . . .

Public Broadcast System

The nonprofit public broadcasting system offers a year-by-year guide to the developmental milestones of the first eight years.

http://www.pbs.org/parents/childdevelopmenttracker/

Center on the Developing Child

Scholars at Harvard University offer a Web site focused primarily on early childhood to translate developmental science for public consumption.

http://developingchild.harvard.edu/

UNICEF

The United Nations Children's Fund (UNICEF) has a Web site devoted to statistical information about children around the world.

http://www.childinfo.org/

Child Trends

Child Trends is a nonprofit research center that provides data and information related to research on child development.

http://www.childtrends.org/

The Children's Defense Fund

The Children's Defense Fund is a nonprofit child advocacy organization that provides research publications related to public policy.

http://www.childrensdefense.org/child-research-data-publications/

National Association for the Education of Young Children

Official site for the National Association for the Education of Young Children, an organization focused on preschool and other forms of early childhood education.

http://www.naeyc.org/

The Character and Education Partnership

The character and education partnership is a coalition trying to promote character education as a way of shaping children to be good citizens.

http://www.character.org/

NYU Child Study Center

This Web site is sponsored by a center at New York University focused on mental health in childhood.

http://aboutourkids.org/

Early Childhood and Middle Childhood

*E*arly childhood (sometimes referred to as toddlerhood) generally encompasses the years between 2 and 6, while middle childhood generally refers to early school years prior to puberty. These ages comprise a gradual transition into the social, psychological, and physical ways of being that orient any lifespan. As such, scholars of development take particular interest in trying to ensure that these ways of being are healthy, hoping to give all children the chance to succeed in an increasingly complex world. The issues in this section focus on three topics that underlie healthy social, psychological, and physical development: our schools, our mental health, and our activities.

- Do Innate Gender Differences Influence How Children Learn?
- Should Bipolar Disorder be Diagnosed and Treated in Children?
- Are Violent Video Games Necessarily Bad for Children?

ISSUE 7

Do Innate Gender Differences Influence How Children Learn?

YES: Kelley King, Michael Gurian, and Kathy Stevens, from "Gender-Friendly Schools," in *Educational Leadership* (November 2010)

NO: Lise Eliot, from "The Myth of Pink and Blue Brains," *in Educational Leadership* (November 2010)

Learning Outcomes

As you read the issue, focus on the following points:

1. There are group-level differences between boys' and girls' performance in school, but many of those differences are relatively recent developments shifting a historical excess of opportunities for boys into an achievement gap favoring girls.

2. Average innate brain-based gender differences do exist, but they initially seem quite small and are difficult to interpret accurately because they always derive from an interaction between nature and nurture.

3. Although some schools and school districts have had success explicitly attending to gender differences, there is research evidence suggesting efforts to emphasize gender equity can also be effective.

4. Average group differences still allow for a great deal of individual variation, meaning that differences in learning related characteristics such as verbal ability and physical activity do not apply to all boys and girls.

ISSUE SUMMARY

YES: Kelley King, Michael Gurian, and Kathy Stevens, all affiliated with an institute that advocates for accommodating gender differences in learning, identify developmental differences between boys and girls that are deep enough to merit distinct educational practices.

NO: Neuroscientist Lise Eliot offers a brain-based perspective to suggest that popular applications of findings on gender differences exaggerate innate tendencies. Instead, Eliot emphasizes that socialization practices are much more influential to the ways boys and girls learn.

Gender is perhaps the central organizing category for lifespan development. From the very earliest prenatal screenings, when parents are asked if they want to know whether they will have a boy or a girl, to differences in infant clothing and toys, to voluntary segregation at school lunch tables and on teams at recess, to the negotiation of particular expectations around work and family in adulthood, gender matters. The very persistence of how greatly gender matters, despite much attention to the importance of gender equity, suggests to some people that gender differences must be hardwired in the brain. Seeing rambunctious boys ignoring calls to focus on their math problems, or chatty girls telling artful tales during story hour, reinforces stereotypes in a way that makes it easy to assume those tendencies derive from natural predispositions. Perhaps, rather than fighting that nature, gender differences should be accommodated?

That line of thinking, however, quickly runs into the problem of history. In regard to learning and educational achievement, for example, it was not too many years back when boys were assumed to be more competent and girls less encouraged toward school achievement. It has only been in recent decades, with a broad emphasis on creating opportunities for girls, that the gender pendulum has swung in schools. Increasingly, girls outperform boys on standardized tests in primary and secondary school, are more likely to attend and complete college, and more regularly pursue graduate degrees. Now for many schools and communities, in stark contrast to just a few decades prior, the concern is less that girls have fewer opportunities and more that boys are adrift.

Contemporary concerns about how gender differences might relate to learning and school achievement are evolving with technology allowing opportunities to better research the potential biological, genetic, and neurological dimensions of gender. Behavioral differences in classroom demeanor or math performance can now be correlated with brain scans analyzing cortical activation. And some studies have indeed found average, group-level differences in aspects of brain functioning between boys and girls. But those differences also turn out to be surprisingly difficult to interpret. One of the wonders of the human brain is its plasticity, meaning that the brain simultaneously causes behavior and responds to experience. When basic gender differences show up in the brain those differences can derive equally from innate predispositions and from lived experience.

The difficulty of interpreting new brain science has not, however, stopped people from trying to apply new research findings to practical settings such as schools. Kelley King, Michael Gurian, and Kathy Stevens have been at the forefront of many such applications through their work at the Gurian Institute, which is devoted to forwarding the lessons of Michael Gurian's many popular books on gender, including titles such as *Boys and Girls Learn Differently! A Guide for Teachers and Parents*. In the YES article, King, Gurian, and Stevens distill their perspectives on gender differences from their experiences working with schools. They observe clear gender differences in tendencies such as physical activity and verbal acuity, noting that those differences seem to correspond with brain-based differences in characteristics such as frontal lobe development and neural rest states. From their perspective, such differences can be accommodated to ensure all children have the chance to thrive in school.

Lise Eliot, on the other hand, is focused less on educational practice and more on the ways neuroscience, her field of expertise, has been misinterpreted. Eliot too has written a popular book on gender differences, but her emphasis in *Pink Brain, Blue Brain* is to emphasize that whatever small gender differences may be hardwired into the brain are insignificant when compared with constant social messages that accentuate and exaggerate the importance of gender. In the NO article, she draws on the concept of epigenetics to argue that most genetic influences on behavior and development only manifest through environmental activation. She thus suggests that concerns about gender differences are best addressed through emphasizing gender equity rather than treating boys and girls as if they are made to learn differently.

This controversy has other implications that go beyond classroom practice to the very design of our school system. In fact, Eliot was recently part of a team of distinguished scholars who published a paper in the prestigious journal *Science* titled "The Pseudoscience of Single-Sex Schooling" arguing against a trend to think of all-boy or all-girl schools as a salve for achievement gaps. Yet, at the level of group averages, those gaps do exist. Although there is a great deal of individual variation, boys and girls do tend to perform differently in school. Now the challenge is to figure out whether old history and new brain science can be reconciled to explain those differences.

YES

Kelley King, Michael Gurian, and Kathy Stevens

Gender-Friendly Schools

Diane Corner had been teaching "forever," so she was confident in her teaching abilities. In 2007, however, confronted with an extraordinarily wiggly group of 2nd grade boys in a chronically low-performing school, Diane told her principal, "I can't even get the boys to sit still for a short phonics lesson. I have to do something."

Desha Bierbaum, her principal, responded with a new possibility. "I've been learning about the differences in how boys and girls learn. Why don't you try letting the fidgety boys stand up and move around while you teach? That helps some boys' brains focus and learn better."

That conversation marked the beginning of the success story we became involved in at Wamsley Elementary School in Rifle, Colorado.

School Improvement Through Gender Equality

Fifty percent of Wamsley's students qualify for free or reduced-price lunch, 30 percent are English language learners, and the mobility rate is 43 percent. In fall 2007, Wamsley was on academic watch for not making adequate yearly progress (AYP).

Because boys underperformed girls by a significant margin at Wamsley, Principal Bierbaum decided to target her school's improvement efforts at achieving gender equality. The school staff acknowledged that it had a better understanding of how to teach girls than boys, but it resolved that any professional development approach the school implemented to give boys more opportunity must also be girl-friendly. Wamsley applied for and received a grant to provide whole-school online classes and strategies-oriented summer institute training for Wamsley's teachers, along with on-site professional development and coaching on the different learning needs of boys and girls. By the end of the first year of the initiative, student performance jumped markedly, and the school was taken off the AYP watch list. Wamsley became a national success story.

A year earlier, the Atlanta Public Schools in Georgia had embarked on a similar effort. In 2006, many Atlanta schools were not meeting AYP, and

From *Educational Leadership*, November 2010, pp. 38–42. Copyright © 2010 by ASCD. Reprinted by permission. The Association for Supervision and Curriculum Development is a worldwide community of educators advocating sound policies and sharing best practices to achieve the success of each learner. To learn more, visit ASCD at www.ascd.org.

previous school reform initiatives had failed. When the district staff disaggregated data for gender, they noticed that gender gaps reflecting lower achievement for boys were present across all subgroups and were largest for boys of color and those living in poverty.

In fall 2007, the school district launched two single-sex middle school academies—the Business Engineering Science Technology Academy for Boys (the B.E.S.T. Academy), and the Coretta Scott King Young Women's Leadership Academy. We became involved at that point. Faculty and staff at the pilot schools received professional development (including coaching, online courses, on-site training, and summer institutes) on how boys and girls learn differently and how to strategically implement gender-friendly teaching strategies into all aspects of the school, from teaching to counseling services to athletics.

Like Wamsley, these schools are now success stories. Within two years, both made AYP. Grades and test scores improved, student attendance increased, discipline referrals decreased, and teachers felt more effective. The district is moving forward with plans to expand their two single-sex middle schools through grade 12.

Looking Through the Gender Lens

In the last two decades, we have supported efforts to close opportunity gaps in more than 2,000 schools across the United States. When educators look closely at test scores, grades, discipline referrals, homework completion rates, special education placements, and student motivation, they consistently realize how gender-related issues intersect and interfere with their ability to achieve school improvement goals. They notice the following areas of difficulty for girls:

- Lower learning and engagement in science and technology classes.
- Relational aggression in school and in cyberspace.
- Problems with self-esteem development in adolescence.

They notice a different set of core areas of difficulty for boys:

- Lower achievement scores in most classes—especially among low-income and racially/ethnically diverse students—with panicular problems in literacy.
- Lagging learning skills in such areas as note taking and listening.
- More struggles with homework.
- Lower grades in all classes, except some math and most science classes.
- Less motivation to learn and lower perception that the curriculum is relevant.

Both boys and girls tend to need help in specific areas. But data show that schools are now failing boys, as a group, in more areas than girls. More and more teachers are expressing the need for assistance in learning to teach boys effectively.

In March 2010, the Center on Education Policy echoed teachers' instincts when it released the report *Are There Gender Differences in Achievement Between*

Boys and Girls? In preparing the report, the center examined state test data from all age groups in all 50 states, finding

> good news for girls but bad news for boys. In math, girls are doing roughly as well as boys, and the differences that do exist in some states are small and show no clear national pattern favoring boys or girls. But in reading, boys are lagging behind girls in all states with adequate data, and these gaps are greater than 10 percentage points in some states.

Dealing with this reality is an important challenge for all of us who care about education reform. If we do not recognize it and work to close the opportunity gaps boys are experiencing, millions of boys and men will lose out over the next decades.

The Elephant in the Room

Boys and girls, like men and women, are not stereotypes; they fall along a wide spectrum of learning preferences and styles. In fact, there is a great deal of overlap. Every day, teachers work with boys who are verbal, collaborative, and more emotive and with girls who are visual, competitive, and less emotive.

As a group, however, boys are much more likely than girls to be graphic thinkers and kinesthetic learners and to thrive under competitive learning structures. Some of the gender differences we observe in the classroom (see a summary at www.ascd.org/ASCD/pdf/journals/ed_lead/el_201011_gurian_figure.pdf) are undoubtedly linked to societal influences, but some also stem from physical differences in the brain identified by neuroscientists.

Most of the teachers we work with realize that the preparation they received in graduate school and teacher certification programs to teach "all students" was in fact training for verbal and sedentary learning. This presents a large elephant in the room for teachers and schools. Given the structures, expectations, and teaching styles in today's classrooms, teachers generally have more difficulty teaching boys than girls. In a classroom of 25 students, we may notice that five to seven boys are having difficulties, whether these are overt issues or a tendency to check out of the learning process. They need a kind of instruction teachers have not been trained to provide, and the lack of such teaching profoundly affects the overall grades, test scores, and behavior of the class, as well as a teacher's sense of whether he or she is teaching effectively.

Strategies for Teaching Boys and Girls Effectively

Here are some examples of strategies that teachers we have worked with are using to close opportunity gaps between boys and girls.

Strategy 1: Add Movement

Chris Zust of Wellington School in Columbus, Ohio, gets her 1st grade boys and girls to stand up for reading group.

I play a game when the children have finished reading. I let them spread out around the room, and I throw a beach ball to them that has eight prompts written on it. Each time a student catches the ball, he or she has to answer a prompt. My boys are far more engaged with this activity than they are when I have them sitting at the reading table.

Pairing learning with movement is especially important for many boys because it helps them stay out of the *neural rest* (boredom) state. But because it increases brain activity, movement can also help girls learn.

In addition to infusing movement into learning activities, teachers might also include regular brain breaks—frequent, brief opportunities to simply get up and move, such as doing jumping jacks, jogging in place, stretching, doing the wave from one side of the room to the other, or dancing in place with music.

Strategy 2: Build on the Visual

Fifth grade teacher Debbie Mathis and her teammates at Edith Wolford Elementary in Colorado Springs, Colorado, noticed that during traditional writing activities, boys were much slower getting started, wrote fewer words, used fewer sensory details, and got lower grades. After learning how graphically oriented boys' brains tend to be, Debbie and her teammates decided to use comic-strip pictures as prompts. "That really got the kids' imaginations flowing," Debbie shares. "The entire class was jazzed and wrote like crazy! Honestly, I was thrilled when even my most reluctant boys were eager to share."

HOW BOYS AND GIRLS LEARN DIFFERENTLY

- *Verbal/graphic differences.* Boys' brains tend to have more cortical areas, mainly in the right hemisphere, wired for spatial/mechanical processing than do girls' brains; girls' brains generally have greater cortical emphasis on verbal processing.
- *Frontal lobe development.* A girl's prefrontal cortex is generally more active than a boy's of the same age, and her frontal lobe generally develops earlier. These are the decision-making areas of the brain, as well as the reading/writing/word production areas.
- *Neural rest states.* Boys' brains tend to go into a more notable *rest state* than girls' brains do. Because the brain's first priority is survival, it scans its environment for information that would alert it to any threat, challenge, or information crucial to its survival. If the classroom is not providing any stimuli that the brain perceives as important, the male brain tends to more quickly slip into a rest state (which manifests itself as boredom, or "zoning out"). In the classroom, boys often try to avoid these natural male rest states by engaging in activities like tapping their pencils or poking at classmates.

Karen Combs, another teacher at Wolford, echoes this approach:

When I explained to my students that they were going to draw pictures as a way to plan their writing content, two of my boys looked at each other and said, "Sweet!" After about 30 minutes of writing, my most reluctant writer came toward me. I expected him to ask, "How much do I have to write?" Instead, he asked, "What if an hour isn't enough time to write everything that I've planned?"

Heather Peter, a language arts teacher at Broomfield High School in Broomfield, Colorado, notes that although boys are vocal about their enthusiasm for visual-spatial projects, girls also flourish when given the opportunity to create visual products to demonstrate their comprehension. Heather shares, "We recently finished a unit on *Hamlet* in which students had the choice to make a video, create a talk show, do a choral reading, or write a screenplay. Of the 38 female students, 35 chose a visual-spatial project."

Visual-spatial activities reach a broader spectrum of learners, harness learner strengths, help to stimulate and develop more neural pathways, and help close gaps for both boys and girls. They can be absolutely essential for some learners.

Strategy 3: Incorporate Student Interests and Choices

Tenth grader Will was like many of the boys struggling in Atlanta Public Schools. Will was not motivated in school, and it required superhuman effort to get him to do his schoolwork. But Will had a passion for sports. His teachers began to identify this passion in his classes and made sure to integrate it into his learning. English, social studies, and other teachers stocked classrooms with sports-relevant reading material, from graphic novels and technical magazines to sports magazines and biographies of football and basketball players.

His teachers reported consistent findings, which we've summarized here:

Since incorporating boys' interests into the curriculum, we have seen a measurable change in Will's body language. He comes in with his head up and is cheerful and making eye contact now. He has something he cares about to focus on in class and homework. Boys like him see school differently when their interests and passions are integrated into classes.

Broomfield's Heather Peter has also used strategies revolving around student interests to close opportunity gaps. She says,

I've had several students over the years tell me that they like literature more now because of all the projects that they were able to do. This is true not just for boys but also for girls. My student Alice told me, "I'll never forget *Hamlet* because I will always remember making my music video."

By bringing in novelty and topics of outside interest, these teachers are boosting all their students' motivation. For both boys and girls, motivation to learn can be the difference between success and failure.

A SNAPSHOT: BOYS IN SCHOOL

- On the most recent National Assessment of Educational Progress (NAEP) writing test, 26 percent of 12th grade males scored *below basic*, compared with 11 percent of females. Just 16 percent of males achieved at the *proficient/advanced* levels, compared with 31 percent of females.
- In reading, one-third of 12th grade males scored *below basic* on NAEP, compared with 22 percent of females; fewer than one-third of males (29 percent) were reading at the *proficient/advanced* levels, compared with 41 percent of females.
- Boys receive two-thirds of the *D*s and *F*s in schools, but fewer than one-half of the *A*s.
- Girls are more likely to attend and graduate from college. In 2003, there were 1.35 females for every male who graduated from a four-year college and 1.30 females for every male undergraduate.
- These and many other gender gaps for boys have been widening over the last decade.

Closing Gaps Now and in the Future

As districts, schools, and teachers close opportunity gaps, teach more effectively, and turn around low-performing schools, they explore and learn solutions they can apply right away—solutions inherent in the boys and girls they teach.

After 20 years of training teachers in both how to help boys and girls learn and strategies for teaching them effectively, we believe the next decade will open greater opportunities for teachers and schools to use the wisdom of the gender lens. This lens is an essential tool for education reform—one that not only enables schools to meet accountability goals in terms of higher test scores for all groups, but also reflects the deep humanity and love of all children that each of us brings to the schoolhouse.

Lise Eliot  **NO**

The Myth of Pink and Blue Brains

Gender differences are a hot topic. But much of the recent discussion about boys' and girls' learning has generated more heat than light. As a neuroscientist who has studied children's cognitive and emotional abilities and, in particular, analyzed gender differences in children's brains, I hope to help set the record straight on this incendiary subject.

Boys and girls differ in many ways—in physical activity level; self-control; and performance levels in reading, writing, and math. Above all, they differ in interests. But most of these differences are nowhere near as large as popular ideas about a "Mars-Venus" gulf imply, nor are they as "hardwired" as current discourse portrays. The truth is that neuroscientists have identified very few reliable differences between boys' and girls' brains. Boys' brains are about 10 percent larger than those of girls, and boys' brains finish growing a year or two later during puberty (Lenroot et al., 2007). But these global differences reflect physical maturation more than mental development.

Few other clear-cut differences between boys' and girls' neural structures, brain activity, or neurochemistry have thus far emerged, even for something as obviously different as self-regulation. Boys and girls, on average, differ in self-regulatory *behavior*, with girls showing better ability to sit still, pay attention, delay gratification, and organize a take-home folder, for instance. We know that self-regulatory abilities depend on the prefrontal cortex of the brain, but neuroscientists have thus far been unable to show that this area develops earlier or is more active in girls (Barry et al., 2004).

The same is true of gender differences in the adult brain. In spite of what you may have read, women do not have a larger corpus callosum,[1] process language in a more symmetrical fashion, or have higher circulating levels of serotonin compared with men. The latest high-resolution MRI studies reveal small differences in brain lateralization or "sidedness" (Liu, Stufflebeam, Sepulcre, Hedden, & Buckner, 2009) and functional connectivity (Biswal et al., 2010), on the order of three-tenths of a standard deviation, meaning there is more overlap between average males' and females' brains than differences between the average brain of each gender. These studies, based on thousands of subjects around the world, give us a better picture of the true size of neurologic sex differences than do the cherry-picked, single studies of a few dozen men and women that are often cited as proof of evolutionarily programmed gender differences.

Our actual ability differences are quite small. Although psychologists can measure statistically significant distinctions between large groups of men and women or boys and girls, there is much more overlap in the academic and even social-emotional abilities of the genders than there are differences (Hyde, 2005). To put it another way, the range of performance within each gender is wider than the difference between the average boy and girl.

Of course, teachers know this. Teachers recognize that girls *or* boys can be strong readers. On the playground, about one-third of girls are physically more active than the average boy. When it comes to academic achievement and even classroom behavior, gender is a very poor predictor of any individual student's performance.

So What's Behind Gender Gaps?

Society as a whole, however, cannot ignore the striking gender gaps in academic performance. Girls have out-performed boys in reading and boys have outscored girls in math (although by a smaller margin) on the National Assessment of Educational Progress (NAEP) in every year assessed since 1971 (U.S. Department of Education, 2005). Similar gender gaps exist on the Program for International Student Assessment (PISA) (Else-Quest, Hyde, & Linn, 2010).

At first glance, this stability suggests there is something inherently different about boys' and girls' academic abilities. But a closer look reveals that the gaps vary considerably by age, ethnicity, and nationality. For example, among the countries participating in PISA, the reading gap is more than twice as large in some countries (Iceland, Norway, and Austria) as in others (Japan, Mexico, and Korea); for math, the gap ranges from a large male advantage in certain countries (Korea and Greece) to essentially no gap in other countries—or even reversed in girls' favor (Iceland and Thailand). What's more, a recent analysis of PISA data found that higher female performance in math correlates with higher levels of gender equity in individual nations.

This suggests that environmental factors are important in shaping gender gaps. The truth is that no mental ability—or ability difference—is "hardwired" into the brain. Abilities develop in a social-cultural context that includes each child's opportunities, relationships, sense of identity, and more. Biologists call such development *epigenetic*. Environmental factors—ranging from diet and chemical exposure to less tangible influences like parenting styles—are known to alter DNA structure, gene expression, and an organism's lifelong brain and behavioral function (Champagne & Curley, 2005). When it comes to gender gaps, boys and girls start out a little bit different, but these differences become rapidly magnified by a culture that sees them—and encourages them to see themselves—as fundamentally different creatures.

Three Little Differences—and How They Grow

Three small, early biases appear to be programmed by prenatal hormone exposure or sex-specific gene expression:

- Baby boys are modestly more physically active than girls (Campbell & Eaton, 1999).
- Toddler girls talk one month earlier, on average, than boys (Fenson et al., 1994).
- Boys appear more spatially aware (Quinn & Liben, 2008).

Such differences contribute to each gender's well-known toy preferences, which surface in the second year of life (Servin, Gohlin, & Berlin, 1999). Boys prefer more active playthings, like trucks and balls; girls choose more verbal-relational toys, especially dolls. In each of these cases, however, boy-girl differences are magnified through parental treatment. For example, parents encourage more physical risk-taking in sons than in daughters (Morrongiello & Dawber, 2000); mothers generally talk more to preschool-aged daughters than sons (Leaper, Anderson, & Sanders, 1998); and parents discourage "gender-inappropriate" play, especially in terms of boys showing too much interest in sister's Barbie collection (Lytton & Romney, 1991).

This is important, because children develop the skills they will bring into the classroom through such early play. Simply put, girls spend more time talking, drawing, and role-playing in relational ways, whereas boys spend more time moving, targeting, building, and role-playing as heroes. Each activity is beneficial, but because of the potency of early experience on children's brain wiring, the differences between typical "girl" and "boy" play have deep consequences for cognitive and emotional function.

For example, as boys and girls progress through childhood, clocking very different amounts of time throwing, catching, constructing, and playing high-speed driving and targeting games, their spatial skills grow increasingly disparate, with boys scoring higher in this area. The ability to visualize three-dimensional objects and their orientations, distances, and trajectories is important in higher math, science, and mechanical work—domains in which boys eventually pull ahead.

Alternatively, consider verbal skills. Thanks to their extra conversation with peers and parents, girls' small verbal advantage balloons by kindergarten into a significant gap in phonological awareness, the key stepping stone for learning to read. By 3rd grade, 20 percent more girls than boys score in the proficient range as readers, according to NAEP data—a gap that grows to 38 percent by 8th grade (Lee, Grigg, & Donahue, 2007) and a startling 47 percent by the end of high school (Grigg, Donahue, & Dion, 2007).

The numbers are stark, but they reveal that the reason boys don't read and write as well as girls has little to do with innate brain wiring and everything to do with the reality that girls engage more than boys with words: talking, reading, journal writing, or endless text-messaging. Only 25 percent of teenage boys around the world cite reading as one of their favorite hobbies, compared with 45 percent of teenage girls (Organisation for Economic Cooperation and Development, 2010).

So if we want to tackle academic gaps between boys and girls, we need to start early, nurturing skills and attitudes that will better prepare both genders for the modern classroom. We also need to make sure that the classroom remains a place where students' potential is broadened, rather than narrowed through misguided beliefs. As always, the best way to do this is to focus on each child's unique combination of cognitive and emotional talents.

Navigating Gender Differences

In spite of claims—and intentions—to the contrary, few parents or teachers are truly gender neutral. The good news is that attempts at gender equity do make a difference. Students develop more stereotyped attitudes in classrooms that emphasize gender (such as by lining up boys and girls separately) and more egalitarian attitudes where it's deemphasized (Hilliard & Liben, in press).

So how should teachers pay attention to gender? Very carefully. As with all types of diversity, the challenge is to respect and honor differences without turning them into self-fulfilling prophecies. Just as we would never try to guess a student's math skill on the basis of skin or eye color, we must avoid prejudging any student's verbal, athletic, scientific, artistic, leadership, analytical, or social ability on the basis of chromosomes.

We must challenge gender stereotypes for *both sexes*. In mainstream U.S. culture, girls are rewarded for behaving like boys more than the other way around—which is great for girls' math and athletic skills, but not for boys' verbal and relational abilities. Boys hear that "girls can do anything" whereas the boys get boxed into smaller corners by their presumed limitations ("Boys are less verbal"); teachers' prohibitions ("No running"); and peers' narrow views of masculinity ("Art is gay"). Might this be why girls excel in many areas, while boys' success is shrinking to sports and a few select curricular zones?

Here are a few suggestions for reducing opportunity gaps between boys and girls:

Avoid stereotyping. I suspect most teachers try to do this, but I fear that the recent focus on boy-girl differences and claims of "hardwiring" have caused things to slip backwards. Some news reports about single-gender programs describe teachers guiding students into stereotyped activities, for instance, giving girls quiet spaces to "sit and discuss their feelings" while boys get extra opportunities for competition and physical play (Tyre, 2005). This approach is wrong: Both sexes need more physical exercise, and both need to be comfortable blending competition and cooperation.

Appreciate the range of intelligences. Beyond the three *R*s lie many zones of performance in which individual students may excel but which aren't typically recognized at school. Howard Gardner brought nontraditional kinds of intelligence and skill to teachers' attention years ago but with the new back-to-basics focus, some important domains—such as the arts and kinesthetic ability—have been forgotten. Broadening the range of abilities that we teach and affirm can help more students feel successful at school.

Strengthen spatial awareness. Spatial skills are arguably the most overlooked nontraditional abilities in the curriculum. Yet spatial cognition is important for understanding such areas as fractions, proportionality, calculus, geography, physics, and chemistry. Research supports the idea that practice in activities requiring spatial awareness improves such skills (Newcombe, Mathason, & Ter-lecki, 2002), but most training in this domain happens outside school. Beginning in preschool, teachers should formally teach spatial and mechanical skills using puzzles, map reading, targeting sports, and building projects that get students thinking in 3D.

Engage boys with the word. Parents and educators alike need to do a better job with this, starting early with the verbal and literary immersion that builds vocabulary, phonologic skill, and a love of books. The simple equation, "Language in = Language out" should remind teachers of the importance of engaging boys in one-on-one dialogue, word play, stories, songs, and every kind of text. Once they begin formal reading instruction, boys benefit from a wide variety of reading material that appeals to their sense of humor and frequent interest in action, adventure, and nonfiction.

Writing ability shows an even larger gender gap, but in a world that produced Shakespeare and Stephen King, it's absurd to suggest that boys are constitutionally incapable of writing as well as girls. The solution is time on task. Beginning in preschool, teachers should emphasize "mark-making" to promote writing using vivid markers, crayons, charcoal, or paint on large surfaces like appliance boxes—or fun ones like portable slates. The goal is not formal printing, but symbolic expression and fine-motor practice. Although penmanship is important, divorce it from composition by allowing students to dictate or type their thoughts.

Recruit boys into nonathletic extracurricular activities. When did the school newspaper, yearbook, and student council become all-female clubs? Unfortunately, many of these activities have reached a tipping point; when the number of boys falls below 25 percent, it becomes—perplexingly—"unmasculine" to join the chorus or run for class president. Just as we'd be appalled to host a science club without girls, we should not accept boys' absence from a wider variety of campus activities.

Bring more men into the classroom. The number of male teachers in elementary school has declined precipitously since the 1980s. We need to increase the ranks of young men who enter teaching, and bring more fathers and adult males into preschool and elementary classrooms as role models for intellectual engagement.

Treat teacher bias seriously. There still are teachers who believe "girls are good at reading and boys are good at math." There still are teachers who cannot tolerate physical exuberance or coloring outside the lines. Considering the potent effect of teacher expectations on student performance, we must train teachers about potential bias and evaluate them with respect to it. Just as girls have benefited from efforts to root out antifemale bias, boys deserve protection from teachers who may—consciously or unconsciously—regard them as "toxic."

In the past 15 years, claims about hardwired differences between boys and girls have propagated virally, with no genuine neuroscientific justification. In reality, culture, attitudes, and practices influence boy-girl academic gaps far more than prenatal testosterone does. The sooner teachers open their eyes to such influences, the sooner we can bring out the best in every child.

Note

1. The corpus callosum is a white matter tract that provides most of the connections between left and right cerebral hemispheres. Some studies have reported that it's larger in the female brain; others have found it larger in the male brain, but a meta-analysis of 49 studies found no significant difference in corpus callosum size between the genders (Bishop & Whalsten, 1997).

CHALLENGE QUESTIONS

Do Innate Gender Differences Influence How Children Learn?

1. King, Gurian, and Stevens identify gender differences in learning and offer suggestions for teaching with those differences in mind. What are the potential advantages and disadvantages to gender-based teaching?
2. Eliot does not deny that gender differences exist; instead, she questions their significance and whether it is fair to consider them "hard-wired." When do gender differences become significant enough to accommodate? If you were a teacher, what kind of evidence would you want to see to understand the development of gender differences?
3. What is the relationship between brain differences and genetic differences? Why is it the case that some brain-based differences may be unrelated to innate predispositions?
4. One of the challenges of confronting gender disparities in schools is that there is much individual variation: How can average differences between boys and girls be respected without condemning individual boys and girls who do not fit with the group norms?

Is There Common Ground?

Gender differences have long provoked contentious discussion, and it seems likely that they always will. Although some radical thinkers have aspired to a gender-free society, most people on all sides of this issue acknowledge that gender differences are real. That includes the authors of the YES and NO selections, who all recognize that schools are a key site for both demonstrating and shaping gender differences. Both sides would likely agree that while girls have historically been marginalized in school, boys are now demonstrating struggles that deserve attention. Both would also likely agree that schools should be constantly working to improve learning outcomes for all boys and girls. The core difference is whether that work requires accommodating or challenging gender norms. And that difference depends on how we understand the origin of those norms. Like all developmental domains, gender is a product of both nature and nurture—but what does our analysis of the relative importance of those forces mean for how our children learn?

Suggested Readings

S. Baron-Cohen, *The Essential Difference: The Truth About the Male and Female Brain*, (Basic Books 2003)

L. Eliot, *Pink Brain, Blue Brain: How Small Differences Grow Into Troublesome Gaps—And What We Can Do About It* (Houghton Mifflin Harcourt 2009)

C. Fine, *Delusions of Gender: How Our Minds, Society, and Neurosexism Create Difference* (W.W. Norton & Company 2010)

D.F. Halpern, C.P. Benbow, D.C. Geary, R.C. Gur, J.S. Hyde, & M.A. Gernsbacher, "The Science of Sex Differences in Science and Mathematics," *Psychological Science in the Public Interest* (August 2007)

D.F. Halpern, L. Eliot, R.S. Bigler, R.A. Fabes, L.D. Hanish, J.S. Hyde, L. Liben, L., & C.L. Martin, "The Pseudoscience of Single-Sex Schooling," *Science* (September 2011)

J. Kleinfeld, "The State of American Boyhood," *Gender Issues* (June 2009)

L. Sax, *Why Gender Matters: What Parents and Teachers Need to Know about the Emerging Science of Sex Differences* (Doubleday 2005)

ISSUE 8

Should Bipolar Disorder be Diagnosed and Treated in Children?

YES: **Child and Adolescent Bipolar Foundation**, from "About Pediatric Bipolar Disorder" at http://www.bpkids.org/learn/library/about-pediatric-bipolar-disorder (October 1, 2010)

NO: **Stuart L. Kaplan**, from "Pediatric Bipolar Disorder" in *Your Child Does Not Have Bipolar Disorder: How Bad Science and Good Public Relations Created the Diagnosis* (Praeger, 2011)

Learning Outcomes

As you read the issue, focus on the following points:

1. Diagnosing bipolar disorder in children and adolescents is a relatively new phenomenon that raises challenging questions about what is "normal" and what is "abnormal."

2. Increasing familiarity with pediatric bipolar disorder can allow for health care workers, families, schools, and others to better intervene with children in distress, and such interventions can come in many forms—only one of which is medication.

3. Increasing rates of diagnoses of bipolar disorder, along with other disorders such as ADHD, have coincided with increasing rates of using psychiatric medications with children in ways that help some children while also posing some risks.

4. Although labeling children as having mental disorders such as bipolar disorder may allow them to access appropriate treatment, there are often less severe diagnoses that might prove less stigmatizing.

ISSUE SUMMARY

YES: The Child and Adolescent Bipolar Foundation offers an overview of how pediatric bipolar disorder is defined, identified, and studied to help parents and others understand this relatively new way of thinking about psychiatric problems among children.

NO: Child psychiatrist Stuart L. Kaplan thinks that the concept of pediatric bipolar disorder is too eagerly embraced considering its newness, and that there is insufficient evidence for labeling children with a serious psychiatric problem that historically only applied to adults.

A 2009 story in the satirical newspaper *The Onion* reported a study finding that "98% of all infants suffer from bipolar disorder." The (fake) study's author claims, "The majority of our subjects, regardless of size, sex, or race, exhibited extreme mood swings, often crying one minute and then giggling playfully the next." Like any good satire, this is funny because it taps at the truth. Infants, and children of all ages, go through phases where the "normal" behavior for them would be extremely "abnormal" for adults. But that obvious and sometimes amusing fact quickly becomes complicated and controversial when trying to make judgments about how to best help children and families who are truly distressed.

Diagnosing mental disorders of any type in children used to be extremely rare. Mental disorders, pervasive disruptions of normal psychological functioning, were assumed to be the province of adults who had matured to the point where consistent judgments about one's psychological state were possible. The thinking was that children, on the other hand, are in the midst of developmental periods inevitably characterized by inconsistency. The moods and interests of a 6-year-old are necessarily different from the moods and interests of a 16-year-old or a 26-year-old. So when the moods of a 6-year-old seem disordered the old thinking was often to consider that a developmental phase—something to be monitored and addressed, but not diagnosed. Increasingly, the new thinking is to take advantage of growing bodies of research and the growing availability of psychiatric medications to identify and treat childhood mental disorders. That trend, however, raises important questions about the very nature of what is normal and abnormal in child development.

The rapid change in thinking about childhood disorders is dramatically evident in statistics on rates of diagnosing and medicating mental disorders in children. In a critical essay titled "The Childhood Bipolar Epidemic: Brat or Bipolar?" Elizabeth J. Roberts cited statistics finding that the number of prescriptions for the types of amphetamines most commonly used to treat attention-deficit/hyperactivity disorder (ADHD) increased by 500 percent between 1991 and 2000. By 2006, Roberts notes, "fully 10 percent of all ten-year-old boys in the United States were being medicated with amphetamines." Likewise, Roberts cites figures noting an "unprecedented, fivefold increase in antipsychotic prescriptions for children" between 1995 and 2002, with antipsychotic drugs typically prescribed to children diagnosed with bipolar disorder (though the same drugs are more commonly used in adults diagnosed with schizophrenia—a diagnoses that is still extremely rare for children).

Both the YES and NO articles for this issue cite similar statistics, but interpret the meaning of those statistics in very different ways. The Child and

Adolescent Bipolar Foundation considers a "40-fold increase in the diagnosis of bipolar disorder in the US in the past ten years" evidence of improved awareness of the presence of the disorder among children, and a move away from dismissing disordered children as simply "bad seeds." The Child and Adolescent Bipolar Foundation also notes that even this increase in diagnosing children does not make rates of bipolar disorder as great for children as for adults. In the book from which the other excerpt is taken, on the other hand, child psychiatrist Stuart L. Kaplan cites the same 40-fold increase and goes further to note that when children and adolescents are discharged from psychiatric hospitals nearly one-third have been diagnosed with bipolar disorder. For Kaplan, however, these dramatic increases are not about increasing awareness but instead about "bad science and good public relations."

For Kaplan a significant factor in the increasing rates of pediatric bipolar disorder is confusion between bipolar disorder and other common childhood mental disorders such as ADHD and oppositional defiant disorder (ODD). This potential confusion highlights the challenges of accurately diagnosing mental disorders of any type. There are no clear biological markers for bipolar disorder, ADHD, ODD, or other common disorders such as depression. As such, there are no blood tests, or brain scans, or x-rays that can currently be used to effectively categorize psychological problems. Instead, clinicians use what is essentially a checklist of diagnostic criteria that require careful observation and accurate reporting of a child's behavior. A similar checklist is included in the article by the Child and Adolescent Bipolar Foundation, and a cursory glance at the list points out the challenges of this endeavor. Although behavior such as "Talk of wanting to die or kill themselves or others" is clearly problematic, other indicators such as "Racing thoughts," "Sleep disturbances," or "Compulsive craving for certain objects or food" can be variants on normal behavior for some children.

In fact, though Kaplan questions the common diagnosis of bipolar disorder, he is moderate compared to some critics who argue that even childhood diagnoses such as ADHD and ODD are rampantly overdiagnosed and overmedicated. Some feel that the simple fact of labeling children as having a mental disorder suggests a permanent state the encourages a reliance on medication, rather than allowing for a recognition that child development can be an erratic process that requires careful attention to environments at home, in school, and elsewhere. As Kaplan notes, the age at which medical practitioners consider it acceptable to diagnosis bipolar disorder has gotten younger and younger to the point where preschool bipolar disorder is well-recognized and *The Onion* satire does not seem too far from reality. Of course, for many children and families that increase in earlier diagnosis may be a good thing; the Child and Adolescent Bipolar Foundation makes a strong case that earlier diagnosis and treatment allows more time and opportunity for healthy change. But in the context of lifespan development the key question is whether there might be other ways of allowing that change to happen?

About Pediatric Bipolar Disorder

Bipolar disorder (also known as manic-depression) is a chronic brain disorder marked by bouts of extreme and impairing changes in mood, energy, thinking, and behavior. The most outwardly apparent symptoms are behavioral; however, the illness often has less visible, but serious, cognitive, cardiac, and metabolic effects. Symptoms may emerge gradually or suddenly during childhood, adolescence, or adulthood. Researchers have identified cases of bipolar disorder in every age group studied, including preschoolers. Here, CABF examines bipolar disorder that emerges in childhood or adolescence.

Bipolar disorder does not affect every child in the same way. The frequency, intensity, and duration of a child's symptoms and the child's response to treatment vary dramatically. As the child grows up, bipolar disorder may affect the size, shape, and function of brain regions and networks. Recent research suggests that pediatric bipolar disorder is a neurodevelopmental disorder. Parts of the brain mature (or come online) at different rates and times; brain maturation is not complete until an individual is 25 or so. Consequently, the symptoms and diagnosis of a psychiatric illness may change as the child grows.

There is presently no cure for bipolar disorder. Yet, there are reasons for optimism. Research to help children and adults with this illness is ongoing. Genetic discoveries are expected to lead to more accurate diagnosing, better treatments, and perhaps a cure. As always, it is wise to expect the best but prepare for the worst. Learn where the road ahead may lead. Develop strategies and contingency plans while staying flexible and confident in the present. Network with other parents. Be involved in CABF. Most importantly, take care of yourself.

Diagnosis

Pediatric Bipolar Disorder

The *Diagnostic and Statistical Manual of Mental Disorders,* the formal psychiatric diagnostic manual referred to as the "DSM-IV," is the standard reference for diagnosing psychiatric disorders. However, when the DSM-IV was first published in 1994, the entire focus was on adult-onset bipolar disorder. In the decade plus since then, rapid research developments in every area of science, especially the brain, have answered many old questions and opened the door to new questions we couldn't even articulate then.

We now understand that children and adolescents can have bipolar disorder. Some of our ill children meet the textbook definition of bipolar disorder. Some of our ill children with severe mood dysregulation might not meet the textbook definition because they don't have distinct episodes of a certain duration or have few clear periods of wellness between episodes. They might have rapid and severe cycling between moods or they might present in a mixed state that produces chronic irritability. Experts have not yet reached consensus as to whether children with chronic irritability and clear mood swings, but without mania, should be classified as having bipolar disorder. CABF urges the research community to agree on a common terminology and a way to communicate with each other and with families about the full spectrum of the severe illness(es) impairing our children. It is imperative that we work together to alleviate the terrible suffering that this disorder wreaks.

The DSM-IV Diagnosis

The *DSM-IV* describes four types of bipolar disorder.

Bipolar I. In this form of the disorder, the individual experiences one or more episodes of mania. Episodes of depression may also occur, but are not required to diagnose bipolar disorder.

Symptoms of **mania** include:

- euphoria (elevated mood)—silliness or elation that is inappropriate and impairing
- grandiosity
- flight of ideas or racing thoughts
- more talkative than usual or pressure to keep talking
- irritability or hostility when demands are not met
- excessive distractibility
- decreased need for sleep without daytime fatigue
- excessive involvement in pleasurable but risky activities (daredevil acts, hypersexuality)
- poor judgment
- hallucinations and psychosis

For an episode to qualify as mania, there must be elevated mood plus at least three other symptoms, or irritable mood plus at least four other symptoms.

Symptoms of depression include:

- lack of joy and pleasure in life
- withdrawal from activities formerly enjoyed
- agitation and irritability
- pervasive sadness and/or crying spells
- sleeping too much or inability to sleep

- drop in grades or inability to concentrate
- thoughts of death and suicide
- fatigue or loss of energy
- feelings of worthlessness
- significant weight loss, weight gain or change in appetite

Stable periods occur between episodes of mania and depression. An episode must last at least one week, or, if hospitalization is necessary, may be of any duration.

Bipolar II. In this form of the disorder, the individual experiences recurrent periods of depression with episodes of normal mood (euthymia) or hypomania between episodes. Hypomania is a markedly elevated or irritable mood accompanied by increased physical and mental energy. Hypomania can be a time of great creativity and energy and may, but not always, progress into full-blown mania if not treated. Some people with bipolar disorder never develop full-blown mania.

Bipolar Disorder NOS (Not Otherwise Specified). Doctors may make this diagnosis when there is severe mood dysregulation with serious impairment, but it is not clear which type of bipolar disorder, if any, is emerging. Perhaps the individual has always been impaired, with cycling apparent since infancy. Maybe there have been no discernable periods of wellness. Perhaps the child is experiencing the emergence of another neurodevelopmental illness and the symptoms of that disorder have not yet been fully expressed. The inability to pinpoint a diagnosis should not be taken as a dismissal of the severity of the child's symptoms.

Cyclothymia. This form of the disorder produces recurrent periods of less severe, but definite, mood swings that seriously impair the individual's life. Cyclothymia may progress into full bipolar disorder.

A Child's Behavior

Since its founding in 1999, CABF has reviewed numerous family accounts that repeatedly report similar behaviors. *If your child exhibits more than a few of these behaviors and you know something is wrong,* follow through with our plan. This is especially crucial if there is a history of mood disorders or substance abuse in your child's family.

- Severe and recurring depression
- Explosive, destructive or lengthy rages, especially after the age of four
- Extreme sadness or lack of interest in play
- Severe separation anxiety
- Talk of wanting to die or kill themselves or others
- Dangerous behaviors, such as trying to jump from a fast moving car or a roof
- Grandiose belief in own abilities that defy the laws of logic (possessing ability to fly)
- Sexualized behavior unusual for the child's age

- Impulsive aggression
- Delusional beliefs and hallucinations
- Extreme hostility
- Extreme or persistent irritability
- Telling teachers how to teach the class, bossing adults around
- Creativity that seems driven or compulsive
- Excessive involvement in multiple projects and activities
- Compulsive craving for certain objects or foods
- Hearing voices telling them to take harmful action
- Racing thoughts, pressure to keep talking
- Sleep disturbances, including gory nightmares or not sleeping very much
- Drawings or stories with extremely graphic violence

Is It Bipolar Disorder, Something Else, or a Mixed Bag?

Bipolar disorder is often accompanied by symptoms of other psychiatric disorders (those other disorders are said to be "comorbid" with the bipolar disorder). In some children, proper treatment for bipolar disorder clears up the symptoms thought to indicate another diagnosis. In other children, bipolar disorder may explain only part of a more complicated case that includes neurological, developmental, and other components. An accurate diagnosis of a child or teen presenting with severely troubled behavior is perhaps the most problematic issue facing families.

Diagnoses that mimic, mask, or co-occur with pediatric bipolar disorder include:

- Attention-deficit hyperactivity disorder (ADHD)*
- Depression**
- Oppositional-defiant disorder (ODD)
- Conduct disorder (CD)
- Pervasive developmental disorder (PDD)
- Generalized anxiety disorder (GAD)
- Panic disorder
- Obsessive-compulsive disorder (OCD)
- Tourette's syndrome (TS)
- Seizure disorders
- Reactive attachment disorder (RAD)

---

*It is estimated that 85% of children with bipolar disorder also have ADHD and up to 22% of children with ADHD have bipolar disorder.

**Depression in children and teens is often chronic and cyclical. A significant proportion of the millions of children and adolescents with depression may actually be experiencing the early onset of bipolar disorder, but have not yet experienced the manic phase of the illness.

Bipolar disorder is often misdiagnosed as:

- ADHD or ADHD with depression
- Depression
- Borderline personality disorder
- Post-traumatic stress disorder (PTSD)
- Substance abuse

Just, as juvenile diabetes is generally a more severe disorder than adult-onset diabetes, pediatric bipolar disorder appears to be more perilous than adult-onset bipolar disorder. The rationale for early intervention is compelling.

Common outcomes of pediatric bipolar disorder are school refusal, suspension, and dropping-out; impulsive acts of aggression; self-injury; substance abuse; and suicide attempts and completions. Teens with symptoms of untreated bipolar disorder are arrested and incarcerated. Suicide is the third leading cause of death among teens. Children as young as six have attempted to hang, shoot, stab, or overdose themselves.

The longest study on pediatric bipolar disorder is ongoing under the direction of Barbara Geller, M.D., a child psychiatrist at Washington University in St. Louis. In the mid-1990s, Dr. Geller began observing 93 children whose average age was 10.8 years. All of the children had mania (Bipolar I) which had begun to onset at an average age of 6.8 years. Assessing the children after four years, Geller and colleagues found that children with mania were sicker than adults, less likely than adults to recover, and relapsed sooner than adults with mania. Differences in symptom severity and frequency of cycling between manic and depressive episodes have presented questions as to whether bipolar disorder in youth is the same illness as in adults. A study published in 2006 by Dr. Geller and colleagues showed that early-onset Bipolar I disorder does appear to be the same illness as adult-onset Bipolar I disorder.

Another study of three major subtypes of bipolar disorder that affect children and adolescents is ongoing under the direction of David Axelson, M.D., a child psychiatrist at Western Psychiatric Institutes and Clinics in Pittsburgh. A report on the 263 children and adolescents, ages 7–17 years, confirmed that bipolar disorder affects children and adolescents more severely than adults. "Study participants had comparatively longer symptomatic stages and more frequent cycling (changing from one mood to another) or mixed episodes. Children and adolescents also converted from a less severe form of bipolar disorder to a more severe form at a much higher rate than seen in adults."

First Steps

Parents with concerns about their child's extreme behaviors should consider the following steps:

- If your child is psychotic, suicidal, or menacing others: take him or her to the emergency room or call 911 for an ambulance (stress that the child needs medical care and an ambulance should be sent). If you are alone, also call a friend or relative to help you immediately.

- Ensure the safety of your family. Find safe havens for siblings. Remove all firearms from the home (this is a matter of life and death, not a political statement). Lock up sharps (knives, razors, whatever). Lock up all prescription and over-the-counter medications. Childproof your home, no matter the physical age of your child.
- Request an urgent appointment to have your child evaluated by a psychiatrist familiar with pediatric bipolar disorder. Start the process now. Your insurance plan might require a referral from your primary care provider. You might also be required to see a social worker or therapist for evaluation before you are permitted to access a psychiatrist. If your child is suspected of abusing substances, a substance abuse evaluation will be needed. Prepare for the initial meeting:

  - Start a mood chart for your child today. Make daily notes of your child's mood, behavior, sleep patterns, events, and medications. Include statements by the child that seem odd or concern you. Share your notes with the professional who evaluates your child and with the doctor who eventually treats your child.
  - Compile a brief family history on both sides. Include family members who have abused alcohol or drugs. Include family members who have been diagnosed with mood disorders, bipolar disorder, or other psychiatric diagnoses. Remember that even if a family member was not diagnosed, it may be a critical link if that person was hospitalized, attempted or completed suicide, or has a history of numerous marriages, fighting, or reckless behavior.

- Keep a notebook or file in which you keep records of each doctor visit and results of lab tests. This notebook will be a good place to keep a list of all medications your child has trialed, the dates, the doses, and the effects. You can keep your mood charts in here, too. And your family history.
- Educate yourself about bipolar disorder. Join CABF and connect with others on CABF's message boards and online support groups. We're here to help you. Later on, you can volunteer to help others!
- Take care of yourself! Remember the flight attendant's safety talk on the airplane: put on your oxygen mask first so that you are in a position to put your children's masks on. Reduce stress, address your own mental health issues, and exercise.

Finding a Doctor

Child psychiatrists are scarce. And few have extensive experience treating pediatric bipolar disorder. Teaching hospitals affiliated with medical schools are often a good place to start looking for an experienced child psychiatrist. Call the hospital's child psychiatry outpatient clinic for an appointment. Perhaps your pediatrician can refer you to a child psychiatrist. An alternative to a child psychiatrist with expertise in mood disorders, is an adult psychiatrist who has a comprehensive background in mood disorders and experience in treating children and adolescents. Check the CABF Directory of Professional Members for doctors and other professionals who list themselves as treating pediatric bipolar disorder in your area. The American Academy of Child and Adolescent Psychiatrists also has an online doctor finder.

Other specialists who may be able to help, at least with an initial evaluation, include psychotherapists and pediatric neurologists. Psychotherapists may recognize symptoms and refer your child to a psychiatrist for evaluation. Neurologists have experience with the anti-convulsant medications often used for treating bipolar disorders.

Some families travel to take their child to nationally known doctors at teaching hospitals for the initial evaluation, diagnosis, and treatment recommendations. They then turn to local professionals for ongoing medical management of their child's treatment and psychotherapy. The local professionals consult with the expert as needed.

Some families enroll their children in research studies run by recognized experts, often providing an in-depth evaluation. The National Institute of Mental Health in Bethesda, Maryland, sometimes has spaces available in approved studies for children with mood symptoms. You can also try consulting other parents through CABF's online forums or seeking information from a member of the CABF Family Response Team.

Goals of Treatment

The initial goals of treatment are to relieve the child's suffering and to stop dangerous behavior. This is accomplished by alleviating the severest symptoms, such as suicidal thoughts and actions, aggression, destructive behavior, psychosis, and sleep disturbances. The long-range goals of treatment are to stabilize mood and extend the period of wellness so that the child is less impaired and may resume developing on a more typical path. Additionally, a successful treatment plan will minimize the side effects of medication.

There are many components to a good treatment plan. Ideally, your menu will include:

- Medication and monitoring of side effects.
- Close monitoring of symptoms.
- Education about the illness for your child and you.
- Psychotherapy for your child and family.
- Treatment of coexisting disorders.
- Accommodations at school.
- Stress reduction.
- Good nutrition and steady exercise.
- Adherence to a regular sleeping schedule and a consistent routine.

Responses to a good treatment plan vary greatly. With appropriate treatment and support at home and at school, many children with bipolar disorder achieve a marked reduction in the severity, frequency, and duration of their episodes. Just as with other chronic illnesses such as diabetes and epilepsy, children who are educated about bipolar disorder can learn how to manage and monitor their symptoms as they grow older, and some experience long periods of wellness. More than a few longtime CABF members report that their children have achieved lengthy remissions, graduated from high school, and are attending college successfully or living and working independently.

Factors that contribute to a better outcome are:

- Early diagnosis and treatment.
- Access to competent medical care.
- Adherence to medication and treatment plan.
- A flexible but consistent low-stress home and school environment
- A supportive network of family and friends
- Family members who are effective advocates for the child's medical, educational, and therapeutic needs

Factors that hinder treatment effectiveness are:

- Time lag between onset of illness and treatment.
- Limited access to competent medical care.
- Not taking medication as prescribed.
- Not having a regular sleep/wake cycle.
- Co-occurrence of other disorders including any use of alcohol or unprescribed drugs.
- Stressful, inflexible, or negative home or school environment.
- Traumatic life events.
- Lack of insight.

In most cases, symptoms can be managed at home with outpatient treatment. Sometimes though, severe episodes require rapid medication adjustments that are best done in an inpatient unit. And some children's illnesses cannot be successfully managed at home. These children and their families may benefit from longer stays in residential treatment centers or therapeutic boarding schools that can provide treatment and education in a safe and highly supervised setting.

Unfortunately, relapses are common even with the best treatment; in fact, relapse is a hallmark of bipolar disorder. Even with treatment by professionals, children may need hospitalization or residential treatment. Upon reaching 18, many young adults with bipolar disorder still require significant support. In fact, CABF advocates that you keep in mind that the adult brain of a typical individual does not fully mature until age 25.

A symptomatic child should not be untreated. If parental disagreement makes treatment impossible, illness education (*psychoeducational therapy*) is recommended. As a last resort, a court order regarding treatment may become necessary.

Medication

Medication is the first line of treatment for any patient with bipolar disorder. CABF recommends that parents and clinicians consult the Treatment Guidelines for Children and Adolescents with Bipolar Disorder. The Guidelines contain specifics of medications currently used to treat children and teenagers with bipolar disorder.

No one medication work in all children. Expect a lengthy trial-and-error process as your doctor may have to prescribe several medications, alone or in combination. CABF advises generally: "Start Low. Go Slow." Two or more mood stabilizers or other medications may be necessary to achieve and maintain the best response. And it is very common that a medication regimen that works might have to be changed as the child grows and the disorder presents differently.

Because of the lack of controlled studies, the Food and Drug Administration has approved only a few psychiatric medications specifically for pediatric use. You might want to keep in mind, however, that few medications used to treat any illnesses—including cancer—have been FDA-approved for children. In many cases, neither pharmaceutical companies nor the government opts to invest in drug trials in children because of the difficulty of finding child subjects or because of the costs or for various other reasons. (Some parents try vitamins or other alternative treatments; research studies have, likewise, not found these effective in reducing the symptoms of bipolar disorder).

Psychiatrists must adapt what they know about treating adults to children and adolescents. The use of FDA-approved psychiatric medications in children is legal and relatively common in the United States. If a medication is FDA-approved for some age or some condition, a doctor may—in his or her professional judgment—prescribe its use for any age or for any condition. Doctors often treat illnesses in children with medications found safe and effective and approved for use in adults with the same illness.

However, more research is needed not only on the effectiveness of these medications on children but also on side effects and dosing strategies. One side effect clearly of concern is metabolic syndrome. As for dosing strategies, children's bodies process drugs differently from adults (they sometimes need more of a medication eliminated by the kidneys or less if the drug is metabolized by the liver). A blood test, the *Cytochrome P-450,* is available to determine how a child's liver processes drugs. The results might be useful to evaluate which drugs may result in adverse effects and to calculate dosing schedules.

The use of psychiatric medications with any child requires close supervision by medical personnel and by caregivers who are knowledgeable, mentally healthy, and organized. Some caregivers may themselves need close supervision and in-home assistance to manage the complex treatment regimens for a child with bipolar disorder.

CABF has heard from many parents that medications used to treat their children have proven effective. Yet it is often hard to accept that your child has a chronic condition that requires long-term treatment with several medications. Remember bipolar disorder has a high mortality rate. Estimates vary but the suicide rate in untreated bipolar disorder is 30 to 60 times higher than that of the general population. The untreated disorder also carries the risk of drug and alcohol addiction, damaged relationships, school failure, difficulty finding and holding jobs, tragic encounters with law enforcement, and even violence. The risks of not treating the illness are known and substantial. These risks must be measured against the risks of using medications whose safety and efficacy have been established in adults but perhaps not in children. CABF advocates for families to have full access to medications to treat bipolar illness—and competent professionals to prescribe and monitor them—because they are life-saving.

In addition to seeing a psychiatrist, the treatment plan for a child with bipolar disorder usually includes regular therapy sessions with a licensed clinical social worker, a licensed psychologist, or a psychiatrist who provides psychotherapy. It is important that the child like the therapist. Cognitive behavioral therapy, interpersonal therapy, and multi-family support groups are an essential part of treatment for children and adolescents with bipolar disorder. These may be offered by a teaching hospital in a large city. Dialectical behavioral therapy, which teaches skills to help the patient learn to tolerate and manage extreme mood states, appears promising.

Therapy might not be effective until mood stabilization occurs. An unstable child is unlikely to be able to absorb the concepts of therapy. While the child is wracked by the turmoil of extreme lows or highs or sudden shifts in mood, cognitive skills are impaired and learning often comes to a standstill until he or she reaches a stable plateau.

Sleep and Exercise

Regular sleep patterns help tackle the fact that your child with bipolar disorder has an out-of-whack biological clock; regular sleep patterns can reduce cycling and mood fluctuations. Provide a child with the necessary routine and deviate only when absolutely necessary. Tell your child (especially your teenager!) to see himself or herself as a farmer: go to bed with the sun and wake up with the sun. Enforce consistent bedtimes and awake times all week long; teens who fall into a weekend pattern of staying up late and sleeping late find that by Monday morning their biological rhythms are out of kilter. Keep to a sleep routine even in the summer. Maybe you can schedule a fun morning activity to motivate your child to get up. Even a few missed wake/sleep cycles can have unfortunate consequences.

Exercise combats depression and can serve as an important tool in stress reduction. Exercise helps your child let go of anger, anxiety, and tension. The naturally occurring beta endorphins that the brain releases during exercise have a calming effect on the body. Trampolines, punching bags, jump ropes, electronic dance mats, and treadmills in front of the TV are some ways to provide an exercise outlet at home.

Here are some ideas for you:

- Learn and use good listening and communication skills.
- Prioritize issues (battles) and let go of less important matters.
- Practice and teach relaxation techniques to your child. Use music, sound, lighting, water, or massage to help your child with falling asleep, waking up, and relaxing.
- Help your child anticipate, and avoid or prepare for, stressful situations by developing strategies in advance.

- Learn safe but firm restraint holds to contain rages
- Advocate at school for stress reduction and other accommodations
- Engage your child's creativity through activities that express their gifts and strengths.
- Provide routine structure while allowing freedom within expressed limits.

Genetics

Bipolar disorder is a complex genetic illness. The illness is highly inheritable. Researchers have uncovered a handful of genes that may elevate the risk of bipolar disorder and are searching for dozens more genes that may be involved. The following statistics support the search for the genetic origins of bipolar disorder:

- For the general population, a conservative estimate of an individual's risk of having Bipolar I disorder is 1% to 3%. Disorders in the bipolar spectrum are thought to affect at least 4% to 6% of the general population.
- When one parent has bipolar disorder, the risk that his or her child will have bipolar disorder is 15% to 30%.
- When both parents have bipolar disorder, the risk increases to 50% to 75%.
- If a sibling (including a fraternal twin) has bipolar disorder, the child's risk is 15% to 25%.
- The risk in identical twins is approximately 85%.

The family trees of many children who develop pediatric bipolar disorder include individuals who suffered from substance abuse or mood disorders (perhaps undiagnosed) or both. Because previous generations were less likely to diagnose bipolar disorder, affected family members may have been written off as "crazy Auntie" or simply as prone to troubling behaviors, such as alcoholism, frequent periods of unemployment, dysfunctional personal relationships bankruptcies, or incarceration. Interestingly, the family tree might also have many members who are highly accomplished, creative, charismatic, and extremely successful in business, politics, and the arts.

Prevalence

Currently, there are very few studies, and none in the US that establish the *prevalence* of bipolar disorder in children. In a review of data in the Netherlands Twin Registry, 4% to 5% of more than 6,000 ten-year-olds were deemed likely to meet criteria for pediatric bipolar disorder.

A recent study showed a 40-fold increase in the *diagnosis* of bipolar disorder in the US in the past ten years. The study reveals that in 1994, very few doctors wished to label children as bipolar (25 bipolar diagnoses per 100,000 people). Yet even the 40-fold increase rate in 2003 (1,003 bipolar diagnoses per

100,000 people) is still well below the rate of bipolar disorder for adults (1,679 bipolar diagnoses per 100,000 people). Further, a long-term NIMH study of adults shows at least 65% felt their illness onset in childhood or adolescence and acknowledges a lag between onset and diagnosis in adults.

As with autism, some of the increase in *diagnosis* is due to greater awareness in the medical community and the public leading to earlier diagnosis. CABF believes that children have been suffering from bipolar disorder all along, but in the past were dismissed as 'bad seeds,' or the product of poor parenting. On the other hand, further research is absolutely necessary to establish the *prevalence* of bipolar disorder in children and the reasons for it. . . .

Stuart L. Kaplan

 **NO**

Pediatric Bipolar Disorder

T he appearance of adult bipolar disorder is so dramatically different from the appearance of child bipolar disorder that it's hard to imagine how the two could be confused. Adults with bipolar disorder have clear-cut episodes of very distinctive behavior: severe overexcitement, irritability, or highs ("mania") that last for weeks followed by crushing lows or depression that also last for weeks. The adult is said to have a "cycle" or "mood swing" when moving from one episode to another. In between the highs and lows are long periods without them. In adults the episodes are recognizable by family, friends, and even the patient as being significantly different from how the patient usually behaves.

The child diagnosed with bipolar disorder, on the other hand, has chronic, almost constant symptoms that characterize, rather than deviate from, the child's usual behavior. The typical elementary school-aged child diagnosed with bipolar disorder tends to be easily angered and can have several angry episodes per day in the form of screaming, tantrums, cursing, and biting. Though the anger may sometimes seem to "come from nowhere," it occurs most often when the child does not get his or her own way, is asked to do something he or she does not want to do, or is criticized or slighted in some way. Not surprisingly, the anger usually ends when the child manages to get what the child wants. Before achieving this goal, the frustrated child can yell, curse, kick, or throw things. The tendency to react to frustration by becoming enraged is constant. In serious cases the child will attack others, including classmates, parents, teachers, or principals. The potential for this kind of behavior is chronic and can flare several times a day. Many parents report feeling as though they are "walking on eggshells" around their children. As these children age, they become more difficult to control because of their increase in size and strength.

How is it possible that two such different disorders could be confused for one another? As discussed earlier, the "A" criterion for a manic episode is defined as a "distinct period of abnormally and persistently elevated, expansive, or irritable mood, lasting at least 1 week (or any duration if hospitalization is necessary)." Proponents of the diagnosis of pediatric bipolar disorder point to the chronic irritability of their patients as evidence of a manic episode. Although it is true that irritability is sufficient to meet the "A" criterion of a manic episode, it is also crucial to the diagnosis that this irritability is a *distinct period* that is different from the patient's normal functioning.

The intense anger typically found in children who have been diagnosed as having bipolar disorder is a chronic problem. These children are not in a distinct state that is different from their usual selves; they are prone to anger or irritability all the time. Often, the problem has been present for many years, and typically it continues long after the diagnosis of bipolar disorder has been made. Unlike adults with bipolar disorder, these children do not have weeks or months of apparently normal behavior. Their irritabiliry, if not always present, is always a felt threat. So while they may meet the "A" criterion for mood—irritability—they do not meet the "A" criterion for a distinct state. This is not insignificant, as these *DSM-IV* criteria must be met in order for the diagnosis to be applicable.

One major group advocating for the diagnosis of pediatric bipolar disorder in children claims to resolve this discrepancy by recasting each angry outburst as a distinct state. In this view, the child with outbursts of anger or irritability is considered to have "cycled" with each outburst. Every minor change in mood that occurs during the ordinary course of a day is counted as a cycle. For children easily provoked to anger, there can be many such cycles per day (Geller, Tillman, & Bolhofner, 2007). Of course, these transient shifts of mood during the course of the child's day are not comparable to the cycles of actual bipolar disorder that usually occur over much longer periods—weeks to months—in adolescents and adults. Instead, the diagnosis of pediatric bipolar disorder in these irritable children is an incorrect interpretation of a frequently observed childhood behavior: temper tantrums. These outbursts are fundamentally different from the complete psychological reorganization that occurs during a bipolar disorder cycle.

Pediatric Bipolar Disorder as ADHD and ODD

Children misdiagnosed with bipolar disorder typically do have serious difficulties that can seem similar to some of the symptoms of mania. These include irritability, distractibility, and talkativeness, among others. But these difficulties are already well known to child psychiatrists and are well described in the *DSM-IV* as the less serious (and far more treatable) diagnoses of attention deficit hyperactivity disorder (ADHD) and oppositional defiant disorder (ODD) (Carlson, 2005). Most of the *DSM-IV* symptoms of mania can easily be matched to one of these disorders. These diagnoses are more fitting still when you consider that, unlike mania, ADHD and ODD are chronic disorders. The symptoms are characteristically present most of the time and do not have to meet the bipolar disorder criterion of being different from the patient's usual self.

It is estimated that anywhere from 60% to 91% of children diagnosed with bipolar disorder are also diagnosed with ADHD (Galanter et al., 2009; Geller et al.,2000; Safer, 2009; Singh et al., 2006). ADHD is characterized by concentration difficulty and often by physical overactivity and difficulty controlling impulses. By *DSM-IV* definition, some symptoms are evident before the age of seven, and the diagnosis becomes a consideration in children having difficulty in the early elementary school years. The children may be restless and fidgety and have difficulty staying in their seats. They often have trouble paying attention, organizing themselves, and finishing their school work. ADHD is found in 7% of elementary school age children. In general, it is diagnosed in boys two times more often than girls and is the most common disorder treated in child psychiatry clinics. The *DSM-IV* criteria for the diagnosis are listed in Table 1.

Table 1

DSM-IV Diagnostic Criteria for Attention Deficit/Hyperactivity Disorder

A.   Either (1) or (2)

    (1) six (or more) of the following symptoms of inattention have persisted for at least 6 months to a degree that is maladaptive and inconsistent with developmental level:

    Inattention

    (a) often fails to give close attention to details or makes careless mistakes in schoolwork, work, or other activities

    (b) often has difficulty sustaining attention in tasks or play activities

    (c) often does not seem to listen when spoken to directly

    (d) often does not follow through on instructions and fails to finish schoolwork, chores, or duties in the workplace (not due to oppositional behavior or failure to understand instructions)

    (e) often has difficulty organizing tasks and activities

    (f) often avoids, dislikes, or is reluctant to engage in tasks that require sustained mental effort (such as schoolwork or homework)

    (g) often loses things necessary for tasks or activities (e.g., toys, school assignments, pencils, books, or tools)

    (h) is often easily distracted by extraneous stimuli

    (i) is often forgetful in daily activities

    (2) six (or more) of the following symptoms of hyperactivity-impulsivity have persisted for at least 6 months to a degree that is maladaptive and inconsistent with developmental level:

    Hyperactivity/Impulsivity

    Hyperactivity

    (a) often fidgets with hands or feet or squirms in seat

    (b) often leaves seat in classroom or in other situations in which remaining seated is expected

    (c) often runs about or climbs excessively in situations in which it is inappropriate (in adolescents or adults, may be limited to subjective feelings of restlessness)

    (d) often has difficulty playing or engaging in leisure activities quietly

    (e) is often "on the go" or often acts as if "driven by a motor"

    (f) often talks excessively

    Impulsivity

    (g) often blurts out answers before questions have been completed

    (h) often has difficulty awaiting turn

    (i) often interrupts or intrudes on others (e.g., butts into conversations or games)

B.   Some hyperactive-impulsive or inattentive symptoms that caused impairment were present before age 7 years.

C.   Some impairment from the symptoms is present in two or more settings (e.g., at school [or work] and at home).

D.   There must be clear evidence of clinically significant impairment in social, academic, or occupational functioning.

E.   The symptoms do not occur exclusively during the course of a Pervasive Developmental Disorder, Schizophrenia, or other Psychotic Disorder and are not better accounted for by another mental disorder (e.g., Mood Disorder, Anxiety Disorder, or a personality disorder).

(Reprinted with permission from the *Diagnostic and Statistical Manual of Mental Disorders, Fourth Edition,* Text Revision [Copyright 2000]. American Psychiatric Association.)

From the perspective of a child psychiatrist, the case of Nathaniel illustrates some of the typical features of ADHD. Nathaniel is a nine-year-old who has always had difficulty remaining in his seat in class. Now in third grade, he frequently leaves his seat to talk to other children and to engage in activities unrelated to the lesson being taught. Even when Nathaniel is in his seat, he is in motion. He drums with his hands and taps his feet. The teacher reports that he is unable to attend to lessons and is in danger of having to repeat the year despite his obviously high intelligence. Often, he fails to bring his homework assignments home, requires his parents' help to complete the assignments when he does bring them home, and then frequently neglects to bring the completed assignments back to school. On those rare occasions when he does complete the assignment at home and return it to school, he often neglects to hand it in to the teacher.

At home, Nathaniel often seems as if he's disobeying his parents. For example, if they ask him to clean up his bedroom, they may find that a half an hour later he's playing with some toys in the bedroom but his clothes remain scattered on the floor. When asked about his failure to clean up his room as they requested, he explains that he "forgot" what they asked him to do. At dinner, Nathaniel prefers to eat standing up in the dining room and frequently runs to the TV room to glimpse the cartoon he had been watching before dinner began. Despite his distractibility, Nathaniel loves to play computer games, and his parents report that he can pay attention to something as long as he's interested in it. If he is not interested, which is frequent, he can't pay attention. Because of his constant talking he is regarded by the family as a "motor mouth." According to the parents, this behavior had been going on at home and at school since Nathaniel was five years old.

The ADHD diagnosis easily includes many of the behaviors described in the misdiagnosis of childhood bipolar disorder. Both the bipolar disorder child and the ADHD child and described as being excessively talkative. In general, people who talk fast also have rapid thoughts. Clinically it is common for children with ADHD to admit to racing thoughts, which is likewise the case for the bipolar disorder child. Both are also described as being easily distracted. The "increase in goal directed activity" of the child with bipolar disorder is similar to the ADHD symptom "is often on the go or often acts as if driven by a motor."ADHD patients have a strong need to be "busy." The item refers primarily to motor activity in ADHD children, but the need to be doing things could be included in that item. Adults with ADHD have a difficult time with beach vacations because lying on a beach doing nothing is very hard for many of them. The mania symptom, "decreased need for sleep," is also reported often by parents, who explain that their ADHD children were always poor sleepers who would rock their cribs, wander the house at night, and now seem to require less sleep than their non-ADHD siblings. Table 2 outlines these similarities, along with the corresponding references to the *DSM-IV* diagnoses for these disorders (see Table 2).

Although the ADHD diagnosis does account for several of the symptoms of mania, it does not account for the angry behaviors that typify children diagnosed with bipolar disorder. Anger, irritability, and aggression are not *DSM*

Table 2

Comparison of Selected DSM-IV Mania and ADHD Symptoms

Mania Symptoms	ADHD Symptoms
(B.3.) more talkative than usual or pressure to keep talking	(2 f) often talks excessively (2 g) often blurts out answers before questions have been completed
	(2 i) often interrupts or intrudes on others (e.g., butts into conversations or games)
(B.4.) flight of ideas or subjective experience that thoughts are racing	(2 f) often talks excessively
(B.5.) distractibility (i.e., attention too easily drawn to unimportant or irrelevant external stimuli)	(1 h) is often easily distracted by extraneous stimuli
(B.6.) increase in goal-directed activity (either socially, at work or school, or sexually) or psychomotor agitation	(2 e) is often "on the go" or often acts as if "driven by a motor"

symptoms of ADHD. Within the universe of ADHD children, however, there is a sizeable group who are very angry and irritable. When this irritability is added to the ADHD symptoms, the child is indistinguishable from the child diagnosed with bipolar disorder. My contention is that irritable children with ADHD are not childhood bipolar disorder patients at all; rather they are ADHD patients who are angry and irritable.

Irritability is a symptom that is found frequently in many psychiatric disorders (Safer, 2009). It is a crucial feature of oppositional defiant disorder (ODD), an extremely common psychiatric disorder of childhood that is closely associated with, and often accompanied by, ADHD. Oppositional defiant disorder is a *DSM-IV* diagnosis that specifies a number of the most important problems found in children misdiagnosed with bipolar disorder. Children with ODD are quick to defy adult request or demands and often refuse to do what they are asked to do. The criteria for diagnosing the disorder include often losing one's temper, often arguing with adults, and often feeling angry and resentful (see Table 3). These children frequently exhibit behavioral problems in school. They refuse to follow school rules and standard social conventions. They may be suspended, expelled, and transferred to special education settings. Aggression in childhood is not tolerated by institutions charged with caring for children. It quickly leads to educational placements outside of regular education classrooms and begins a journey of stigmatization that puts the aggressive child at an important disadvantage compared to the child's nonaggressive peers.

I work as a consultant to a special education school, and it is not unusual to encounter at least a few 7- to 12-year-old children with combined ADHD

Table 3

DSM-IV Diagnostic Criteria for Oppositional Defiant Disorder

A. A pattern of negativistic, hostile, and defiant behavior lasting at least 6 months, during which four (or more) of the following are present:
    (1) often loses temper
    (2) often argues with adults
    (3) often actively defies or refuses to comply with adults' request or rules
    (4) often deliberately annoys people
    (5) often blames others for his or her mistakes or misbehavior
    (6) is often touchy or easily annoyed by others
    (7) is often angry and resentful
    (8) is often spiteful or vindictive
    Note: Consider a criterion met only if the behavior occurs more frequently than is typically observed in individuals of comparable age and developmental level.
B. The disturbance in behavior causes clinically significant impairment in social, academic, or occupational functioning.
C. The behaviors do not occur exclusively during the course of a Psychotic or Mood Disorder.
D. Criteria are not met for Conduct Disorder, and, if the individual is age 18 years or older, criteria are not met for Antisocial Personality Disorder.

(Reprinted with permission from the *Diagonostic and Statistical Manual of Mental Disorders, Fourth Edition,* Text Revision [Copyright 2000] American Psychiatric Association.)

and ODD in the hallways outside of the classroom during class time. Their behaviors exemplify the ODD diagnosis. These children have defiantly left the class, refusing to return. They are found kicking lockers, cursing at adults who attempt to intervene, and in general making every effort to disobey and disrupt school routines. When they are in class, they are often impulsive, restless, rude, loud, threatening, and defiant.

The diagnosis of ODD is easy to recognize, and the *DSM-IV* criteria are self-explanatory. The recommended treatment for ODD is behavior modification, sometimes in combination with medication. ODD often seems to account for the aggressive behavior in children that leads to the incorrect diagnosis of pediatric bipolar disorder.

This was the case for Lucy, a girl diagnosed with bipolar disorder whose symptoms clearly indicated the presence of ADHD and ODD. Lucy was a 12-year-old girl with eight previous child psychiatric hospitalizations. I saw her as a consultant on an inpatient unit during her ninth hospitalization. She had recently been expelled from a special education setting for severely misbehaving children after she had been in the program for less than one week. She was then placed in a day hospital program but only lasted there for two days as her frequent and severe aggression required readmission to the hospital.

Lucy had a long-standing history of violence. Her symptoms included constant refusal to conform to rules, cursing, physical aggression against teachers, throwing chairs, and biting peers. She repeatedly ran out of classrooms and she ran away from home on a weekly basis. Lucy's anger, defiance, and temper tantrums were first noted at age three. At that time she was also noted to be restless, overactive, and talkative, which continued throughout her childhood and was clearly evident during the interview. As a young child, Lucy was placed in a special education preschool program for emotionally disturbed children. She cursed frequently in the classroom and challenged her teachers constantly by not following classroom routines. She was diagnosed with bipolar disorder at the age of five and had been treated since then with a number of medications used for adult bipolar disorder. Despite these medications, her many hospitalizations, and an array of special education and mental health services, she did not respond to treatment.

When I interviewed Lucy during her most recent hospitalization, she reported that she *could* sit still and pay attention but that she intentionally chose not to. Although she very clearly met the criteria for ADHD, she seemed to need to maintain the illusion for herself that she had control over her behavior. ADHD had not been considered as a diagnosis, and she had never been treated with medication for it.

This case illustrates many of the aspects of behavior that lead to the misdiagnosis of child bipolar disorder. The most conspicuous feature of this case, and of most children who receive the diagnosis, is excessive irritability and anger. The symptoms of ODD dominate the appearance of the so-called childhood bipolar disorder patient. Most of the *DSM-IV* symptoms of mania can also easily be matched to those of ADHD and ODD. There doesn't seem to be much difference between combined ODD and ADHD and the description of the child bipolar disorder patient. The clinical reality is that there is no difference.

My view of pediatric bipolar disorder is that it is almost always severe oppositional defiant disorder combined with severe ADHD. These two *DSM-IV* diagnoses account for all of the observed "bipolar" symptoms. Also, both ADHD and ODD are relatively common diagnoses for elementary school-aged children. The co-occurrence of these two disorders is frequently encountered as well, in contrast to the rarity of an actual case of bipolar disorder in childhood. The combined diagnosis of ADHD and ODD is the best and most likely explanation for the anger found in these elementary school age children. There is no need to add the additional diagnosis of bipolar disorder; it is confusing and misleading to do so.

There are three critical reasons for redefining most cases of child bipolar disorder as ADHD and ODD.

First, and most important, ADHD and ODD are the diagnoses these children seem to have; together they provide a better measure of the children's actual difficulties than does the diagnosis of bipolar disorder. The symptoms of ADHD and ODD are characteristically present most of the time and do not have to meet the bipolar disorder criterion of being distinctly different from the patient's usual self. ADHD symptoms, in particular, must appear early in the child's life and persist over time. By *DSM-IV* definition, they are stable and must have been present since before the age of seven. In contrast, the *DSM-IV* symptoms of mania must represent a change from usual behavior—that is, to count as mania, an increase or decrease in symptoms must occur with the change in mood. Most advocates for the childhood bipolar disorder diagnosis ignore this requirement. Yet it is a major violation of *DSM-IV* to label what are essentially long-standing symptoms of ADHD or ODD as transitory symptoms of bipolar disorder.

Second, ADHD and ODD are relatively easy to treat compared to bipolar disorder. Bipolar disorder can be treated in adults, but often it is difficult. Lithium, the most effective treatment known, only works in 50% of adult patients. Antiseizure medications, also used in adults, have not been researched sufficiently for use in the treatment of pediatric bipolar disorder patients. What little is known is not encouraging; there is little evidence that they work in children. Antipsychotic medications are used increasingly in bipolar disorder children, and some have very recently been FDA approved in the 10–17-year-old age range. Yet these have an array of side effects that many parents and children find unacceptable.

In contrast to the lack of understanding of the treatment of child bipolar disorder, the treatment of ADHD is very well understood. It is effective and safe. Many hundreds of studies on the treatment of the disorder with stimulant medications have been conducted since the 1930s, and they have demonstrated that these medications are an effective treatment for the disorder. One of the most stern clinical rules in medicine is that it is vital not to fail to recognize and diagnose a treatable condition. In Lucy's case, as in a number of cases of childhood bipolar disorder, ADHD was missed as a diagnosis; often it is not treated even when it is identified. Effective treatment of ADHD often resolves many of the symptoms that led to the child's diagnosis of bipolar disorder. As a clinician, I am always interested in redefining a problem that is untreatable into a problem that is treatable.

Third, an older tradition in child psychiatry suggests that when there is ambiguity about a diagnosis, a less serious diagnosis is preferable to a more malignant diagnosis. With time, the clinical situation might become more clear and the malignant diagnosis might indeed have not been selected. In the interim, the child and family would not have been burdened with the anxiety and the more hazardous treatments of the more serious diagnosis.

The Development of the Diagnosis of Pediatric Bipolar Disorder

For many years the general view among child psychiatrists was that aggressive, hyperactive school age children usually had ADHD and often had ODD as well. Sometime around the middle part of the 1990s this view began to change. At that time, two distinguished child psychiatrists, Joseph Biederman, MD, at Harvard University, and Barbara Geller, MD, at Washington University, independently began to report that there was something more than ADHD and ODD that was troubling severely disruptive school age children and adolescents. The additional crucial diagnosis that had been overlooked, according to Drs. Geller and Biederman, was bipolar disorder. They went on to define pediatric bipolar disorder for child psychiatrists, creating a large amount of excitement in the profession and in the public. Working independently, they and their colleagues continue to study and write frequent articles about the disorder.

It is significant that these two prominent research groups differ in their descriptions and criteria for the diagnosis. Dr. Biederman and his colleagues argue that pediatric bipolar disorder is defined by severe aggression; Dr. Geller and her colleagues argue that pediatric bipolar disorder is defined by grandiosity and elation. That two of the leading child psychiatric investigators of this area could not agree on the fundamentals of the clinical appearance of these children does nothing to allay misgivings about the accuracy of this novel diagnosis. The difficulty in pinpointing exactly what characterizes pediatric bipolar disorder is one of the crucial issues in the controversy surrounding the diagnosis. It will be useful for our purposes, therefore, to understand exactly how these independent conclusions were drawn.

Dr. Biederman and his colleagues (including distinguished child psychiatric researchers Timothy Wilens, MD, Janet Wozniak, MD, and Stephen Faraone, PhD), published numerous studies of pediatric bipolar disorder in rapid succession in the mid- to late 1990s, as noted by Geller (Geller, 1997). The first study, which served as a model for many of the subsequent studies, evaluated all 262 children aged 12 years and younger who had been referred to the Pediatric Psychopharmacology Unit of the Child Psychiatry Service at Massachusetts General Hospital for evaluation and treatment. The data collection began in 1991, but the authors do not provide an end date. The children had not been referred because of a particular diagnosis but simply for evaluation and possible treatment with medication. Each child received an evaluation that consisted of a clinical interview of the parent about the child and a psychiatric research interview of the parent about the child. The psychiatric research interview assessed symptoms for all psychiatric disorders. The children themselves were not interviewed.

Of the 262 children who had been referred for evaluation and treatment, 43 (16%) were declared by the authors to have mania. Forty-two of the 43 manic children (98%) also had ADHD. More than threefourths of the children who met the criteria for mania (77%) did so because of extreme and persistent irritability (33 of the 43). These manic patients were notable, in particular, for their marked levels of aggression. The young age of mania onset was dramatic as well. The authors report the age of onset of the mania in 70% of the manic subjects to have been before the age of five. At that time the diagnosis of mania in a child that young was very rare (Wozniak et al., 1995). Although the authors used a number of careful research procedures in an effort to reach an accurate diagnosis, incredibly, they did not interview the child patients. Instead, information about the children's behavior was gathered in interviews with their parents. In clinical work, it is legally required that the patient be seen during a patient evaluation. I doubt that there is a managed care company in the country that would pay for a child psychiatric evaluation in which the patient was not seen. It is also a traditional part of medical culture for the doctor always to see the patient. It becomes habitual during long nights of providing care during internships and years of post-graduate medical education. It is a source of specific professional pride for child psychiatrists that they can gain meaningful information from interviewing child patients. It is not uncommon for the physician or diagnostician to see a patient quite differently from how the patient has been described by the parent. In a research study purporting to describe a new diagnosis, it is hard to imagine relying solely on parent reporting and not interviewing the patients.

In the discussion section of the article, the authors noted that the children seemed to have a level of aggression that qualified them for a diagnosis of mania, and the authors laid down the challenge for the child psychiatric field to recognize these aggressive children as having early bipolar disorder, based on the severity of their aggression. In later articles, the Biederman group continued the position that aggressive severity differentiated pediatric bipolar disorder from ADHD (Biederman, 1995; Biederman et al., 1999; Faraone et al., 1997; Wozniak & Biederman, 1996). Bipolar disorder, however, is an entirely different type of disorder. According to the *DSM-IV*, ADHD is classified as a "Disruptive Behavior Disorder" while bipolar disorder is an "Affective [mood] Disorder"—a completely different category. The Biederman group mistakenly treats what is only a difference in severity as a major difference in type of disorder. *DSM-IV* bipolar disorder is not on a continuum with ADHD or ADHD plus ODD, as these studies incorrectly suggested. Aside from the issue of severity of aggressive symptoms, which is insufficient for confirming a *DSM-IV* diagnosis of mania, Biederman's group failed to provide any persuasive evidence that the children had bipolar disorder.

In a related study (Biederman et al., 1995), Biederman and his group again did not interview the child patients (Biederman et al., 1995). In this new study, the authors had the same group of parents mentioned above complete a symptom checklist, called the Child Behavior Checklist (CBCL), to determine whether or not the children's scores corresponded to the diagnosis of mania that had been made in the first study. Not surprisingly, as that initial diagnosis was based exclusively on parent reporting, they did correspond. The authors conclude that the CBCL questionnaire can be used to diagnose bipolar disorder. Although the CBCL was designed to analyze a child's emotional and behavioral health, it is not intended to assess for mania or bipolar disorder. Investigators who study bipolar disorder in children, however, continue to use it (Biederman et al., 2009; Luby & Belden, 2006).

The studies of the 262 children, of course, do not tell us whether any of the children actually had bipolar disorder. The studies merely confirm that the parents told an interviewer in the first study approximately the same material about their children that they wrote on a paper-and-pencil questionnaire in the second study. The children in these two studies were not interviewed, and Biederman's group failed to provide any other persuasive evidence that the children had bipolar disorder. Perhaps because of the enormous amount of influence Dr. Biederman and his group have in the field, many child psychiatrists nonetheless adopted his views on the existence of the disorder following the publication of these and similar studies.

Barbara Geller, MD, began to write and speak about pediatric bipolar disorder at about the same time Dr. Biederman began to present his work. She is well known in child psychiatry as a distinguished academic psychiatrist who recently retired from the prestigious Washington University of St. Louis. She has received numerous grants from NIMH and has published prolifically on bipolar disorder in children. She, too, is a strong and major influence on contemporary child psychiatric views of pediatric bipolar disorder.

Dr. Geller has criticized the pediatric bipolar disorder work of Dr. Biederman and his colleagues on similar grounds to the criticisms made here. She highlights the fact that there were no interviews of children. She also makes the point that irritability is a frequently encountered symptom found in many different diagnoses and thus cannot be helpful in making the specific diagnosis of bipolar disorder.

Nonetheless, Dr. Geller and colleagues continued to support the validity of the diagnosis. Initially, she and her colleagues believed that children with bipolar disorder had several symptoms of mania beyond what are found in aggressive children with ADHD and ODD. Eventually they settled on two: grandiosity and elation. Whether they appeared independently or combined, these two symptoms were seen by Dr. Geller as the "cardinal symptoms" of pediatric bipolar disorder. "Cardinal" is not a *DSM-IV* term. It is not in the index of the *DSM-IV* and is not part of day-to-day mental health jargon. Dr. Geller defines a "cardinal symptom" as one that is unique to a diagnosis in *DSM-IV* terms (Geller et al., 2004). Grandiosity, however, which is an over-inflated sense of self-worth or self-importance, is found in a number of *DSM-IV* diagnoses. Narcissistic personality disorder, for example, refers to a condition in which patients have an excessive self-regard, sense of entitlement, and belief that others are inferior. Grandiosity is found in normal child development as well. It is not unique to mania and therefore is not a cardinal symptom by Dr. Geller's own definition (Wozniak et al., 2005).

The case of Alexis demonstrates some of the misconceptions about grandiosity and how it is sometimes misinterpreted as diagnostic of pediatric bipolar disorder.

Alexis was an 11-year-old girl who attended a private school for troubled children. She had been diagnosed with bipolar disorder at a center for the study of child bipolar disorder and had been placed on a variety of mood-stabilizing agents, including lithium, valproic acid, and carbamazepine. The medications had been initiated about two years previously, which roughly coincided with her admission to the school. The medications were not working. During her two years at the school she performed poorly and had not demonstrated academic or clinical improvement. Her parents had requested a private psychiatric consultation. When I first met Alexis, she had been refusing to attend class or do any work for many months. Her failure to participate in the classroom or in any other school activity led the school to decide to terminate her enrollment in two months at the end of the school year.

Alexis came from a high-achieving, upper-social-class family. Her parents and close relatives served on the boards of her city's largest corporations. The family's power and affluence lent a larger-than-life quality to much of what they did. For the most part Alexis refused to talk with me during our sessions, which made it difficult to develop a coherent understanding of her current problems. Information gathered from the parents and other relatives was also of little help in clarifying the diagnosis. Alexis was a talented artist and spent her sessions with me drawing very elaborate Renaissance-like drawings of people in a large leather-bound book. She was also a child actor in an adult Shakespearean theatrical group in the city and spent long hours at play rehearsals. The family felt that she was talented and highly intelligent but was bored by schoolwork and by the activities of children her own age.

During Alexis's early elementary school years, doctors and other professionals had suggested that she might have ADHD because of her difficulties concentrating on schoolwork. Her parents disagreed with these diagnostic impressions because of the mistaken belief that their daughter's many talents were inconsistent with ADHD.

In school, the teachers reported that Alexis did not do her work. She seemed unable to concentrate on it. This was less than clear, however, because she rarely made any effort in class. Her main activity during the day was to leave class and go to the teachers' lounge. Here, she tried to engage in conversations with the teachers. She preferred the teachers to the other children and had no friends at the school.

I consulted with some of the doctors who had treated her in the past. Although they felt unsure about the diagnosis of bipolar disorder, they had nevertheless treated her for it with mood stabilizers. She had been seen for several years and had placements in a day treatment program for bipolar disorder. Though she did not respond to the treatment, she was still given the diagnosis, and the family believed the diagnosis was correct.

Clinically, Alexis's apparently arrogant refusal to participate in class work, her preference for socializing with teachers over classmates, and her preoccupation with art and Shakespearean acting suggested an element of grandiosity possibly consistent with bipolar disorder. No other symptoms of bipolar disorder, however, were present. Alexis did not have mood swings, had never had a clear-cut episode of depression or mania, had never had a week-long period of elated mood or irritability, and had no symptoms of bipolar disorder other than the possible grandiosity, which was chronic rather than episodic.

Consistent with the diagnosis of ADHD was the suggestion that her refusal to do schoolwork may have reflected difficulties in concentrating that she tried to disguise by feigning a lack of interest. Another behavior that suggested ADHD was her walking out of class, which could have reflected a symptom of overactivity. An urge to move is often concealed by leaving class to get a drink of water, go to the bathroom, or in her case, visit the teachers' lounge. Finally, the doctors who saw her in her early childhood believed she had ADHD.

Faced with certain expulsion from school, a trial of stimulant medication seemed warranted in an effort to forestall this undesirable outcome. Her mood stabilizers were stopped, and she was placed on a moderate dose of a stimulant medication. Her behavior changed immediately and dramatically. Within two or three days of starting the stimulant, she began attending classes regularly and began to work in class. The school decided to re-enroll her for the fall semester.

From a technical perspective, the response to stimulant medication alone does not confirm the diagnosis of ADHD. Performance is improved for almost everyone on stimulant medication. To merit the diagnosis of ADHD, she would have to meet other criteria for the disorder. With careful probing, it became clear that these criteria were met.

This is a good example of the not-uncommon situation in which a family avoids the diagnosis of ADHD but willingly accepts the more serious diagnosis of bipolar disorder. An inclination to be disdainful of those with ADHD and to associate bipolar disorder with the more creative interests of their daughter may have contributed to missing the ADHD diagnosis.

Alexis's case provides some information about the fate of children incorrectly diagnosed as having bipolar disorder. Had she not been diagnosed and treated for her ADHD, Alexis's problems would likely have remained intractable. For this affluent family, more expensive private boarding school for the educationally disabled would have been the next intervention. Without the correct diagnosis and treatment Alexis's pattern of failure would have continued. A persistent pattern of academic and personal failure is the fate of many children with untreated ADHD who have been diagnosed incorrectly as having bipolar disorder.

Although grandiosity is not a *DSM-IV* symptom of ODD, it is nonetheless common in patients with ODD. For example, I once had a session with a nine-year-old boy, Andrew, who had been diagnosed with ADHD and ODD and was brought in for evaluation of his severe disruptive behavior. It quickly became clear that prior to the visit Andrew had extracted an agreement from his mother that he would decide upon the medication and its dose because he knew best. When I tried to discuss various medication options, he became enraged at his mother and insisted that she abide by her promise to him. The mother acceded to his wishes and demanded that the child, rather than the child psychiatrist, decide upon the medication and dose. Andrew was grandiose in his belief that he knew more and was more powerful than his doctor. He had coerced his mother and tried to coerce me into getting his way. This mother always acceded to his wishes, and this served to confirm his distorted belief in his own power, making it virtually impossible for those outside of the home to control his behavior. This form of grandiosity is common in ODD children. As this case suggests, any challenge to authority by an oppositional child involves some degree of grandiosity.

Andrew's belief that he could refuse the demands of his powerful protectors and providers and exercise his own will required at least some overestimation of his own power. The same could be said of children who refuse to go to bed at assigned times, refuse to do homework, or refuse to comply with household rules. Any of these situations suggests that these children believe that they have the power to extract what they want from unwilling providers. Insofar as this belief is true, the need for parent counseling or family therapy to toughen parent limit-setting ability seems clear. Insofar as this belief is false, there is an element of grandiosity at play in these children's minds. Of course, in the real world there is usually a mixture of overindulgent parents combined with elements of grandiosity in the children. A parent's difficulty in setting limits on a child tends to reinforce the child's grandiosity and perception of power in the family.

The role of grandiosity in the psychology of the everyday life of the child may not be well understood. Grandiosity, expressed in the form of ambition, could play a critical role in normal child development. Geller felt that a child with no musical talent who persisted in practicing a musical instrument and had aspirations for a great musical career could be considered grandiose. It certainly seems possible, however, perhaps even likely, that such a child would find, over time, that he or she was not suited for such a career and would go on to other things. This type of grandiosity is inextricably linked to normal ambition in early adulthood as well. The belief that one can become a successful artist, excel at a sport, have a great love, or raise a child may entail some grandiosity. A modest amount of grandiosity, at least, may even be necessary for success in the world. Given these considerations, grandiosity does not seem to be a cardinal symptom of bipolar disorder because it is found in many other *DSM* disorders as well as in nonpathological situations in everyday life.

Geller's second "cardinal symptom," elated mood, is not necessarily abnormal. Elation means extreme happiness. Geller notes that the emotion is found in normal children on holidays such as birthdays or Christmas, at amusement parks, and during other joyous times of childhood. It is when this intense happiness occurs without reason or far beyond what would be expected for the circumstances that it becomes a potential psychiatric symptom. Geller and colleagues describe the elation as brief periods of silliness and giggling (Geller et al., 2002). Silliness and giggling, however, are a normal part of childhood and can be engaged in by children for a variety of reasons unrelated to bipolar disorder. Precise criteria for diagnosing pleasant mood feelings as abnormal are difficult to establish. It seems unlikely that the giggling and silliness described by these authors would be easily recognized as pathological elated mood; furthermore, the fact that the periods are brief counters characterizing them as constituting the elation of bipolar disorder, as this elation needs to last seven days or longer in *DSM-IV* to count as an episode of mania.

In adult mania, a great deal of scholarly psychiatric study has been devoted to the subject of episode length (time the symptoms are present) and cycle length (time from beginning of one episode to beginning of next), and there is considerable precedent in using these words according to the agreed-upon definitions. On several occasions Geller and her colleagues have recommended a major redefinition of these concepts in order to reflect their observations of children they have diagnosed as having pediatric bipolar disorder. They believe pediatric bipolar disorder patients switch moods more often than adult bipolar disorder patients. The shortest episode length in adult bipolar disorder is the rapid cycler who has about four cycles per year. An exceptionally rare set of adult patients with an extremely high number of cycles a year has also been described. Rather than being exceptionally rare, Geller and colleagues believe it is common for pediatric bipolar disorder patients to be "ultrarapid cyclers" (with 5–364 cycles per year) or even "ultraradian cyclers" (with more than 365 cycles a year) (Geller, Tillman, & Bolhofner, 2007; Tillman & Geller, 2003).

The contrast between adult patients having cycles lasting six months to several years and child patients having numerous cycles throughout a day is striking. It is obviously a mistake to identify these very different phenomena as the same.

Parents of patients often come to believe that every temporary shift in mood is a "mood swing" or "cycle" and anxiously point to a childish pout or temper tantrum as evidence that their child has bipolar disorder. During an evaluation session a parent may point to a grumpy child and announce, "See? It's starting again. He's having another mood swing." Geller's concept of ultraradian cycles lends credibility to this obvious parental misinterpretation. These "mood swings" or "cycles" are entirely different from those seen in *DSM-IV* bipolar disorder.

A recent publication by several NIMH psychiatrists stated unambiguously that *DSM-IV* criteria had to be met in order to diagnose bipolar disorder in children and adolescents (Leibenluft et al., 2003). The paper strongly underscored the necessity of episodic behaviors in which *all* of the child's behaviors changed depending upon the change in the mood of the child, as *DSM-IV* requires. All mood swings, even the briefest, require that there is a shift of the patient's B group of *DSM-IV* symptoms such as elation, distractibility, grandiosity, etc. The mood and the behaviors cannot be the usual mood and behaviors the child displays. The child has to be different from his or her usual self. The NIMH group is confident that such patients exist during adolescence but seems uncertain that prepubertal children could actually meet the *DSM-IV* criteria for episodes. Rapid mood shifts in children, such as those described above, do not include changes in these other symptoms and therefore cannot count toward a diagnosis of bipolar disorder.

Bipolar Disorder in the Very Young

The risks, failures of judgment, and bad science of pediatric bipolar disorder are even more apparent in preschool children than they are in elementary school age children. There is more of a divorce from *DSM-IV* criteria, and the risks of medication may be greater because of the preschool child's lower weight and physical immaturity. The potential for diagnostic error is also greater; there is a greater chance of incorrectly deciding that behavioral issues are due to a serious psychiatric disorder rather than due to simple developmental, psychological, or family problems. It is widely appreciated that preschoolers are more sensitive than are older children to fluctuations in family functioning, which can result in a variety of troublesome behaviors.

Preschool children are less well studied than older children in psychiatry. There are less medication studies in these age groups and less clinical prescribing experience. The leading scholar of bipolar disorder in preschool children is Joan Luby, MD, of Washington University. A colleague of Dr. Geller, Dr. Luby has published several important studies on bipolar disorder in preschool children.

In an elaborate and careful NIMH-funded study, Dr. Luby had the parents of 305 preschool children interviewed by trained raters using an interview specifically designed to study depression and mania in preschool children (Luby & Belden, 2006). The children themselves were not interviewed. Based on the parental interviews, 21 of the preschool children were diagnosed as having bipolar disorder, and all of these children had depression as well. Fifty-four additional children had depression without bipolar disorder. The children diagnosed with both bipolar disorder and depression had more severe depression than the children diagnosed with depression without bipolar disorder. It has been my experience that these subtle distinctions are difficult enough to make in adults with a cooperative adult patient speaking directly to a psychiatrist. It strains credibility to believe they can be made accurately in preschoolers without ever having seen the child.

In another study based largely on the same group of patients, Dr. Luby reported that preschool children with grandiosity, elation, and hypersexuality (precocious interest in sex and sexual behaviors) were likely to have bipolar disorder (Luby & Belden, 2008). Again, the existence of these symptoms is based solely on parent reports, which are surely open to alternative interpretations than the children having bipolar disorder. It also seems unlikely that the parents were capable of evaluating symptoms such as grandiosity and elation in their preschool children. Most child psychiatrists, including myself, would be challenged when asked to weigh the significance of elation, grandiosity, and hypersexuality behaviors in an evaluation of a preschool child that they were actually observing. Asking parents of preschool children to report on these behaviors in the absence of some confirmatory professional observation of the child makes the assessment incomplete. This is especially significant because Dr. Luby asks the reader to believe in an entirely new disorder that has not been previously described in the psychiatric literature.

As was mentioned in discussion of Dr. Biederman's studies of mania in childhood, it is common knowledge that children must be seen in order to be evaluated. Dr. Luby acknowledges the failure to evaluate the children as a limitation of her study yet nonetheless seems confident in her findings. Absent some direct observation of the child, however, it is difficult to be persuaded that these preschool children actually had bipolar disorder.

Dr. Biederman's group also reported a study of 165 preschool children aged four years to six years who were diagnosed with ADHD. Of these preschool children, 26%, or 42, were also diagnosed as having bipolar disorder. This group of children was compared with an older group of 381 children aged seven to nine years who were diagnosed with ADHD. Of these older children, 69 (18%) were also diagnosed with bipolar disorder (Wilens et al., 2002). In general, these are high rates of bipolar disorder. The Biederman group also reported that the preschoolers had an average onset of their bipolar disorder at about two and a half years of age and the school age children at three years, seven months. The authors warn that reluctance to treat bipolar disorder children in their preschool years will lead to disturbed children in the future.

These types of cautions about the consequences of failing to treat the disorder at younger and younger ages are undoubtedly contributing to the dramatic increases in the diagnoses of the disorder in these age groups. As a consequence of these dire warnings, more children (and younger children) are exposed to the risk of misdiagnoses and treatment with potentially dangerous medications to little purpose.

A different view of psychopathology in the preschool years is offered by Drs. Speltz, McClellan, and colleagues. They studied 92 boys age four years to five years, five months, whom they believed were similar to the preschool group studied by the Biederman group. All of the children had ODD and about half also had ADHD. The Speltz and McClellan group followed their preschoolers for two years and, unlike the Biederman group, did not find a single case of bipolar disorder at the beginning or end of their study (Speltz et al., 1999).

The difference in the results of the two studies produced a fascinating exchange of letters between the two research groups. The Speltz group expressed the concern that the study of the Biederman group would contribute to the overdiagnosis of bipolar disorder (McClellan & Speltz, 2003). The Biederman group stood by their results and made a comment that is especially relevant to this book: "We find perplexing the notion of Drs. McClellan and Speltz that publishing data in peer-reviewed journals on a particular subject leads to an epidemic of diagnosis in children. Since when does awareness cause a disorder?" (Wilens et al., 2003, p. 129). The Biederman group seemed to minimize the powerful effect of the combination of the persuasiveness of a scientific finding with the prestige of Harvard University and the exceptional influence of this particular group of investigators on the field of child psychiatry.

Another useful corrective to the preschooler studies of Luby and Biederman is a recent published work of Birmaher and colleagues (2010). Dr. Birmaher is a longtime investigator of pediatric bipolar disorder and the recipient of numerous NIMH grants on the disorder. He is regarded as a careful, thoughtful, and highly capable researcher and one who regularly diagnoses pediatric bipolar disorder in his research studies. He studied 121 two- to five-year-old children in families in which one parent had bipolar disorder and 102 two- to five-year-old children in families in which neither parent had bipolar disorder. The interviewers of the children did not know if the parents had bipolar disorder. None of the preschool children from the bipolar disorder parent group had a bipolar I disorder diagnosis. This runs counter to what many pediatric bipolar disorder proponents would have predicted.

One Authoritative View

Dr. Gabrielle Carlson, MD, a professor of psychiatry and pediatrics and director of the division of child and adolescent psychiatry at State University of New York at Stony Brook, has been investigating bipolar disorder in children and adolescents for decades. She has authored numerous studies and articles about the disorder and serves almost as an unofficial referee regarding the diagnosis. She regularly chairs national conferences about research on the disorder. She recently authored the pediatric bipolar disorder sections in the authoritative Goodwin and Jamison textbook, *Manic-Depressive Illness* (Carlson, 2007a, 2007b; Goodwin & Jamison, 2007).

In a recent article about the high reported rates of pediatric bipolar disorder in child psychiatric inpatients, Carlson was critical of interpreting irritability symptoms of childhood disorders as an expression of childhood bipolar disorder.

> Impulse control deficits and affective instability in young people is now often conceptualized as bipolar disorder. However, there is broad, recognition that . . . this presentation . . . differs from BD [bipolar disorder] seen in adults. . . . Euphoria, expansiveness, supreme self-confidence, self-importance . . . are rarely seen among children. Intense, mission-driven efforts to undertake projects . . . are also rare among children. (Blader & Carlson, 2007, p. 107)

Dr. Carlson continues in this vein to note that episodes of mood disorder in children differ greatly from episodes of mood disorder in adults with bipolar disorder.

In 2006, Dr. Carlson chaired a research forum at the meeting of the American Academy of Child and Adolescent Psychiatry. The findings were published, and Dr. Carlson, who is the senior author of the article, stated,

> Impulsive, affective aggression is difficult to classify. Reframed as mood instability, it is no less complicated. Unfortunately, fitting what is likely a multitude of childhood disorders into one diagnostic category originally developed for the study of adult [bipolar disorder] remains unsatisfactory at best and destructive at worst. It is destructive both because we do not know which children are being described and thus do not know how to understand research findings, and because the valid scientific questions that have arisen have been framed in ways that cast doubt on the entire profession. (Carlson et al., 2009, p. 4)

Dr. Carlson has the well-deserved trust of a large segment of child psychiatry about bipolar disorder in children and adolescents; her beliefs about it are highly influential in the field. If she has begun to doubt the diagnosis of pediatric bipolar disorder, it likely has a poor prognosis.

References

Biederman, J. (1995). Developmental subtypes of juvenile bipolar disorder. *Harv Rev Psychiatry, 3*(4), 227–230.

Biederman, J., Faraone, S.V., Chu, M.P., & Wozniak, J. (1999). Further evidence of a bidirectional overlap between juvenile mania and conduct disorder in children. *J Am Acad Child Adolesc Psychiatry, 38*(4), 468–476.

Biederman, J., Petty, C.R., Monuteaux, M.C., Evans, M., Parcell, T., Faraone, S.V., & Wozniak, J. (2009). The child behavior checklist-pediatric bipolar disorder profile predicts a subsequent diagnosis of bipolar disorder and associated impairments in ADHD youth gowing up: A longitudinal analysis. *J Clin Psychiatry, 70*(5), 732–740.

Biederman, J., Wozniak, J., Kiely, K., Ablon, S., Faraone, S., Mick, E., Mundy E., & Kraus., I. (1995). CBCL clinical scales discriminate prepubertal children with structured interview-derived diagnosis of mania from those with ADHD. *J Am Acad Child Adolesc Psychiatry, 34*(4), 464–471.

Birmaher, B., Axelson, D., Goldstein, B., Monk, K., Kalas, C., Obreja, M., Hickey, M.B., Iyengar, S., Brent, D., Shamseddeen, W., Diler, R., & Kupfer, D. (2010). Psychiatric Disorders in Preschool Offspring of Parents with Bipolar Disorder: The Pittsburgh Bipolar Offspring Study (BIOS). *Am J Psychiatry, 167,* 321–330.

Blader, J.C., and Carlson, G.A. (2007). Increased rates of bipolar disorder diagnoses among U.S. child, adolescent, and adult inpatients, 1996-2004. *Biol Psychiatry, 62*(2), 107–114.

Carlson, G. (2007a). Children and Adolescents. In F.K. Goodwin & K.R. Jamison (Eds.) *Manic-Depressive Illness: Bipolar Disorders and Recurrent Depression.* New York: Oxford University Press.

Carlson, G. (2007b). Treatment of Children and Adolescents. In F.K. Goodwin & K.R. Jamison (Eds.) *Manic-Depressive Illness: Bipolar Disorders and Recurrent Depression.* New York: Oxford University Press.

Carlson, G.A. (2005). Early onset bipolar disorder: Clinical and research considerations. *J Clin Child Adolesc Psychol, 34*(2), 333–343.

Carlson, G.A., Findling, R.L., Post, R.M., Birmaher, B., Blumberg, H.P., Correll, C., DelBello, M.P., Fristad, M., Frazier, J., Hammen, C., Hinshaw, S.P., Kowatch, R., Leibenluft, E., Meyer, S.E., Pavuluri, M.N., Wagner, K.D., & Tohen, M. (2009). AACAP 2006 Research Forum—Advancing research in early-onset bipolar disorder: barriers and suggestions. *J Child Adolesc Psychopharmacol, 19*(1), 3–12.

Faraone, S.V., Biederman, J., Wozniak, J., Mundy, E., Mennin, D., & O'Donnell, D. (1997). Is comorbidity with ADHD a marker for juvenile-onset mania? *J Amz Acad Child Adolesc Psychiatry, 36*(8), 1046–1055.

Galanter, C.A., Pagar, D.L., Oberg, P.P., Wong, C., Davies, M., & Jensen, P.S. (2009). Symptoms leading to a bipolar diagnosis: A phone survey of child and adolescent psychiatrists. *J Child Adolesc Psychopharmrmacol, 19*(6), 641–647.

Geller, B. (1997). Discussion of "Attention-Deficit Hyperactivity Disorder with Bipolar Disorder: A Familial Subtype?" *J. Am. Acad Child Adolesc Psychiatry, 36*(10), 1387–1388.

Geller, B., Tillman, R., & Bolhofner, K. (2007). Proposed definitions of bipolar I disorder episodes and daily rapid cycling phenomena in preschoolers, school-aged children, adolescents, and adults. *J Child Adolesc Psychopharmacol, 17*(2), 217–222.

Geller, B., Zimerman, B., Williams, M., DelBello, M., Bolhofner, K., Craney, J. L., Frazier J., Beringer L., & Nickelsburg, M.J. (2004). DSM-IV Mania Symptoms in a Prepubertal and Early Adolescent Bipolar Disorder Phenotype Compared to Attention-Deficit Hyperactive and Normal Controls. *Focus,* 2, 586–595.

Geller, B., Zimerman, B., Williams, M., Bolhofner, K, Craney, J. L., DelBello, M.P., & Soutullo, C.A. (2000). Diagnostic characteristics of 93 cases of a prepubertal and early adolescent bipolar disorder phenotype by gender, puberty and comorbid attention deficit hyperactivity disorder. *J Child Adolesc Psychopharmacol, 10*(3), 157–164.

Geller, B., Zimerman, B., Williams, M., DelBello, M.P., Frazier, J., & Beringer, L. (2002). Phenomenology of prepubertal and early adolescent bipolar disorder: examples of elated mood, grandiose behaviors, decreased need for sleep, racing thoughts and hypersexuality. *J Child Adolesc Psychopharmacol, 12*(1), 3–9.

Goodwin, F. K., & Jamison, K. R. (2007). *Manic-Depressive Illness: Bipolar Disorders and Recurrent Depression.* Oxford: Oxford University Press.

Leibenluft, E., Charney, D.S., Towbin, K.E., Bhangoo, R.K., & Pine, D.S. (2003). Defining clinical phenotypes of juvenile mania. *Am J Psychiatry, 160*(3), 430–437.

Luby, J., & Belden, A. (2006). Defining and validating bipolar disorder in the preschool period. *Dev Psychopathol, 18*(4), 971–988.

Luby, J.L., & Belden, A.C. (2008). Clinical characteristics of bipolar vs. unipolar depression in preschool children: An empirical investigation. *J Clin Psychiatry, 69*(12), 1960–1969.

McClellan, J.M., & Speltz, M.L. (2003). Psychiatric diagnosis in preschool children. *J Am Acad Child Adolesc Psychiatry, 42*(2), 127–128; author reply, 128–130.

Safer, D.S. (2009). Irritable mood and the Diagnostic and Statistical Manual of Mental Disorders. *Child Adolesc Psychiatry Ment Health, 3.*

Singh, M.K., DelBello, M.P., Kowatch, R.A., & Strakowski, S.M. (2006). Co-occurrence of bipolar and attention-deficit hyperactivity disorders in children. *Bipolar Disord, 8*(6), 710–720.

Speltz, M.L., McClellan, J., DeKlyen, M., & Jones, K. (1999). Preschool boys with oppositional defiant disorder: Clinical presentation and diagnostic change. *J Am Acad Child Adolesc Psychiatry, 38*(7), 838–845.

Tillman, R., & Geller, B. (2003). Definitions of rapid, ultrarapid, and ultradian cycling and of episode duration in pediatric and adult bipolar disorders: A proposal to distinguish episodes from cycles. *J Child Adolesc Psychopharmacol, 13*(3), 267–271.

Wilens, T.E., Biederman, J., Brown, S., Tanguay, S., Monuteaux, M.C., Blake, C., & Spencer, T. J. (2002). Psychiatric comorbidity and functioning in clinically referred preschool children and school-age youths with ADHD. *J Am Acad Child Adolesc Psychiatry, 41*(3), 262–268.

Wilens, T., Biederman, J., Spencer T.J., & Monuteaux, M. (2003). Psychiatric Diagnosis in Preschool Children: In reply. *J. Am. Acad Child Adolesc Psychiatry, 42,* 128–129.

Wozniak, J., & Biederman, J. (1996). A pharmacological approach to the quagmire of comorbidity in juvenile mania. *J Am Acad Child Adolesc Psychiatry, 35*(6), 826–828.

Wozniak, J., Biederman J., Kiely K., Ablon J.S., Faraone S.V., Mundy E., & Mennin, D. (1995). Mania-like symptoms suggestive of childhood-onset bipolar disorder in clinically referred children. *J Am Acad Child Adolesc Psychiatry, 34*(7), 867–876.

Wozniak, J., Biederman, J., Kwon, A., Mick, E., Faraone, S., Orlovsky, K., Schnare, L., Cargol, C., & van Grondelle, A. (2005). How cardinal are cardinal symptoms in pediatric bipolar disorder? An examination of clinical correlates. *Biol Psychiatry, 58*(7), 538–583.

CHALLENGE QUESTIONS

Should Bipolar Disorder be Diagnosed and Treated in Children?

1. Drawing off the descriptions provided by the Child and Adolescent Bipolar Foundation, where does it seem reasonable to draw the line between a child with "normal" mood swings and emotional volatility and a child with pediatric bipolar disorder?
2. What are the potential advantages and disadvantages to giving younger children psychiatric medications? What alternative treatments seem most promising?
3. The Child and Adolescent Bipolar Foundation suggests that the huge increase in rates of pediatric bipolar disorder in recent decades derive from increased awareness. What are other possible explanations for the changing prevalence rates?
4. Stuart L. Kaplan argues that pediatric bipolar disorder is often confused with ADHD and ODD. Why might those disorders be confused for each other, and what are the likely advantages of each diagnosis?

Is There Common Ground?

When any child suffers from the signs and symptoms of mental disorders, it is heartbreaking to see. No one would suggest that distressed children and their families do not deserve guidance and help. The question here is whether diagnosing what had previously been almost exclusively adult afflictions in children makes that help possible. Both the Child and Adolescent Bipolar Foundation and Stuart L. Kaplan clearly want to help children and families, but what would make that possible? And what do our efforts to help in "abnormal" situations say about how we think about the very nature of "normal" child development? A core tenant of lifespan development is that the human mind is qualitatively different throughout a progression of ages and stages. Accordingly, both sides of this issue would agree that children with the symptoms of pediatric bipolar disorder are different from adults with bipolar disorder. But how can we best take those differences into account for the sake of healthy child development?

Suggested Readings

K. Chang, "Challenges in the Diagnosis and Treatment of Pediatric Bipolar Depression," *Dialogues in Clinical Neuroscience* (vol. 11, no. 1, 2009)

H.L. Egger and R.N. Emde, "Developmentally Sensitive Diagnostic Criteria for Mental Health Disorders in Early Childhood," *American Psychologist* (February-March 2011)

M.M. Gleason, et al., "Psychopharmacological Treatment for Very Young Children: Contexts and Guidelines," *Journal of the American Academy of Child and Adolescent Psychiatry* (December 2007)

B.I. Goldstein, "Pediatric Bipolar Disorder: More Than a Temper Problem" *Pediatrics* (June 2010)

J. Groopman, "What's Normal? The Difficulty of Diagnosing Bipolar Disorder in Children," *The New Yorker* (April 9 2007)

J.L. Luby, "Preschool Depression: The Importance of Identification of Depression Early in Development," *Current Directions in Psychological Science* (April 2010)

S. Olfman (Ed.), *Biploar Children: Cutting-Edge Controversy, Insights, and Research* (Praeger 2007)

E. Parens and J. Johnston, "Troubled Children: Diagnosing, Treating, and Attending to Context," Special Report, *Hastings Center Report* (March-April 2011)

E. Parens, J. Johnston, and G.A. Carlson, "Pediatric Mental Health Care Dysfunction Disorder?" *New England Journal of Medicine* (May 20 2010)

E. Roberts, *Should You Medicate Your Child's Mind? A Child Psychiatrist Makes Sense of Whether or Not to Give Kids Meds* (Da Capo Press 2006)

J. Warner, *We've Got Issues: Children and Parents in the Age of Medication* (Riverhead Press 2010)

ISSUE 9

Are Violent Video Games Necessarily Bad for Children?

YES: Craig A. Anderson, from "Violent Video Games and Other Media Violence (Parts 1 & 2)" in *Pediatrics for Parents* (January/February & March/April 2010)

NO: Cheryl K. Olsen, Lawrence Kutner, and Eugene Beresin, from "Children and Video Games: How Much Do We Know?" in *Psychiatric Times* (October 2007)

Learning Outcomes

As you read the issue, focus on the following points:

1. Research has established a consistent association between violent video game play and aggression, though it is difficult to ascertain if that association is long-term and causal.
2. Violent video games are not likely to cause significant problems for normal children doing well in other contexts, but may exacerbate existing problematic tendencies for children prone to aggression.
3. Children themselves, most particularly boys, often identify significant benefits to video game play, including having relatively safe outlets for aggression and opportunities for shared social experiences.

ISSUE SUMMARY

YES: Psychologist and researcher Craig A. Anderson finds that violent video game play consistently associate with aggression and problematic behavior, arguing that there is no good reason for making them available to children.

NO: Cheryl K. Olsen, Lawrence Kutner, and Eugene Beresin have all been affiliated with a Harvard Medical School center devoted to studying mental health and the media. In their work they recognize the potential risks of violent video games, but find that most children play video games in ways that pose little risk and offer some potential benefit.

Though debate about the value or harm of video games has existed since the first video games became widely distributed, the issue has rarely been as prominent as it was in 2011 when the U.S. Supreme Court decided a case called "*Brown v. Entertainment Merchants Association.*" The case derived from a proposed law in the state of California prohibiting the sale of violent video games to children. Ironically, the legislation was originally signed into law in 2005 by the then governor of California Arnold Schwarzenegger, who garnered fame largely through playing violent action heroes in Hollywood movies. During the process Schwarzenegger was reported as saying "We have a responsibility to our kids and our communities to protect against the effects of games that depict ultraviolent actions," taking for granted that those effects are negative. Although the Supreme Court ultimately sided with the video games makers and ruled the California prohibition on the sale of violent games unconstitutional, the decision was based largely on protecting free speech rather than protecting children. The case did, however, put a spotlight on much research relevant to lifespan development addressing the effects of video games on children.

New media of all types inundates the lives of today's children and youth, generating much debate among scholars about the developmental effects. How much television should children watch? Does time spent surfing the Internet erode social skills? Do social networking sites such as Facebook enhance or detract from personal relationships? Are video games more likely to be an engaging forum for fun and imagination or an addictive distraction that imparts questionable values? All of these questions are crucial issues for anyone concerned with healthy child and youth development, and accordingly they have received much scholarly attention. But they are also surprisingly challenging questions to research effectively.

Perhaps the single most challenging research issue is the classic social science question of causality. For questions about the effects of video game violence, the issue is to isolate video game play as a causal agent—if aggressive children indulge themselves in violent video games, does the aggression or the video game play come first? The usual way researchers isolate causality is to do experimental studies where one randomly assigned group is exposed to violent media and another randomly assigned group is not; a classic example here is Alfred Bandura's famous "Bobo Doll" experiment where he found that children who watched an adult act aggressively toward a blow-up doll were more aggressive themselves than children who watched the adult act playfully with the doll. But although studies such as these have established that watching aggression can produce more aggression in the short-term, they are virtually impossible to undertake in the long term. It is both unethical and unfeasible to randomly assign children to long-term exposure to violent media. This means most research relies on short-term experiments or long-term observations comparing groups that may already differ in the predilection toward aggression and violence.

The challenges of researching media violence have not, however, stopped many scholars from specializing in studying the effects of media violence.

Prominent among these is psychologist Craig A. Anderson, who summarizes his perspective on the research in the YES article. Based on decades of his own research, Anderson finds that the evidence convincingly demonstrates an association between aggression and violent video games. He acknowledges that some studies and researchers have found limited effects, but asserts that when quality studies are combined in meta-analyses, the results clearly show negative effects. Anderson also identifies potential mechanisms that are relevant to developmental processes, suggesting that extensive exposure to video game violence serves to make such violence familiar and acceptable.

In the NO article, Cheryl K. Olsen, Lawrence Kutner, and Eugene Beresin offer a contrasting perspective, acknowledging that violent video games can exacerbate preexisting problems, but focusing on ways that violent video games do not necessarily harm children who are otherwise doing well. As they note, "The biggest fear of clinicians and the public alike—that violent video games turn ordinary children and adolescents into violent people in the real world—is not borne out by the data." They also draw on focus group research with video game players to identify potential benefits of video game play, including providing a reasonably safe outlet for aggressive feelings and providing opportunities for shared social experiences (particularly among boys).

Ultimately, while the U.S. Supreme Court addressed this issue as a constitutional question, the issue for children and families is developmental. What is it about violent video games that actually has the power to shape or alter a developmental trajectory? Is it what Arnold Schwarzenegger seemed to fear as Governor of California: that the games have the potential to desensitize children to violence and socialize them to see aggression as a way to solve problems? Or is it what Arnold Schwarzenegger seemed to enjoy in his days as an actor: that violence in the media offers a chance to be engaged in ways that allow both entertainment and escape?

YES

Craig A. Anderson

Violent Video Games and Other Media Violence

Violent Video Games and Other Media Violence (Part I)

For my 2003 article on *The Influence of Media Violence on Youth,* a group of media scholars and I, selected by the National Institute of Mental Health, reviewed 50 years of research on media violence and aggression.

Early Research

Most of the early research focused on two questions:

1. Is there a significant association between exposure to media violence and aggressive behavior?, and
2. Is this association causal? (That is, can we say that violent television, video games, and other media are directly causing aggressive behavior in our kids?)

The results, overall, have been fairly consistent across types of studies (experimental, cross-sectional, and longitudinal) and across visual media type (television, films, video games). There is a significant relation between exposure to media violence and aggressive behavior.

Exposing children and adolescents (or "youth") to violent visual media increases the likelihood that they will engage in physical aggression against another person. By "physical aggression" we mean behavior that is intended to harm another person physically, such as hitting with a fist or some object.

A single, brief exposure to violent media can increase aggression in the immediate situation. Repeated exposure leads to general increases in aggressiveness over time. This relation between media violence and aggressive behavior is causal.

Early aggression researchers were interested in discovering how youth learn to be aggressive. Once they discovered observational learning takes place not only when youth see how people behave in the real world but also when they see characters in films and on television, many began to focus on exactly how watching such violent stories increases later aggression. In other words, more recent research really focused on the underlying psychological mechanisms.

Current Research

In the last 10 years there has been a huge increase in research on violent video games. Based on five decades of research on television and film violence and one decade of research on video games, we now have a pretty clear picture of how exposure to media violence can increase aggression in both the immediate situation as well as in long-term contexts.

Immediately after consuming some media violence, there is an increase in aggressive behavior tendencies because of several factors:

1. Aggressive thoughts increase, which in turn increase the likelihood that a mild or ambiguous provocation will be interpreted in a hostile fashion
2. Aggressive (or hostile) emotion increases
3. General arousal (e.g., heart rate) increases, which tends to increase the dominant behavioral tendency
4. Youth learn new forms of aggressive behaviors by observing them, and will reenact them almost immediately afterwards if the situational context is sufficiently similar.

How Media Violence Increases Aggression

Repeated consumption of media violence over time increases aggression across a range to situations and across time because of several related factors. First, it creates more positive attitudes, beliefs, and expectations regarding aggressive solutions to interpersonal problems. In other words, youth come to believe that aggression is normal, appropriate, and likely to succeed.

It also leads to the development of aggressive scripts, which are basically ways of thinking about how the social world works. Heavy media violence consumers tend to view the world in a more hostile fashion. Additionally, it decreases the cognitive accessibility of nonviolent ways to handle conflict. That is, it becomes harder to even think about nonviolent solutions.

Media violence also produces an emotional desensitization to aggression and violence. Normally, people have a pretty negative emotional reaction to conflict, aggression, and violence, and this can be seen in their physiological reactions to observation of violence (real or fictional, as in entertainment media). For example, viewing physical violence normally leads to increases in heart rate and blood pressure, as well as to certain brain wave patterns. Such normal negative emotional reactions tend to inhibit aggressive behavior, and can inspire helping behavior. Repeated consumption of media violence reduces these normal negative emotional reactions.

Finally, repetition increases learning of any type of skill or way of thinking, to the point where that skill or way of thinking becomes fairly automatic. Repetition effects include learning how to aggress.

Effect of Violence in Passive Versus Active Media

Most of the research has focused on TV/film violence (so-called "passive" media), mainly because it has been around so much longer than video games.

However, the existing research literature on violent video games has yielded the same general types of effects as the TV and cinema research.

At a theoretical level, there are reasons to believe that violent video games may have a larger harmful effect than violent TV and film effects. This is a very difficult research question, and there currently is no definite answer. But, recent studies that directly compare passive screen media to video games tend to find bigger effects of violent video games.

Violent Video Games and School Shootings

Mainstream media violence researchers do not believe that an otherwise normal, well-adjusted child who plays violent video games is going to become a school shooter. The best way to think about this issue is the risk factor approach. There are three important points to keep in mind.

First, there are many causal risk factors involved in the development of a person who frequently behaves in an aggressive or violent manner. There are biological factors, family factors, neighborhood factors, and so on. Media violence is only one of the top dozen or so risk factors.

Second, extreme aggression, such as aggravated assault and homicide, typically occurs only when there are a number of risk factors present. In other words, none of the causal risk factors are "necessary and sufficient" causes of extreme aggression. Of course, cigarette smoking is not a necessary and sufficient cause of lung cancer, even though it is a major cause of it. People with only one risk factor seldom (I'm tempted to say "never") commit murder.

Third, consumption of media violence is the most common of all of the major risk factors for aggression in most modern societies. It also is the least expensive and easiest risk factor for parents to change.

Playing a lot of violent games is unlikely to turn a normal youth with zero, one, or even two other risk factors into a killer. But regardless of how many other risk factors are present in a youth's life, playing a lot of violent games is likely to increase the frequency and the seriousness of his or her physical aggression, both in the short term and over time as the youth grows up.

Risk Groups for Aggression

There is some research that suggests that individuals who are already fairly aggressive may be more affected by consumption of violent video games, but it is not yet conclusive. Similarly, video game effects occasionally appear to be larger for males than females, but such findings are rare. Most studies find that males and females are equally affected, and that high and low aggressive individuals are equally affected.

One additional point is worth remembering: Scientists have not been able to find any group of people who consistently appear immune to the negative effects of television, film, or video game violence.

Realistic Versus Fantasy Violence

One of the great myths surrounding media violence is this notion that if the individual can distinguish between media violence and reality, then it can't have an adverse effect on that individual. Of course, the conclusion does not logically follow from the premise. And in fact, most of the studies that have demonstrated a causal link between exposure to media violence and subsequent aggressive behavior have been done with individuals who were fully aware that the observed media violence was not reality. For instance, many studies have used young adult participants who knew that the TV show, the movie clip, or the video game to which they were exposed was not "real." These studies still yielded the typical media violence effect on subsequent aggressive behavior.

Contradictory Studies

In any field of science, some studies will produce effects that differ from what most studies of that type find. If this weren't true, then one would need to perform only one study on a particular issue and we would have the "true" answer. Unfortunately, science is not that simple.

Why have different researchers found different results? Well, part of the problem is that many studies have used a sample size that is much too small to produce consistent results. But even with a larger sample sizes, we still would not get the exact same results in every study. Chance plays some role in the outcome of any experiment. So even if all the conditions of the test are exactly the same, the results will differ to some extent. Test conditions are complex. Each study differs somewhat from every other study, usually in several ways.

Given that scientific studies of the same question will yield somewhat different results, purely on the basis of chance, how should we go about summarizing the results of a set of studies? One way is to look at the average outcome across studies. This is essentially what a meta-analysis does. And when one does a comprehensive meta-analysis on the video game violence research literature, the clear conclusion is that the results are quite consistent. On average, there is a clear effect: exposure to violent video games increases subsequent aggression. This has been found for each of the three major research designs (experimental, cross-sectional, and longitudinal), for youth and for young adults, and for youth in North America, Japan, and Western Europe. Similar meta-analyses of the television and film violence research literatures produce the same, generally consistent effects.

In addition to the small sample size and chance factors, a third factor is that some of the few contradictory studies can be explained as being the result of poor methods. For example, one frequently cited study that failed to find a video game effect did not actually measure aggressive behavior; instead, it measured arguments with a friend or spouse. That same study also failed to show that participants in the "high video game violence" condition actually played more violent games than participants in the "low video game violence" condition.

When you separate studies into those that were well conducted versus those that had major flaws, you find that the well-conducted studies found bigger average effects of violent video games on aggression than did the poorly conducted studies. Some well-conducted, and some poorly conducted, studies suffer from a too-small sample size. But the main point is that even well-conducted studies with appropriate sample sizes will not yield identical results. For this reason, any general statements about a research domain must focus on the pooled results, not on individual studies.

Violent Video Games and Other Media Violence, (Part II)

Marketing Violence

Clearly, violence sells, at least in the video game market. But it is not clear whether the dominance of violent video games is due to an inherent desire for such games, or whether this is merely the result of the fact that most marketing dollars are spent on promoting violent games instead of nonviolent ones.

One great irony in all of this is that the industry belief that violence is necessary in their product in order to make a profit may be hurting their overall sales by failing to satisfy the market for nonviolent games. Another unfortunate consequence of the extreme marketing emphasis on violence is that the media industries have convinced many people in the U.S. that they like only violent media products. But nonviolent and low-violent products can be exciting, fun, and sell well.

Myst is a good example of an early nonviolent video game that sold extremely well for quite some time. More recent examples include The Sims, many sports and racing games, and many simulation games. In some of our studies, college students are required to play nonviolent video games. Interestingly, some of these students report that they have never played nonviolent games, and are surprised to learn that they like some of the nonviolent ones as much as their violent games.

Even more intriguing is recent research on the psychological motivations that underlie judgments about which games are the most fun and worthy of repeat business. Scholars at the University of Rochester conducted six studies on game players' ratings of game enjoyment, value, and desire for future play. They found that games that give the player a lot of autonomy (lots of choices within the game) and feelings of competence (for example, success in overcoming difficulties with practice) were rated much more positively than games without these characteristics, regardless of whether or not the games included violence. In other words, violent games are so popular mainly because such games tend to satisfy both autonomy needs and competence needs, not because they contain violence.

Media Violence "Experts"

The media industries seek out, promote, and support "experts" who make claims that there is no valid scientific evidence that links media violence to aggression. There are several such "experts" who have made their careers by bashing legitimate research. Examining their credentials is quite revealing.

Many do not have any research training in an appropriate discipline. Of those who do have advanced degrees in an appropriate discipline (for example, social psychology), almost none of them have ever conducted and published original media violence research in a top-quality peer-reviewed scientific journal; they have never designed, carried out, and published a study in which they gathered new data to test scientific hypotheses about potential media violence effects. In other words, they are not truly experts on media violence research. To get at the truth, one must distinguish between actual versus self-proclaimed (and often industry-backed) experts.

Interestingly, a number of professional organizations have asked their own experts to evaluate the media violence research literature. One of the most recent products of such an evaluation was a "Joint Statement on the Impact of Entertainment Violence on Children," issued by six medical and public health professional organizations at a Congressional Public Health Summit on July 26, 2000. This statement noted that ". . . entertainment violence can lead to increases in aggressive attitudes, values, and behavior, particularly in children." The statement also noted that the research points ". . . overwhelmingly to a causal connection between media violence and aggressive behavior in some children." The six signatory organizations were: American Academy of Pediatrics, American Academy of Child & Adolescent Psychiatry, American Medical Association, American Psychological Association, American Academy of Family Physicians, and the American Psychiatric Association.

Along the same line, several reports by the U.S. Surgeon General have concluded that exposure to media violence is a significant risk factor for later aggression and violence. Both the American Academy of Pediatrics and the American Psychological Association have specifically addressed the violent video game issue; both concluded that playing violent video games is a causal risk factor for later aggression against others, and called for a reduction in exposure of youth to this risk factor.

Public's Perception of Causal Effect

Some people claim the media violence/aggression issue today is very similar to the tobacco/lung cancer issue of 30 years ago. The tobacco industry was quite effective at keeping the public confused regarding the true causal effect of tobacco on lung cancer, and there are still sizable numbers of smokers who don't really believe this scientific fact. Among other tactics, the tobacco lobby promoted "experts" who claimed that the research was badly done, or was inconsistent, or was largely irrelevant to lung cancer in humans. The media industries have been doing much the same thing: seeking out, promoting, and supporting "experts" willing to bash legitimate media violence research.

The tobacco industry successfully defended itself against lawsuits for many years. There have been several lawsuits filed in the U.S. against various video game companies in recent years. As far as I know, none have been successful yet.

One big difference between the tobacco industry cases and the violent media cases is that the main sources of information to the public (e.g., TV news shows, newspapers, magazines) are now largely owned by conglomerates that have a vested interest in denying the validity of any research suggesting that there might be harmful effects of repeated exposure to media violence.

The tobacco industry certainly had some influence on the media because of their advertising revenues, but the violent media industries are essentially a part of the same companies that own and control the news media. Thus, it is likely to be much more difficult for the general public to get an accurate portrayal of the scientific state of knowledge about media violence effects than it was to get an accurate portrayal of the tobacco/lung cancer state of scientific knowledge.

Given that it took 30-some years for the public to learn and accept the tobacco/lung cancer findings, it seems unlikely that we'll see a major shift in the public's understanding of media violence effects in the near future. Indeed, a study that my colleague Brad Bushman and I published in 2001 suggests that the media violence/aggression link was firmly established scientifically by 1975, and that news reports on this research have become less accurate over time.

Another big difference between the tobacco case and the media violence case is in the proportion of people who were hooked on these risk factors as children. The vast majority of youth repeatedly consume violent media, well before they turn 18; this was never true of tobacco products. This is important in part because of the "third-person effect," a psychological phenomenon in which people tend to think that they personally are immune to risk factors that can affect others.

Current Video Game Research

Since 2000, a large number of new video game studies have been published. One of the most important developments is that now there have been several major longitudinal studies of violent video game effects on youth. In such studies, the research team gathers information about a child's video game habits and his typical level of aggressiveness at two separate points in time. The two time points may be separated by months or years.

Sophisticated statistical techniques are used to answer a simple question: Do those who played lots of violent video games at the first time measurement show larger increases in aggression over time than those who played few violent video games? Such longitudinal studies from North America, Europe, and Japan have all found the same answer: Yes.

In addition, my colleagues and I have done several meta-analyses of all of the video game studies. It is even clearer today than it was in 2000 that violent video games should be of concern to the general public. That is, even stronger statements can now be made on the basis of the scientific literature.

Advice

My colleagues and I are expert media violence researchers, not policy advocates. So, we tell the U.S. Senate (or anyone else who asks) what current scientific research literature shows as plainly and clearly as possible, and generally do not promote specific public policies.

Nonetheless, I believe that we need to reduce the exposure of youth to media violence. My preference for action is to somehow convince parents to do a better job of screening inappropriate materials from their children. It is not always an easy task for parents—in part because of poor ratings systems—and perhaps there are appropriate steps that legislative bodies, as well as the media industries, could take to make it easier for parents to control their children's media diet.

As long as the media industries persist in denying the scientific facts and persist in keeping the general public confused about those facts, many parents won't see a need to screen some violent materials from their children. Ironically, the industry's success in keeping parents confused and in making parental control difficult is precisely what makes many citizens and legislators willing to consider legislation designed to reign in what they perceive to be an industry totally lacking in ethical values. My colleagues and I recently published several pieces on the complexity of the public policy issues.

Conclusion

A well-designed video game is an excellent teaching tool. But what it teaches depends upon its content. Some games teach thinking skills. Some teach math. Some teach reading, or puzzle solving, or history. Some have been designed to teach kids how to manage specific illnesses, such as diabetes, asthma, and cancer.

But all games teach something, and that "something" depends on what they require the player to practice. If the player practices thinking in violent ways, deciding to solve conflicts with violent action, and then physically carrying out violent game actions, then those types of thinking, deciding, and behaving are what is learned and reinforced.

However, there are many nonviolent games that are fun, exciting, and challenging. Children, adolescents, and adults like them and can learn positive things from them. Some even get you to exercise muscles other than those in your hands. In moderation, such positive nonviolent games are good for youth. But parents and educators need to check the content of the games they are considering for the youth in their care. You can't simply use the game ratings, because many games rated by the industry as appropriate for children and for teens contain lots of violence. But with a bit of parental effort, and some household rules about game playing, the youth's gaming experience can be fun and positive.

Cheryl K. Olsen, Lawrence Kutner, and Eugene Beresin

 **NO**

Children and Video Games: How Much Do We Know?

There is no shortage of hyperbole when politicians of all stripes describe the nature and effects of video games. Republican presidential candidate Mitt Romney proclaimed, "Pornography and violence poison our music and movies and TV and video games. The Virginia Tech shooter, like the Columbine shooters before him, had drunk from this cesspool." Democratic presidential candidate Hillary Clinton spoke of the game, *"Grand Theft Auto,* which has so many demeaning messages about women, and so encourages violent imagination and activities, and it scares parents."

Some researchers have echoed similar sentiments, noting that Columbine High School shooters Dylan Harris and Eric Klebold were avid computer gamers. Several television pundits quickly drew a link between the recent Virginia Tech shootings and video games, as well. (Ironically, Seung-Hui Cho's college roommates found it odd that he never joined them in playing video games.)

Do these assumptions about video-game violence leading to similarly violent behavior among child and adolescent players make sense? A review of the research gives us insights into which patterns of video game play may serve as potential markers of more serious problems among children and adolescents, and which are normal or even possibly beneficial.

Additional research and case studies may shed some light on parents' concerns, such as whether video games are addictive or dangerous. Finally, we will offer recommendations on what parents can do to reduce potential risks and to maximize potential benefits of video game play.

The biggest fear of clinicians and the public alike—that violent video games turn ordinary children and adolescents into violent people in the real world—is not borne out by the data. Analyses of school shooting incidents from the US Secret Service and the Federal Bureau of Investigation National Center for the Analysis of Violent Crime do not support a link between violent games and real-world attacks. But what does research show about more subtle behaviors, such as bullying or changes in game players' perceptions of violence?

Going from Lab to Street

An August 2007 search of the OVID database for titles incorporating some variation on "video game" yielded 30 articles; a similar search of PsycINFO (limited to peer-reviewed journals) found 418 articles. Most reports focused on studies of the effects of violent video games on aggressive cognitions, emotions, and behavior.

This body of research, however, is of limited use to clinicians for a range of reasons. The most-cited studies are laboratory experiments on college students, generally involving brief exposures to a single violent game. Correlational studies typically involve small, nonrepresentative samples, and assess playing time rather than game content. The terminology is vague, and some researchers use "aggression" and "violence" interchangeably, implying that one inevitably leads to the other. Studies done in the 1980s and 1990s are outdated because of rapidly evolving content and technologies. Recent studies that involve child or adolescent exposure to violent game content represent a tiny fraction of this literature.

In the sections below, we review some findings relevant to clinicians, including our own surveys and focus groups with young adolescents. Unless otherwise specified, "video games" refers to console and handheld games as well as games played on computers.

Normal Use

In a 2005 national sample, the Kaiser Family Foundation surveyed 2032 children in grades 3 to 12 about their media use, including computers and video games. On average, children aged 8 to 18 years spent 49 minutes per day on video games (console or handheld) and 19 minutes on computer games. Boys aged 8 to 10 years were the heaviest users of video games; 73% played on a typical day for an average of an hour and a half.

To learn more, we surveyed 7th- and 8th-grade students at two middle schools in Pennsylvania and South Carolina. Virtually all eligible children attending school on that day participated. For most, electronic game play was a routine activity. Of 1254 children surveyed, only 6% had not played any electronic games in the 6 months before the survey. (These nonplayers were excluded from most analyses.) Gender differences were striking. Boys typically said they played video games 6 or 7 days per week; girls typically played 1 day per week.

To assess exposure to various types of game content, we asked children to list the games they had played "a lot in the past months." We found that 68% of boys and 29% of girls aged 12 to 14 years included at least one M-rated (for those aged 17 years and older, often because of violent or sexual content) game on this list of frequently played games.

Why Kids Play

We presented children and adolescents with a list of 17 possible reasons for playing video games. More than half cited creative reasons for play, such as "I like to learn new things" and "I like to create my own world."

"To relax" was chosen as a reason to play by the majority of boys and close to half of girls. "To get my anger out" was selected by 45% of boys and 29% of girls; 25% of boys and 11% of girls said that they played to "cope with anger." Violent video games might provide a safe outlet for aggressive and angry feelings.

This use of video games to manage emotions came up repeatedly in focus groups we conducted with 42 young adolescent boys. A typical comment was, "If I had a bad day at school, I'll play a violent video game, and it just relieves all my stress."

Children also play violent electronic games for predictable developmental reasons, such as rebellion, curiosity about the forbidden, and testing the limits of acceptable behavior in a safe environment. "You get to see something that hopefully will never happen to you," said one boy in our focus groups. "So you want to experience it a little bit without actually being there."

In both surveys and focus groups, boys described video game play as a social activity. Although most boys played games alone at times, most also routinely played with one or more friends. Just 18% of boys and 12% of girls surveyed said they always played alone.

Markers of Problems

Our survey results, combined with other research, hint at some markers of abnormal (though not necessarily unhealthy) game play patterns. It is uncommon for girls to be frequent, heavy players of video games, especially violent games. One third of girls in our survey played electronic games for less than an hour per week on average. By contrast, it was unusual for boys to rarely or never play video games; just 8% of boys played for less than an hour per week. (Since game play is often a social activity for boys, nonparticipation could be a marker of social difficulties. These boys were also more likely than others to report problems such as getting into fights or trouble with teachers.) Finally, boys and girls who exclusively play games alone are atypical.

In our survey of young adolescents, we found significant correlations between routine play of M-rated games and greater self-reported involvement in physical fights, with a stronger association for girls. It is likely that aggressive or hostile youths may be drawn to violent games. There is limited but suggestive evidence that persons with trait anger or aggression may be affected differently by violent games. In one study, players tended to be less angry after playing a violent game, but this was not true for subjects who scored high on trait anger and aggression. Thus, another possible marker of unhealthy video game use may be increased anger after a round of play.

It must be emphasized that correlational studies, including ours, cannot show whether video games cause particular behaviors. Far too frequently, this important distinction between correlation and causation is overlooked.

Case Vignette: Games and Attention/Learning Disorders

Alex, a 13-year-old boy, spends 6 to 7 hours a day playing video games. He locks himself in his room, misses meals, and often stays up most of the night, which results in school tardiness. He learns "cheats" (tricks to find quick solutions to game-based problems) online, converses with players in chat rooms, and has accumulated a great deal of knowledge about the intricacies of the many, often violent, games he plays.

Although very bright, Alex has a nonverbal learning disability, social difficulties, poor athletic skills, and attention problems, and he was often made fun of at school. The primary source of his self-esteem, beyond academic achievement, is his video game prowess.

His parents have no understanding of the games, nor of the video games' central importance in his life. Other children in school often come to him for advice about games and strategies and ask to play with him. This has become his claim to fame in and out of school.

While his parents need to educate themselves about the games he is play-ing and to set limits on his game play, their initial response to curtail them has been modified over time, allowing for an important avenue in the socializa-tion of their son.

Therapy for Alex and his parents involved their appreciation of the role and meaning of games in his life. His parents needed to understand that com-petence is a crucial component of positive self-esteem—something Alex needed tremendously in order to take on academic and social challenges. Video games provided a means for Alex to feel more confident in moving ahead in these areas. With a greater understanding of the role the games played in his life, his parents were much more tolerant of his game playing.

The therapist continues to work with Alex and his parents and teachers to find additional ways for him to build a stronger sense of himself, improve his self-worth, and learn new ways of connecting with peers. His increased sense of competence has translated into greater academic achievement and the development of friendships outside the realm of video games.

Little research has been done on how subgroups of children, including those with diagnosed mental illness or learning difficulties, may be differen-tially affected by video games—for better or worse. Our survey included Pedi-atric Symptom Checklist subscales on attention and internalizing symptoms. Boys whose responses put them over a threshold level for attention-deficit/ hyperactivity disorder (ADHD) symptoms were more likely than others to use games to cope with angry feelings.

Among girls with ADHD symptoms, twice as many (almost 1 in 4) played games to make new friends compared with girls who did not have ADHD. In moderation, these are probably healthy uses of video games. As in the case of Alex above, children with ADHD often are adept at playing video games and using computers. This can provide a highly valued source of self-esteem.

Might video games be helpful with other illnesses, such as depression? In our survey, children who endorsed internalizing symptoms, such as feeling sad, hopeless, and worthless were much more likely to select "to forget my prob-lems" as a reason for playing video games. These children did not spend signif-icantly more time with video games, but they were more likely to play alone. Unfortunately, we do not know enough to say whether using video games to manage emotions is healthy or unhealthy for depressed children in general, or any child in particular. It may be that temporary or intermittent immersion in a game is therapeutic, while playing games alone for hours most days after school makes matters worse. Talking with a child about where, when, why, and how he or she uses electronic games could provide some useful insights.

Parental Perceptions and Concerns

In our survey, more than three quarters of respondents said their parents "rarely" or "never" played video games with them. In focus groups, many parents expressed frustration about being too much in the dark about the games their children were playing. Many worried that their child spent too much time in game play to the detriment of homework, socializing, or sports.

For their part, boys liked the action, challenge, and excitement of their violent games. While *Grand Theft Auto* was the most popular game series among the boys we surveyed, the second most-cited series was *Madden NFL* football. For many, and perhaps most boys in middle school, violent and/or sports games are a key to initiating and structuring social interactions. As one boy in a focus group told us, "If I didn't play video games—it's like a topic of conversation—and so I don't know what I'd talk about, 'cause I talk about video games a lot."

Contrary to parental concerns, our focus groups—as well as a British study of college students—suggest that realistic sports games may actually encourage interest and participation in real-world sports.

CHALLENGE QUESTIONS

Are Violent Video Games Necessarily Bad for Children?

1. One reason this issue has been an ongoing controversy is because it is challenging to research. Based on the readings, which types of research seem most convincing, and what more would you want to know about the relationship between video game play and child development?
2. The question of whether it should be illegal to sell violent video games to children was the target of a major case for the U.S. Supreme Court in 2011, which decided that the risks of the games did not trump free speech rights. From a developmental perspective, does this seem like the right decision? What would you say to the Supreme Court if they asked your opinion?
3. If it is problematic for children to play violent video games, is it also problematic for teens and adults? What are likely to be key effects of violent video game play that are particular to children in earlier developmental stages?
4. The readings on both sides of this issue essentially agree that violent video games are unlikely by themselves to turn normal children into violent or aggressive deviants. Does that mean only certain types of children should be allowed to play violent video games? How would you distinguish between those who might and might not be harmed?

Is There Common Ground?

Playing violent video games is probably not anyone's idea of an ideal activity for children—except for some children themselves. The simple popularity of violent video games suggests that they may be serving some need, even if that need is antisocial. A key question thus becomes whether there are other ways to fill those needs. Craig A. Anderson thinks there are, suggesting that creative and educational video games can be an entertaining substitute rendering violent games pointless. Cheryl K. Olsen, Lawrence Kutner, and Eugene Beresin agree that other types of video games can be entertaining and worthwhile, but are not as concerned if some children still choose more violent games. Both sides also agree that violent video games can be a bad idea for some children who seem otherwise at risk. So ultimately the difference comes down to a matter of who we can trust to ensure violent video games don't take development off track?

Suggested Readings

American Academy of Pediatrics Council on Communications and Media, "Policy Statement—Media Violence," *Pediatrics* (November 1 2009)

C.A. Anderson et al., "Violent Video Game Effects on Aggression, Empathy, and Prosocial Behavior in Eastern and Western Countries: A Meta-Analytic Review," *Psychological Bulletin* (March 2010)

C.A. Anderson, D.A. Gentile, and K.E. Buckley, *Violent Video Game Effects on Children and Adolescents: Theory, Research, and Public Policy* (Oxford University Press 2007)

C.J. Ferguson and J. Kilburn "The Public Health Risks of Media Violence: A Meta-Analytic Review," *Journal of Pediatrics* (May 2009)

C.J. Ferguson, "Blazing Angels or Resident Evil? Can Violent Video Games be a Force for Good?" *Review of General Psychology* (June 2010)

D. Grossman and G. Degaetano, *Stop Teaching Our Kids to Kill: A Call to Action Against TV, Movie, and Video Game Violence* (Crown Archetype 1999)

G. Jones, *Killing Monsters: Why Children Need Fantasy, Super Heroes, and Make-Believe Violence* (Basic Books 2002)

L. Kutner and C. Olson, *Grand Theft Childhood: The Surprising Truth About Violent Video Games and What Parents Can Do* (Simon & Schuster 2008)

C.K. Olson, "Children's Motivations for Video Game Play in the Context of Normal Development," *Review of General Psychology* (June 2010)

D. Pollard Sacks, B.J. Bushman, and C.A. Anderson, "Violent Video Games and Children: Comparing the Scientific "Experts" in Brown v. Entertainment Merchants Association," *Northwestern University Law Review* (May 27, 2011)

Internet References . . .

The Society for Research on Adolescence

The Society for Research on Adolescence provides information for academics, clinicians and students.

http://www.s-r-a.org/

The National Clearinghouse on Families & Youth

The National Clearinghouse on Families & Youth (NCFY) offers free information related to teens, youth, and families, and offers relevant links at their Web site.

http://www.ncfy.com/links/

After-school Programs

This site presents "promising practices in afterschool" programs, and is managed by the Academy for Educational Development's Center for Youth Development and Policy Research.

http://www.afterschool.org/

Public/Private Ventures

Public/Private Ventures is a research group that has information about out-of-school time and adolescent development available on their Web site.

http://www.ppv.org/ppv/outofschooltime.asp

The MacArthur Foundation Research Network

This site offers research reports related to adolescence and delinquency.

http://www.adjj.org/content/index.php

Psychology Central

This site provides articles summarizing research about mental health as related to adolescent development.

http://psychcentral.com/blog/archives/category/children-teens/

The Society for Neuroscience

This Web site offers information and links to contemporary brain science research.

http://www.sfn.org/

Youth Today

Youth Today is an independent newspaper and network that focuses on youth work.

http://www.youthtoday.org/

Adolescence

*A*dolescence is a distinctive stage in the lifespan because it is marked by a clear biological change: puberty. Developing adolescents cope with dramatic physical changes that often seem to combine a mature body with an immature mind. Further, because adolescence is associated with increasing independence and responsibility, adolescents seem both powerful and vulnerable. Society is compelled to provide adolescents care and opportunity, while simultaneously fearing that they will rebel. The issues in this section deal with the nature of success and failure in adolescence by asking two questions about the range of adolescent experiences.

- Should Contemporary Adolescents Be Engaged in More Structured Activities?

- Does the Adolescent Brain Make Risk Taking Inevitable?

ISSUE 10

Should Contemporary Adolescents Be Engaged in More Structured Activities?

YES: Joseph L. Mahoney, Angel L. Harris, and Jacquelynne S. Eccles, from "Organized Activity Participation, Positive Youth Development, and the Over-Scheduling Hypothesis," *Social Policy Report* (August 2006)

NO: Alvin Rosenfeld, from "Comments on 'Organized Activity Participation, Positive Youth Development, and the Over-Scheduling Hypothesis'," . . . .

Learning Outcomes

As you read the issue, focus on the following points:

1. Though children and adolescents are participating in more structured activities than was historically the case, most participate because they genuinely enjoy them.

2. Although a minority of children spend an overwhelming amount of time in structured activities, the average American youth spends less time on activities than on less constructive things such as watching television.

3. The increasing popularity of structured activities as enrichment activities seems to have corresponded with more stress among parents, less free play, and less family time.

4. Research finds a consistently positive relationship between activity participation and healthy development, such that emphasizing "overscheduling" may actually be detrimental to positive opportunities for children.

5. To this point, simply identifying overscheduling as a phenomenon does not seem to be causing cuts in activity programming.

ISSUE SUMMARY

YES: Psychologist Joseph Mahoney and colleagues recognize the concern about "over-scheduling" but present research suggesting that the benefits to structured activities outweigh any costs.

NO: Child psychiatrist Alvin Rosenfeld asserts that all of the data suggest that most youth and adolescents need less structured activity and more balance.

Structured activities, including sports, music, academics, drama productions, and more, have become a standard part of many adolescent experiences. These activities, with their promise of a safe environment for enriching experiences, are popular with diverse constituencies from parents and educators to policymakers and scholars. From a developmental perspective, however, the phenomenon of a highly structured youth brings both opportunities and risks. While structured activities and youth organizations provide many rich opportunities for adolescents, structured time also has the potential to put stress on youth and families while taking away the joy and creativity that can come from free leisure.

Because of these two potential outcomes, the growing availability of structured activities has been accompanied by a growing concern that some children are over-scheduled. News outlets are reporting on youth and families that spend so much time with structured activities that the teens end up deprived of sleep and the families end up without any significant time together. Scholars have also been pointing out concerns in books such as *The Hurried Child* and *The Power of Play* by developmental psychologist David Elkind and *Unequal Childhoods* by sociologist Annette Lareau. This work describes fatigued and overwhelmed youth whom child psychiatrist Alvin Rosenfield and journalist Nicole Wise categorized in a 2000 book as *The Over-Scheduled Child*.

While the image of the over-scheduled child may seem familiar from the media, developmental psychologists Joseph Mahoney et al. realized that there was little direct research investigating broad issues related to the scheduling of today's youth. They thus compiled a review of new and existing research addressing specific issues related to structured activity participation, and empirically tested what they phrase "the over-scheduling hypothesis." In the selection, which is excerpted from their work, they find that overall, youth seem more likely to be under-scheduled than over-scheduled.

Mahoney and colleagues frame their work in relation to the emerging scholarly field of "positive youth development," which focuses on how to create environments for successful development. The general consensus is that structured activities are part of such environments, and few would disagree that activities can be a beneficial part of anyone's childhood years. But that does not necessarily mean the more the better.

Perhaps we are at a point where the quantity of structured activities has become too much of a good thing? This is the position articulated by child psychiatrist Alvin Rosenfeld in response to Mahoney and his colleagues. Rosenfeld thinks that Mahoney et al. have over-simplified the issue by comparing youth who participate in activities with youth who participate in no activities. Rosenfeld notes that structured activities are such a common part of growing up today that the children who do not participate at all are the exception. From Rosenfeld's perspective, the important thing is to balance reasonable amounts of structured activity participation with free leisure and family life.

POINT

- Most children participate in activities because they enjoy them, and do not experience undue pressure.
- On average, American youth actually spend very little time directly participating in structured activities.

- There is a consistently positive relationship between activity participation and healthy developmental outcomes.

- By claiming that children are over-scheduled there may be an impetus to cut much-needed funding for positive youth development programs.

COUNTERPOINT

- The effects are not just on youth, but also on stressed parents and family life in general.
- The real goal is a balance of activities and free time. It is unreasonable to compare youth who are participating in no activities because the contemporary norm is to participate in some.
- Data suggest that moderation is best regarding structured activity participation, and there have been notable declines in family life during recent decades.
- Identifying over-scheduling does not seem to lead to cuts in funds for activity programs.

YES ⤹ Joseph L. Mahoney, Angel L. Harris, and Jacquelynne S. Eccles

Organized Activity Participation, Positive Youth Development, and the Over-Scheduling Hypothesis

School-aged children in the U.S. and other Western nations average 40–50% of their waking hours in discretionary activities outside of school. There has been increasing awareness that how young people use this time has consequences for their development. As a result, research on the risks and benefits of a variety of after-school activities has been expanding rapidly and considerable attention has been devoted to school-aged children's (ages 5–11) and adolescents' (ages 12–18) involvement in organized activities. Organized activities occur outside of the school day and are characterized by structure, adult-supervision, and an emphasis on skill-building. Common activities include school-based extracurricular activities (e.g., sports, clubs, and fine arts), after-school (i.e., programs, often targeted to youth between the ages 5–14, that provide participants with adult supervision during the afternoon hours while many parents are working and offer opportunities for academic assistance, recreation, and/or enrichment learning) and community-based programs and youth organizations (e.g., 4-H, Boys & Girls Clubs of America, and Girls, Inc). Organized activities can be contrasted with alternative ways that young people spend their discretionary time such as educational activities, household chores, watching television, playing games, hanging out, and employment.

Participation in organized activities is a common developmental experience for young people. For example, the 1999 National Survey of America's Families (NSAF) reported that 81% of 6- to 11-year-olds and 83% of 12- to 17-year-olds participated in one or more sports, lessons, or clubs during the past year. Approximately 7 million children are enrolled in after-school programs. Millions more participate in community-based programs and youth organizations such as 4-H, Boys & Girls Clubs of America, and Girls Inc. Moreover, national studies show that participation in some organized activities such as sports and before/after-school programs has increased significantly in recent years.

The growth of organized activities has resulted from several factors. First, there has been an expansion of local, state, and Federal expenditures to support organized activities. A well–known example is the increase in Federal support for 21st-Century Community Learning Center grants that support after-school programs. This funding grew exponentially from $40 million in

From *Social Policy Report*, vol. XX, no. IV, 2006. Copyright © 2006 by Society for Research in Child Development. Reprinted by permission. Reference omitted.

1998 to $1 billion in 2002. Second, the historic rise in maternal employment has resulted in a gap between the school day of children and work day of their parents. This fact, coupled with research pointing to dangers for children who are unsupervised during the after-school hours, has called attention to organized activities as a means to provide safety and supervision for children with working parents. Finally, on balance, the bulk of research on organized activities has shown positive consequences of participation for academic, educational, social, civic, and physical development.

In combination, these factors have increased awareness that organized activities represent a valuable resource for promoting positive youth development. This is evident in the out-of-school initiatives of major research intuitions (e.g., Chapin Hall Center for Children, Harvard Family Research Project), granting institutions and foundations (e.g., C. S. Mott Foundation, W. T. Grant Foundation), advocacy and lobbying groups (e.g., Afterschool Alliance, Fight Crime Invest in Kids, National Institute on Out-of-School Time, National School-Aged Care Alliance), as well as the initiation of a bipartisan Congressional After-school Caucus in March 2005.

The Over-Scheduling Hypothesis

At the same time that initiatives to expand opportunities for organized activity participation have been increasing, concern exists that some youth are participating in too many organized activities. Written and televised media reports and popular parenting books suggest that the lives of many young people are now replete with hurry, stress, and pressure brought on, in part, because of their involvement in too many organized activities. These articles maintain that an over-scheduling of organized activity participation may undermine family functioning and youth well-being.

With respect to organized activities, the over-scheduling hypothesis is based on three interrelated propositions. First, the motivation for participation in organized activities is viewed as extrinsic. Youth are seen as taking part in a variety of activities because of the perceived pressure from parents or other adults to achieve and attain long-term educational and career goals (e.g., a college scholarship). Second, the time commitment required of children and parents to participate in organized activities is believed to be so extensive that traditional family activities—dinnertime, family outings, and even simple discussions between parents and children—are sacrificed. Finally, owing to the assumed pressures from parents, coupled with the extensive time commitment and disruption of family functioning, youth devoting high amounts of time to organized activity participation are thought to be at risk for developing adjustment problems and poor relationships with parents.

Although the basis for these propositions has been seldom anchored by empirical research, scientific evidence has been used to advance the notion that some youth (particularly middle class and affluent youth) are over-scheduled in some cases and that such over-scheduling can be detrimental to the optimal development of young people and their families. This evidence draws on qualitative studies of how organized activity participation affects family life and quantitative studies suggesting that perceived pressure from parents and other adults (e.g., coaches, teachers) may lead to poor adjustment particularly for affluent youth (i.e., families whose annual household earnings are at least twice as high the medium annual income for families in the US). As far as we know, the argument has not been directed to poor or working-class youth and there have been no studies of this issue focused on less advantaged populations.

Whether youth participate in organized activities depends, in part, on the behavior of their parents. Studies of children and adolescents suggest that they are more likely to become involved and to stay involved in organized activities when parents value and encourage their participation, provide the necessary material resources, and are participants themselves. However, a recent ethnographic study conducted with children (ages 9–10) from 12 diverse families suggests that organized activity schedules can determine the pace of life for all family members. The findings from Lareau's study show that the time budgeting and schedule commitments required of parents to support their children's activity participation can be challenging—particularly for working parents with several children. The qualitative accounts also suggest that participation in many organized activities can limit children's down time and constrain the nature parent-child interactions. While her study has been used to justify the inference that such scheduling might be problematic, Lareau did not actually investigate the children's well-being. Moreover, a systematic evaluation of how time spent in organized activities may affect discretionary time or parent-child interactions was not a goal of this study. Finally, although provocative, the findings are based on a small number of families and this raises concern about whether the results can be generalized beyond the study sample.

Quantitative studies suggesting possible risks for affluent adolescents have also been cited in support of the over-scheduling hypothesis. For example, in one of a few relevant studies, Luthar and her colleagues concluded, first, that adolescents (6th and 7th graders) from affluent homes can be at greater risk for substance use, depression, and anxiety as they enter adolescence than children living in less affluent homes, and, second, that excessive achievement pressures and isolation from parents may help to explain these associated risks. However, this research did not assess the association between time spent participating in organized activities and achievement pressures or adolescent adjustment. Accordingly, these studies neither intended to nor do they provide evidence that adolescents (affluent or otherwise) perceive pressure to participate in organized activities from their parents or are at-risk for adjustment problems as a result of their participation.

Our interest in conducting an evaluation of the scientific underpinnings of these propositions is twofold: First, these propositions suggest negative consequences resulting from too much organized activity participation. This has the potential to undermine recent efforts to support and expand opportunities for youth to participate in organized activities. Because policy decisions concerning children and families will be made with or without the use of scientific knowledge, this concern holds despite the limited evidence on which the over-scheduling hypothesis is based.

Indeed, the response to findings from the national evaluation of 21st-Century Community Learning Centers show that substantial reductions in funding for organized activities can be proposed on the basis of a single study with controversial findings.

Second, despite research available to inform propositions of the over-scheduling hypothesis, the scientific community has been relatively silent on this issue. As the value and worth of psychological research depends increasingly on an appropriate and timely integration of science with policy, it is essential that the existing research informing this matter be communicated. To that end, one of our major goals is to evaluate the scientific basis of the over-scheduling hypothesis. Our second major goal is to evaluate the evidence for the alternative positive youth development perspective; namely, that participation in organized activities facilitates positive development and that more participation is associated with more positive development. . . .

Discussion

In this paper, we have explored two perspectives regarding the relation of organized activity participation and development: the positive youth development perspective and the over-scheduling perspective. On the one hand, advocates of positive youth development have argued that participation in organized activities facilitate optimal development and therefore policymakers should provide more opportunities for American youth to be involved in such activities. On the other hand, some writers have suggested that participating in organized activities has become excessive for some young people, owing, in part, to achievement pressures from parents and other adults. These authors maintain that external pressures, along with the activity-related time commitment, can contribute to poor psychosocial adjustment for youth and to undermine relationships with parents. If this is the case, then attention from scientists, practitioners, and policymakers are warranted. Our goal was to bring scientific evidence to bear on both of these perspectives.

The available research base provides far more support for the positive youth perspective than for the over-scheduling perspective. To begin, the belief that organized activity participation is often motivated by parental pressure to achieve or attain long-term educational and career goals is not supported by the limited available empirical data. Overwhelmingly, the primary reasons adolescents give for participating in organized activities are intrinsic and focus on the here and now. This holds for the few studies that sampled affluent and suburban youth with relatively high levels of involvement in organized activities. However, there is a paucity of information on whether the reasons for participation vary according to either the amount or type of organized activity participation, or the age and other demographic characteristics of the participants and their families. We need to know much more about the relation between the participants' and their parents' motivations, goals, values, and expectations and the choices children/adolescents make about their discretionary time, in general, and the amount of time they devote to various types of organized activities, more specifically.

On the basis of time alone, very few American youth devote enough time to organized activities to be classified as "over-scheduled." For example, youth in the PSID-CDS—the only nationally representative sample of American youth with time use data—averaged about 5 hours/week in organized activities on any given week during the school year; furthermore, roughly 40% of the PSID-CDS youth did not participate in any organized activities and those who did typically spent fewer than 10 hours/week doing so. Comparable estimates emerged in the other studies we reviewed. These findings suggest that organized activities do not dominate the vast majority of American youth's free time. Instead, the majority of their time is consumed by other leisure pursuits such as watching television, educational activities, playing games, hanging out, and personal care. In other words, given the considerable amount of discretion time typically available to young Americans, most appear able to balance their organized activity participation effectively with school-related tasks, family time, informal socializing with peers, and relaxing. Nevertheless, there was evidence in some of the studies reviewed as well as in the PSID-CDS analyses reported in this paper, of a subgroup of youth (3% of children and 6% of adolescents) who spend a very high amount of time (20 or more hours/ week) participating in organized activities. Are these youth poorly adjusted as a result of their high levels of participation in organized activities? By and large the evidence suggests not. Like their slightly less involved peers, they appear to be functioning better than non-involved youth. We discuss this more later.

In general, youth who participate in organized activities score better on a variety of indicators of healthy development than youth who do not participate. For example, those PSID-CDS youth who participated in organized activities for fewer than 20 hours/week scored better than the youth who did not participate in any activities on all of the indicators of well-being. This finding was true for all of the studies we reviewed and is consistent with the evidence summarized by Eccles and Gootman in their 2002 report for the National Research Council and the Institute of Medicine on the Community Based Programs for Youth. Thus, reliable support for the benefits of participation in organized activities emerged across studies and these benefits, by and large, become stronger with increased participation. Although the scheduling of responsibilities surrounding organized activities can sometimes be challenging for families, the associated benefits of participation are apparent nonetheless.

What about those youth who participate a great deal? Once again the findings across studies provide very limited support for the hypothesis that too much participation can be harmful. Many of the existing studies find a linear increase in the psychological, social, and academic well-being of youth as the number of organized activities or weekly hours of participation increases. Other studies report a curvilinear trend such that the well-being of youth with very extreme levels of involvement may level off or decline somewhat; however, these studies do not provide evidence that even very high amounts participation confers risk. The findings regarding the well-being of the extreme 6% of PSID-CDS youth who participated in organized activities 20 or more hours/week are generally consistent with these other studies. Clearly, the White youth who participated for 20 or more hours/week were better off than those White youth who did not participate in any activities on all but one of the indicators assessed: They reported higher levels of self-esteem and psychological and emotional well-being; lower alcohol, marijuana, and cigarette use; and ate meals with their parents and engaged in discussion with them more frequently. The only potentially negative finding for these White youth was that shared activities with their parents occurred less frequently. The findings for PSID-CDS Black youth were less consistent. On the one hand, the Black youth who participated in organized activities for 20 or more hours/week had higher reading achievement; reported higher emotional well-being; lower alcohol, marijuana, and cigarette use; and ate meals together with their parents more frequently than their Black peers who did not participate in any organized activities. On the other hand, these Black youth also reported less frequent parent-adolescent discussions and lower self-esteem and psychological well-being than their Black peers who did not participate.

The reasons for few the negative findings from the PSID-CDS and other studies need to be investigated before policy implications can be drawn. They may or may not be indicators of a negative impact of over-scheduling on adolescent development. For example, in the PSID-CDS, the fact that older adolescents may spend somewhat less time with their parents is not necessarily an indication of problems. Instead it could reflect normative increases in autonomy among competent young people. Thus, more needs to be known about the causes and consequences of this association before drawing any conclusions about whether they imply a developmental risk in these adolescents' lives. Likewise, the finding by Luthar et al. that a very small group of early adolescent females from affluent families demonstrated high internalizing symptoms and poor school adjustment when they were both highly involved in academic activities and perceived their parents as critical and overly achievement-oriented requires additional study before conclusions concerning over-scheduling can be made. One possibility is that a high amount of activity participation is associated with adjustment problems primarily for youth who do not receive positive support from their parents. This is consistent with research showing that activity-related support and encouragement from parents plays an important role in youths' enrollment and continued participation in organized activities. Parent-adolescent relations may also help to explain why the PSID-CDS findings showed that a very high amount of organized activity participation was associated with lower self-esteem and psychological well-being for Black adolescents; these same youth also reported a low frequency of parent-adolescent discussions. However, other studies have found have found a positive, linear association between the amount of organized activity participation and self-esteem during adolescence. Thus, to understand better what underlies these associations, process-oriented longitudinal research is needed. Moreover, given the many associated benefits of participation for other areas of their adjustment, follow-up studies are required to assess whether these highly involved adolescents are at risk for poor adjustment in the long term.

Despite these few possible risks of very high levels of activity participation, we do not believe efforts to limit adolescents' participation in organized activities are warranted for several reasons. First, across all studies reviewed, those few youth with very high levels of organized activity participation did not show negative adjustment in most of the indicators assessed and they demonstrated significantly healthier functioning than non-participants on many indicators of well-being. Furthermore, there is evidence that greater amounts of participation are positively associated with civic engagement, high school graduation, and college attendance, and are negatively related to antisocial behaviors and criminal offending. Therefore, even if a causal relation exists between very high amounts of participation and some negative outcomes, it is not clear that the cumulative effect of limiting participation for this extreme subgroup would be positive or negative.

Second, none of the studies reviewed in this report focused on stability and change in the amount of organized activity participation over time. Therefore, they tell us nothing about whether the very high amounts of participation that characterizes a small subgroup of youth is stable or transient across adolescence. It is possible that some youth extend their time commitment in organized activities to a very high level for a limited time. During this time, certain indicators of well-being may decline somewhat. However, this does not imply that such youth maintain a very high level of participation across all of adolescence or that their long-term well-being is compromised as a result. To evaluate whether this is the cause, longitudinal data measuring adolescents' time use and well-being over time are required.

Third, the existing research concerning amount of organized activity participation and youth adjustment has only begun to examine whether findings vary according to individual characteristics or features of the activity context. For example, studies of high-risk youth show that a lack of organized activity participation predicts poor academic adjustment and high rates of obesity, school dropout, and crime. For these youth, even a very high amount of organized activity participation may be better than spending time in arrangements that lack adult supervision or do not provide opportunities to build competencies. Likewise, the consequences of high amounts of participation are certain to depend on the features of the activity considered. Participation in high-quality organized activities is likely to be associated with positive youth development across the full range of hours considered in this report. In contrast, participation in activities that are poorly designed is predictive of relatively poor adjustment. Thus, attention to person and program features is needed before making decisions concerning the small proportion of youth who demonstrate very high amounts of organized activity participation.

Fourth, attention to person and program features is also relevant when interpreting the somewhat small effect sizes reported in some studies reviewed in this report. For example, results from Marsh's study indicate that, across the multiple significant and positive outcomes, the well-being of youth who were highly involved in organized activities youth was, on average, .22 *SD* (range .05–.58) above that of youth who did not participate. Results from the PSID-CDS showed that the time spent in organized activities explained an average of 8.8% of variance in the adolescent outcomes considered. Because youth typically spend much less time in organized activities than in other contexts (e.g., school and family), the associated impact of participation in any one area of adjustment should ordinarily be modest. However, in regard to the positive youth development perspective, such effects sizes are reported consistently across a broad array of outcomes and, therefore, are large enough to be of practical importance. In addition, research suggests that the magnitude of activity-related benefits may be greatest for: 1) youth who show stable participation over time; 2) those at the highest risk for poor developmental outcomes; 3) when long-term indicators of well-being are considered; and 4) when the quality of the program is high. Thus, there are likely to be many youth for whom participating in organized activities has a very large and positive effect. Similarly, to the extent that some youth participate in low-quality organized activities, the average effect sizes reported may have been diminished. Given the positive associations identified in the PSID-CDS and the other studies reviewed, one conclusion that is possible is that we need to provide America's youth with more, rather than less, opportunities to participate in high-quality, organized activities.

Finally, we note some parallels between the findings connected to organized activity participation and those pertaining adolescent participation in the paid labor force. Both become normative developmental experiences during adolescence, show variability according the family earnings and race, are viewed as a source of preparation for adult roles and responsibilities, and call attention to a small proportion of youth with very high levels of involvement—the consequences of which appear mixed. In the youth employment literature, research on working conditions and quality, reasons that motivate long hours of work, and long-term follow-ups have helped to clarify the pros/cons of young people who work extended hours. These types of studies suggest next steps for research aimed at understanding better the consequences of very high amounts of organized activity participation.

Our overall conclusion is that there is scant support for the over-scheduling hypothesis and considerable support for the positive youth development perspective. As such, we recommend that recent efforts to expand opportunities for organized activity participation should stay the course. For the vast majority of young people, participation in organized activities is positively associated with indicators of well-being. Of greater concern than the over-scheduling of youth in organized activities is the fact that many youth do not participate at all. The well-being of youth who do not participate in organized activities is reliably less positive compared to youth who do participate.

Alvin Rosenfeld

 **NO**

"Organized Activity Participation, Positive Youth Development, and the Over-Scheduling Hypothesis," by Mahoney, Harris, and Eccles

Testing sociological hypotheses is difficult, so Mahoney, Harris, and Eccles should be commended for trying to approach a very complex child rearing question in a scientific fashion. Although these authors follow many well-accepted standards for empirical research, their study is based, in part, on an inaccurate account of Wise and my work and a questionable interpretation of their own data. The authors' conclusions are overly broad and their recommendations may misinform readers, persuading ambitious parents that over-scheduling their children is a scientifically validated way to raise emotionally well, academically successful children. In my opinion, that could have very unfortunate consequences.

Mahoney, Harris, and Eccles' paper contains serious shortcomings. I will name those I consider most important:

1. *Mahoney, Harris, and Eccles misrepresent our work:* Mahoney, Harris, and Eccles' paper tests "the overscheduling hypothesis," attributed in part to *The Over-Scheduled Child* (Griffin/St. Martin's, 2001) by Rosenfeld and Wise. Unfortunately, this "over-scheduling hypothesis" is a creation of their own that bears only scant resemblance to our work. For instance, Mahoney, Harris, and Eccles write that "the overscheduling hypothesis predicts that youth with very high amounts of organized activity participation will demonstrate poor adjustment relative to both those **with little or no participation** [italics added] and those with moderate amounts of participation." In their opinion, testing that contention will test the validity of what Wise, I, and others have said. Wise and I have never suggested that children do better if they participate in no activities nor have we posited that children who are in numerous organized activities do worse than **those who do none**. In fact, we repeatedly call for balance in families, where activities, education, family time, and down time all get sufficient attention. We write that up to a point, enrichment activities can benefit children. When asked, we have responded that

young children who participate in no activities should be urged—even forced—to try some out. We also write that the contemporary pressure to fill every moment with activities can frazzle children *and parents,* diminish the amount of quiet time families spend together, make parents and children resentful and critical, and de-emphasize the importance of creativity and character development.

2. *After creating an inaccurate, simplistic version of Wise and my work and labeling it "the overscheduling hypothesis," the authors design a study—using existing time-use survey data collected for other purposes—to test it:* After grossly misrepresenting our work, Mahoney, Harris, and Eccles compare children who participate in many activities to those in a "no activity" group, arguing—erroneously—that we say the "no activity" group should be doing better. In addition to misrepresenting our position, this comparison is highly flawed. Likely, the "no activity" group is quite diverse; some percentage of it probably does no activities because they are drop-outs, acting out, have failed at school subjects and so are not allowed to participate, etc. Comparing these kids to almost any other group—other than perhaps to foster children and incarcerated youth—would prove the second group, however composed, to be doing better. Mahoney, Harris, and Eccles have selected a well-known marker of poor adjustment—as indicated by the children's partaking in no activities that are normative for their age—and used it as a normative comparison group. They then reverse cause and effect, saying that these children are doing less well because they are not in activities.

3. *Some of Mahoney, Harris, and Eccles' findings support our actual position:* What does Mahoney, Harris, and Eccles' data actually show? In some ways, rather than contradicting our ideas, it supports the position that we put forth, suggesting that balance is best. In published reports, Mahoney maintains that "the more activities they do, the better kids stack up on measures of educational achievement and psychological adjustment" (Newsweek). However, some of Mahoney, Harris, and Eccles' own data suggests the opposite: Black youth spending over 20 hours a week in organized activities had self-esteem lower even than those who participated in no organized activities and far lower than those who participate in a moderate number. Adolescents in 15 or more hours of scheduled activities drink more alcohol than those with 5–15 hours. White youth with 20 or more hours of organized activities report fewer shared activities with parents and doing fewer favorite activities with parents than did youth with 5–15 hours of activities. Black youth with more than 15 hours of organized activities reported fewer shared activities with parents than did those with 5–15 hours of activities; those with more than 20 hours of scheduled activities spent less time with parent-child favorite activities than did those with 10–20 hours of scheduled activities. Black youth with more than 20 hours of activities had fewer parent-adolescent discussions than did any other group, even those with no activities. Reading achievement for black youth doing over 15 hours of organized activities is significantly below those of adolescents doing 5–15 hours. Reading achievement for white youths doing over 20 hours a week of organized activities is almost identical

to those doing *no* organized activities and substantially below those doing moderate activity (though the authors' state that this did not reach statistical significance.) To us, this data seems to support our contention that a balanced number of activities is best rather than the idea that the more the better.

4. ***The Mahoney, Harris, and Eccles study lacks observational data and does not include travel time:*** The study analyzes data based on self-reports. As such, the data is subject to all the well known difficulties non-observational studies are prone to. It relies on time diaries asking people to put down everything they did in a 24 hour period. However, these diaries are written up to three days after a weekday set of activities and up to a week after a weekend day. It is highly questionable that a week after the events, people can accurately remember their activities and how much time they spent on each for an entire 24 hour period which may explain why Mahoney, Harris, and Eccles' study cannot account for how 13–14% of the time is spent. Furthermore, the study does not include travel time. Mahoney, Harris, and Eccles overlook the reality that many families have several children. A parent with three children each with three activities may spend four hours a day driving between activities. In our experience, this driving schedule creates substantial irritation, particularly among highly educated mothers; they love their kids but resent feeling they have become chauffeurs. It also leads to some siblings becoming "car potatoes."

5. ***Mahoney, Harris, and Eccles approach the subject simply from the active child's perspective, discounting the effects on other family members:*** The omission of travel time is part of Mahoney, Harris, and Eccles' general discounting of parental stress. Their study states, "although the scheduling of responsibilities surrounding organized activities can sometimes be challenging for families (Lareau, 2003), the associated benefits of participation are apparent nonetheless." It seems that they regard a child or adolescent seeming to be doing well by questionnaire report as a sufficient outcome marker. This runs diametrically against observational data, including our own clinical observations. Our books stress the importance of the whole family's needs being taken into account, ***including the parents'***. Mahoney, Harris, and Eccles seem to contend that no matter how much the parents sacrifice and no matter how resentful they may feel, their kids do well in the long run if they have more activities. Much of the literature about over-scheduled children speaks of the ways the parents *feel* about leading stressed, overscheduled, and often frenzied lives. Mahoney, Harris, and Eccles do not take these into account.

In contrast, our books, and my talks since the book was published, speak of the need for parents to be sure that they are enjoying their lives because in my clinical experience parents who are satisfied with their situation—rather than feeling frenzied much of the time—have kids who do better. We repeatedly argue against one-size-fits-all solutions and speak of how in arriving at the number and types of activities that are suitable for the family as a whole, each family needs to balance the child's temperament and desires with the number of children in the family and the parents' abilities, capacity, needs, and schedules. We have said that some children—in our experience, often ambitious first born children—want to do everything and need to be reined in a bit. Other children are "couch potatoes" and need to be encouraged, even forced, to partake in organized activities.

6. *Mahoney, Harris, and Eccles discount a large body of data to the contrary and feel that results from their single, flawed study are sufficiently robust to conclude that the more scheduled activities children have, the better:* The conclusions Mahoney, Harris, and Eccles draw from this study seem to run contrary to what numerous experienced observers have noted. We will note just a few: Studies show that in just the past 20 years household conversations have become far less frequent and family dinners have declined 33%. Numerous observers have spoken of sleep deprivation among high achieving adolescents. This study does not even acknowledge that sleep deprivation may be a significant issue among over-scheduled children, nor does it note that as children's sports have become professionalized, orthopedic surgeons have reported an alarming increase of stress related sports and overuse injuries among 5–14 year olds. They ignore work that shows that homework among middle schoolers has grown dramatically and that some scholars feel that the high amount spent could actually harm children. They report but discount the findings, including their own, of higher levels of alcohol use among adolescents with many activities. We have noted that resumes are being shaped for what elite colleges supposedly expect; we and others have commented that community service no longer is a sign of a good heart but a box that must be checked. Speaking of over-scheduled youth, Harvard University's admissions director said that admitted freshman, and we paraphrase, look like the dazed survivors of a life long boot camp. MIT's admissions director has concurred. Parents and adolescents we speak to seem well aware of the pressure they are under. Mahoney, Harris, and Eccles acknowledge none of this as valid.

7. *Mahoney, Harris, and Eccles raise a concern that "the over-scheduling hypothesis," attributed in part to us, could lead to programs for the underprivileged being cut. In almost seven years since our book was first published, this has not happened even once:* Mahoney, Harris, and Eccles state, "These propositions [the "over-scheduling hypothesis"] suggest negative consequences resulting from too much organized activity participation. This has the potential to undermine recent efforts to support and expand opportunities for youth to participate in organized activities" (P 10 draft) particularly for the underprivileged.

A. We agree with the authors' contention that one of the cases in which activity-related benefits may be greatest is for "those at the highest risk for poor development," and when the program's quality is high (35). As a child advocate who has worked with—and written extensively about—indigent and high risk populations, I am quite sensitive to the needs of people in these situations. Whenever Wise and I have been asked about underprivileged populations, we have said that they needed *more—not fewer—* organized activities.

B. Several months back, I wrote a letter to Dr. Mahoney after reading the final draft of this paper: "I would appreciate knowing where and when I—or my work—has been used *in any way* in opposition to these initiatives. In the almost seven years since our book was first published, *I have not once received a single contact or communication from any group or individual asking that my ideas, writings, or speeches be used as support for decreasing activity programs or funding* [italics added]. If such an attempt has ever occurred, I would be grateful if you could inform me of it." To date, I have not received a reply.

In summary, Mahoney, Harris, and Eccles take complex, nuanced ideas and try to make them one-dimensional caricatures. Our books have subtle ideas and a social commentary about the way American families are living their lives and the pressures they are responding to. To name just a few, our books speak of "hyper-parenting," a cultural pressure to involve children in increasing activities so that they turn out "winners" not "losers." We speak of how, from birth on, media play on parents' uncertainty, and how marketers use the idea that the more "enrichment" the better to sell unnecessary products to new parents. We note how individual families and children differ, how what benefits one may be counter-productive for another. Some families thrive on endless activities and sports while others prefer quiet down time. *We suggest that each individual family needs to assess what suits it; when activities are getting parents or the children frenetic, we suggest that they try cutting back 5–10%, hardly a notion that scheduled activities be eliminated.* We speak of needing down time to develop imagination, and of how focusing on activities and accomplishments often de-emphasizes relationships, character, and play which we consider critical to a good life. Our books have recommendations, such as trusting yourself, rather than relying on the experts who don't know you or your family. We suggest that parents do not rely on the most recent "scientific" study whose recommendations may change tomorrow. Mahoney, Harris, and Eccles take all this and create a one-dimensional "over-scheduling hypothesis" which attributes to us the idea that simply counting the number of activities a child participates in accurately and inversely reflects their mental health and life success.

We could discuss many other serious limitations in Mahoney, Harris, and Eccles' paper, but that would serve little purpose. As I wrote to Dr. Mahoney: "It is excellent that you are trying to do reliable, valid scientific work that criticizes my position and refutes my contentions. That keeps the academic process vigorous. If I turn out to have been mistaken, I will shamefacedly admit that I was in error. Nothing I see in my daily observation in our communities makes me think that I am. However, I would appreciate it if in trying to test a hypothesis you ascribe to me, you at the very least represent my positions accurately."

If competitive, affluent parents take to heart Dr. Mahoney's assertion that the more activities kids do the better—as they are wont to do with "expert, scientific" advice from a professor at an elite university—they may be following a path that leads them to more resentment, criticism of their children, and ultimately to damaging them. That would truly be a very unfortunate outcome.

CHALLENGE QUESTIONS ⟳

Should Contemporary Adolescents Be Engaged in More Structured Activities?

1. Some commentators have noted that much of this issue seems to depend upon socioeconomic status—with wealthier children being at risk of having too much structured activity and children from other families being at risk of having too little. How do you think socioeconomic status may influence one's position on this controversial issue?
2. Mahoney, Harris, and Eccles suggest that only a very small portion of youth participate in significant weekly hours of structured activities. Does that seem to be true among your friends and neighbors? Why or why not?
3. What do you make of Rosenfeld's claim that structured activities influence the whole family, not just the involved youth? Why do you think Mahoney and colleagues did not test effects on family life more generally?
4. If you were giving advice to parents about activity participation, what would you say? What does the research allow you to conclude?
5. What might be the benefits of not having structured activities as part of adolescence? What might be the costs?

Is There Common Ground?

Hypothetically, both sides of this issue agree that too much structured activity participation can be a bad thing. It can be stressful to children and adolescents, it can be stressful to families, and it could take away from other types of healthy, unstructured leisure. Hypothetically, both sides of this issue would also likely agree that too little structured activity participation can be a bad thing. Activities offer rich developmental spaces for children and adolescents to explore sports, arts, service, and many other healthy opportunities they might otherwise miss. So the point of contention here is whether that hypothetical resembles the real lives of most teens. Are they really "overscheduled," or is "underscheduling" the greater risk? And where exactly is the cutoff between the two? Is there any way to research and prescribe the optimal quantity of structured activities for positive adolescent development?

Suggested Readings

D. Brooks, "The Organization Kid," *The Atlantic Monthly* (April 2001)

D. Elkind, *The Power of Play* (Da Capo Books, 2007)

K. Ginsburg and the Committee on Communications and the Committee on Psychosocial Aspects of Child and Family Health, from "The Importance of Play in Promoting Healthy Child Development and Maintaining Strong Parent-Child Bonds," *Pediatrics* (January 2007)

R. Larson, "The Tip of an Iceberg?" *Society for Research in Child Development Social Policy Report* (2006)

S. Luthar, "Over-Scheduling Versus Other Stressors: Challenges of High Socioeconomic Status Families," *Society for Research in Child Development Social Policy Report* (2006)

J. Mahoney, R. Larson, and J. Eccles (Eds.), *Organized Activities as Contexts of Development: Extracurricular Activities, After-school and Community Programs* (Lawrence Erlbaum & Associates, 2005)

A. Rosenfeld and N. Wise, *The Over-scheduled Child: Avoiding the Hyper-parenting Trap* (St. Martin's Griffin, 2000)

J. Roth, "Next Steps: Considering Patterns of Participation," *Society for Research in Child Development Social Policy Report* (2006)

ISSUE 11

Does the Adolescent Brain Make Risk Taking Inevitable?

YES: **Laurence Steinberg**, from "Risk Taking in Adolescence: New Perspectives from Brain and Behavioral Science," *Current Directions in Psychological Science* (April 2007)

NO: **Michael Males**, from "Does the Adolescent Brain Make Risk Taking Inevitable?: A Skeptical Appraisal," *Journal of Adolescent Research* (January 2009)

Learning Outcomes

As you read the issue, focus on the following points:

1. Adolescent risk taking has long been a concern, and whether or not that concern is valid advances in brain science have added a new dimension to our understanding of the issue.
2. Brain science does carry with it a risk of "biodeterminism," oversimplifying the complicated reality of why people at any age take risks.
3. Purely educational efforts to mitigate adolescent risk taking have had little success in fully engaging adolescents, perhaps because the efforts do not adequately account for the challenges of impulse control or perhaps because teens are already more aware of risks than adults give them credit for.
4. There is significant variation in rates of risk taking among teens, with some of the variation accounted for by immediate context and some accounted for by broad socioeconomic differences.

ISSUE SUMMARY

YES: Although adolescent risk taking has proved difficult to study and explain, psychology professor Laurence Steinberg claims brain science is now demonstrating that basic biological changes explain much about the issue.

NO: Sociologist Michael Males rejects "biodeterminism" as an over-simplification that exaggerates the effects of brain age and ignores the realities of social and economic differences.

One of the most common stereotypes of adolescents is that they are prone to take risks without adequately accounting for consequences. Much attention has been directed toward influencing adolescents to be more careful and safe. But despite all the attention, the stereotypes persist. Which raises the interesting developmental question of whether the stereotypes are true to begin with.

The idea of adolescence as a tumultuous period that inevitably results in "storm and strain" has long been a controversial issue for developmental research. It has also long been popular to attribute whatever tumult research finds to biological changes—most often to "raging hormones." In fact, adolescence is the rare stage in the life-span with a clear biological marker: puberty. And because puberty does produce dramatic physical changes, it is not hard to imagine that psychological changes would follow.

Advances in technology and brain science seem to have only perpetuated debates about the nature of adolescent behavior. There are ways in which the adolescent brain seems, on average, to function differently than the brain at other ages. Unfortunately, while those differences are often interpreted as indicating biological inevitabilities, patterns of brain activity alone tell us very little about the causes of behavior: social experiences activate the brain just as do genetic programs. Brain activity is both a cause and an effect of behavior. So one of the great challenges that comes with technological advancement is the art and science of interpretation.

Laurence Steinberg explains, the brain's ability to reason and logically think through problems matures more consistently than its ability to manage social and emotional stimulation. Steinberg thinks this difference helps explain a paradox of adolescent risk taking: despite effective educational efforts to help teens logically understand the consequences of risk taking, they often act as if they do not care. From his perspective, the maturation of function in the teen brain makes risk taking nearly inevitable.

Another interpretation is that the facts of biological change distract our attention from the social realities of teenage life. Thus, as Michael Males explains, there are many ways in which adolescents take less risks than adults—particularly when it comes to risk outcomes such as accidental deaths and drug overdoses. In fact, Males argues, there is much more variation in risk taking *within* the stage of adolescence than there is *between* adolescents and adults. Males is particularly concerned that artificially inflating the importance of the brain, which does change with experiences, puts too much emphasis on biology and not enough emphasis on the types of socioeconomic disadvantage that really influence risky adolescent behavior.

However we interpret the findings of modern brain research, it is clear that new technologies raise as many questions as they answer. And some of those questions may allow us to re-evaluate stereotypes about adolescence.

POINT

- There has been much study of adolescent risk taking, but no satisfactory explanation until recent advances in brain science.
- Adolescents are able to engage in mature logical reasoning, but their psychosocial capacities often remain more immature.
- Puberty seems to accelerate socioemotional networks associated with risk taking, overwhelming cognitive-controls—particularly in group contexts.
- Increases in risk taking are closely associated with the biological changes of puberty regardless of chronological age.
- Educational interventions to minimize adolescent risk taking have been largely ineffective, suggesting it is not about rational thinking.

COUNTERPOINT

- Claims of adolescent risk taking are regularly exaggerated, often in service of other social or political agendas.
- Focusing on the adolescent brain as the cause of risk taking is a type of "biodeterminism" that over-simplifies complicated issues; brain science is still not advanced enough to really make clear links between biology and behavior.
- Teenagers have lower rates of risk compared to adults for suicide, drug overdoses, and accidents—yet those statistics are often ignored when making claims about adolescent risk.
- Researchers such as Steinberg fail to control for the most important cause of risk taking: socioeconomic differences predict risk taking better than age.

YES

Laurence Steinberg

Risk Taking in Adolescence: New Perspectives from Brain and Behavioral Science

. . . **A**dolescents and college-age individuals take more risks than children or adults do, as indicated by statistics on automobile crashes, binge drinking, contraceptive use, and crime; but trying to understand why risk taking is more common during adolescence than during other periods of development has challenged psychologists for decades. . . . Numerous theories to account for adolescents' greater involvement in risky behavior have been advanced, but few have withstood empirical scrutiny. . . .

False Leads in Risk-Taking Research

Systematic research does not support the stereotype of adolescents as irrational individuals who believe they are invulnerable and who are unaware, inattentive to, or unconcerned about the potential harms of risky behavior. In fact, the logical-reasoning abilities of 15-year-olds are comparable to those of adults, adolescents are no worse than adults at perceiving risk or estimating their vulnerability to it . . ., and increasing the salience of the risks associated with making a potentially dangerous decision has comparable effects on adolescents and adults. . . . Most studies find few age differences in individuals' evaluations of the risks inherent in a wide range of dangerous behaviors, in judgments about the seriousness of the consequences that might result from risky behavior, or in the ways that the relative costs and benefits of risky activities are evaluated. . . .

Because adolescents and adults reason about risk in similar ways, many researchers have posited that age differences in actual risk taking are due to differences in the information that adolescents and adults use when making decisions. Attempts to reduce adolescent risk taking through interventions designed to alter knowledge, attitudes, or beliefs have proven remarkably disappointing, however. . . . Efforts to provide adolescents with information about the risks of substance use, reckless driving, and unprotected sex typically result in improvements in young people's thinking about these phenomena but seldom change their actual behavior. Generally speaking, reductions in adolescents' health-compromising behavior are more strongly linked to changes in

From *Current Directions in Psychological Science,* April 2007, pp. 55–59. Copyright © 2007 by the Association for Psychological Science. Reprinted by permission of Wiley-Blackwell.

the contexts in which those risks are taken (e.g., increases in the price of ciga-rettes, enforcement of graduated licensing programs, more vigorously imple-mented policies to interdict drugs, or condom distribution programs) than to changes in what adolescents know or believe.

The failure to account for age differences in risk taking through studies of reasoning and knowledge stymied researchers for some time. Health educa-tors, however, have been undaunted, and they have continued to design and offer interventions of unproven effectiveness, such as Drug Abuse Resistance Education (DARE), driver's education, or abstinence-only sex education.

A New Perspective on Risk Taking

In recent years, owing to advances in the developmental neuroscience of adole-scence and the recognition that the conventional decision-making framework may not be the best way to think about adolescent risk taking, a new perspective on the subject has emerged. . . . This new view begins from the premise that risk taking in the real world is the product of both logical reasoning and psychoso-cial factors. However, unlike logical-reasoning abilities, which appear to be more or less fully developed by age 15, psychosocial capacities that improve decision making and moderate risk taking—such as impulse control, emotion regulation, delay of gratification, and resistance to peer influence—continue to mature well into young adulthood. . . . Accordingly, psychosocial immaturity in these respects during adolescence may undermine what otherwise might be competent deci-sion making. The conclusion drawn by many researchers, that adolescents are as competent decision makers as adults are, may hold true only under conditions where the influence of psychosocial factors is minimized.

Evidence from Developmental Neuroscience

Advances in developmental neuroscience provide support for this new way of thinking about adolescent decision making. It appears that heightened risk tak-ing in adolescence is the product of the interaction between two brain networks. The first is a socioemotional network that is especially sensitive to social and emotional stimuli, that is particularly important for reward processing, and that is remodeled in early adolescence by the hormonal changes of puberty. It is local-ized in limbic and paralimbic areas of the brain, an interior region that includes the amygdala, ventral striatum, orbitofrontal cortex, medial pre-frontal cortex, and superior temporal sulcus. The second network is a cognitive-control network that subserves executive functions such as planning, thinking ahead, and self-regulation, and that matures gradually over the course of adolescence and young adulthood largely independently of puberty. . . . The cognitive-control network mainly consists of outer regions of the brain, including the lateral prefrontal and parietal cortices and those parts of the anterior cingulate cortex to which they are connected.

In many respects, risk taking is the product of a competition between the socioemotional and cognitive-control networks . . . , and adolescence is a period in which the former abruptly becomes more assertive (i.e., at puberty) while the latter gains strength only gradually, over a longer period of time. The socioemotional network is not in a state of constantly high activation during adolescence, though. Indeed, when the socioemotional network is not highly activated (for example, when individuals are not emotionally excited or are alone), the cognitive-control network is strong enough to impose regulatory control over impulsive and risky behavior, even in early adolescence. In the presence of peers or under conditions of emotional arousal, however, the socioemotional network becomes sufficiently activated to diminish the regulatory effectiveness of the cognitive-control network. Over the course of adolescence, the cognitive-control network matures, so that by adulthood, even under conditions of heightened arousal in the socioemotional network, inclinations toward risk taking can be modulated.

It is important to note that mechanisms underlying the processing of emotional information, social information, and reward are closely interconnected. Among adolescents, the regions that are activated during exposure to social and emotional stimuli overlap considerably with regions also shown to be sensitive to variations in reward magnitude. . . . This finding may be relevant to understanding why so much adolescent risk taking—like drinking, reckless driving, or delinquency—occurs in groups. . . . Risk taking may be heightened in adolescence because teenagers spend so much time with their peers, and the mere presence of peers makes the rewarding aspects of risky situations more salient by activating the same circuitry that is activated by exposure to nonsocial rewards when individuals are alone.

The competitive interaction between the socioemotional and cognitive-control networks has been implicated in a wide range of decision-making contexts, including drug use, social-decision processing, moral judgments, and the valuation of alternative rewards/costs. . . . In all of these contexts, risk taking is associated with relatively greater activation of the socioemotional network. For example, individuals' preference for smaller immediate rewards over larger delayed rewards is associated with relatively increased activation of the ventral striatum, orbitofrontal cortex, and medial prefrontal cortex—all regions linked to the socioemotional network—presumably because immediate rewards are especially emotionally arousing (consider the difference between how you might feel if a crisp $100 bill were held in front of you versus being told that you will receive $150 in 2 months). In contrast, regions implicated in cognitive control are engaged equivalently across decision conditions. . . . Similarly, studies show that increased activity in regions of the socioemotional network is associated with the selection of comparatively risky (but potentially highly rewarding) choices over more conservative ones. . . .

Evidence from Behavioral Science

Three lines of behavioral evidence are consistent with this account. First, studies of susceptibility to antisocial peer influence show that vulnerability to peer pressure increases between preadolescence and mid-adolescence, peaks in mid-adolescence—presumably when the imbalance between the sensitivity to socioemotional arousal (which has increased at puberty) and capacity for cognitive control (which is still immature) is greatest—and gradually declines thereafter. . . . Second, as noted earlier, studies of decision making generally show no age differences in risk processing between older adolescents and adults when decision making is assessed under conditions likely associated with relatively lower activation of brain systems responsible for emotion, reward, and social processing (e.g., the presentation of hypothetical decision-making dilemmas to individuals tested alone under conditions of low emotional arousal. . . . Third, the presence of peers increases risk taking substantially among teenagers, moderately among college-age individuals, and not at all among adults, consistent with the notion that the development of the cognitive-control network is gradual and extends beyond the teen years. In one of our lab's studies, for instance, the presence of peers more than doubled the number of risks teenagers took in a video driving game and increased risk taking by 50% among college undergraduates but had no effect at all among adults. . . . In adolescence, then, not only is more merrier—it is also riskier.

What Changes During Adolescence?

Studies of rodents indicate an especially significant increase in reward salience (i.e., how much attention individuals pay to the magnitude of potential rewards) around the time of puberty . . ., consistent with human studies showing that increases in sensation seeking occur relatively early in adolescence and are correlated with pubertal maturation but not chronological age. . . . Given behavioral findings indicating relatively greater reward salience among adolescents than adults in decision-making tasks, there is reason to speculate that, when presented with risky situations that have both potential rewards and potential costs, adolescents may be more sensitive than adults to variation in rewards but comparably sensitive (or perhaps even less sensitive) to variation in costs. . . .

It thus appears that the brain system that regulates the processing of rewards, social information, and emotions is becoming more sensitive and more easily aroused around the time of puberty. What about its sibling, the cognitive-control system? Regions making up the cognitive-control network, especially prefrontal regions, continue to exhibit gradual changes in structure and function during adolescence and early adulthood. . . . Much publicity has been given to the finding that synaptic pruning (the selective elimination of seldom-used synapses) and myelination (the development of the fatty sheaths that "insulate" neuronal circuitry)—both of which increase the efficiency of information processing—continue to occur in the prefrontal cortex well into the early 20s. But frontal regions also become more integrated with other brain regions during adolescence and early adulthood, leading to gradual improvements in many aspects of cognitive control such as response inhibition; this integration may be an even more important change than changes within the frontal region itself. Imaging studies using tasks in which individuals are asked to inhibit a "prepotent" response–like trying to look away from, rather than toward, a point of light—have shown that adolescents tend to recruit the cognitive-control network less broadly than do adults, perhaps overtaxing the capacity of the more limited number of regions they activate. . . .

In essence, one of the reasons the cognitive-control system of adults is more effective than that of adolescents is that adults' brains distribute its regulatory responsibilities across a wider network of linked components. This lack of cross-talk across brain regions in adolescence results not only in individuals acting on gut feelings without fully thinking (the stereotypic portrayal of teenagers) but also in thinking too much when gut feelings ought to be attended to (which teenagers also do from time to time). In one recent study, when asked whether some obviously dangerous activities (e.g., setting one's hair on fire) were "good ideas," adolescents took significantly longer than adults to respond to the questions and activated a less narrowly distributed set of cognitive-control regions. . . . This was not the case when the queried activities were not dangerous ones, however (e.g., eating salad).

The fact that maturation of the socioemotional network appears to be driven by puberty, whereas the maturation of the cognitive-control network does not, raises interesting questions about the impact—at the individual and at the societal levels—of early pubertal maturation on risk taking. We know that there is wide variability among individuals in the timing of puberty, due to both genetic and environmental factors. We also know that there has been a significant drop in the age of pubertal maturation over the past 200 years. To the extent that the temporal disjunction between the maturation of the socioemotional system and that of the cognitive-control system contributes to adolescent risk taking, we would expect to see higher rates of risk taking among early maturers and a drop over time in the age of initial experimentation with risky behaviors such as sexual intercourse or drug use. There is evidence for both of these patterns. . . .

Implications for Prevention

What does this mean for the prevention of unhealthy risk taking in adolescence? Given extant research suggesting that it is not the way adolescents think or what they don't know or understand that is the problem, a more profitable strategy than attempting to change how adolescents view risky activities might be to focus on limiting opportunities for immature judgment to have harmful consequences. More than 90% of all American high-school students have had sex, drug, and driver education in their schools, yet large proportions of them still have unsafe sex, binge drink, smoke cigarettes, and drive recklessly (often more than one of these at the same time . . .). Strategies such as raising the price of cigarettes, more vigilantly enforcing laws governing the sale of alcohol, expanding adolescents' access to mental-health and contraceptive services, and raising the driving age would likely be more effective in limiting adolescent smoking, substance abuse, pregnancy, and automobile fatalities than strategies aimed at making adolescents wiser, less impulsive, or less shortsighted. Some things just take time to develop, and, like it or not, mature judgment is probably one of them.

The research reviewed here suggests that heightened risk taking during adolescence is likely to be normative, biologically driven, and, to some extent, inevitable. There is probably very little that can or ought to be done to either attenuate or delay the shift in reward sensitivity that takes place at puberty. It may be possible to accelerate the maturation of self-regulatory competence, but no research has examined whether this is possible. In light of studies showing familial influences on psychosocial maturity in adolescence, understanding how contextual factors influence the development of self-regulation and knowing the neural underpinnings of these processes should be a high priority for those interested in the well-being of young people.

Michael Males  **NO**

Does the Adolescent Brain Make Risk Taking Inevitable?: A Skeptical Appraisal

...**I**f grown-ups are paragons of mature restraint, our discussion of teenagers and the "teenage brain" must be an exception. A survey of stories in the popular press on the teenage brain and risk taking found reporters and commentators, including experts, lambasting teens as "reckless," "stupid," "irrational," "callous," "lazy," "violent;" even "alien". . . . Psychologist Michael Bradley's . . . *Yes! Your Teen Is Crazy!* brands teens "stupid," "crazy," and "brain damaged" on virtually every page, wildly exaggerates the tolls of teens killed by guns (by 200%) and drunken driving (by 600% . . .), and still wins endorsement from psychologist Jay Giedd of the august National Institutes of Health. University of California public health professors Martha Campbell and Malcolm Potts . . . blame global violence on young men's aggressive natures, as if political and military leaders played no part. The March 2008 *Developmental Review*'s special issue contains eight articles on "risk and decision making;" six of these entirely concern adolescents and the remaining two mostly so, and all adopt the framework of developmental theory. . . . The National Research Council . . . held a forum on the "emerging . . . science of adolescence" led by physician Ronald Dahl warning of "the tinderbox of the teenage brain."

Adolescence, this new science holds . . . is a mélange of biohazard, a frightening mistake of nature. Temple University psychologist Laurence Steinberg . . . declares, "Heightened risk taking during adolescence is likely to be normative, biologically driven, and, to some extent, inevitable." . . . The age range designated as biologically inferior is expanding rapidly. From minimum-subject experiments maximally interpreted, Steinberg . . . has suggested no one less than the age of 25 years should be allowed to drive, Giedd . . . has questioned the rights of persons under that age to drive or vote, and Harvard School of Public Health assistant professor Deborah Yurgelun-Todd suggests even older teens should not be allowed to hold licenses or employment in such areas as lifeguard or military service. . . . Lobbies across the spectrum find the idea of biodetermined teenage incompetence useful to promote varied agendas, including imposing sweeping curfews on young people, requiring parental consent for adolescents' abortions, abolishing the death penalty for juveniles, and soliciting funding for youth management industries.

From *Journal of Adolescent Research*, January 2009, pp. 3–20 excerpted. Copyright © 2009 by Sage Publications. Reprinted by permission via Rightslink.

This article will argue that this new biodeterminist "science of adolescence" . . . now cascading through American media and political forums incorporates major violations of scholarly ethics, research fundamentals, critical scientific debate, and the right of young people to objective and accurate treatment. A future Stephen Jay Gould applying a science historian's skepticism is likely to find ample reason for alarm in the way brain research has proven "vulnerable to over-simplification, over-interpretation, and the confirmation of prior prejudices." . . .

Is "Adolescent Risk Taking" Scientifically Founded?

Claims about the "teenage brain" depend on the theory of "adolescent risk taking:" that "adolescents, on average, engage in more reckless behavior than do individuals of other ages." . . . If adolescent behaviors are not generally riskier than those of adults when relevant factors are controlled, then interpreting teenage biologies as provoking riskier behavior would be a torturous exercise indeed.

"If kids are as smart as adults, why do they do such dumb things?" Steinberg asks . . . , presaging a biodeterminist explanation:

> The temporal gap between puberty, which impels adolescents toward thrill seeking, and the slow maturation of the cognitive control system, which regulates these impulses, makes adolescence a time of heightened vulnerability for risky behavior . . . Risk taking is the product of a competition between the socio-emotional and cognitive control networks . . . and adolescence is a period in which the former abruptly becomes more assertive at puberty while latter gains strength only gradually, over a longer period of time. . . .

Theorists then link risk-prone teenage brain biology to enhanced social hazard:

> Studies of susceptibility to antisocial peer influence show that vulnerability to peer pressure increases between preadolescence and mid-adolescence, peaks in mid-adolescence, presumably when the imbalance between the sensitivity to socio-emotional arousal (which has increased at puberty) and capacity for cognitive control (which is still immature) is greatest, and gradually declines thereafter." . . .

However, the biodeterminist views presented by Steinberg . . . and others as scientific consensus are disputed. Eminent researchers caution that we know too little about brain biology to make sweeping claims, Asked, "How much do we know about the relationship between the anatomy or biology of the brain and behavior?" Kurt W. Fischer, Professor of Education and Human Development and director of the Mind, Brain, & Education Program at the Harvard Graduate School of Education replied,

We do not know very much! . . . Most of the recent advances in brain science have involved knowledge of the biology of single neurons and synapses, not knowledge of patterns of connection and other aspects of the brain as a system . . . but we have a very long way to go . . . People naturally want to use brain science to inform policy and practice, but our limited knowledge of the brain places extreme limits on that effort. . . .

Daniel Siegel of the University of California, Los Angeles's (UCLA) School of Medicine, coinvestigator at UCLA's Center for Culture, Brain, and Development, and director of the Center for Human Development, agreed: "We are just beginning to identify how systems in the brain work together in an integrated fashion to create complex mental processes." . . . Richard Lerner, director of Tufts University's Institute for Applied Research in Youth Development, likewise points out that brain research is "in its infancy" and "it's way too premature to make those specific links" between biology and behavior. . . .

In addition to being premature, biological risk theories fail fundamental tests. What objective evidence shows that "adolescent risk taking" exists at all? What, in fact, is an "adolescent"?

Here arises the first major contradiction: True "adolescents" whose puberty-impelled risk taking would be highest and cognitive control systems the least developed according to biodeterminist theory, do not display inordinately high risks. Puberty now occurs from around the age of 10 to 13 years for girls and 12 to 15 years for boys. Thus, developmental, cognitive, and social influences should combine to render "mid-adolescence a time of heightened vulnerability to risky and reckless behavior." . . . Second, modern "teenagers spend so much time with their peers." . . . If the theory of greater thrill seeking driven by immature cognitive control, more peer association, and increasing independence from adults is correct, we would expect that adolescents would account for an increasing share of society's risks.

However, few of the results we would expect from this "adolescent risk" theory turn out to be true either in cross section or longitudinally. Modern, presumably peer-socialized adolescents are not acting riskier than their parent-socialized counterparts of the past; the highest rates for most teenage ills occurred 30 to 40 years ago. Today, the parent generation seems more at risk. The latest statistics for rates of violent death—those from accidents, suicides, homicides, and those of undetermined intent—reveal that teens aged 15 to 19 years (49.7 deaths per 100,000 population in 2005) have lower rates than every adult age group. The worst rates are for ages 20 to 24 years (73.8 deaths per 100,000 population), followed closely by what had been assumed the safest grown-up ages: 45 to 49 years (70.1), 40 to 44 years (67.6), and 50 to 54 years (65.0). . . . For unintentional deaths (accidents) thought to be the scourge of reckless youth, age 45 to 49 years (44.6 deaths per 100,000 population) is the worst, followed by age 20 to 24, 50 to 54, and 40 to 44 years; age range 15 to 19 years (31.4) is safer than every adult age group. Even for the risk for which teenagers show the most excessive rate, motor vehicle fatality, travel survey, and accident reports show a 16-year-old would have to drive from Boston to Los Angeles and back 1,000 times to run even odds of being in a fatal traffic crash. . . .

More than 99.5% of all 16-year-olds live to be 17—a higher annual survival rate than for any single year of adult age to the next even if only violent deaths are considered. Indeed, the safest ages from accidental death for ages from 16 to 64 years are 16, followed by 17, and 35; middle-age now is riskier even than age 18. Yet authorities have failed to mention these trends and continue to insist that "statistics" prove adolescence is the time of greatest risk. . . .

That there are very few areas in which even the riskiest adolescent ages, 16 and 17 years, suffer the worst risk outcomes clearly is not due to adults' effective control. Such large majorities of high schoolers report alcohol, cigarettes, firearms, sex, and other risk enhancers are easy to obtain and/or frequently indulged that those who abstain must be doing so voluntarily. If self-reports such as Monitoring the Future's . . . indicating adolescents experience widespread opportunities to take risks are creditable, then, it's hard to attribute the day-to-day safety of the overwhelming majority of teenagers to anything other than self-restraint. The argument that legal protections and supervision shield adolescents from the opportunities to engage in risky behaviors does not explain why, as noted later, teenagers do commit crimes and get in car wrecks at higher rates than adults do but experience lower rates of other risks.

Because adolescents of the ages that developmentalists and biodeterminists predict would be suffering the highest risks actually display relatively safe behavior, theorists have extended the definition of "adolescence" into the 18 to 25 age range when, paradoxically, risk outcomes are worse even though puberty is long past and cognitive controls more advanced. Indeed, Giedd . . . has questioned the rights of young people to vote before the age of 25 years and both Giedd and Steinberg . . . have questioned the rights of young people to drive before that age, though neither has produced research findings justifying such radical assertions. In any case, the peculiar reality is that "adolescent risk taking" now is driven by emerging adults, not adolescents. Adding in statistics of age group 18 to 25 years or 20 to 24 years to artificially boost adolescent and teenage risk numbers should no longer be tolerated in the literature.

What Behaviors Define "Risk Taking?"

Beyond the extension of adolescence well into adulthood, the second troubling question involves why only certain risk behaviors, and only when adolescents engage in them, are considered evidence for biodeterminist theories. If the prevalence of certain risk behaviors demonstrates teenagers' developmental and/or cognitive immaturity, then how do we explain the similar or greater prevalence of these same or equally perilous behaviors in adult populations? For example, teenagers display lower risks than do adults for outcomes such as suicide, drug overdose, and accidents in general. . . . Why not use these measures as indexes of "risk taking?" We might then term teenagers' relative safety *adolescent prudence* and credit the cautionary influence of the amygdala.

Even when assessing the same behavior, characterizations of teenage and adult risks often seem inconsistent. For example, claims that teenagers' greater tendency than adults to commit crimes in groups demonstrates the developmental dangers of youthful peer associations become dubious when applied to similar variations by race. The National Crime Victimization Survey . . ., considered our best measure of crime, shows that victims report that around one fourth of the violent offenses perceived as involving offenders less than the age of 21 years were perpetrated by groups, triple the proportion for perceived older offenders. However, in addition to showing massive declines in group offending by teens in recent decades, the same survey shows an even larger proportion (one third) of violent offenses by perceived African American offenders of all ages involved groups. The most logical inference is that group offending is a feature not of age or race, but of conditions common to both Blacks and young people, such as high rates of poverty.

In a particularly strange assertion, Steinberg . . . argues that adolescents' low rates of suicide do not imply low risks; rather, the fact that "the rate of attempted suicide is higher among teenagers than adults" . . . means "adolescents take more risks; adults are merely more competent, so to speak—consistent with the brain science." . . . True, teens in the age group of 15 to 19 years perpetrate around 40 self-inflicted injuries requiring medical attention for every actual suicide, compared with a 10:1 ratio for adults aged from 25 to 64 years. . . . But the NCIPC also reports 33 suicide "attempts" per completion for women of all ages versus 6 for men. If we accept Steinberg's logic that greater success in committing suicide reflects greater cognitive competence, then male brains are far more competent at every age than females'; teenage boys are more competent than women in their 30s and 40s; Whites' brains are more competent than those of Blacks; and Black females of all ages (averaging over 60 attempts for every suicide) are the least biologically competent of all. Alternatively, we could look at "suicide attempts" not as evidence of cognitive incompetence but as stemming from motives other than to die, as research on survivors finds. . . .

Similarly, a small study (widely cited in media stories) reported that adolescents perceived a wider variety of emotions in pictured "fearful faces" than adults did, yielding researchers' assertion that teenagers' reliance on the brain's "primitive" amygdala leads them to misjudge basic social cues such as fear. . . . However, similar picture-image studies have found that economically disadvantaged subjects also are more prone to interpret facial expressions as communicating aggressiveness . . ., suggesting that reactions to facial expressions stem more from differing social environments than differing brains. Likewise, video-game simulation experiments supposedly showing that teenagers react in more reckless, peer-pressured, unempathic, lazy, or otherwise objectionable ways compared with adults . . . may "have nothing to do with the process of emotions and everything to do with a difference in the way teenagers process *simulations*" stemming from "generational differences in the experience teenagers and adults have" with visual media. . . . Notably, even large racial differences in risk taking found in these studies . . . are not similarly attributed to brain differences.

Still another contradiction involves positing teenage behavior as "risky" if it fails to meet absolute standards of perfection.

More than 90% of all American high school students have had sex, drug, and driver education in their schools, yet large proportions of them still have unsafe sex, binge drink, smoke cigarettes, and drive recklessly (some all at the same time). . . .

Antidrunken driving, antidrug, safe sex, and similar messages have also been directed at grown-ups, yet tens of millions of adults engage in risky behaviors now extending well into middle age. It seems peculiar to brand "incompetent" adolescents as reckless for failing to meet standards stricter than those expected of "competent" grown-ups.

Ignoring Socioeconomic Context

Teenage brain and adolescent risk-taking theories seem to have been developed with a disregard for alternative explanations. "Brain research needs to be pulled alongside other established cognitive and sociological research, rather than common prejudice," Sercombe . . . contends. Risk outcomes must be assessed not as absolutes but in the context of risk exposure—that is, the social factors governing teens' and adults' risk opportunities. Yet when behavior contexts are incorporated into the analysis, the entire "adolescent risk taking" construct becomes shaky indeed. Researchers who assert unique adolescent risk, whether blaming it on biology, peer pressure, developmental singularities, or some combination have failed to control even for the most rudimentary socioeconomic conditions.

Let us examine the two major behaviors cited by Steinberg and widely considered gold standards of adolescent risk: crime and automobile crashes. Compared straight across, older adolescents and emerging adults aged from 16 and 19 years do indeed display worse rates than do older adults for these behaviors. But even if we accept criminal arrest and traffic crashes as seminal indexes of risk, how do we know older adolescents' worse outcomes result from their teen age and not some other covariate? After all, males, African Americans, and urban dwellers of all ages display high arrest rates and males, Southerners, and Native Americans suffer excess traffic fatality, yet very few scientists (any longer) blame these on inferior biologies. Compelling warning signs loom that teenagers' higher rates of criminal arrest and traffic accidents are not "adolescent" at all. Here, I will cite California's statistics, which are similar in magnitude and provided in greater demographic detail compared with those nationally.

If adolescents were generically miswired, we would expect teenagers from varied backgrounds to act more like each other and less like adults—in mathematical terms, the within-group risk variation for separate adolescent populations should be significantly less than the between-group risk variations for adolescent versus adult populations. Yet the opposite is the case. At the microlevel, teenagers from unstable, violent, drug- and alcohol-abusing, tobacco-using, mentally troubled families and communities are many times more likely to display corresponding problems than teenagers from nurturing, peaceful, healthy, nonsmoking homes, and communities. . . .

These parallels also show up in macrostatistics. The state-by-state correlations between teenage and adult rates of drinking, binge drinking, smoking, marijuana use, unwed births, drunken-driving deaths, firearms deaths, homicide, suicide, criminal arrest, and a host of other major risks are powerful, ranging from 0.70 to 0.95. . . . If teenage and adult brains reason so fundamentally differently, we would not expect teenage behaviors to be better predicted by the behaviors of adults around them than by those of teenagers elsewhere.

If there is a consensus of literature and statistics, it is that teenage troubles are not randomly distributed, but highly concentrated. Most serious risks track socioeconomic inequalities more closely than age. For example,

- California's Black adolescents suffer felony arrest rates five times higher, including murder arrest rates 14 times higher, than do White non-Hispanic adolescents. The felony arrest rate for older African Americans (ages 30 to 69 years) is double that of older White teens, including homicide arrest rates four times higher. . . .
- Firearms homicide death rates are 25 times higher among California teens in areas in which adolescent poverty rates exceed 30% than among teenagers in areas in which their poverty levels are below 5%. African Americans in their 50s and 60s suffer gun murder rates five times higher than even the riskiest ages of White teens and emerging adults, while White teens have lower firearms mortality rates than every age group of White adults. . . .
- Teen drivers aged between 16 to 19 years in California's poorest major counties suffer fatal traffic crash rates averaging six times higher per mile driven (the best measure of risk exposure) than teens in the richest counties. Middle-aged adults in poorer counties suffer fatal crash rates averaging three times higher per mile driven than do teenagers in wealthier counties. . . .

Such wide variations in behavior within all ages along socioeconomic lines should raise a red flag to those asserting unique adolescent risk. . . .

Socioeconomic status predicts risk outcome more consistently than age. When poverty rates are held constant for California's major counties, adolescents and emerging adults even at the riskiest ages generally are less prone to risk taking than are middle-aged adults, with adults aged from 25 and 39 years, in between. For many serious risks—including, murder, rape, and assault arrest; homicide and motor vehicle death; and external injury—adolescents' and middle-aged adults' rates become startlingly similar under equalized levels of poverty. Some adolescent and emerging adult excesses do remain; robbery arrest, property crime arrest, and firearms injury (but not death) rates remain higher for older adolescents than for middle-agers. However, these teenage risks are dwarfed by middle-agers' much higher rates of risk outcome across a broad spectrum: violent death, accidental death, suicide, drug overdose, and firearms death as well as white-collar crimes that cost society far more than street crime. If "the cognitive control system of adults is more effective than that of adolescents" and "some things just take time to develop, and, like it or not, mature judgment is probably one of them" . . . , why do adults do such dumb things?

The best generalization seems to be that most risks are tied to external conditions, and each age level displays its own particular hazards. In short, "adolescent risk" disappears on a level playing field. Unfortunately, the field is far from level. More than any other Western society, American grown-ups render youth a time of poverty and middle age a time of wealth, a political choice exposing our young to greater dangers. This suggests that claims of innate "adolescent risk" and "teenage brain" flaws not only reflect "a bias in interpretation that privileges the age, class, and culture position of the researcher" . . . but serve to defend older age groups' economic privileges as well.

The Danger of New "Adolescent Science"

Theories affirming innate adolescent risk-taking benefit adults in many ways. "By emphasizing the irrationality and disturbance of young people we affirm our own basic rationality, peacefulness, conformity, and decency." . . . Biodeterminist claims about adolescents shift attention away from social inequalities that form the genuine bases for the risky behaviors now mislabeled "adolescent risk," including the large and widening gap between the economic fortunes of young versus middle-aged Americans. They allow the dismissal of unsettling youthful complaints against adults as merely the products of faulty teenage thinking. . . . They obscure the troubling eruptions in drug abuse, criminal arrest, imprisonment, HIV, family breakup, and related difficulties among middle-aged Americans over the last 25 to 35 years.

Ever-more restrictive policies against young people are being proposed and rationalized by claims that "new scientific discoveries" show teenagers and even emerging adults must be custodialized like children rather than afforded adult rights. The United States has instituted an unprecedented barrage of youth-control measures that are increasing in prevalence and intensity even as long-term research finds them ineffective or even harmful. Raising drinking ages to 21 years was initially associated with reduced traffic crashes among 18- to 20-year-olds, but later study associated it with even greater increases among 21- to 24-year-olds. . . . Graduated driver licensing laws were followed by fewer traffic deaths among 16-year-olds, but 18-year-old driver fatalities rose even more sharply. . . . Mandatory drug testing of public school students not only has proven ineffective, it may foster greater use of harder, less detectible drugs. . . . Research consistently finds curfews neither improve youth safety nor reduce crime. . . . School uniforms and zero tolerance policies are associated with negative effects on school participation and academics and no demonstrable benefits. . . . Policies banning teenagers and emerging adults from legally acquiring lodging, transportation, and an increasing array of products, services, and medications pose distinct threats to their well-being.

Far from justifying antiprecocity measures, emerging brain science, viewed in social contexts, indicates the dangers of efforts to restrict youth and to banish them from adult behaviors and public spaces. Preliminary analyses of brain physiology suggest that "taking risks is precisely the experience that develops the prefrontal cortex . . . you don't learn what you need for adulthood by being excluded from it until you can demonstrate that you have got the right circuits." . . . Viewed as a system, American social and health policies built on age-segregating measures may well be contributors to the extraordinarily high-risk behaviors prevailing among American youths and adults well into middle age compared with their counterparts in peer nations.

There may be a price to pay in the adaptability of larger society as well. If brain science is to be credited with biodeterminist findings, neuroscannings and cognitive tests reveal developments in the middle-aged brain that make worry over teenage brains look silly. Significant losses in key memory and learning genes . . ., mental fluidity . . ., and measurable losses in IQ show up in middle age and accelerate in senior years. Although some research indicates that myelinization (the pruning and selection of certain cerebral nerve fibers for myelin sheathing) aids adult brains in handling familiar situations more efficiently, it also renders them less able to address new challenges than more flexibly circuited younger brains. Adults' difficulty in changing unhealthy behaviors as they age could be seen as a brain-based developmental stage promoting greater risk taking.

That young people's "brains are different because the experience of young people is different" than that of older adults . . . confers distinct advantages in a changing, diversifying society. In the face of aging, adults "managing clumsily and often unsuccessfully the tasks imposed on them by the new conditions" argued Mead . . ., changing societies must learn to share leadership with the more flexible young informed by "experiential knowledge." Unfortunately, both young people's well-being and the adaptive value to a changing society of integrating the diverse capacities of older and younger thinking are threatened by today's resurgence of biological determinism that, like its discredited predecessors, reveals more popular prejudice than scientific rigor. . . .

CHALLENGE QUESTIONS

Does the Adolescent Brain Make Risk Taking Inevitable?

1. Is the debate about the adolescent brain just another version of the old debate about whether teens are at the mercy of "raging hormones?"
2. Steinberg focuses on age differences in risk taking, where Males focuses on socioeconomic differences; what are the relative advantages for understanding development of each approach?
3. Males argues that claims of adolescent risk taking are exaggerated because many researchers include young adults in their calculations. How do the teenage years seem meaningfully different from young adulthood in regard to risk taking, and is that enough to explain this controversy?
4. What qualifies as "risk taking" in adolescence? Why does Males think researchers often manipulate categories of risk to suggest adolescents take more risks?
5. Both authors discuss the public policy implications of their perspectives; what are the important public policies that might change depending on how we come to understand adolescent risk taking?

Is There Common Ground?

Brain-based research is extremely popular in most areas of contemporary developmental science, and that research has advanced quickly amidst technological improvements. Both authors in the YES and NO selections recognize that interpreting this brain science is a key skill for those interested in adolescent development. For Laurence Steinberg, however, those interpretations offer practical suggestions about mitigating risk. For Michael Males, in contrast, those interpretations themselves pose a risk in distracting us from broader social issues around adolescence as a stage. In some ways, then, this issue becomes a matter of different levels of analysis. At the microlevel of neuronal activity in the brain, risk taking looks very different from the macro level of societal inequalities. Though these two authors clearly disagree, the prominence of brain-based research makes it important to think about ways those different levels of analysis might become complementary rather than contentious.

Suggested Readings

J. Bessant, "Hard Wired for Risk: Neurological Science, 'the Adolescent Brain' and Developmental Theory," *Journal of Youth Studies* (June 2008)

R. Epstein, "The Myth of the Teen Brain," *Scientific American Mind* (April 2007)

J.N. Giedd, "The Teen Brain: Insights from Neuroimaging," *Journal of Adolescent Health*, (April 2008)

D. Yurgelun-Todd, "Emotional and Cognitive Changes during Adolescence," *Current Opinion in Neurobiology* (April 2007)

M. Payne, "'Teen Brain' Science and the Contemporary Storying of Psychological (Im)maturity," *inter-disiplinary.net* (July 2009)

D. Offer and K.A. Schonert-Reichl, "Debunking the Myths of Adolescence: Findings from Recent Research," *Journal of the American Academy of Child and Adolescent Psychiatry* (November 1992)

L Steinberg, "A Social Neuroscience Perspective on Adolescent Risk Taking," *Developmental Review* (March 2008)

M. Gardner and L. Steinberg, "Peer influence on risk taking, risk preference, and risky decision making in adolescence and adulthood: An experimental study," *Developmental Psychology* (July 2005)

R. Restak, *The secret life of the brain* (Joseph Henry 2001)

J.J. Arnett, "Adolescent storm and stress, reconsidered," *American Psychologist* (May 1999)

Internet References . . .

The Forum for Youth Investment

The Forum for Youth Investment uses research to promote the idea that all young people should be "Ready by 21" and offers a variety of related information on their Web site.

http://www.forumforyouthinvestment.org/

The Network on Transitions to Adulthood

The Network on Transitions to Adulthood is a scholarly effort sponsored by the MacArthur Foundation and offers data and resources at their Web site.

http://www.transad.pop.upenn.edu/

The Narcissism Epidemic

The Web site for the book *The Narcissism Epidemic* by Jean Twenge and W. Keith Campbell offers information about related research.

http://www.narcissismepidemic.com/

The Narcissism Epidemic

The Web site for the book *The Narcissism Epidemic* by Jean Twenge and W. Keith Campbell offers information about related research.

http://www.narcissismepidemic.com/

Jeffrey Arnett on Emerging Adulthood

A list of useful references related to "emerging adulthood" by the originator of the concept, Jeffrey Jensen Arnett.

http://www.jeffreyarnett.com/articles.htm

The Society for the Study of Emerging Adulthood

This Web site is the home for a relatively new scholarly group named the Society for the Study of Emerging Adulthood.

http://www.ssea.org/

Emerging Adulthood Blog

An academic's blog about emerging adulthood as a life-span stage between adolescence and adulthood.

http://emergingadulthood.blogspot.com/

The Social Science Research Council

The Social Science Research Council Web site has extensive information from a 2007 Forum on the Religious Engagement of American Undergraduates.

http://religion.ssrc.org/reforum/

Youth and Emerging Adulthood

*A*lthough we often talk about "youth" in everyday conversation, it is an ill-defined concept as a stage of the lifespan. Generally, "youth" refers to a period when a person is developing the characteristics of adulthood but does not yet have adult responsibilities (such as a career and marriage) nor the full psychological sense of responsibility. In many contemporary societies, this period of life seems longer and more intense because of increasing educational expectations, later average ages for starting a family, and more time allocated to self-exploration. Thus, youth and emerging adulthood are primarily times where people gradually make the transition to fully adult roles. That transition involves both psychological and practical challenges, several of which are dealt with in the issues covered in this section.

- Is There Such a Thing as "Emerging Adulthood"?

- Is There a "Narcissism Epidemic" Among Contemporary Young Adults?

- Are Today's College Students Interested in Engaging with Religion and Spirituality?

ISSUE 12

Is There Such a Thing as "Emerging Adulthood"?

YES: **Jeffrey Jensen Arnett**, from "Emerging Adulthood: What Is It, and What Is It Good For?" *Child Development Perspectives* (December 2007)

NO: **Leo B. Hendry and Marion Kloep**, from "Conceptualizing Emerging Adulthood: Inspecting the Emperor's New Clothes," *Child Development Perspectives* (December 2007)

Learning Outcomes

As you read the issue, focus on the following points:

1. "Emerging adulthood" has quickly, and relatively recently, become a popular way to describe and understand the age period from the late teens through at least the mid-twenties.
2. Historical and cultural differences in the nature of the transition from childhood to adulthood make it challenging to generalize about discrete developmental stages, leading some to focus instead on gradual change throughout the lifespan.
3. Although the process of identity development has often been associated with adolescence and early adulthood, our identities are constantly evolving throughout the lifespan.
4. At least in most Western countries, the transition into full adult status does seem to have gotten longer, leading to new challenges for both individuals and societies.

ISSUE SUMMARY

YES: Developmental psychologist Jeffrey Jensen Arnett has earned wide acclaim among scholars for defining an "emerging adulthood" as a distinctly modern stage of the life-span.

NO: Life-span research scholars Lew B. Hendry and Marion Kloep argue that defining emerging adulthood as a discrete stage provides a misleading account of the age period between the late teens and the mid- to late twenties.

Is there something different about today's young adults? Although this is a perennial question in many social and historical settings, psychologist Jeffrey Jensen Arnett thinks that the characteristics of the age period from the late teens through the mid- to late twenties in contemporary society are so distinct that they merit a new stage of life-span development. He calls this stage "emerging adulthood" and argues that it is qualitatively different from the transitional period that has long characterized life between adolescence and full adulthood. With increasing educational demands, later ages for marriage, and more instability in work, Arnett thinks that post-high school life is now a distinct time of exploration in work, relationships, and the self. Although exploring options related to work and relationships may be something of a necessary process during the transition to adulthood, the prominence of self-exploration during one's twenties has raised more serious questions and concerns.

Among those interested in the study of life-span development, perhaps the most interesting question is about what qualifies as a distinct stage in the life-span? Stage theories have a long history in the study of development, including famous examples posited by Sigmund Freud, Erik Erikson, and Jean Piaget. But while those theories offer useful shortcuts for identifying important characteristics of different ages, they also may create a false sense that development occurs in orderly steps. Is there really a clear point where adulthood begins? Although we often define people by broad stages of the life-span that correspond to chronological age, we also recognize that there is much individual variation and that social markers matter as much as biological age.

It was only around the turn of the twentieth century that the concept of "adolescence" as a transition period between childhood and adulthood came to be considered a distinct stage of the life-span. The need for the concept of adolescence, similar to Arnett's argument for emerging adulthood, depended on changing social conditions, including increased access to education and changing community responsibilities.

From Hendry and Kloep's perspective, however, the study of life-span development has progressed to the point where rather than adding "new" stages, it makes more sense to move away from stage theories entirely. They do acknowledge that stage theories have had some usefulness but, they note, many significant contemporary theories of development recognize that such change occurs in dynamic and nonlinear ways.

The question of stages is important to the study of life-span development at all ages. In thinking about development, how much attention should go to consistent patterns across broad groups of people, and how much attention should go to individual variations? Although the concept of "emerging adulthood" is relatively new, and worth understanding as product of a particular cultural and historical context, being able to evaluate the concept of life-span stages is central to understanding development at any time or age.

POINT

- "Emerging adulthood" has quickly become a popular way to describe and understand the age period from the late teens through at least the mid-twenties.

- Changes in the nature of the transition between adolescence and adulthood for people growing up in modern industrialized societies necessitates marking a new life stage.

- Emerging adulthood is not an entirely discrete stage, but it is an important transition period that overlaps with both adolescence and adulthood.

- Many of the life events that used to happen in adolescence, such as the "identity crisis," have been delayed due to more extensive educational expectations and later normative ages for marriage.

COUNTERPOINT

- It is inaccurate to claim development occurs toward a comprehensive stage of adulthood since rates of development are different across domains and are reversible.

- The process of identity development does not define one stage because it is ongoing throughout the life-span.

- Generalizing about emerging adulthood discounts variations between social and cultural groups.

- Promoting emerging adulthood as a stage may mean promoting an unhealthy prolongation of wayward exploration that has negative social implications.

YES

Jeffrey Jensen Arnett

Emerging Adulthood: What Is It, and What Is It Good For?

It is now 7 years since I first proposed the term *emerging adulthood* for the age period from the late teens through the mid- to late 20s (roughly ages 18–25) in an article in *American Psychologist*. . . . I had mentioned the term briefly in two previous articles . . ., but the 2000 article was the first time I presented an outline of the theory. It was not until 2004 that I proposed a full theory in a book on emerging adulthood. . . . In a short time, the theory has become widely used, not just in psychology but in many fields. At the recent Third Conference on Emerging Adulthood . . ., a remarkable range of disciplines was represented, including psychology, psychiatry, sociology, anthropology, education, epidemiology, health sciences, human development, geography, nursing, social work, philosophy, pediatrics, family studies, journalism, and law.

The swift spread of the term and the idea has surprised me because normally any new theoretical idea meets initial resistance from defenders of the reigning paradigm. Perhaps, the acceptance of emerging adulthood has been so swift because there really was no reigning paradigm. Instead, there was a widespread sense among scholars interested in this age period that previous ways of thinking about it no longer worked and there was a hunger for a new conceptualization. In any case, now that emerging adulthood has become established as a way of thinking about the age period from the late teens through at least the mid-20s, the theory is attracting commentary and critiques. . . . This is a normal and healthy part of the development of any new theory, and I welcome the exchange here with Leo Hendry and Marion Kloep.

The Configuration of Emerging Adulthood: How Does It Fit into the Life Course?

When I first proposed the theory of emerging adulthood . . . , one of my goals was to draw attention to the age period from the late teens through the mid-20s as a new period of the life course in industrialized societies, with distinctive developmental characteristics. The dominant theory of the life course in developmental psychology, first proposed by Erikson . . . postulated that adolescence, lasting from the beginning of puberty until the late teens, was

From *Child Development Perspectives*, Vol. 1, No. 2, 2007, pp. 68–72. Copyright © 2007 by Wiley-Blackwell. Reprinted by permission.

followed by young adulthood, lasting from the late teens to about age 40 when middle adulthood began. This paradigm may have made sense in the middle of the 20th century when most people in industrialized societies married and entered stable full-time work by around age 20 or shortly after. However, by the end of the century, this paradigm no longer fit the normative pattern in industrialized societies. Median ages of marriage had risen into the late 20s, and the early to mid-20s became a time of frequent job changes and, for many people, pursuit of postsecondary education or training. Furthermore, sexual mores had changed dramatically, and premarital sex and cohabitation in the 20s had become widely accepted. Most young people now spent the period from their late teens to their mid-20s not settling into long-term adult roles but trying out different experiences and gradually making their way toward enduring choices in love and work.

The theory of emerging adulthood was proposed as a framework for recognizing that the transition to adulthood was now long enough that it constituted not merely a transition but a separate period of the life course. I proposed five features that make emerging adulthood distinct: it is the *age of identity explorations,* the *age of instability,* the *self-focused age,* the *age of feeling in-between,* and *the age of possibilities.* . . . But I emphasized from the beginning that emerging adulthood is perhaps the most heterogeneous period of the life course because it is the least structured, and the five features were not proposed as universal features but as features that are more common during emerging adulthood than in other periods.

In this light, of the possible configurations A–D in Figure 1 of how emerging adulthood might fit into the adult life course, I would reject D

Figure 1

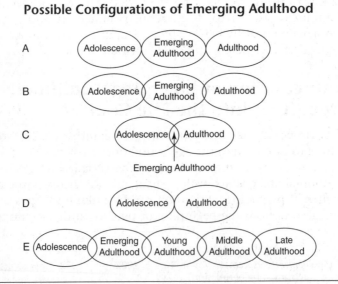

Possible Configurations of Emerging Adulthood

because it does not show a distinct period between adolescence and adult-hood. C does not work because it slights emerging adulthood, inaccurately portraying it as a brief transition between adolescence and adulthood. A is better, but it shows the transitions from adolescence to emerging adulthood and from emerging adulthood to young adulthood as more discrete than they actually are in some respects. It applies to transitions from adolescence to emerging adulthood such as finishing secondary school and reaching the legal age of adult status, and perhaps to transitions from emerging to young adulthood such as marriage. However, B works best in my view because the five features described above are entered and exited not discretely but gradually. Furthermore, of the three criteria found in many countries and cultures to be the most important markers of reaching adult status—accept-ing responsibility for oneself, making independent decisions, and becoming financially independent—all are attained gradually in the course of emerging adulthood. . . .

This gradual passage from one period to the next may apply not just to emerging adulthood but to the entire adult life course. Theorists have emphasized how in recent decades the life course in industrialized societies has become increasingly characterized by *individualization,* meaning that insti-tutional constraints and supports have become less powerful and important and people are increasingly left to their own resources in making their way from one part of the life course to the next, for better or worse. . . . Emerging adulthood is one part of this trend. So, in Figure 1, an improvement on B might be E, showing gradual transitions into and out of different periods throughout the adult life course.

Do We Really Need the Term *Emerging Adulthood*?

I believe the rapid spread of the term *emerging adulthood* reflects its useful-ness and the dissatisfaction of scholars in many fields with the previous terms that had been used. There were problems with each of those terms, including *late adolescence, young adulthood, the transition to adulthood,* and *youth.* . . . *Late adolescence* does not work because the lives of persons in their late teens and 20s are vastly different from the lives of most adoles-cents (roughly ages 10–17). Unlike adolescents, 18- to 25-year-olds are not going through puberty, are not in secondary school, are not legally defined as children or juveniles, and often have moved out of their parents' house-hold. *Young adulthood* does not work because it has been used already to refer to such diverse age periods, from preteens ("young adult" books) to age 40 ("young adult" social organizations). Furthermore, if 18–25 are "young adulthood," what are people who are 30, 35, or 40? It makes more sense to reserve "young adulthood" for the age period from about age 30 to about age 40 (or perhaps 45) because by age 30 most people in industrialized socie-ties have settled into the roles usually associated with adulthood: stable work, marriage or other long-term partnership, and parenthood.

The transition to adulthood has been widely used in sociology and in research focusing mostly on the timing and sequence of transition events such as leaving home, finishing education, marriage, and parenthood. Certainly, the years from the late teens through the 20s are when the transition to adulthood takes place for most people, not only as defined by transition events but also by a more subjective sense of having reached adulthood. . . . But why call this period merely a "transition" rather than a period of development in its own right? If we state, conservatively, that it lasts 7 years, from age 18 to 25, that makes it longer than infancy, longer than early or middle childhood, and as long as adolescence. Furthermore, calling it "the transition to adulthood" focuses attention on the transition events that take place mainly at the beginning or end of the age range, whereas calling it "emerging adulthood" broadens the scope of attention to the whole range of areas—cognitive development, family relationships, friendships, romantic relationships, media use, and so on—that apply to other developmental periods as well.

Finally, *youth* has been used as a term for this period, especially in Europe but also among some American psychologists and sociologists. However, *youth* suffers from the same problem as *young adulthood,* in that it has long been used to refer to a wide range of ages, from middle childhood ("youth organizations") through the 30s. Furthermore, in its American incarnation, it was promoted by Keniston . . . on the basis of his research with student protesters in the late 1960s, and his description of it as a time of rebellion against society bears the marks of his time but does not apply widely.

Emerging adulthood is preferable because it is a new term for a new phenomenon. Across industrialized societies in the past half century, common changes have taken place with respect to the lives of young people: longer and more widespread participation in postsecondary education and training, greater tolerance of premarital sex and cohabitation, and later ages of entering marriage and parenthood. As a consequence of these changes, a new period of the life course has developed between adolescence and young adulthood. Furthermore, *emerging adulthood* reflects the sense among many people in the late teens and early 20s worldwide that they are no longer adolescent but only partly adult, emerging into adulthood but not there yet. . . .

Some aspects of the theory of emerging adulthood are likely to be modified with further research, and the main features of emerging adulthood will no doubt vary among cultures. There are certainly psychosocial differences among emerging adults related to socioeconomic status and ethnic group, and cross-national differences have only begun to be explored. . . . But there is some degree of heterogeneity in every developmental period, and overarching terms and general descriptions for those periods are nevertheless useful for understanding them. . . .

Is Emerging Adulthood Experienced Positively or Negatively by Most People?

The fact that it takes longer to reach full adulthood today than it did in the past has been subject to various interpretations, mostly negative. In American popular media, the term "quarterlife crisis" has been coined to describe the alleged difficulties experienced by emerging adults as they try to find a place in the adult world. . . . Within academia, some sociologists have asserted that

Figure 2

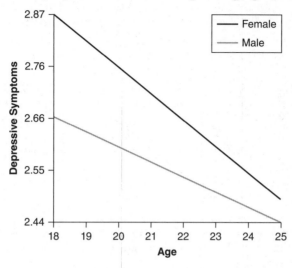

Depressive Symptoms Decline During Emerging Adulthood

Note. The sample was drawn from Grade 12 classes in six high schools in a western Canadian city, followed over the next 7 years. *N* = 920 at age 18 and 324 at age 25. The sample was diverse in socioeconomic status background; at Time 1, 10% were from families in which both parents had a university degree, and 16% had one parent with a university degree. Among the participants themselves, by age 25, 30% had a university degree, 14% had a college diploma, 24% had a technical degree, and the remaining 32% had no postsecondary educational credential. . . .

higher ages of marriage and parenthood indicate that "growing up is harder to do" than in the past.

Yet, the bulk of the evidence is contrary to these assertions. . . . Numerous studies show that for most, well-being improves during the course of emerging adulthood. An example is shown in Figures 2 and 3, which demonstrate a decline in depressive symptoms and a rise in self-esteem in a longitudinal Canadian study of emerging adults. . . . Similar results have been found in the longitudinal Monitoring the Future studies in the United States. . . . Emerging adults enjoy their self-focused freedom from role obligations and restraints, and they take satisfaction in their progress toward self-sufficiency. I think they also benefit from growing social cognitive maturity, which enables them to understand themselves and others better than they did as adolescents. . . .

Nevertheless, although I believe the notion of a "quarterlife crisis" is exaggerated, I do not dismiss it entirely. It is true that identity issues are prominent in emerging adulthood and that sorting through them and finding satisfying alternatives in love and work can generate anxiety. The idea of a "quarterlife crisis" can be seen as recognizing that the identity crisis Erikson . . . described over a half century ago as central to adolescence has now moved into emerging adulthood. It is also true that entry into the labor market is often stressful and frustrating, especially for emerging adults with limited educational credentials. . . . Furthermore, even among the most advantaged emerging

Figure 3

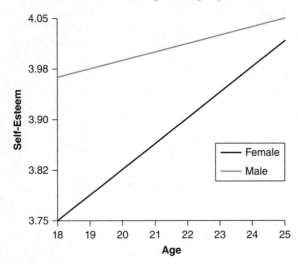

Self-Esteem Rises During Emerging Adulthood

Note. The sample was drawn from Grade 12 classes in six high schools in a western Canadian city, followed over the next 7 years. N = 920 at age 18 and 324 at age 25. The sample was diverse in socioeconomic status background; at Time 1, 10% were from families in which both parents had a university degree, and 16% had one parent with a university degree. Among the participants themselves, by age 25, 30% had a university degree, 14% had a college diploma, 24% had a technical degree, and the remaining 32% had no postsecondary educational credential. . . .

adults, the graduates of 4-year colleges and universities, their extraordinarily high expectations for the workplace—their aspirations of finding work that not only pays well but also provides a satisfying and enjoyable identity fit—are difficult for reality to match and often require compromises of their hopes and dreams. . . . Nevertheless, the evidence of rising well-being during the course of emerging adulthood indicates that most people adapt successfully to its developmental challenges.

Here as elsewhere, we must take into account the heterogeneity of emerging adults. Even as well-being rises for most emerging adults, some experience serious mental health problems such as major depression and substance use disorder. . . . A possible interpretation is that the variance in mental health functioning becomes broader in the course of emerging adulthood. . . . This may be because emerging adults have fewer social roles and obligations than children and adolescents, whose lives are structured by their parents and other adults, or adults (beyond emerging adulthood), whose lives are structured by work, family, and community roles and obligations. Although most emerging adults appear to thrive on this freedom, some find themselves lost and may begin to experience serious mental health problems. Emerging adults may also struggle if they are part of especially vulnerable populations, such as those aging out of foster care, coming out of the criminal justice system, or experiencing disabilities. . . .

Although I have made a case that emerging adulthood is experienced positively by most people, I hasten to add that my perspective is based mainly on my interviews and other data obtained from emerging adults in the United States and (recently) Denmark. Studies on emerging adults in other countries, such as Argentina . . ., Czech Republic . . ., and China . . . show some similarities as well as some differences. An exciting prospect for the new field of emerging adulthood is examining the forms it takes in different countries and cultures worldwide. . . .

Is Emerging Adulthood Good for Society?

Even if it is true that most people seem to enjoy their emerging adulthood, is the advent of this new period of life good for society? Certainly, there are complaints about it in American popular media. "They Just Won't Grow Up" sniggered a *TIME* magazine cover story on emerging adults in 2005. In the 2006 movie *Failure to Launch,* a young man shows so little inclination to take on adult responsibilities that his parents hire an attractive young woman to lure him out of their household. Advice writers warn that emerging adults are refusing to give up their teenage pleasures and take on adult responsibilities, with "catastrophic" results. . . .

Here, as with "quarterlife crisis," a grain of truth is exaggerated to the point of caricature. . . . It is true that many emerging adults are ambivalent about taking on adult roles and responsibilities. . . . Although they take a certain satisfaction in moving toward self-sufficiency, they also find it burdensome and onerous to pay their own bills and do all the other things their parents had always done for them. Furthermore, they often view adulthood as dull and stagnant, the end of spontaneity, the end of a sense that anything is possible.

Nevertheless, their ambivalence is not an outright refusal or rejection of adult roles. It may be that they are wise to recognize the potentials of emerging adulthood and to wait until at least their late 20s to take on the full range of adult obligations. Although adulthood may have more satisfactions and rewards than they recognize, they are right that entering adult roles of marriage, parenthood, and stable full-time work entails constraints and limitations that do not apply in emerging adulthood. Once adult roles are entered they tend to be enduring if not lifelong. It seems sensible for emerging adults to wait to enter them until they judge themselves to be ready, and meanwhile to enjoy the freedoms of emerging adulthood while they last.

It should also be added that few emerging adults fail to "grow up" and take on the responsibilities of adulthood. By age 30, three fourths of Americans are married, three fourths have at least one child, nearly all have entered stable employment, nearly all have become financially independent from their parents, and almost none live in their parents' household. . . . Similarly, by age 30 nearly all (about 90%) feel that they have fully reached adulthood, no longer feeling in-between. . . . Thus, the claim that a long and gradual process of taking on adult responsibilities during emerging adulthood results in permanent rejection of adulthood is clearly overblown. The great majority of emerging adults become contributing young adult members of society by age 30, fulfilling stable family and work roles.

Here again, my perspective is based mainly on my research with American emerging adults. However, there are some indications that similar patterns exist in most other industrialized countries, with some variations. Across industrialized societies emerging adulthood is a period of many changes in love and work but most people settle into enduring adult roles by about age 30. . . .

So, emerging adulthood may not be harmful to societies, but is it actually *good* for them? Yes and no. On the one hand, it would be nice to think that if people spend most of their 20s looking for just the right job and just the right love partner, they will have a better chance of finding happiness in love and work than if they had made long-term commitments in their late teens or very early 20s out of duty, necessity, or social pressure. On the other hand, emerging adults' expectations for love and work tend to be extremely high—not just a reliable marriage partner but a "soul mate," not just a steady job but a kind of work that is an enjoyable expression of their identity—and if happiness is measured by the distance between what we expect out of life and what we get, emerging adults' high expectations will be difficult for real life to match. So, it cannot be said with confidence that the existence of emerging adulthood ensures that most people in a society will be happier with their adult lives.

Furthermore, emerging adulthood is the peak age period for many behaviors most societies try to discourage, such as binge drinking, illegal drug use, and risky sexual behavior. . . . If people still entered adult commitments around age 20, as they did in the past, rates of risk behaviors in the 20s would undoubtedly be lower. Such behavior may be fun for emerging adults, but it can hardly be said to be good for their society. However, one way emerging adulthood is good for society is that it allows young people an extended period that can be used for post-secondary education and training that prepares them to contribute to an information and technology-based global economy.

Conclusion

Already in its short life, emerging adulthood has been shown to bear the marks of a good theory: It has generated research, ideas, and critiques that have advanced science and scholarship. Like all theories, it is an imperfect model of real life, and will no doubt be subject to alterations, revisions, and elaborations in the years to come. Especially important will be investigating the different forms it takes in cultures around the world. The theory of emerging adulthood that I have presented is offered as a starting point, and I look forward to the contributions and further advances to come, from scholars around the world. . . .

**Leo B. Hendry and
Marion Kloep**

 **NO**

Conceptualizing Emerging Adulthood: Inspecting the Emperor's New Clothes

Academics worldwide have congratulated Arnett . . . for focusing over the last decade or so on a previously under-researched phase of the life span. Societal and economic changes and shifts inspired him to ask what these forces meant to the transition from adolescence to adulthood. Arguably, this theory has been hailed by some as the most important theoretical contribution to developmental psychology in the past 10 years. . . .

Nevertheless, in this article, we want to play the part of the little boy in Hans Christian Andersen's story who points out the Emperor's lack of clothes, because in our view, his ideas on this period of transition contain several limitations, which should be addressed if future research is to advance on firmer theoretical grounds. To examine these points, we concentrate on the following issues:

1. The configuration of adolescence, early adulthood, and adulthood.
2. Retrospect and prospect: Do we really need the term?
3. Is emerging adulthood experienced positively or negatively by most young people?
4. Is emerging adulthood good for society?

The Configuration of Emerging Adulthood

Arnett . . . is right in suggesting that the transition to adulthood has become increasingly prolonged as a result of economic changes, with many young people staying in education longer, marrying later, and having their first child later than in the past and that in present day society, it is difficult to determine when adolescence ends and adulthood begins. However, he is not the first to make this observation:

> The distinction between youth status and adult status is gradually blurring: Over the last fifteen years, the behavioural differences between youth and adults have drastically diminished. In a growing number of life spheres (sexuality, political behaviour, etc.) young people behave like adults or claim the same rights as adults. . . .

From *Child Development Perspectives,* vol. 1, no. 2, 2007, pp. 74–78. Copyright © 2007 by Wiley-Blackwell. Reprinted by permission.

Figure 1

Arnett's Conceptualization of Emerging Adulthood

What is new in Arnett's theory is the proposal of a new stage in human development, distinct from adolescence and adulthood, overlapping with both stages (see Figure 1).

We do not agree with this model for several reasons. First, Arnett suggests that adulthood (however defined) is fully attained at a certain stage, though there is wide agreement among psychologists that development is domain specific and demonstrates plasticity. . . . Thus, not all areas of human functioning are affected to the same degree, in the same direction, or at the same time. Young people might reach adult status early in some domains, later in others, and in some aspects, never. Further, development is nonlinear and reversible. . . . Young people having reached adulthood according to their own perceptions and by societal markers may find themselves in circumstances where they have to "regress" both subjectively and objectively. For example, it is not uncommon that after cohabitation, some young people return to their familial house when the relationship breaks up, losing the feelings of independence associated with adult status. This can even happen temporarily when young (and not so young) people pursuing a career and feeling completely independent of their parents might in times of illness happily assume the role of cared-for child. . . . The transition from adolescence to adulthood is not as smooth as Arnett proposes, being domain specific, variable, and reversible.

Second, given the few, if any, normative shifts in present-day life, the search for identity is a process of recurring moratoria and achievements extending over the entire life span. . . . Fauske . . . noted that if youth can no longer be interpreted as a bridge between childhood and adulthood as two stable statuses (as Arnett proposes), there is an alternative scenario, which is some kind of perpetual youth. Adults behave like young people, undergo cosmetic surgery, return to college, fall in love with new partners, start a different career, have exciting leisure pursuits, follow youth fashions, and even give birth in advanced biological age:

> Next time you visit the supermarket, you may encounter . . . newborn infants with their mothers who are aged fifteen and sixteen and newborn infants with mothers aged thirty-five to forty. You may encounter, in fact, grandparents in their early forties as well as parents in their sixties and seventies. . . .

If there have to be stages to describe the human life course, the idea of emerging phases between them should be applied to the whole life course. In

Figure 2

Hendry and Kloep's Conceptualization of Life Transitions

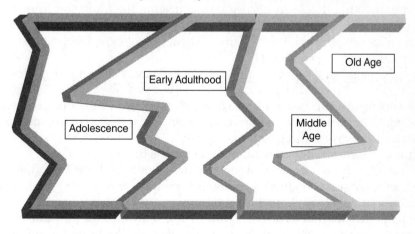

other words, most of us are almost always in the state of being in between or emerging:

> Adult life, then, is a process—a process, we must emphasise, which need not involve a predetermined series of stages of growth. The stages or hurdles, which are placed in front of people and the barriers through which they have to pass (age-specific transitions) can be shifted around and even discarded. . . .

In Figure 2, we illustrate our conceptualization of transitions (though the connections between phases should be in a continual state of dynamic fluctuation to indicate plasticity and reversibility).

Do We Really Need the Term?

Arnett . . . is right that in today's rapidly changing world, traditional developmental tasks such as gaining independence from parents, making personal living arrangements, orienting to a career, and developing new sets of relationships with parents, peers, romantic partners, and so on are differently ordered and present young people with significant challenges in gaining adult status. However, modern developmentalists have claimed that emerging adulthood is not a universal stage but depends on the cultural context in which young people develop and the social institutions they encounter. . . . Findings from studies of non-Western cultures and ethnic minorities suggest that generalizations about emerging adults do not capture the variations that exist within individuals and across cultures. . . . In many countries, young people, particularly women in rural areas, are granted no moratorium for identity exploration but glide quickly from childhood into adulthood. For example, in Turkey, the mean age for marriage is 21 years. . . . Lloyd . . . has stated that the largest generation of young people in history is now making the transition from childhood to adulthood, with 86% of this cohort, nearly 1.5 billion individuals, living in developing countries. Many of them do not experience adolescence, much less emerging adulthood!

The fact that socioeconomic conditions heavily influence the lifestyles and options of individuals in a given society is not new. Apart from Marx's well-known historic materialism, social scientists have repeatedly observed this, and Rindfuss, Swicegard, and Rosenfeld . . . stated that the life course deviates from an idealized "normal" pattern from time to time because the shaping of early adulthood is conditioned by the historical context.

To give a few examples of varying transitional pathways to adulthood with an extended period of moratorium for some, centuries ago Jane Austen wrote about how many upper class youngsters never followed an occupation and remained dependent on their parents until they died. In the same historical period, many 12-year-old children left their families to join a ship's crew or go mining or serve as maids in wealthy households, whereas some women only became "independent" adults when they married. In the political sphere, Queen Mary of Scotland married the French Dauphin (aged 14) at age 15 and a year later became Queen of France.

Considering the points above, the theory of emerging adulthood is merely a description limited to a certain age cohort in certain societies at a certain historical time with particular socioeconomic conditions. This implies that the concept will almost certainly become outdated, given that Western societies are bound to change and new cohorts emerge with different developmental characteristics in different social contexts. New technologies have an impact on young peoples' socialization and learning. There are effects of the "war on terror" on family life, a changing work–leisure balance together with demographic shifts, and increasing migration, to name but a few possible societal trends into the future that will require new theories of development.

As such, Arnett's construct of emerging adulthood does not advance our knowledge and understanding of human development. On the contrary, by elevating it to the status of a theory, we are repeating an error psychology made decades ago when it regarded male behavior as the norm. We are now in danger of having a psychology of the affluent middle classes in Western societies, with other groups being seen as deviating from that norm.

This is not a problem of Arnett's theory alone. All age-bound stage theories, from Freud to Erikson, have been criticized for being ethnocentric and having social class and gender biases. There is a great diversity among people across the life span, and as Valsiner . . . has said, whereas median trends are useful to observe, it is the error variance that is crucial to our understanding of human development. Age, like other structural variables such as gender, social class, or ethnicity, may predict, but do not explain, developmental phenomena. It is not age in itself that causes development; it is the experiences, and not necessarily associated with chronological age, that cause developmental change. Bynner . . . proposed that there is a need to

> move away from a blanket categorisation of individuals in terms of stages bounded by chronological age towards a broader conception based on a range of trajectories or pathways. . . .

In other words, how useful is it to create yet another age stage into existing theories that are neither universal nor explanatory? Rather, we need to investigate the processes and mechanisms of developmental change and abandon age stage theories altogether if we want to go beyond descriptions and seek explanations about development.

Is the Experience of Emerging Adulthood a Positive or Negative One?

Relying on young people's own optimistic perspectives of the future, Arnett . . . sees the period of emerging adulthood as mainly positive for the individual. Whether the experience of a prolonged moratorium is positive, however, depends to a large extent on what societal group they belong to and how they use this period of moratorium.

Castells . . . observed that the contemporary contours of diffuse social, economic, and cultural conditions present new challenges because people must lead their lives without a road map. In Western societies, the signposts and symbols of approaching adulthood are inconsistent and difficult for the young person to understand and interpret. These complexities led Coles . . . to compare adolescent transitions to a deadly serious game of snakes and ladders, where the main transitions are the ladders through which young people gradually move toward adult status. Although this may sound as if growing up in modern societies is risky, we often forget that many more young people survive childhood, adolescence, and emerging adulthood than in previous ages. It is true that young people are confronted with a range of challenges on their way to adulthood and that these challenges create anxieties. One of the significant contributions stage theorists have made to developmental psychology has been to pinpoint that without challenges, conflicts, and crises, there is no developmental change.

Thus, young people face a range of choices, challenges, and risks in relationships, schooling, higher education, and work. . . . Although this may open up opportunities for some, there are fewer safety nets for others, with inequalities in the distribution of resources such as social class, ethnicity, gender, health, and education . . .:

> It can be misleading to present society as changing with all elements; in effect, "marching in step". We need to recognise that the traditional routes to adulthood, with far fewer signs of its emergent status, are still very much in place. . . .

Although it may be true that independence, possibilities, and choices are available for those who can access consumer markets, this may hold only for the young person who has an income or, better yet, supportive parents: Wealthy middle-class youths do have better options. . . .

Similar to Heinz's . . . variety of pathways to occupational roles, we propose from our own research of 18- to 30-year-olds in Wales, who were either working or unemployed and not attending any school . . ., at least three broad subgroups of young people in Western societies, each experiencing the period of emerging adulthood very differently. Of these, 74% stated that they considered themselves to be adult and only 13% felt "in-between" (whereas Arnett's . . . study found 60% feeling in-between).

One of the three groups identified was in extended moratorium, which was similar to Arnett's . . . affluent, middle-class students. With parental support, they could afford a prolonged moratorium, live at home, seek new opportunities, delay in choosing a career, "have fun," and not be fully adult. Although this sounds a pleasant experience, the danger is that these young people would not develop adult skills and might experience "happy" developmental stagnation through overprotection. . . . With regard to education, Levine . . . argued that many young people in their mid-20s have not learned planning, organizational, decision making, and interpersonal skills that are necessary for the transitions into working life. He believes that education leaves these young people unprepared to move into adulthood because they are both overindulged and pressured by parents to excel in all life domains, leaving them uncommitted to deep, focused, and detailed learning. Relatively speaking, this group is forever emerging but never adult. The increasing number of young and middle-aged adults who cannot manage their credit card debts seems to point to a lack of life skills in the wider population.

A second subgroup found in the Wales sample was disadvantaged by their lack of resources, skills, and societal opportunities, though superficially they exhibited a somewhat similar lifestyle to the more affluent subgroup, living with parents and occasionally accepting temporary unskilled jobs. The difference here was that they were in this rut not through choice but through lack of opportunities. Rather than being in a state of emerging adulthood, they were more likely in a state of "prevented adulthood" and in "unhappy stagnation." Lack of affordable housing, education, and suitable jobs prevented them from gaining independence and self-reliance. Many noted that choices and possibilities were available *but not for them,* and this was unlikely to change in the near future. Members of this group not only lacked adult skills but also felt bitter and alienated from society. In drawing attention to the economic and social factors that keep some dependent until at least their mid-20s, Côté . . . concluded that a significant number of young adults have transitional difficulties and greatest problems come to those with least economic, intellectual, and psychological resources.

Finally, there was a third, small subgroup that exhibited early maturity developed through "steeling experiences." . . . These are life events that include parental illness or divorce, having to look after younger siblings or their own children, finding a responsible job, or being forced to become financially independent because their parents could not afford to support them. . . . Growing up early added psychosocial resources and influenced their views of adult status. Barry and Nelson . . . reported that those who perceived themselves to be adult had a better sense of their own identity, were less depressed, and engaged in fewer risk behaviors than those who saw themselves as in-between.

In general, internal markers of adulthood (taking responsibility for one's actions, making independent decisions, becoming financially independent, establishing equal relations with parents) appear to be of greater salience to young people than external markers (marriage, parenthood, beginning full-time work. . . . Hence, there are several other developmental tasks than those traditionally seen as markers of adulthood. Experiencing and coping with different nonnormative shifts can enhance maturity in exactly the same way as these normative shifts achieve: These experiences are causes, not consequences, of becoming adult.

In summary, the experience of emerging adulthood depends on whether a prolonged moratorium is the result of choice or constraints and whether it is used effectively to gain experiences. Some may acquire skills for adult living, whereas others idle their time away. Overall, it seems as if the long-term consequences are more beneficial to those who do not spend lengthy years in identity exploration.

Is Emerging Adulthood Good for Society?

What might be the societal effects of young people delaying their entry into adult roles? On this we can only speculate, though Arnett makes clear that he sees it as a positive experience for young people.

Large numbers of young adults not participating in the labor market and not being economically active in their first 30 years of life (as well as in their last) would cost Western societies dearly. Some emergent adults would fail to realize their full potential throughout life because they failed to acquire skills and qualifications needed for modern living. It will certainly place large financial and emotional burdens on middle-aged parents having to support their ever-emerging children at the same time as having to care for aging parents. The current increase in divorce and the decrease in fertility rates . . . may also be a reflection of current trends in extended identity exploration. Further, emerging adults of today may not be particularly affluent parents, because they left both career and child bearing to their early 30s, and if many remain single parents, they will be unable to indulge their own children in a 30-year-long period of identity exploration. In other words, we predict that the current situation of emerging adulthood will regulate itself over time.

Already several European governments have reacted by increasing university fees, placing limits on time allowed to complete a degree course (United Kingdom and Germany), and establishing laws on cohabiting very similar to marriage laws (Ireland, United Kingdom, Sweden). These emerging adults, in extended moratorium, may also create opportunities for well-qualified non-Western immigrants within the labor markets of Western societies.

Concluding Comments

In our view, Arnett's concept does not add to our understanding of human development. Instead of simply describing the effects of certain societal conditions on certain individuals belonging to a certain cohort, we should better understand and investigate the interactive processes and mechanisms (of which societal transformation is only one) that are involved in human development. Social scientists have already moved away from age-bound stage theories toward more systemic approaches. Significant in this have been Bronfenbrenner's (1979; Bronfenbrenner & Morris, 1998) interactive micro- to macrolevel theory; Elder's (1974, 1999) emphasis on both historical time and the timing of life events; Baltes' (1987, 1997) concepts of plasticity, multidirectionality, multifunctionality, and nonlinearity; Lerner's (1985, 1998) views on proactivity and self-agency; and Valsiner's (1997) explorations of systemic developmental changes. Understanding human development and life course transitions demands that we examine the interplay among many factors and forces, including structural factors, individual agency and experience, encounters with social institutions, and cultural imperatives. This is more complex than descriptions of age stages, which cannot embrace all facets of developmental changes. In other words, contemporary developmental scientists should consider human interaction within cultural, historical, and psychosocial shifts and the peculiarities of time and place and embrace dynamic, systemic, interactive models as a way of charting and understanding development across the adolescent–adult transition and, indeed, across the whole life span (e.g., Côté, 1996, 1997; Hendry & Kloep, 2002; Magnusson & Stattin, 1998). . . .

Today, young people are increasingly required to take the initiative in forming work and personal relationships, gaining educational credentials and employment experience, and planning for their future. Those who actively address these issues with self-agency may be most likely to form a coherent sense of identity toward their subsequent life course. . . . On the other hand, an inability to shape identity is linked to heightened risks, insecurity, and stress. . . . Arnett's descriptions of a new age stage do not penetrate the layers of variations in transitional trajectories. A complementary perspective is necessary, and we would claim that a dynamic, systemic framework would suit.

To finally return to Hans Christian Andersen's story, it is fair to say that Arnett's ideas on emerging adulthood are not denuded of value. However, a new fashion designer is needed to clothe the emerging framework in the more sophisticated drapes of interactive processes and mechanisms if we are going to research and interpret the many variations within this transitional period accurately and sensitively.

CHALLENGE QUESTIONS

Is There Such a Thing as "Emerging Adulthood"?

1. What is the purpose of defining life-span stages at any age? In defining stages, will we always add more or might there be cause to eliminate what used to be considered a characteristic stage of the life-span?
2. What else might we call emerging adulthood? Are there other terms that might better describe aspects of this age period?
3. Arnett criticizes popular claims of a "quarterlife crisis" as an exaggeration, and claims many dimensions of mental health improve during emerging adulthood. If this is the case, why has the idea of a "quarterlife crisis" achieved some popularity?
4. Arnett claims that emerging adulthood leads to higher expectations in domains such as love and work, but does this seem to be a necessary result of delaying full adult responsibilities?
5. Many of Hendry and Kloep's criticisms of emerging adulthood could also apply to other stages—what are the advantages and disadvantages of thinking about the lifespan in stages despite significant individual and cultural variation?

Is There Common Ground?

Historical epochs and cultural norms do shape what it means to become an adult. Jeffrey Jensen Arnett, Leo B. Hendry, and Marion Kloep would likely all agree that the transition to adulthood in modern Western societies is qualitatively different from that same transition a century ago, and that transition in turn is qualitatively different from what happens in many non-Western societies. The question is whether those changes merit a distinct developmental stage, and whether stage theories are even helpful in making sense of lifespan development. Arnett has convinced a lot of scholars that his concept of "emerging adulthood" is helpful, and the term has come into common usage. But Hendry and Kloep also offer the valuable service of making scholars think about whether a shared vocabulary around emerging adulthood limits our ability to account for ongoing change. Emerging adulthood as a stage is characterized by questions and exploration, so perhaps it is only appropriate that the concept itself is also subject to questioning.

Suggested Readings

J. Arnett, *Emerging Adulthood: The Winding Road From the Late Teens Through the Twenties* (Oxford University Press, 2004)

J. Arnett and J. Tanner (eds.) *Emerging Adults in America: Coming of Age in the 21st Century.* APA Books.

P. Baltes, "Theoretical Propositions of Life-Span Developmental Psychology: On the Dynamics Between Growth and Decline." *Developmental Psychology* (September 1987)

J.C. Coleman and L.B. Hendry, *The Nature of Adolescence.* (Routledge, 1999)

A. Robbins and A. Wilner, *Quarterlife Crisis: The Unique Challenges of Life in Your Twenties,* (Tarcher, 2001).

J. Côté, *Arrested Adulthood: The Changing Nature of Maturity and Identity in the Late Modern World,* (New York University Press, 2000).

Lloyd, C.B., *Growing Up Global: The Changing Transitions to Adulthood in Developing Countries,* (National Academies Press, 2005)

ISSUE 13

Is There a "Narcissism Epidemic" Among Contemporary Young Adults?

YES: Jean M. Twenge and Joshua D. Foster, from "Mapping the Scale of the Narcissism Epidemic: Increases in Narcissism 2002–2007 within Ethnic Groups," *Journal of Research in Personality* (December 2008)

NO: M. Brent Donnellan, Kali H. Trzesniewski, and Richard W. Robins, from "An Emerging Epidemic of Narcissism or Much Ado About Nothing?" *Journal of Research in Personality* (June 2009)

Learning Outcomes

As you read the issue, focus on the following points:

1. There is some evidence that college student scores on the Narcissistic Personality Inventory have risen significantly in recent decades to reflect more self-centeredness, though the magnitude of those changes depends some upon the data being interpreted.

2. Rates of narcissism do not seem consistent across ethnic groups, with Asian-American college students in particular demonstrating lower narcissism scores.

3. Harmful components of narcissism, such as a pervasive sense of entitlement, may not be increasing as much as a more benign self-focus.

ISSUE SUMMARY

YES: Jean M. Twenge and Joshua D. Foster present evidence from surveys of college students that reinforces their claim of a "narcissism epidemic."

NO: Research psychologists M. Brent Donnellan, Kali H. Trzesniewski, and Richard W. Robins take the evidence used by Twenge and colleagues and draw different conclusions, arguing claims of an epidemic are greatly exaggerated.

In the hit 2004 Disney movie *The Incredibles,* Dash, the boy child in a family of superheroes, finds himself frustrated by his mother's insistence that he not use his super-speed to beat other children in running races—despite his father telling him his powers make him "special." His mother explains to Dash that beating the other children would make them feel bad, and that "everyone's special." "Which," according to Dash, "is another way of saying that nobody is." Though the movie was imaginary, it touches on a very real issue for contemporary children and youth: emphasizing the idea that "everyone is special" may create a culture where young people believe they are extraordinary regardless of their actual accomplishments or aptitudes.

Many scholars attribute the contemporary emphasis on ways that "everyone is special" to the prominence of the self-esteem movement and to the importance of individualism in Western cultures. Although the value of individual rights have long been emphasized, there is a sense that the priority on individualism in contemporary society is new and extreme. Self-reflection, self-awareness, and self-esteem are now considered basic needs. Jean Twenge points out in her 2006 book *Generation Me*, in the 1950's only 12 percent of teenagers agreed with the statement "I am an important person," but thirty years later 80 percent of teenagers agreed with the same statement.

Twenge thinks our contemporary emphasis on self-esteem and individualism has created an entire group characterized by self-absorption: a phenomena leading her, along with psychologist W. Keith Campbell, to title their 2009 book *The Narcissism Epidemic*. Narcissism, according the book's Web site, "is a positive, inflated and grandiose sense of self . . . Along with this inflated sense of self is a lack of warm, emotionally intimate or caring relationships with others. This does not mean a lack of social relationships—often the opposite is the case—but a lack of emotionally deep relationships." Psychologists also have a technical classification for "Narcissistic Personality Disorder" that highlights the traits associated with narcissism as problematic for normal functioning.

M. Brent Donnellan, Kali H. Trzesniewski, and Richard W. Robins, think that claims of a narcissism epidemic are an exaggeration. They have engaged in an ongoing empirical debate with Twenge and colleagues, consistently taking similar data and drawing very different conclusions. While Donnellan and colleagues acknowledge there may be some small generational differences for a few specific groups in scores on narcissism inventories, they question whether those differences are meaningful enough to warrant claims of an epidemic that describes an entire generation.

The broader issue here relates to other controversial questions in the study of life-span development. The fact that there may be significant differences in narcissism between ethnic groups, for example, raises questions about the influence of cultural differences in child rearing. In addition, the question of whether the term "generation me" is accurate relates to questions about how to characterize age groups at any point in the life-span. And finally, the broad question of self-esteem has been the subject of much debate. Scholars have realized that while emphasizing self-esteem for children is popular, that emphasis produces mixed results.

POINT

- National data suggests that college students' scores on the Narcissistic Personality Inventory have risen significantly between 1982 and 2006.
- Other data suggesting few cohort changes in narcissism have not adequately accounted for differences between ethnic groups.
- Though Asian-American students score lower overall on narcissism than other ethnic groups, within ethnic groups narcissism scores have increased significantly even if only considering the years between 2002 and 2007.

COUNTERPOINT

- The evidence of a "narcissism epidemic" is mixed, depending on who has analyzed the data.
- Claims of generational changes would not fit with differences between 2002 and 2007—since those young adults would essentially be of the same generation.
- When looking at changes in scores on sub-scales of the Narcissistic Personality Inventory, there seem to be no significant differences in "entitlement"—which would likely be the most harmful characteristic of narcissism.

YES  Jean M. Twenge and Joshua D. Foster

Mapping the Scale of the Narcissism Epidemic: Increases in Narcissism 2002–2007 within Ethnic Groups

1. Introduction

Several authors have argued that American culture has become more individualistic over the past few decades. . . . Perhaps as a result, young people's self-views have grown more positive and agentic over the generations. . . . But has young Americans' increasing individualism recently crossed the line into narcissism?

Two recent papers reported conflicting findings on whether narcissism has increased among American college students during the past 25 years. Twenge, Konrath, Foster, Campbell, and Bushman . . . found that Narcissistic Personality Inventory (NPI) scores rose by 0.33 standard deviations between 1982 and 2006 among 16,475 students attending 31 colleges throughout the United States. However, Trzesniewski, Donnellan, and Robins . . . found that NPI scores remained unchanged between 1982 and 2007 in samples of 26,887 college students from the University of California (primarily UC Davis). Trzesniewski et al.'s paper received widespread media attention, including stories in *The New York Times* and *USA Today,* with the *Times* declaring that "young Americans are not more self-absorbed than earlier generations, according to new research challenging the prevailing wisdom."

In our reply to their set of results . . ., we argued that Trzesniewski et al. . . . failed to find an increase in narcissism because Asian-American enrollment at the UC campuses nearly doubled over the time of their investigation, and Asians typically score lower on individualistic traits . . ., including narcissism. . . . For example, among college age (18–23) participants in Foster et al.'s . . . data, Asian-Americans scored 0.21 SDs lower on the NPI than White Americans. Thus as proportionally more Asian-American students entered the samples used by Trzesniewski et al., NPI means would appear to remain constant (or go down) even if scores within ethnic groups actually increased.

Unfortunately, Trzesniewski et al. did not report their data broken down by ethnic group. Trzesniewski et al. did report that the interaction between ethnicity and time was not significant. However, that is a different question: If NPI means increased similarly within each ethnic group, there would indeed be no interaction between time and ethnicity. Examining the pattern of change within ethnic groups, however, eliminates the possible confound of samples changing in ethnic composition over time (e.g., the percentage of Asian-Americans in the samples rising over time). Both generational differences and ethnic group membership reflect the impact of culture on the individual. . . . These effects can be additive (or, in this case, subtractive), so if both change over time, generational effects might not appear. Because ethnicity data were only available for the 2002–2007 samples, we examined change in NPI scores over only this 5-year period, another difference from Trzesniewski et al., who concentrated on the change between 1982 and 2007.

2. Method

Trzesniewski et al. graciously provided the NPI means for their UC Davis samples separated into four ethnic groups: Whites, Blacks, Hispanics, and Asians. Respondents who did not answer the ethnicity question or who chose "other" are not included in this analysis. Trzesniewski et al. noted that means broken down by ethnic group were only available for the 2002–2007 samples; thus the 1996 and 1979–1985 datapoints from their paper are not included here. The 1979–1985 datapoint is from Raskin and Terry . . . , also the first datapoint in the Twenge et al. . . . analysis, and Raskin and Terry did not report means by ethnic group nor the percentage of their sample from each ethnic group. The participants in the present analysis, collected every year 2002–2007 in introductory psychology classes at UC Davis, were 48.3% Asian-American, 37.6% White, 11.4% Hispanic, and 2.7% Black.

3. Results and Discussion

We examine two questions critical to our theory: (1) Did Asian-Americans score lower on the NPI than other ethnic groups in Trzesniewski et al. . . . samples of UC Davis undergraduates? And, more importantly, (2) did narcissism increase over time among UC Davis undergraduates when examined within ethnic group?

The answers to both questions were unambiguous. First, using all of the data from 2002 to 2007, Asian-American undergraduates at UC Davis ($M = 13.75$, SD = 6.85, $n = 9969$) scored significantly lower in narcissism than Whites ($M = 15.77$, SD = 6.82, $n = 7747$), $t(17,715) = 19.50$, $p < .001$, $d = 0.30$, and lower than Whites, Hispanics, and Blacks combined ($M = 15.97$, SD = 6.78, $n = 10,658$), $t(20,626) = 23.40$, $p < .001$, $d = 0.33$.

Second, when the data were separated by ethnicity, the UC Davis samples showed a significant increase in narcissism between 2002 and 2007. White students' NPI scores increased significantly between 2002 ($M = 15.30$, SD = 6.59) and 2007 ($M = 16.42$, SD = 7.05), $t(1916) = 3.57$, $p < .001$, $d = 0.17$. Fifty-nine percent of White students in 2007 scored higher on narcissism than the average White student in 2002. Because this change occurred over only 5 years—compared to 24 years in the Twenge et al. . . . meta-analysis—

this modest d represents a large yearly increase of $d = .034$, more than twice the yearly increase in narcissism found in the Twenge et al. . . . . meta-analysis ($d = .014$, which totals 0.33 over 24 years). If the 5-year change in the Davis samples continued for 24 years, it would result in an increase of $d = 0.82$ (about 5 points on the NPI), or 81% of White students in 2007 scoring higher than the 1980s average. For comparison, this rate of change is three times larger than the increase in Americans' body mass index over the same time period, often referred to as the "obesity epidemic" ($d = 0.31$ . . .).

A regression equation for the 6 yearly means weighted by sample size also showed a significant effect for year among Whites, Beta = .96, $p < .002$; using the individual-level SD, the $d = 0.14$. These results are consistent with Twenge et al. . . . , which found that the rise in narcissism was apparently accelerating in recent years, with an increase of $d = 0.18$ between 2000 and 2006 (a year-by-year change of $d = 0.03$, vs. $d = 0.014$ for 1982–2006).

Asian-Americans' narcissism scores also increased significantly from 2002 ($M = 13.26$, SD = 6.67) to 2007 ($M = 14.04$, SD = 6.93), $t(2416) = 2.81$, $p < .01$, $d = 0.12$, with 57% of Asian students in 2007 scoring higher than the average Asian student in 2002 (extrapolated for 24 years, $d = 0.58$, or 74% of Asian 2007 students scoring higher than the average Asian student in the 1980s). The regression equation yielded Beta = .68, $p = .14$, $d = 0.07$. With lower n's, the t-tests for year among Hispanic and Black students were not significant, though the trends were in the same direction ($d = 0.14$ for Hispanics, with Beta = .72, $p = .10$; and $d = 0.10$ for Blacks, with Beta = .56, $p = .25$). Fig. 1 shows the data centered within ethnic group, illustrating the change over time within each ethnic group. Because the change was similar across ethnic groups, this is consistent with Trzesniewski et al.'s . . . finding that time by ethnicity did not produce a significant interaction.

Even when the data are collapsed across ethnicity, UC Davis students' NPI scores were higher in 2007 ($M = 15.24$, SD = 6.90) than in 2002 ($M = 14.48$, SD = 6.65), $t(5051) = 3.99$, $p < .001$, $d = 0.11$. This is a yearly change of $d = .022$, still larger than the yearly increase found in Twenge et al. . . . , and would total $d = 0.53$ over 24 years. Across all six datapoints, the Beta for year was .79, $p = .06$; using the individual-level SD, $d = 0.08$. This change is smaller than those within ethnic groups, but is still significant.

Why did Trzesniewski et al. . . . . come to different conclusions?[1] Analyzing the data within ethnic groups to avoid the confound of changing populations explains only some of the discrepancy. The difference in our conclusions is not due to using means vs. individual-level data, as Trzesniewski et al. . . . . argued,[2] as those analyses yield identical results (e.g., for Whites, the regression equation using means produces $d = 0.14$, the same as the regression equation Trzesniewski et al. . . . . provided to us that used individual-level data). One clear difference between our approaches is that Trzesniewski et al. . . . . did not report analyses examining change over time between 2002 and 2007, only over the entire time period 1982–2007.

Because ethnic breakdowns were not available before 2002, we cannot be sure how narcissism changed at the UC campuses before that time. Although the overall mean from UC Davis in 2007 was similar to the 1979–1985 mean

Figure 1

**NPI Scores at UC Davis 2002–2007, Centered within Ethnic Group.
Dataset from Trzesniewski et al (2008).**

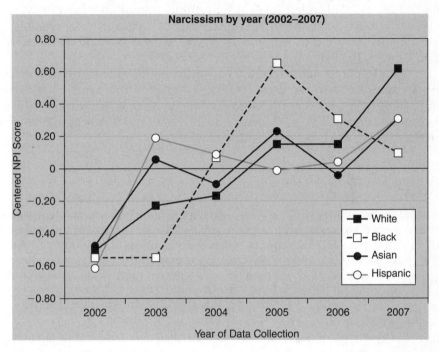

for UC Berkeley and UC Santa Cruz . . . , Asian-American enrollment doubled (and White enrollment was cut in half) at the UCs between the early 1980s and 2007. Raskin and Terry did not report the ethnic makeup of their sample, but Asian-Americans were 23% and Whites 61% of Berkeley undergraduates in 1983, compared to 52% Asian and 38% White in the 2007 Davis data (note that this excludes those who identified their ethnic group as "other"). This is a much larger shift in ethnic composition than that between 2002 and 2007 (from 44% to 52% Asian), and we do not know what impact these changes had on NPI scores—even for non-Asian students, if the shift in ethnic composition created a different campus culture. In addition, Berkeley and Davis are different campuses with different cultures and populations; this is a particular problem because year is perfectly confounded with campus in Trzesniewski et al. . . . dataset (the two earliest datapoints are from Santa Cruz and Berkeley and the last six are from Davis). Thus the lack of change between 1979 and 2002 could be caused by the switch from one campus to another. Another problem is the small number of samples in Trzesniewski et al. . . . dataset, with just two datapoints for the 22-year period between 1979 and 2001, and only one between 1996 and 2001. This sparse coverage, combined with the changes in ethnic composition and the change in campus, make it very difficult to draw conclusions about changes in narcissism in this dataset before 2002. Another difficulty in discerning the pattern of change is that the Davis NPI means are outliers compared to means from other campuses. Recent Davis students ($M = 15.24$) score significantly lower than recent students from other campuses [$M = 17.65$ for 2006 from the Twenge et al. . . . meta-analysis], $t(3625) = 9.64$, $p < .001$, $d = .35$. This is not solely due to ethnic composition; even the White students at Davis score lower ($M = 16.42$ in 2007). Thus it is not possible to combine the Davis means with the nationwide data to examine change across both datasets; the two must be examined separately.

The 85 college student samples available nationwide show an increase in narcissism between the early 1980s and 2006. . . . The trends in our data and that of Trzesniewski et al. lead to the conclusion that narcissism increased nationwide among college students between the early 1980s and 2006 and increased at UC Davis between 2002 and 2007. . . .

Notes

1. Trzesniewski et al. . . . also reported finding no change in self-enhancement over the generations in a nationally representative dataset of high school students. Most measures of self-enhancement use the residual of subjective performance and objective performance. In this dataset, however, Trzesniewski et al. . . . relied on self-reported high school grades as the measure of "objective" performance rather than SAT scores, transcripts, or GPA reported by others. Thus it is difficult to interpret these results (see Twenge et al. . . . for further discussion of this issue).

2. Trzesniewski et al. . . . incorrectly state that cross-temporal meta-analysis [the technique used in Twenge et al. . . .] commits the ecological fallacy (or alerting correlations . . .), in which mean-level data shows larger changes because the standard deviation (SD) of groups is lower than that of individuals. However, cross-temporal meta-analysis does not calculate the effect size using the correlation or Beta. Instead, it uses the unstandardized B and the SD of the individual samples—the variance in a sample of people—*not* the SD among groups. Thus the ecological fallacy is not an issue. We use the same technique here for calculating the d for change in mean-level data regressions, relying on the individual-level SD.

M. Brent Donnellan, Kali H.
Trzesniewski, and Richard W. Robins

 **NO**

An Emerging Epidemic of Narcissism or Much Ado About Nothing?

0. Introduction

Twenge and colleagues have recently raised concerns about an epidemic of narcissism among today's college students and Twenge . . . has argued that this increase is an unintended effect of the self-esteem movement. In fact, Twenge . . . has suggested that, "the self-esteem movement has created an army of little narcissists." . . . In a series of articles, including a recent one entitled, "Mapping the Scale of the Narcissism Epidemic" . . ., Twenge and colleagues claim that narcissism levels have been rising dramatically over the past decade or two. . . . However, the evidentiary basis of this claim has been the subject of much controversy within the scientific literature . . . as well as in the popular media. . . . The aim of this brief report is to re-examine the evidence for secular increases in narcissism in light of the issues, criticisms, and findings presented in Twenge and Foster. . . .

1. Previous Research on Secular Changes in Narcissism

In a previous article . . ., we presented data that failed to support Twenge's . . . assertion that "narcissism is much more common in recent generations." . . . Specifically, we found nearly the same average score on the 40-item Narcissistic Personality Inventory (NPI . . .) for data collected on large samples of college students: (a) from 1979 to 1985 at the University of California (UC) Berkeley and UC Santa Cruz; (b) in 1996 at UC Berkeley; and (c) from 2002–2007 at UC Davis. In a response to Trzesniewski et al. . . .; Twenge et al. . . . re-analyzed secular trends in their meta-analytic database after restricting their analyses to the seven samples from California universities (all but one sample were from UC campuses) and replicated our original finding that college students in California have not shown an increase in narcissism. In an attempt to explain this null result, Twenge and Foster . . . speculated that the secular increase in narcissism that they believe is occurring in society as a whole has been

From *Journal of Research in Personality,* Vol. 43, 2009, pp. 498–501. Copyright © 2009 by Elsevier Science Ltd. Reprinted by permission.

obscured at California universities because of countervailing increases in the proportion of Asian-American students, who tend to score lower on measures of narcissism than White students.

Whether secular trends vary across racial/ethnic groups is an important question, albeit one that has been largely ignored by all of the participants in this debate . . . did not evaluate ethnicity as a moderator of secular trends in their meta-analysis). In Trzesniewski et al. . . . ., we reported that Asian–Americans students scored lower on the NPI than White students, but we found no evidence that ethnicity moderated the secular trends. However, based on a reanalysis of our UC Davis data (the only data for which ethnicity was available to them), Twenge and Foster . . . concluded that narcissism levels actually increased from 2002 to 2007 for Whites and Asian Americans (but not African Americans or Latinos/as). They interpreted this result as supporting their contention that there is an epidemic of narcissism among today's college students.

The goal of this brief report is to revisit this question of whether there is an epidemic of narcissism among today's youth by examining changes in narcissism from 1996 to 2008 as a function of ethnicity using potentially more meaningful and easier to understand effect size measures. In addition, we examined whether any observed trends held across gender and across several specific facets of narcissism.

2. Method

NPI scores were drawn from prescreening sessions conducted at U.C. Berkeley in 1996 and at U.C. Davis from 2002 to 2008. We restricted the analyses to the 30,073 participants between 18 and 24 years of age who completed the NPI and self-identified their racial/ethnic background. The dataset used for some of these analyses differs from the dataset analyzed by Twenge and Foster . . . with additional data collected in 2007 ($n = 2025$) and 2008 ($n = 2405$) and with ethnicity data analyzed for the 1996 sample ($n = 571$).[1] Given the number of comparisons and the large sample sizes we set the alpha level to 0.01 to evaluate statistical significance.

3. Results

There are two general ways to analyze secular trends in narcissism. First, mean scores can be computed each year and then correlated with year of data collection. This analysis produces what is referred to as an "ecological correlation" (the N in these analyses is the number of years that data were collected). Second, the individual participants' scores can be correlated with the year each score was collected (the N in these analyses is the number of participants). This kind of analysis produces the kind of correlation coefficient that is commonly used in personality research (i.e. the unit of analysis is individual scores rather than yearly averages). Both approaches presumably reflect the degree of association between narcissism levels and year of assessment, and thus tell us something about secular trends. As we will show, however, the two approaches produce dramatically different effect sizes.

The method that Twenge and Foster . . . used to obtain their most impressive effects sizes was the ecological approach. Specifically, to test their assumption that ethnicity confounds the general trend, they predicted yearly means broken down by ethnicity from the 6 years of data collection (2002–2007) reported in Trzesniewski et al. . . . From this analysis, they reported large standardized regression coefficients (i.e. correlations) for each ethnic group (β = 0.96, 0.68, 0.72, and 0.56 for Whites, Asian Americans, Latinos/as, and African Americans, respectively). One problem with the ecological approach is that the effect size can be quite large because individual-level variability is not factored into the standardization of the regression weight.[2]

When individual-level effects were computed using the second approach, the resulting standardized coefficients (i.e., correlations) were considerably smaller (β = 0.045, 0.002, 0.021, and 0.048 for Whites, Asian Americans, Latino/a, and African Americans, respectively).[3] In contrast to Twenge and Foster's analysis of the same data, these coefficients suggest that little secular change has occurred, even when the trends were analyzed within ethnic groups. Twenge and Foster . . . suggest that these small effects could amount to potentially substantial changes if they played out at the same rate over 24 or so years. However, such an extrapolation might be unwarranted given the restricted timeframe, moreover, it is unclear from a "generational change" perspective why college students in 2002 or 2003 should be much different from college students in 2006 or 2007.

Based on these concerns, we evaluated within-group secular changes in narcissism by extending the sample analyzed by Twenge and Foster . . . to include data from 1996, Fall 2007, and Winter and Spring of 2008. Specifically, our goal was to examine secular trends within ethnic group, within gender, and across the NPI subscales for this longer interval. Table 1 displays mean NPI scores as a function of ethnicity and year of data collection. Averages were based on a 0–40 metric for scoring the NPI. To quantify changes over time, we calculated the individual–level correlations between NPI scores and year (1996–2008). This information is reported in row labeled $r_{overall}$. For example, the association between individual scores for Whites and year of data collection was 0.019 (p = 0.067) and the correlation between year of data collection and NPI score in the total sample was 0.024 (p < 0.01). These correlations between year and NPI scores were quite small (range = 0.019–0.044) and they provided little indication of a meaningful secular increase in narcissism from 1996 to 2008.

We next analyzed the trends separately for men and women of each ethnicity. This is an instructive analysis because Twenge et al. . . . . found that only women showed a statistically significant increase in NPI scores. The correlations for women are reported in the row labeled r_{women} and the correlations for men are reported in the row labeled r_{men}. For example, the correlation between individual scores for White women and year of data collection was 0.021 (p = 0.111), whereas the corresponding correlation for White men was 0.024 (p = 0.184). All of the correlations were small and none exceeded 0.10, the conventional threshold for a "small" effect. As another illustration of the magnitude of the effect, year of data collection accounted for 0.1% of the variance,

Table 1

Means, Standard Deviations, and Correlations of NPI Scores with Year of Data Collection (1996–2008), Separately for Each Ethnic Group.

Year	African–American			Asian–American			Latino/a			White			"Other"			Total Sample	
	M	SD	N	M	SD	N	M	SD	N	M	SD	N	M	SD	N	M	SD
1996	18.24	5.98	28	13.53	6.84	254	15.82	6.22	82	17.78	6.71	163	14.12	5.84	44	15.35	6.86
2002	17.38	6.55	70	13.26	6.67	1133	15.51	6.82	252	15.30	6.59	1107	16.64	7.03	535	14.85	6.84
2003	17.38	6.89	109	13.79	6.92	1818	16.32	6.65	420	15.58	6.66	1644	16.57	6.93	817	15.18	6.90
2004	17.99	7.30	92	13.64	6.87	1884	16.23	6.70	438	15.64	6.88	1505	16.54	6.90	830	15.10	6.98
2005	18.58	6.23	92	13.96	6.84	1769	16.12	6.89	437	15.96	6.87	1332	16.45	7.03	777	15.31	6.97
2006	18.24	6.48	119	13.70	6.77	2080	16.17	6.61	487	15.97	6.96	1348	16.48	6.86	924	15.19	6.94
2007	18.57	6.47	125	14.34	6.98	2171	16.40	6.61	528	16.56	7.15	1287	16.76	7.11	967	15.68	7.10
2008	18.65	5.92	48	14.33	6.73	1049	16.32	6.69	267	16.00	7.00	585	17.18	6.81	456	15.58	6.89
Overall	18.12	6.56	683	13.87	6.85	12158	16.18	6.68	2911	15.88	6.87	8971	16.61	6.95	5350	15.27	6.96
	African–American			Asian–American			Latino/a			White			"Other"			Total sample	
$r_{overall}$	0.044			0.036*			0.021			.019			0.027			0.024*	
r_{women}	0.073			0.039*			0.015			.021			0.042			0.030*	
r_{men}	0.001			0.028			0.047			.024			–0.013			0.016	

Note: $r_{overall}$ is the correlation for both men and women, whereas r_{women} is the correlation for women and r_{men} is the correlation for men.
*$p < 0.01$.

Table 2

Correlations of NPI Sub-Scales with Year of Data Collection (1996–2008), Separately for Each Ethnic Group.

	Authority	Exhibitionism	Superiority	Entitlement	Exploitativeness	Self-sufficiency	Vanity
African–American	0.053	0.029	0.038	–0.017	–0.008	0.070	–0.004
Asian–American	0.017	0.016	0.044*	0.006	0.029*	0.037*	0.021
Latino/a	0.002	–0.003	0.056	–0.003	0.012	0.039	–0.002
White	0.011	0.013	0.022	–0.008	0.037*	–0.007	0.026
Other	0.021	–0.003	0.040*	–0.002	0.017	0.026	0.029
Total sample	0.010	0.009	0.031*	0.005	0.024*	0.020*	0.017*

*$p < 0.01$.

whereas gender accounted for 1.2% (i.e., 12 times as much) in a regression analysis predicting NPI scores.

It is possible that only certain facets of narcissism have been increasing over time. To explore this possibility, we computed correlations between the seven NPI subscales . . . and year of data collection, separately in the total sample and for each ethnic group. The vast majority of the 42 correlations were below 0.05 (median $r = 0.017$) and none were above 0.10 (see Table 2). Of note, the weakest correlations, hovering around zero (e.g., $r = 0.005$ in the total sample, $p = 0.351$), were found for the Entitlement subscale. Konrath, Bushman, and Campbell . . . identified Entitlement as the best predictor of laboratory aggression, even outperforming the overall NPI score. Thus, this particularly socially toxic aspect of narcissism showed no increase from 1996–2008, contrary to the characterization of the current generation of college students as "Generation Me." . . .

4. Discussion

Based on the overall pattern of results in this report, we are not convinced that there has been either a widespread or a substantial secular increase in narcissism. All of the effect sizes were well below the conventional threshold for a "small" effect and, even in our very large sample, there was no statistically detectable increase for men ($p = 0.105$) or for Latinos and African Americans ($p = 0.252$ and $p = 0.253$, respectively). Although very small effects can be highly meaningful in some contexts, in the present context, we prefer to follow recommendations by Hyde . . . who has argued that Cohen's criteria . . . (e.g., 1988) for "small" ($r = 0.10$), "medium" ($r = 0.30$), and "large" ($r = 0.50$) effects are reasonable for interpreting contentious findings such as the presence of gender differences. . . . In this case, the observed correlations are even smaller than "small," which argues for erring on the side of caution before making pronouncements about an entire generation of young adults.

Moreover, it is occasionally overlooked that the secular increase in narcissism reported by Twenge et al. . . . held only for women; the association between year and mean NPI scores was not statistically detectable for men whereas it was statistically detectable for women based on their sub-analyses of the 44 studies that had information separately reported by gender (out of 85 total studies). The present analyses further hinted at this gender difference, although the trend was miniscule even for women. Thus, even if we were to accept Twenge et al.'s claim that narcissism levels are rising, this trend seems to be restricted to women. Such an apparent boundary condition raises questions about how to best interpret the reported secular effect as scores on the NPI can reflect heightened social potency as well as more socially toxic aspects of personality. . . .

Finally, we emphasize that there is nothing in any of these data that suggests an epidemic of narcissism. Why? The NPI is measured on an arbitrary metric . . . and there is no basis for declaring when an average score indicates "excessively" high levels of the characteristic in question. In fact, even in the most recent time point . . . , when the epidemic was presumably raging, participants on average endorsed fewer than half (about 40%) of the narcissistic responses; whether this value should be considered high or low in an absolute sense is impossible to determine with the arbitrary metric of the NPI. Indeed, claims about an "epidemic of narcissism" essentially boil down to quite small changes over a fairly restricted range of scores all of which typically average below the midpoint of the scale. Based on these considerations, we do not believe that "epidemic" is an appropriate adjective in this context.

5. Conclusion

We continue to believe that a conservative approach is warranted with respect to the empirical status of generational increases in narcissism. Our extensive analyses of data from over 30,000 participants showed uniformly small secular trends, which failed to reach statistical significance for men, for two of the four ethnic groups, and for three of the facets of narcissism. Moreover, all of the existing NPI evidence is based on convenience (i.e., non-probability) samples, and such samples are highly problematic for making inferences about trends in the general population. Thus, evidence for an increase in narcissism is far from clear-cut and there are good reasons why researchers should be wary of labeling any apparent changes in this multifaceted dimension of personality as evidence of an epidemic. . . .

Notes

1. The 1996 data were not included in the Twenge and Foster . . . analysis because ethnicity information was not readily available when requested by Dr. Foster in February of 2008. We tracked these down in light of the

Twenge and Foster . . . analysis and provided them to their team in September of 2008.

2. We are not claiming the Twenge and her colleagues are committing the *ecological fallacy* with these analyses (i.e., the error of assuming that effects at an aggregated level generalize to a lower level). Rather, we are pointing out that correlating two variables at an aggregated level yields an effect size that is quite different from the traditional correlation used in personality research, which is based on individual-level data. . . . Ecological correlations are typically much larger than individual-level correlations (and can even reverse signs) and it is not clear how personality researchers should interpret the magnitude of these effects.

3. These results are based on analyses conducted using the exact same set of data analyzed by Twenge and Foster . . ., which consists of the 20,627 participants between 18 to 24 years of age who completed the NPI between 2002 and Spring of 2007 and self-identified their racial/ethnic background as African American (n = 553), Asian American (n = 9969), Latino/Latina (n = 2,358), or White (n = 7,747). These regression results were also provided to Dr. Twenge in Spring of 2008.

CHALLENGE QUESTIONS

Is There a "Narcissism Epidemic" Among Contemporary Young Adults?

1. What qualifies as a "generation" of young adults? What types of social forces might have influenced the increasing emphasis on self-esteem leading to the potential for "generation me?"
2. Twenge thinks that high rates of narcissism among college students relate to a gradual shift toward more emphasis on the self and individualism. Are there other factors that might contribute to her findings?
3. Donnellan, Trzesniewski, and Robins suggest that any increases in narcissism seem to have mostly occurred for females rather than males. Why might there be more generational change for females?
4. Some of the differences between the sides for this issue are a matter of whether to be assertive or cautious when interpreting data about generational differences. What are the relative advantages and disadvantages of each approach?

Is There Common Ground?

No one questions whether there are generational differences that influence the nature of young adulthood, though there are many questions about what exactly constitutes a generation. The inexact science of labeling a generation means that concepts such as "Generation Me," as coined by Jean M. Twenge, are bound to generate debate. Both sides of this debate would likely agree that college students today have come of age amidst social trends that are meaningfully different from those of past decades. The issue here is whether data supports the suggestion that narcissism particularly characterizes this generation. Or are there other possibilities? If you had to define a generation of contemporary college students, what characteristics would you highlight and what data would want to gather as your evidence?

Suggested Readings

J.M. Twenge, "Generation Me, The Origins of Birth Cohort Differences in Personality Traits, and Cross-Temporal Meta-Analysis," *Social and Personality Psychology Compass* (May 2008)

M.B. Donnellan and K.H. Trzeniewski, "How Should We Study Generational 'Changes'—Or Should We? A Critical Examination of the Evidence for 'Generation Me'," *Social and Personality Psychology Compass* (September 2009)

J.M. Twenge and W.K. Campbell, *The Narcissism Epidemic: Living in the Age of Entitlement* (Free Press 2009)

J.M. Twenge, *Generation Me: Why Today's Young Americans are More Confident, Assertive, Entitled—and More Miserable Than Ever Before* (Free Press 2006)

K.H. Trzesniewski, M.B. Donnellan, and R.W. Robins, "Do Today's Young People Really Think They Are so Extraordinary? An Examination of Secular Changes in Narcissism and Self-Enhancement," *Psychological Science* (February 2008)

K.H. Trzesniewski, M.B. Donnellan, and R.W. Robins, "Is 'Generation Me' Really More Narcissistic Than Previous Generations?" *Journal of Personality* (August 2008)

E. Russ, J. Shedler, R. Bradley, and D. Westen, "Refining the Construct of Narcissistic Personality Disorder: Diagnostic Criteria and Subtypes," *American Journal of Psychiatry* (November 2008)

J. Crocker, L. Park, "The Costly Pursuit of Self-Esteem," *Psychological Bulletin* (2004)

D. DuBois, B. Flay, "The Healthy Pursuit of Self-Esteem: Comment on and Alternative to the Crocker and Park (2004) Formulation," *Psychological Bulletin* (2004)

R. Baumeister, J. Campbell, J. Krueger, K. Vohs, "Exploding the Self-Esteem Myth," *Scientific American* (January 2005)

P. Bronson, "How Not to Talk to Your Kids: The Inverse Power of Praise," *New York Magazine* (February 9, 2007)

ISSUE 14

Are Today's College Students Interested in Engaging with Religion and Spirituality?

YES: Diane Winston, from "iFaith in the Amen Corner: How Gen Y Is Rethinking Religion on Campus," in the Social Science Research Council Essay Forum on the Religious Engagements of American Undergraduates (May 11, 2007, http://religion.ssrc.org/reforum/index .html)

NO: Tim Clydesdale, from "Abandoned, Pursued, or Safely Stowed?" in the Social Science Research Council Essay Forum on the Religious Engagements of American Undergraduates (February 6, 2007, http://religion.ssrc.org/reforum/index.html)

Learning Outcomes

As you read the issue, focus on the following points:

1. In past decades, college has been associated with a decline in religious involvement, but contemporary college students may be countering that trend through new forms of religious engagement.

2. College students are increasingly aware of religious traditions different from their own, though that awareness has not necessarily led to the widespread adoption of new practices or beliefs.

3. Subgroups of college students are heavily engaged with religion and spirituality, though the size and importance of those subgroups is the subject of debate.

4. Although religious involvement may decline during college, religious identification with one's childhood religion often continues. This identification, however, may not involve a critical engagement with one's values and beliefs.

ISSUE SUMMARY

YES: Religion scholar Diane Winston describes interacting with students at her university and finding that the students have vibrant religious engagements despite eschewing traditional types of religiosity.

NO: Tim Clydesdale, a sociologist who studies young adults transitioning from high school, finds instead that most college students "stow" away their religious engagements and generally immerse themselves in other identity commitments.

From a lifespan perspective, young and emerging adulthood is often the nadir of people's religious engagement. Most Americans still grow up in households that identify with a religious denomination, and children often have little choice about church attendance. In middle and later adulthood, when most have settled into routines and communities, church and religious involvement offers an anchor. But in-between, with the relative independence that often accompanies leaving home and finding one's own path, religious involvement has been considered easy to set aside. That ease does not, however, make the relationship between young adults and religion a simple one.

One complication is the challenge of defining religious engagement. Does it necessarily require involvement in religious congregations and church attendance? Or can religious engagement encompass more general spiritual explorations that involve searching for meaning in ways that may or may not include God? In fact, scholars (and young adults) often make a distinction between "religiosity" and "spirituality," with the former referring more to traditional religious practice and the latter referring more to personal attention to values, meanings, and one's "inner life." It is almost a cliché among young adults to define oneself as "spiritual but not religious," and social scientists have usually observed that same pattern: contemporary young adulthood is often characterized less by traditional religious involvement than by exploring spiritual interests.

Another complication is that explorations of religious interest take place in the context of broader identity explorations in regard to careers, relationships, political values, and more. Such explorations are often facilitated, if not encouraged, by college life—where students have the freedom to try on different identities and explore new ideas in a relatively safe environment during a time that is understood to be a transition. Yet, colleges and universities have long been considered bastions of secularism, disproportionately populated by atheists. In fact, contemporary scholars are often quite interested in religion— at least intellectually, if not personally.

One manifestation of scholarly interest in religious life was a 2007 forum on "The Religious Engagements of American Undergraduates" sponsored by the Social Science Research Council (SSRC), a prominent independent organization "devoted to the advancement of social science research and scholarship." In introducing the forum, the president of the SSRC noted that although academia has had a mixed interest in religion in recent decades, "Renewed attention to religion has been driven largely by the extent to which it has assumed manifest importance in public life." The necessity of understanding diverse religious traditions in a globalized world, the prominent public role of Evangelical Christians, and debates about evolution and creation are all part of the world today's college students confront and seek to understand.

The YES and NO articles addressing this issue are both from the SSRC forum on religious engagement, and offer distinct scholarly perspectives on the role of religion in contemporary college life. In the YES article, Diane Winston, a professor of media and religion at the University of Southern California, offers the perspective of a teacher interacting with students around issues of religion and spirituality. She finds her students engaged in religion in innovative ways, committed to their own religious orientation while also intrigued to learn about other traditions. At one point, Winston notes, she had thought students would start merging religious traditions into a personal faith, but she finds that "cafeteria-style" religion less common than she expected. Drawing on both surveys and personal experience, Winston finds many college students committed to their faith while simultaneously curious about others.

In the NO article, sociologist Tim Clydesdale, in contrast, argues that claims of religious interest among college students are overstated. He does not deny that college students often identify as religious. Instead, he thinks such identification is superficial. It is born of convenience and a disinterest in engaging critically with religious identity—or with other types of engagement. Of college freshmen, Clydesdale claims that "Issues of religion, philosophy, ethics, or meaning are of no concern to them." Instead, they are "practical credentialists" focused on what it will take to get a job and stay on track. Clydesdale acknowledges some exceptions to this pattern, but argues that most college students put religion in an "identity lockbox" that he sees as problematic to healthy development.

Returning to our lifespan perspective, the concept of an identity lockbox seems directly against the characteristics most scholars associate with emerging adulthood. Transitioning from the protections of childhood, but not yet committed to one's own family life, college can be a time of healthy exploration. Certainly many college students want to include religion in those explorations—Clydesdale himself notes the popularity of faith-based colleges and universities in recent decades. But does that interest constitute genuine engagement, or just following along?

YES

Diane Winston

iFaith in the Amen Corner: How Gen Y Is Rethinking Religion on Campus

I had to ask.

If you saw one student, then another and another wearing an "I am a Whore" tee shirt around campus, wouldn't you want to ask?

My chance came when a young woman wore the eye-popping black shirt to class. But a big red patch now hid the bold letters of sexual provocation. The new message? "FORGIVEN."

Was it an upcoming film? A fabulous new scent? A velvet-roped all-night bar?

No, the reference was to the Biblical story of Hosea, the Hebrew prophet whom God commanded to marry a faithless prostitute. The account, understood as an allegory of God's unwavering love for Israel, is shocking on many levels—which is why 250 students chose it for their religious witness that spring.

The students, members of Campus Crusade for Christ, wanted to be asked what the shirts meant. That opening would allow them to share the good news that God loves and forgives us, whether or not we deserve it.

I work at the University of Southern California (USC) where 77 religious groups, representing everyone from Asian evangelicals to Wiccans vie for student support. That support is both greater and more tenuous than in years past. According to recent surveys, members of Generation Y—which includes today's college students—exhibit a deep and thoughtful commitment to religion and spirituality. But since they also are, in the words of one study, "redefining faith in the iPod era," they're not in the market for package deals. Instead they want to create their own playlists. So even if youthful fervor is growing, don't count on a new crop of listeners for the Old Time Gospel Hour.

The combination of religious commitment and intellectual independence initially confounded me. As a journalist and historian, I have tracked American religion for more than two decades. I thought I knew what an evangelical was. Sarah Glass, who'd worn the black tee to the class I teach on American religious history, obviously was one. She'd averred the need to reach people—however, wherever—with the gospel message. But then she said she wanted to be a minister—an unlikely career choice for a female true believer.

"You can't limit God to whom he's going to call," Sarah told me, explaining why she did not agree with the evangelical prohibition against ordaining women. "The Bible is full of contradictions. In I Timothy, women are told to submit to men, but in Acts women teach men. God changes his mind all the time."

That's not the standard view at Campus Crusade, a 56-year old mission "to turn lost students into Christ-centered laborers." One of the largest Christian ministries in the world, the US arm of the international organization works on 1,300 campuses with over 55,000 students. Still, despite its immersion in the edgy richness of campus life, the group is not known for pushing the envelope on either social or theological issues.

But Sarah's mix of religious commitment and social progressivism squares with the findings of "OMG! How Generation Y is Redefining Faith in the iPod Era," as well as data collected by UCLA's Higher Education Research Institute on collegiate religion and spirituality. Both studies found a high level of religious tolerance and acceptance among college students. The UCLA survey focused more on beliefs, while Greenberg examined social and political attitudes, too. Her bottom line? "Respect for difference and diversity" is a core value. Members of Generation Y—even the most "Godly"—tend to be more liberal on social issues than their elders. Recent HERI data supports similar findings.

This coincides with what I've heard in classes. These new religious conservatives are eloquent in defense of gay rights and women's ordination. They are happy, even eager, to discuss their own faith, but go to great lengths to understand others: a staunch Catholic gingerly explained Mormonism's three-tiered heaven, an evangelical explored why some Muslim women choose to veil, and a young Jew grappled with the Religious Right. I teach in three different departments—Religion, Journalism, and Communications—and students in each one invariably are curious about what others believe and why.

While other contributors to the SSRC Forum on Religion and Higher Education have analyzed the sociological, historical, theological and pedagogical issues surrounding religion on campus; the relationship between faith and reason, and the moral development of today's young people, my focus is the classroom. I am interested in how my colleagues' analyses look on the ground. And having compared my own observations with those from a range of colleges and universities nationwide, my experiences do not appear out of the ordinary.

Here at USC, some 10,000 out of 33,000 undergraduate and graduate students are on the campus' religious organization listserv, and 4,200 of these are actively involved in faith groups. Forty-seven percent of students consider themselves "above average" in seeking to integrate spirituality into their lives, and 67 percent say they understand other religions better since coming to USC.

Seventeen percent list their religious choice as different from either of their parents.

In 2006, freshmen completed an online assignment as part of orientation and were invited to state their religious interests. Of the 3,637 new students, 1,087 used the website to state a religious interest and 149 chose instead to fill in a low-tech postcard. Of the 1,236 responses, the largest number (1,072) identified as Christian: 235 Roman Catholics, 126 non-denominational and 99 Presbyterian (followed by 23 other denominations). The next largest number of freshman were Jewish (198), Buddhist (99) and atheist/agnostic (77)—followed by 14 other designations including Falun Gong, Pagan, Unitarian and Zoroastrian.

My own classes do not reflect such diversity. Although I teach in three different areas, the subject matter of my classes (writing about religion, religion in American history, religion and the entertainment media) leads to self-selection among students. The majority has some religious inclination (ranging from deeply committed to marginally identified) and a minority want to know why religion is such a big deal. This year's class in American religious history—the same one Sarah Glass attended two years ago—had 21 students who identified as Protestant (8), Jewish (5), Catholic (4), Muslim (1) and None (3).

This spring I also taught "Religion, Media and Hollywood," a Communications class that explored religion, spirituality and ethics in post 9/11 television drama. At the end of the semester I asked the 33 students to answer a short questionnaire I had written. Of the 20 who participated, 13 identified as Christian, 5 as nothing, one as Muslim and one as Jewish. Asked to select how religious and spiritual they were on a scale of 1 to 5 (one being the lowest and five highest), they arrayed themselves evenly over the religious spectrum, but clustered at the high end of the one measuring spirituality. Twelve said this was their first college religion course while two were Religion majors or minors.

When I gave the Religion class the same questionnaire, 16 responded. Eight were taking a religion course for the first time while six were Religion majors or minors. This group skewed less religious and less spiritual than the Comm. students. Members of both classes listed prayer as a central religious practice, and several said they followed their own spiritual practices. A handful expressed a preference for the term religion over spirituality, noting the two were intertwined. Those who listed a religious affiliation were quite clear: They were Catholic, Methodist, Lutheran, Jewish or Muslim. Evangelicals called themselves Christian. But no one identified with more than one faith tradition. Overall, my modest data collection tracked with UCLA's findings from 112,232 students.

That was far from the experience I had when interviewing college students about religion and spirituality in the late 1990s. Working on a research project for Robert Wuthnow, I found many young people (and older ones too) who had constructed a spiritual regime based on religious sampling. One young woman—the epitome of this trend—was a Methodist, Taoist, Native American, Quaker, Russian Orthodox, Jew. But she was faithful in her fashion. She worked for world peace, practiced yoga and meditation, attended church, sat in sweat lodges, and participated in additional spiritual activities with her housemates.

At the time, I speculated that the growth of religious diversity in our society was paralleled by an increased diversity in individual religious practice.

Inveighing against language that demeaned such eclecticism—specifically the whimsical yet market-driven description of "cafeteria-style" religion, I suggested the term "transreligiousity," a concept used by African scholars to describe conjoined spiritual beliefs and ritual practices.

Sadly, my bid to expand our descriptive vocabulary was no more prescient than my prediction of a new religious phenomenon. There has been no groundswell of students identifying in religious multiples. They are interested in learning about others' practices but not in adopting them. When I send out my class to explore local religious sites—visiting hitherto unfamiliar traditions from Sikhism and Hinduism to Wiccan and Self-Realization, they come back enthused by new discoveries but disinclined to integrate them into their lives.

Rather, students will try out variations within a familiar theme—Christians will go to InterVarsity, Campus Crusade and a Bible student fellowship—and stick with the one that feels right for them. If there aren't a lot of options, students make do with what exists: Jewish students attend Hillel, and Muslims gather at on-campus Islamic groups or nearby mosques. Religious students don't mix and match, they practice and participate. Even those from interfaith marriages fall on one side of the fence or the other.

At least most do, and those who don't are often seeking.

"My dad comes from a Jewish family in New York and my mom is a German Methodist," said one senior, who grew up in Santa Monica. Although his parents celebrated holidays from both traditions, he identified as a Christian—partly to distinguish himself in his heavily Jewish neighborhood. "Now I don't associate with a church but I'm graduating in two weeks so I've been thinking a lot about spirituality. I want something to hold onto before my life falls apart so I'm on a quest."

The USC students seem similar to their peers nationwide. The UCLA/HERI results—on the heels of 9/11, the Iraqi war and the upsurge of "values voters"—inspired a spate of stories on campus religion. Most reported an upswing in student interest and activity. At Stanford University, the Office of Religious Life reported half of the student body claim religious affiliation. The Rev. Scotty McLennan, Dean of Religious Life and a Unitarian Universalist minister told Stanford magazine that student interest in religion had doubled over the past 20 years, "The immigration laws of the '60s brought a lot of people from other religious traditions and our student body mirrors that. And another part is the failure of science and rationality to answer and solve all our problems."

At Oberlin College, Catholic chaplain Father Edward Kordas saw a similar rise in religious interest. "Some of them are flipping back to the spiritual forms of their grandparents," he told the college alumni magazine. Erica Seager, a senior when interviewed, agreed, "There has always been spirituality here. Ties to nature, service to others, people doing yoga. But definitely, in the last several years, there has been more interest in traditional religion and, along with that, an increasing desire of religions to work together."

It's the same story further east at Rensselaer Polytechnic Institute. According to the university magazine, "the Institute's religious population is larger, more active and more diverse than it was a decade ago." Rick Hartt, director of the Rensselaer Union and a member of RPI's class of 1970, reported significant differences between religion on campus then and now, "It used to be that your religious beliefs were private—except for Mass on Sunday morning. Now we try to create an environment where [students] can feel comfortable exploring their faith. I've really seen interest grow in the last five years. These students see the big picture."

The big picture, as the UCLA/HERI survey suggests, is that today's students "show a high degree of spiritual interest and involvement." To understand why, I tried an in-class experiment. After lecturing on the large sweep of 20th century American religion—highlighting post-war events including the Second Vatican Council, changed immigration laws, the Age of Aquarius, the integration of Jews and Catholics into the religious mainstream and the rise of evangelicalism—I asked students how their own family histories fit in.

Nick Street, my teaching assistant, and I began by discussing how our religious odysseys crossed paths with the Vietnam anti-war movement, psychedelicism, feminism, gay liberation, new religious movements, Southern Baptists, yoga, Buddhism and Reconstructionist Judaism.

I'd never before asked students to speak personally about their families or their religious identities, but the stories that Nick and I told established a level of trust and intimacy that enabled class members to speak freely. We subsequently discovered that five were children of first generation immigrants (who tended to have strong religious backgrounds) while another five had parents who had been "60s hippies" and wanted nothing to do with organized religion. Three were from intermarried families (one was raised Jewish and the other two Christian) and another five, who came from conservative Christian homes, remained so. Students raised in non-religious homes had little interest in becoming religious; several who had some religious education were still "searching."

"I'm open to everything," said a student who had attended Catholic, Lutheran and Baptist primary and secondary schools. "I've done lots of reading in Christian apologetics but I still have no idea what I believe."

Afterwards, students questioned each other. A non-believer asked an evangelical, "Can you accept me?" A Jew asked a Christian how she reconciled religious truths that were different from her own. A born-again asked an atheist why she got out of bed in the morning; in other words, what gave her life meaning. Great questions all, they underscored the challenges that religion poses in a secular, pluralist environment as well as the reasons why its study and practice has experienced a renaissance on many American campuses.

Two years ago, Stanley Fish, Dean Emeritus at the University of Illinois at Chicago, opined that religion "is now where the action is." While some may agree, others—steeped in the culture of secular fundamentalism—remain unconverted. Last fall, when a Harvard task force on curriculum reform proposed a "faith and reason" requirement, many faculty responded as if Al Queda had breached the ivy-covered walls.

Given longstanding intellectual paradigms, emotional prejudices and a pervasive system of financial rewards that work against the academic study of religion, can the field move from side show to center stage in secular research universities? When I posed the question at an American Academy of Religion meeting in 2003, I spoke from my position as a program officer at the Pew Charitable Trusts. Pew invested more than $30 million in ten centers of excellence to mainstream the study of religion at ten, top-tier research universities. As part of my portfolio I helped select and oversee the centers that the foundation hoped would end the ghettoization of religious studies.

On my own campus, the Pew-supported Center for Religion and Civic Culture (CRCC) has reinvigorated the academic discussion of religion through high-profile programming, funding for interdisciplinary research and leveraging Pew support to garner additional funding. Is religion center stage at USC? That is for others to decide, but CRCC's research and academic programs combined with extracurricular activities through the Office of Religious Life and faculty and student interest provide a high profile.

That's not to say that religion holds the same hallowed spot that engineering, business, and the sciences do. These areas attract the most funding, some of the best students and a significant slice of cultural capital. Yet religion has made inroads in each of these fields through programming, research and interdisciplinary projects that remind faculty (as well as students) that some of our most pressing questions—*why do you get up in the morning*—are religious in nature.

For me, these questions exemplify why religion has a central role to play in the academy. All our studies must be leavened by inquiries into the ethical and existential meaning of the knowledge we seek and the responsibilities it bears. But even though I believe these questions are fundamentally religious in nature, I am cautious about framing the discussions that follow lest I—or anyone else—appear to have ultimate answers. I balk when others try to impress their truth claims on me, as when evangelical colleagues claim that all truth is mediated through the Christian revelation. I am glad that many of our great universities are no longer religious institutions and I pray they remain so. I want my students to be free to choose which tee shirts to wear around campus.

"If Jesus came back he would be just as liberal for today as he was for his time," Sarah told me. "He'd go to the people whom nobody loves just like he went to the prostitutes and those who were unclean and unworthy. That's his example."

To drive home her point, Sarah wore another black tee shirt to a Campus Crusade meeting. This one read, "Gay? Fine By Me."

The leadership immediately pulled her aside.

"They wanted to talk about it and look at the Bible," she recalled. "I never saw anything in the Bible that said being a homosexual is evil. It says two guys having sex is bad, but not that you're going to hell if you're born gay."

After much discussion, Sarah and the leadership agreed to disagree.

"They gave me the postmodern view that everyone has to come to the truth their own way," she observed. "But I'm socially liberal and most of them aren't."

Me, I'm still coming to terms with a generation that doesn't automatically tie Biblical truth to social conservatism. If my students are indicative, these young believers may have more in common with nineteenth century evangelicals, crusaders for abolition, suffrage and labor reform—than with the today's Christian right. Now can somebody say Amen?

NO

Abandoned, Pursued, or Safely Stowed?

There is certainly no shortage of passionate opinions about what happens to the religious commitments of college students. Some religious conservatives allege that liberal professors undermine student faith, that college administrators permit conditions that foster sexual promiscuity and alcohol abuse, and that the result is a deliberate weakening of students' religious commitments. College professors and administrators respond that college is a time when students explore new possibilities and reflect critically on their new *adult* lives, and that any change in religious commitment is a result of these adults' own choices and individual learning processes. Left unstated, of course, is the opinion of many professors that traditional religious faiths are incompatible with liberal education, and the opinion of many religious conservatives that professors lead morally vacuous lives. This longstanding and deeply-rooted difference of opinion has undoubtedly helped to fuel the two-decade-plus expansion of religious college and university enrollments; that is, expansion at educational institutions that combine faith development with a liberal arts education.

But popular recognition of religion's influence in America, especially after the 2004 election, has given rise to a new interpretation. Several observers, who previously ignored religion, now argue that the vast majority of American college students "report high levels of spiritual interest and involvement," that over half affirm "reducing pain and suffering in the world" as a life goal, that "nearly half" of American college students "are on a quest" to identify a spiritual purpose for their lives, and that spiritual traditions provide resources which can inspire students' educational efforts. By framing religion as "spirituality," this interpretation grants religious life legitimacy as an (optional) component in college student "wellness," and provides market-savvy colleges with a rationale for expanding support of religious life on their campuses.

There is just one problem with this view, which is the same problem that the longer-standing views have: woefully inadequate evidence. For all the fears of religious conservatives, and all the claims of students' critical thinking by professors and college administrators, there is precious little evidence that college students either abandon their faith commitments *or* develop intellectual curiosity. And the evidence offered in support of claims about

From *Social Science Research Council Essay Forum on the Religious Engagements of American Undergraduates*, February 6, 2007. Copyright © 2007 by Social Science Research Council. Reprinted by permission.

widespread pursuit of spiritual purpose or social justice among college students is as compelling as a survey about world peace completed by beauty pageant contestants. The real issue is not how many college students check off "an interest in spirituality," but how many actualize that interest in their everyday priorities. Social survey results need to be checked against grounded and contextualized understandings of college student lives—particularly if one wishes to draw conclusions about the lived culture of American college students. Such grounded and contextualized understandings are what this author has undertaken and summarizes here.

What in-depth, longitudinal interviews and field research with college freshmen reveal is that most freshmen are thoroughly consumed with the everyday matters of navigating relationships, managing gratifications, handling finances, and earning diplomas—and that they stow their (often vague) religious and spiritual identities in an *identity lockbox* well before entering college. This lockbox protects religious identities, along with political, racial, gender, and civic identities, from tampering that might affect their holders' future entry into the American cultural mainstream. If religious identities were to shift to a religious or anti-religious extreme, for example, they could ruin a teen's mainstream standing and future trajectory. The same holds true for political, racial, gender, and civic identities. "Wrong" choices in any of these areas could put freshmen seriously out of step with mainstream culture, and endanger their odds of attaining the privatized, consumer happiness that American youth have long been socialized to seek.

Not all college students make use of the lockbox to store religious identities, and these exceptions deserve close attention. But most college students do so because they view religion not unlike vegetables—as something that is "good for you" and part of adult life, but not as something all that relevant to their current stage as college students. As one freshman put it, "I feel like God dropped me off at college and said, 'I'll be back to pick you up in four years'." Note that this student, like many of his peers, planned to be picked up when he graduated—in the same place and by the same driver. It is not that his religious identity was unimportant (quite the contrary), only that he did not see its relevancy to his college education and campus experience. The same holds true of students' political, civic, racial, and gender identities. These identities, as undeveloped as they often are, play a critical role in guiding youth into the cultural mainstream of the United States. College students, of course, are not one-dimensional. There are those who peek inside their identity lockboxes, with varying frequency, and who consider some or all of its contents. Those who do this in a sustained manner, however, are proportionately few, and qualify as one of three exceptional types described below.

Religious Involvement vs. Religious Identification

There is, to be sure, well-documented research on college students' decline in attendance at religious services and in other forms of involvement in organized religious life. This is not in dispute. But a decline in religious involvement is not equivalent to a decline in religious identification, and needs to be understood carefully. Freshmen whose religious involvements declined offer various reasons for their reduced involvement: a few choose to behave in keeping with the nonreligious identities they had established previously, though as high school students they attended religious services to please their parents. Others visit a few religious services "out at college," do not find a service they "like," but still attend "every time" they are "back home." And many continue to attend worship services—just "a little less often" because "it can be really hard to get up that early on Sundays." (A national survey of college freshmen, in fact, found 57 percent reported attending religious services "frequently" or "occasionally" at the *end* of their first year of college.) What freshmen do *not* say, however, is that they have gained a critical perspective on religion because of attending college, and thus have ceased to identify themselves as a religious person. Religious identifications are not questioned during the freshman year, not because they are held to in widespread piety, but because doing so would require freshmen to give attention to these identities, and few have any interest in doing so.

Asking students the summer after their freshman year to describe their spiritual and religious beliefs brought forth nearly identical answers to those they gave as high school seniors. Post-freshman year interviewees still did not relate to the terms "spiritual" or "spirituality," and they still struggled to define such terms. "Being spiritual" meant "having morals" or "being religious," and fewer than half offered even that definition. As others have well-documented, the vast majority of American teens are *not* spiritual seekers, and the few interviewees who identified as spiritual did so within established religious traditions (e.g., "I pray the rosary and meditate every night"). Likewise, freshmen's religious identifications had not shifted in the slightest. It was as if these rising sophomores peeked inside their identity lockboxes, dusted off their religious identifications, and reported, "Yeah, I'm still religious." This was quite striking. Why would freshmen choose to preserve what were often vague religious identifications, and which often diminished as aspects of their regular activities? The answer lies in understanding the powerful effects of popular American moral culture on mainstream American teens.

Religion and Popular American Moral Culture

The American mainstream can be defined in many ways; it is defined here as including American households earning $25,000 or more a year, but excluding independently wealthy households. Members of mainstream households have a toehold (or better) in the "American dream," and they have been fully socialized into American culture. Culture, to use a computer analogy, is humanity's operating system. Without it, there would be no language, no communication, no knowledge, and no meaning. And like a computer operating system, culture gets installed with certain "default" settings that, unless overridden, determine how humans view their world and structure their everyday behavior. In the United States, the current default settings install a popular American moral culture that celebrates personal effort and individual achievement, demonstrates patriotism, believes in God and a spiritual afterlife, values loyalty to family, friends, and co-workers, expects personal moral freedom, distrusts large organizations and bureaucracies, and conveys that happiness is found primarily in personal relationships and individual consumption. Unless these default settings are altered, typically to install more specific religious or nonreligious sub-cultural settings, this constellation of beliefs and practices is characteristic of most Americans.

Thus, one national study reports that most American teens consider religion to be "a very nice thing," and despite their specific religious tradition, essentially adhere to a faith in "divinely underwritten personal happiness and interpersonal niceness." There are, to be sure, nonreligious teens who have no need for the divine and theistic elements of popular American moral culture: national surveys estimate 12–18 percent of American teens consider themselves *nonreligious*. And there are also, to be sure, strongly religious teens who subscribe to elaborate religious doctrines and particular moral codes: national surveys estimate 25–35 percent of American teens are *strongly religious*. The majority of American teens, however, about 55 percent, comprise the *semireligious* middle ground. These teens believe in God and identify with a religious tradition, but their practical creed is essentially a combination of Benjamin Franklin's "God helps those who help themselves" and the "Golden Rule." In other words, their semireligious identities provide divine reinforcement for pursuing individual achievement and, as one interviewee put it, for "trying to be a nice person."

Semireligious identities therefore serve a specific purpose: they underwrite a popular American moral culture that has been inculcated since birth. Semireligious identities reinforce the mainstream cultural script that graduating from college leads to a good job, which leads to marriage, which leads to children, comfortable housing, and a good standard of living. To question these religious identities is thus to question the whole of the mainstream cultural script and the popular American moral culture that created it, and these college students see no benefit in doing so. Besides, given the myriad of personal relationships to navigate, gratifications to manage, money to earn and spend, and credentials to complete—there are more pressing daily matters to which college students must attend. Semireligious identities are therefore stowed in college students' identity lockboxes, often alongside political, racial, gender, and civic identities, and all are left undisturbed.

It is not just semireligious college freshmen who stow identities, however. So do many strongly religious and nonreligious freshmen. Many strongly religious freshmen do so because they have become proficient *compartmentalizers*. That is, they stow religious identities when in educational settings, and stow educational identities when in religious settings, and readily switch one with the other. And most nonreligious freshmen stow identities because they not only lack interest in religion, they also lack interest in their *non*-religion. Issues of religion, philosophy, ethics or meaning are of no concern to them. These nonreligious, religious, and strongly religious freshmen use identity lockboxes for the same reasons as semireligious teens: they too subscribe to popular American moral culture (with a few minor adjustments), and they too possess more than enough everyday concerns to occupy their attentions.

Hence, the vast majority of college freshmen approach their education not as intellectual explorers but as *practical credentialists;* they focus on degree completion (and on grades if they seek high-status credentials), and view the rest of their education as little more than a necessary nuisance. Popular American moral culture is dubious of large organizations and bureaucracies, and especially of higher education, and college students are both products and proponents of this moral culture.

Religious and Educational Exceptions

There *are* exceptions to the above pattern. There are teens who enter college seeking to understand their own lives more fully and the wider world more thoughtfully. They take advantage of educational opportunities because they enjoy learning for its own sake, they pursue creative opportunities because these express deeper realities, or they serve needy communities because they desire a more just society. In short, they refuse to stow critical identities in identity lockboxes. Who are they? Some are the *future intelligentsia*—that is, the next generation of professors and allied professionals like psychologists, deans, journalists, and guidance counselors. Some are *religious skeptics* and atheists—that is, a subset of nonreligious teens who consider religion to be the chief obstacle to achieving social justice and equity. And some are *religious emissaries*—that is, a subset of strongly religious teens who refuse to stow or compartmentalize faith but are driven to understand it and engage it with the world. The existence and inclusion of this last category here may be surprising to some, but as scholars of contemporary American religion demonstrate repeatedly, religious communities thrive in American pluralism because they engage it thoughtfully, not retreat from it. Even members of the most conservative religious communities know they possess the option to pursue any religion, or none—thus religious communities put much effort into attracting and keeping adherents, including intellectual appeals, and their teen emissaries become quite conversant in these matters.

What all of these teen exceptions share is a critical perspective on popular American moral culture. That perspective may be rooted in their possession of inquisitive and self-reflective minds, and in parental and educational nurturance of the same. It may be rooted in their alienation from "mindless" theism and in their relationships with like-minded mentors. Or it may be rooted in their personal and deep identification with a religious community that decries the superficiality of American culture. (Those in the first category, in fact, frequently qualify for one of the latter two categories.) Whatever its cause, these teens grow up doubting core elements of popular American moral culture and thus reflecting upon their deeper identities and broader perspectives on the world regularly. When they enter college, this does not change. They become highly desirable students, because they genuinely engage with class materials and because they demonstrate intellectual curiosity, creative engagement, social awareness, or all three.

Some professors will point to these intellectually engaged students as evidence of the value of liberal education. But these students' patterns of engagement pre-date their arrival at college, and while they take advantage of educational, creative, and service opportunities during their college years, college is not the cause of their engagement. Further confounding some professors' perceptions is the temporary nature of the intellectual curiosity, creative engagement, or social awareness that many students demonstrate in class. Sometimes this temporariness has more genuine roots—for example, the marketing student who becomes enraptured with her opera performance course, but who subsequently pushes aside that interest to concentrate on her "more realistic" educational goals. And sometimes this temporariness is more Machiavellian—that is, a pose that grade-obsessed practical credentialists strike because they know intellectual curiosity, creative engagement, and social awareness are precisely what their professors want to see.

The actual proportion of American teens who possess both genuine and sustained intellectual curiosity, creative engagement, or social awareness is quite small. About 1–2 percent of American teens are atheists or religious skeptics (i.e., nonreligious teens with an active and sustained interest in their non-religiosity), another 10–15 percent are religious emissaries (i.e., non compartmentalizing, religiously driven teens), and perhaps one percent more are future intelligentsia (i.e., intellectually engaged teens not already included above, often in semireligious transition), giving a total estimate of 12–18 percent. Their representation on college campuses, moreover, is uneven. These exceptional teens often enroll in more selective colleges, with religious skeptics gravitating to nonreligious colleges, and religious emissaries to religious colleges. None of this should undermine the importance of professors' efforts to encourage intellectual, creative, or social engagement among students, only professors' self-aggrandizing assumptions that liberal education is the cause of such engagement.

Implications

The enemy of developing critical thinking, creative engagement, and social awareness among college students is therefore not students' possession of religious identities—it is their widespread use of identity lockboxes. So, too, the enemy of a thoughtful and lasting religiosity among college students is not their pursuit of college education, but their widespread use of identity lockboxes. Thus, what hinders college students' development is neither religion nor liberal education, but the use of these lockboxes. College educators need to understand that religion, and devout religion in particular, can indeed be an ally in the cause of critical thinking and social awareness. Correspondingly, religious leaders need to understand that college education, and a liberal education in particular, can aid in the development of a thoughtful and meaningful religious identity.

College students are not, however, likely to end their use of identity lockboxes anytime soon. The power of college students' desire to keep within the American cultural mainstream is not likely to diminish, and may even enlarge, as America's new economic realities make entering the cultural mainstream even more difficult. College students know that companies are quick to reorganize, to relocate to less costly areas or nations, and to release even diligent and long-term employees. They know that downward mobility is a real possibility, and that better odds of attaining economic security come with a college diploma. Thus, college students are not, save for the exceptions above, going to risk using college as a time for developing intellectual curiosity, reflecting on identities—religious or otherwise, or understanding their interdependence with communities large and small. Doing so could move students outside the cultural mainstream and jeopardize their long-term futures—a risk too great for most college students to take.

Pleading with freshmen to swim against these economic and cultural currents is not the solution. Colleges and religious communities already do this extensively, and have likely seen as much gain as they will from such appeals. Freshman interviewees were quite aware of these appeals, and had long developed immunity to them. There is anecdotal evidence that once the daily life management project of freshman year is mastered, a window of opportunity opens to engage sophomores and juniors more deeply in both religious and nonreligious pursuits. But the established, everyday patterns of college student lives, combined with the narrowing of social circles during the freshman year, makes this a narrow window indeed.

Rather than "curse the cards" American culture has dealt, college educators and religious leaders should play the hand they have. Because higher education does not possess the cultural authority in America that it does in other societies, its educators need to become public intellectuals. College educators need to realize that the same cultural pluralism that challenges religious truth claims also challenges scholarly truth claims. It is not enough for college educators to be members of scholarly disciplines, where knowledge claims are accepted when they meet the criteria of that discipline. College educators must also earn the right to be heard by larger publics because they speak plainly, marshal evidence, evaluate dispassionately, and lead their audience to logical conclusions. And the first place where that right must be earned is with their most immediate audience: college students. In the same way, religious leaders must earn the right to be heard by larger publics by the same methods. College students should be respected as the individual arbiters of truth that they are, and encouraged to see that the skills of critical thinking, creative expression, and social engagement are as useful for faith as they are for learning.

Stowed identities benefit no one—not educators, not religious communities, and certainly not college freshmen. There exists no quick fix, either. Broad cultural and economic forces will ensure that the vast majority of American college freshmen continue to follow mainstream scripts that offer no guarantee of success or satisfaction. Still, it is better to know the real problem confronting freshmen development than to continually waste energy and resources addressing the wrong issues.

CHALLENGE QUESTIONS

Are Today's College Students Interested in Engaging with Religion and Spirituality?

1. Many explanations have been offered for the fact that college is often a low point of an individual's religious involvement, ranging from the college environments that discourage religious engagement to individual priorities shifting during the college years. Which explanations do you find most convincing? Which best fit what you have observed among your friends and peers?
2. Both authors note the differences between "religiosity" and "spirituality," highlighting the difficulty of making that distinction. How do you understand each concept, and what are the ways in which religiosity and spirituality do and do not overlap?
3. Winston describes several personal experiences with college students engaging religion in surprising, nontraditional ways. Have you seen examples of nontraditional religious engagement among college students? What do such engagements say about religion in the lives of contemporary college students.
4. Clydesdale argues that in addition to "stowing" religious identities, college students often stow "political, civic, racial, and gender identities." Do these processes seem analogous? Is there anything different about explorations of religious identity when compared with other types of identity exploration?

Is There Common Ground?

American colleges and universities have not historically been considered bastions of religious involvement, but these selections from Diane Winston and Tim Clydesdale suggest that is not for lack of scholarly curiosity. Scholars may debate the reasons for religious engagement and disengagement, but they often share an appreciation for college as a time when young adults could potentially explore their religious and spiritual life—something integral to development across the lifespan. Winston seems to think this is increasingly likely, while Clydesdale thinks it is more of a missed opportunity, but they both see attitudes toward religion as an interesting dimension of college life. Both also acknowledge that it may not be fair to talk about college students as a whole when thinking through this issue: there are always subgroups of students who are particularly engaged with religion and spirituality, and subgroups who demonstrate no interest whatsoever. In the end, then, it may be worth thinking not just about whether or not college students take an interest in religion and spirituality, but also about whether more should?

Suggested Readings

J.P. Hill, "Faith and Understanding: Specifying the Impact of Higher Education on Religious Belief," *Journal for the Scientific Study of Religion* (September 2011)

G.D. Kuh and R.M. Gonyea, "Spirituality, Liberal Learning, and College Student Engagement," *Liberal Education* (Winter 2006)

D. Mayrl and F. Oeur, "Religion and Higher Education: Current Knowledge and Directions for Future Research," *Journal for the Scientific Study of Religion* (June 2009)

P. Schwadel, "The Effects of Education on Americans' Religious Practices, Beliefs, and Affiliations," *Review of Religious Research* (July 28, 2011)

M.D. Regnerus, *Forbidden Fruit: Sex & Religion in the Lives of American Teenagers* (Oxford University Press 2007)

C. Smith and P. Snell, *Souls in Transition: The Religious and Spiritual Lives of Emerging Adults* (Oxford University Press 2009)

R. Wuthnow, *After the Baby Boomers: How Twenty- and Thirty-Somethings are Shaping the Future of American Religion,* (Princeton University Press 2007)

Internet References . . .

Division 20

This Web site provides information from Division 20 of the American Psychological Association, the division focused on adult development and aging.

http://apadiv20.phhp.ufl.edu/apadiv20.htm

The Society for Research on Adult Development

The Society for Research on Adult Development brings together researchers interested in positive adult development.

http://www.adultdevelopment.org/

The Alternatives to Marriage Project

The Alternatives to Marriage Project advocates for diversity in adult relationships.

http://www.unmarried.org/

The Institute for American Values

The "Institute for American Values" promotes, among other things, marriage and traditional families.

http://americanvalues.org/

The International Research Association for Talent Development and Excellence

The International Research Association for Talent Development and Excellence is "a professional organization of scientists working in the fields of talent development, creativity, excellence and innovation."

http://www.iratde.org/

Tufts University Child and Family Web Guide

Information and links, vetted by the Eliot-Pearson Department of Child Development at Tufts University, for information about parenting.

http://www.cfw.tufts.edu/

Working Mother Magazine

The Web site for Working Mother magazine offers information and links for adult women trying to balance parenting and careers.

http://www.workingmother.com/

Parenting Blog

The author of the New York Times parenting blog, Lisa Belkin, wrote a controversial article bringing the "opt-out revolution" into popular use—and offers regular articles about issues related to balancing family with work.

http://parenting.blogs.nytimes.com/

Middle Adulthood

*I*n conventional terms, middle adulthood is often the most productive portion of the lifespan. During middle adulthood, most people deeply engage with families, the world of work, and communities. As such, some versions of the lifespan present middle adulthood (generally conceptualized as being between the mid-30s and the mid-60s) as the peak of development. But middle adulthood also produces significant challenges and new expectations. This section focuses on the relationship between healthy development and three challenges and expectations confronted by most adults in contemporary society: marriage, parenthood, and career success.

- Do Adults Need to Place More Value on Marriage?
- Is Parenthood a Detriment to Well-being?

ISSUE 15

Do Adults Need to Place More Value on Marriage?

YES: W. Bradford Wilcox et al., from *Why Marriage Matters: Thirty Conclusions from the Social Sciences—3rd ed.* (Institute for American Values, 2011)

NO: Kathleen E. Hull, Ann Meier, and Timothy Ortyl, from "The Changing Landscape of Love and Marriage" *Contexts* (vol. 9, no. 2, Spring 2010)

Learning Outcomes

As you read the issue, focus on the following points:

1. The dramatic increases in divorce rates during the second half of the twentieth century have now leveled off, such that some social scientists consider cohabitation a more significant threat to traditional marriage.

2. Although adults increasingly see cohabitation as a viable option for long-term relationships, there is evidence to suggest that cohabitation does not associate with as positive of outcomes as marriage.

3. When surveyed, most young Americans still express a desire for stable, long-term love relationships, even if those relationships take increasingly diverse forms.

4. When thinking about long-term relationships, many adults have somewhat conflicting desires for love, security, and independence that are not always compatible with marriage.

5. Long-term relationship norms vary significantly across historical periods and cultural settings, suggesting that it may be worth devoting attention to providing social support for relationships other than traditional marriage.

ISSUE SUMMARY

YES: Sociologist W. Bradford Wilcox led a team of prominent family scholars to draw conclusions about the contemporary state of marriage as an institution, and the consequences of being married. They conclude that although marriage patterns are changing, traditional marriages still benefit adults and society.

NO: Kathleen E. Hull, Ann Meier, and Timothy Ortyl from the sociology department at the University of Minnesota survey findings suggesting that most contemporary adults value committed relationships even if social forces are changing the nature of marriage itself.

Marriage is one of the most significant markers of the adult lifespan. Both historically and cross-culturally, adulthood is often defined by getting married and starting a family. In contemporary society, this norm is gradually changing. Although there has always been a diversity of family types, the general expectation that a person will get married immediately upon becoming an adult has waned. It is much more likely for people to wait to get married, or to not get married at all. This trend has generated tremendous controversy among those interested in considering the relationship between marriage and lifespan development.

Some of the controversy derives from divorce rates that are astonishingly high. It is common to hear that half of all marriages in the United States end in divorce—though that figure is generally used more as a high-end estimate rather than the probability of any particular marriage working out. For example, by some estimates, college-educated people are half as likely to get a divorce than the less educated. Likewise, people who marry at a young age are significantly more likely to get divorced. Although such statistics can be manipulated to serve varying agendas, it is true that divorce is a common outcome of contemporary marriage. And divorce is hard on people—it is hard on the people getting divorced, and it is hard on any children who may be involved. Although the long-term impact of divorce is another controversial area of study, few people would argue divorce is a good outcome.

In addition to controversy around divorce, a current trend toward adults choosing cohabitation over marriage is raising new and interesting questions. In *Why Marriage Matters: Thirty Conclusions from the Social Sciences*, W. Bradford Wilcox and a team of family scholars note that the prevalence of cohabitation in the United States "has risen fourteen-fold since 1970." They see this rise as the major current threat to marriage, having overtaken divorce. In fact, they go on to note, "today's children are much more likely to spend time in a cohabiting household than they are to see their parents divorce." And data does find that cohabitation on average associates with more negative outcomes than marriage. Even when comparing divorce rates among couples who had initially cohabited and those who had not, for example, many have been surprised to learn that prior cohabitation associates with less successful marriages.

As Wilcox and colleagues note, however, "social science is better equipped to document whether certain facts are true than to say why they are true." In this case, while it is easy to assume that adults need to put more value on marriage and avoid cohabitation, there may be other social forces at play. It may well be the case, for example, that cohabiting couples and others in nontraditional forms of adult relationships have had less success than married couples precisely because such relationships have been marginalized. Because marriage has long been a normative marker of adulthood, many social support systems focus on marriage: accessing health care, financial planning, parental duties, and more may all be easier for those in traditional marriages.

The influence of social forces and social supports upon adults' attitudes toward marriage is of much interest to sociologists including Kathleen E. Hull, Ann Meier, and Timothy Ortyl. Their article presents theory and data raising the possibility that individuals continue to value marriage and long-term committed relationships, but those values are negotiated with a desire for independence and changing social norms. In fact, although Hull, Meier, and Ortyl are sociologists, some of the points they make offer psychological insight. In particular, they note that adults are often conflicted by competing impulses: in this case, people aspire to the romantic love and stability of a healthy marriage, but also want to freedom of leaving or changing a relationship over time. These competing impulses may contribute to some problematic statistics on the state of marriage, but they are consistent with broader cultural values simultaneously prioritizing security, love, and freedom.

Rather than encouraging adults to place more value on marriage, Hull, Meier, and Ortyl imply that we would all to well to recognize and accommodate changing relationship norms. They highlight, for example, the issue of same-sex marriage—which proponents of traditional marriage have often opposed despite the possibility that "same-sex marriage would bring some Americans into the marital fold, benefiting the adults and children in these families and society more generally." But data does suggest that traditional marriage still associates with positive outcomes, and some worry that more change could diminish those associations. So is there something special and enduring about marriage, or are there other viable models and markers of successful adulthood?

YES

W. Bradford Wilcox et al.

Why Marriage Matters: Thirty Conclusions from the Social Sciences

Executive Summary

In the latter half of the twentieth century, divorce posed the biggest threat to marriage in the United States. Clinical, academic, and popular accounts addressing recent family change—from Judith Wallerstein's landmark book, *The Unexpected Legacy of Divorce,* to Sara McLanahan and Gary Sandefur's award-winning book, *Growing Up with a Single Parent,* to Barbara Dafoe Whitehead's attention-getting *Atlantic* article, "Dan Quayle Was Right"—focused largely on the impact that divorce had upon children, and rightly so. In the wake of the divorce revolution of the 1970s, divorce was the event most likely to undercut the quality and stability of children's family lives in the second half of the twentieth century.

No more. In fact, as divorce rates have come down since peaking in the early 1980s, children who are now born to married couples are actually more likely to grow up with both of their parents than were children born at the height of the divorce revolution (see figure 1). In fact, the divorce rate for

Figure 1

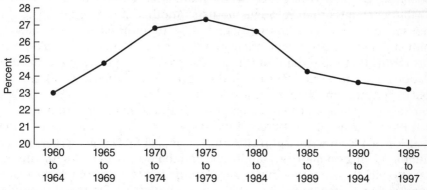

Percentage of Children Experiencing Parental Divorce by Age 10 by Parents' Year of Marriage (1960–1997)

Source: SIPP Data, 2001, 2004, and 2008. Women with premarital births excluded.

From *Why Marriage Matters: Thirty Conclusions from the Social Sciences* by Bradford W. Wilcox (Institute for American Values, 2011). Copyright © 2011 by Institute for American Values. Reprinted by permission.

Figure 2

Percentage of Children Experiencing Parental Divorce/Separation and Parental Cohabitation, by Age 12; Period Life Table Estimates, 2002–07

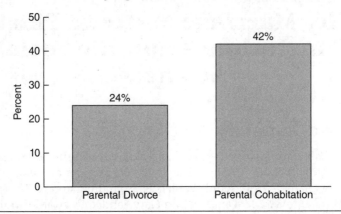

Source: Kennedy and Bumpass, 2011. Data from National Survey of Family Growth. Note: The divorce/separation rate only applies to children born to married parents.

married couples with children has fallen almost to pre-divorce revolution levels, with 23 percent of couples who married in the early 1960s divorcing before their first child turned ten, compared to slightly more than 23 percent for couples who married in the mid 1990s.

Today, the rise of cohabiting households with children is the largest unrecognized threat to the quality and stability of children's family lives. In fact, because of the growing prevalence of cohabitation, which has risen fourteen-fold since 1970, today's children are much more likely to spend time in a cohabiting household than they are to see their parents divorce (see figure 2).

Now, approximately 24 percent of the nation's children are born to cohabiting couples, which means that more children are currently born to cohabiting couples than to single mothers. Another 20 percent or so of children spend time in a cohabiting household with an unrelated adult at some point later in their childhood, often after their parents' marriage breaks down. This means that more than four in ten children are exposed to a cohabiting relationship. Thus, one reason that the institution of marriage has less of a hold over Americans than it has had for most [of] our history is that cohabitation has emerged as a powerful alternative to and competitor with marriage.

For this reason, the third edition of *Why Marriage Matters* focuses new attention on recent scholarship assessing the impact that contemporary cohabitation is having on marriage, family life, and the welfare of children. This edition also picks up on topics that surfaced in the first two editions of the report, summarizing a large body of research on the impact of divorce, stepfamilies, and single parenthood on children, adults, and the larger commonwealth. The report seeks to summarize existing family-related research into a succinct form useful to policy makers, scholars, civic, business, and religious leaders, professionals, and others interested in understanding marriage in today's society.

Figure 3

Incidence Per 1,000 Children of Harm Standard Abuse by Family Structure and Living Arrangement, 2005–2006

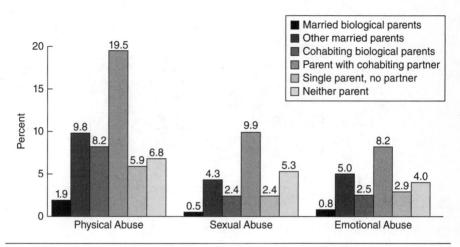

Source: Figure 5-2 in Fourth National Incidence Study of Child Abuse and Neglect (NIS-4): Report to Congress.

Five New Themes

1. *Children are less likely to thrive in cohabiting households, compared to intact, married families.* On many social, educational, and psychological outcomes, children in cohabiting households do significantly worse than children in intact, married families, and about as poorly as children living in single-parent families. And when it comes to abuse, recent federal data indicate that children in cohabiting households are markedly more likely to be physically, sexually, and emotionally abused than children in both intact, married families and single-parent families (see figure 3). Only in the economic domain do children in cohabiting households fare consistently better than children in single-parent families.

2. *Family instability is generally bad for children.* In recent years, family scholars have turned their attention to the impact that transitions into and out of marriage, cohabitation, and single parenthood have upon children. This report shows that such transitions, especially multiple transitions, are linked to higher reports of school failure, behavioral problems, drug use, and loneliness, among other outcomes. So, it is not just family structure and family process that matter for children; family stability matters as well. And the research indicates that children who are born to married parents are the least likely to be exposed to family instability, and to the risks instability poses to the emotional, social, and educational welfare of children.

3. *American family life is becoming increasingly unstable for children* (see figure 4). Sociologist Andrew Cherlin has observed that Americans are stepping "on and off the carousel of intimate relationships"

Figure 4

Percent of 16-Year-Olds Living with Mother and Father, 1978–1984 and 1998–2004

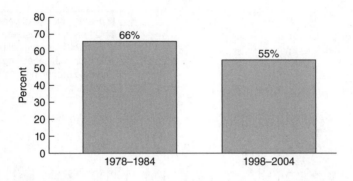

Source: General Social Survey, 1980–2010.

with increasing rapidity. This relational carousel spins particularly quickly for couples who are cohabiting, even cohabiting couples with children. For instance, cohabiting couples who have a child together are more than twice as likely to break up before their child turns twelve, compared to couples who are married to one another (see figure 5). Thus, one of the major reasons that children's lives are increasingly turbulent is that more and more children are being born into or raised in cohabiting households that are much more fragile than married families.

4. *The growing instability of American family life also means that contemporary adults and children are more likely to live in what scholars call "complex households,"* where children and adults are living with people who are half-siblings, stepsiblings, stepparents, stepchildren, or unrelated to them by birth or marriage. Research on these complex households is still embryonic, but the initial findings are not encouraging. For instance, one indicator of this growing complexity is multiple-partner fertility, where parents have children with more than one romantic partner. Children who come from these relationships are more likely to report poor relationships with their parents, to have behavioral and health problems, and to fail in school, even after controlling for factors such as education, income, and race. Thus, for both adults and children, life typically becomes not only more complex, but also more difficult, when parents fail to get or stay married.

5. *The nation's retreat from marriage has hit poor and working-class communities with particular force.* Recent increases in cohabitation, nonmarital childbearing, family instability, and family complexity have not been equally distributed in the United States; these trends, which first rose in poor communities in the 1970s and 1980s, are now moving rapidly into working-class and lower-middle-class communities.

Figure 5

Percent of Children Experiencing Parental Separation by Age 12 by Mother's Relationship Status at Birth; Period of Life Table Estimates, 2002–07

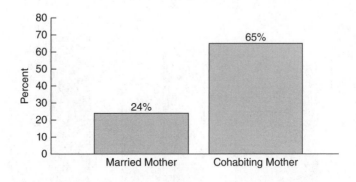

Source: Kennedy and Bumpass, 2011. Data from National Survey of Family Growth.

But marriage appears to be strengthening in more educated and afflu-ent communities. As a consequence, since the early 1980s, children from college-educated homes have seen their family lives stabilize, whereas children from less-educated homes have seen their family lives become increasingly unstable (see figure 6). More generally, the stratified character of family trends means that the United States is "devolving into a separate-and-unequal family regime, where the highly educated and the affluent enjoy strong and stable [families] and everyone else is consigned to increasingly unstable, unhappy, and unworkable ones."

We acknowledge that social science is better equipped to document whether certain facts *are* true than to say *why* they are true. We can assert more definitively that marriage is associated with powerful social goods than that marriage is the sole or main cause of these goods.

A Word About Selection Effects

Good research seeks to tease out "selection effects," or the preexisting differ-ences between individuals who marry, cohabit, or divorce. Does divorce cause poverty, for example, or is it simply that poor people are more likely to divorce? Scholars attempt to distinguish between causal relationships and mere correla-tions in a variety of ways. The studies cited here are for the most part based on large, nationally representative samples that control for race, education, income, and other confounding factors. In many, but not all cases, social sci-entists used longitudinal data to track individuals as they marry, divorce, or

Figure 6

Percent of 14-Year-Old Girls Living with Mother and Father, by Mother's Education and Year

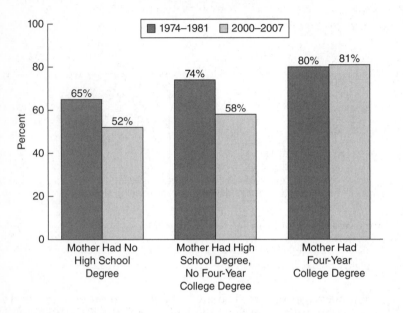

Source: National Survey of Family Growth, 1982 and 2006–08.

stay single, increasing our confidence that marriage itself matters. Where the evidence appears overwhelming that marriage *causes* increases in well-being, we say so. Where marriage probably does so but the causal pathways are not as well understood, we are more cautious.

We recognize that, absent random assignment to marriage, divorce, or single parenting, social scientists must always acknowledge the possibility that other factors are influencing outcomes. Reasonable scholars may and do disagree on the existence and extent of such selection effects and the extent to which marriage is causally related to the better social outcomes reported here.

Yet, scholarship is getting better in addressing selection effects. For instance, in this report we summarize three divorce studies that follow identical and nonidentical adult twins in Australia and Virginia to see how much of the effects of divorce on children are genetic and how much seem to be a consequence of divorce itself. Methodological innovations like these, as well as analyses using econometric models, afford us greater confidence that family structure exercises a causal influence for some outcomes.

Departures from the norm of intact marriage do not necessarily harm most of those who are exposed to them. While cohabitation is associated with increased risks of psychological and social problems for children, this does not mean that every child who is exposed to cohabitation is damaged. For example, one nationally representative study of six- to eleven-year-olds found that only 16 percent of children in cohabiting families experienced serious emotional problems. Still, this rate was much higher than the rate for children in families headed by married biological or adoptive parents, which was 4 percent.

While marriage is a social good, not all marriages are equal. Research does not generally support the idea that remarriage is better for children than living with a single mother. Marriages that are unhappy do not have the same benefits as the average marriage. Divorce or separation provides an important escape hatch for children and adults in violent or high-conflict marriages. Families, communities, and policy makers interested in distributing the benefits of marriage more equally must do more than merely discourage legal divorce.

But we believe good social science, despite its limitations, is a better guide to social policy than uninformed opinion or prejudice. This report represents our best judgment of what current social science evidence reveals about marriage in our social system.

Our Fundamental Conclusions

1. *The intact, biological, married family remains the gold standard for family life in the United States,* insofar as children are most likely to thrive—economically, socially, and psychologically—in this family form.
2. *Marriage is an important public good,* associated with a range of economic, health, educational, and safety benefits that help local, state, and federal governments serve the common good.
3. *The benefits of marriage extend to poor, working-class, and minority communities,* despite the fact that marriage has weakened in these communities in the last four decades.

Family structure and processes are only one factor contributing to child and social well-being. Our discussion here is not meant to minimize the importance of other factors, such as poverty, child support, unemployment, teenage childbearing, neighborhood safety, or the quality of education for both parents and children. Marriage is not a panacea for all social ills. For instance, when it comes to child well-being, research suggests that family structure is a better predictor of children's psychological and social welfare, whereas poverty is a better predictor of educational attainment.

But whether we succeed or fail in building a healthy marriage culture is clearly a matter of legitimate public concern and an issue of paramount importance if we wish to reverse the marginalization of the most vulnerable members of our society: the working class, the poor, minorities, and children.

Kathleen E. Hull, Ann Meier,
and Timothy Ortyl

 **NO**

The Changing Landscape of Love and Marriage

Celebrities breaking up, making up, and having kids out of wedlock. Politicians confessing to extramarital affairs and visits to prostitutes. Same-sex couples pushing for, and sometimes getting, legal recognition for their committed relationships. Today's news provides a steady stream of stories that seem to suggest that lifelong love and (heterosexual) marriage are about as dated as a horse and carriage. Social conservatives continue sounding the alarm about the consequences of the decline of marriage and the rise of unwed parenting for children and for society at large. Are we really leaving behind the old model of intimacy, or are these changes significant but not radical? And what are the driving forces behind the changes?

In the United States, marriage historically has been an important and esteemed social institution. Historian Nancy Cott argues that, since colonial times, Americans have viewed marriage as the bedrock of healthy families and communities, vital to the functioning of democracy itself. But today, nearly half of all marriages end in divorce. People are getting married later than they used to; the median age at first marriage is now 28 for men and 26 for women, compared to 23 and 20 in 1960. The proportion of adults who never marry remains low but is climbing; in 2006, 19% of men and 13% of women aged 40–44 had never married. Roughly one-third of all births are to unmarried parents, and unmarried cohabitation has gone from a socially stigmatized practice to a normal stage in the adult life course (more than half of all American marriages now begin as cohabitations). Many of the same patterns are seen in Europe, although divorce is lower there.

These demographic trends raise two seemingly undeniable conclusions: marriage has lost its taken-for-granted, nearly compulsory status as a feature of adult life, and, as a result, both adults and children are experiencing more change and upheaval in their personal lives than in the post. Sociologists have entered the fray to try to make sense of these trends, both by offering causal explanations and by predicting the depth and future direction of changes in intimacy.

Rethinking Commitment

Prominent sociologists offer two different but related theories about what is happening to intimacy in modern Western nations today. The British theorist Anthony Giddens argues that we are witnessing a "transformation of intimacy," while the American family scholar Andrew Cherlin suggests that we are witnessing the "deinstitutionalization" of marriage.

In his 1992 book *The Transformation of Intimacy*, Giddens observes that intimacy is undergoing radical change in contemporary Western societies. The romantic love model, which emphasizes relationship permanence ("till death do us part") and complementary gender roles, is being displaced by what Giddens calls "confluent love." The confluent love model features the ideal of the "pure relationship," one that's entered into for its own sake and maintained only as long as both partners get enough satisfaction from it to stick around. Partners in a pure relationship establish trust through intense communication, yet the possibility of breakup always looms. Giddens sees the rise of confluent love resulting from modernization and globalization. As family and religious traditions lose influence, people craft their own biographies through highly individualized choices, including choice of intimate partners, with the overarching goal of continuous self-development. Giddens argues that pure relationships are more egalitarian than traditional romantic relationships, produce greater happiness for partners, and foster a greater sense of autonomy. At the same time, the contingent nature of the relationship commitment breeds psychological insecurity, which manifests in higher levels of anxiety and addiction.

Cherlin's deinstitutionalization argument focuses more specifically on marriage now and in the future. The social norms that define and guide people's behavior within the institution of marriage are weakening, he writes. There's greater freedom to choose how to be married and when and whether to marry at all. The deinstitutionalization of marriage can be traced to factors like the rise of unmarried childbearing, the changing division of labor in the home, the growth of unmarried cohabitation, and the emergence of same-sex marriage. These large-scale trends create a context in which people actively question the link between marriage and parenting, the idea of complementary gender roles, and even the connection between marriage and heterosexuality. Under such conditions, Cherlin argues, people feel freer to marry later, to end unhappy marriages, and to forego marriage altogether, although marriage stills holds powerful symbolic significance for many people, partly as a marker of achievement and prestige. The future of marriage is hard to predict, but Cherlin argues it is unlikely to regain its former status; rather, it will either persist as an important but no longer dominant relationship form or it will fade into the background as just one of many relationship options.

Marriage's Persistent Pull

Recent empirical studies suggest that the transformation of intimacy predicted by Giddens is far from complete, and the deinstitutionalization of marriage described by Cherlin faces some powerful countervailing forces, at least in the

U.S. In her interview study of middle-class Americans, sociologist Ann Swidler found that people talking about love and relationships oscillated between two seemingly contradictory visions of intimacy. They often spoke about love and relationships as being hard work, and they acknowledged that relationship permanence is never a given, even in strong marriages. This way of talking about intimacy reflects the confluent love Giddens describes. But the same people who articulated pragmatic and realistic visions of intimacy also sometimes invoked elements of romantic love ideology, such as the idea that true love losts forever and can overcome any obstacles.

Swidler speculates that people go back and forth between these two contradictory visions of love because the pragmatic vision matches their everyday experience but the romantic love myth corresponds to important elements in the institution of marriage. In other words, the ongoing influence of marriage as a social institution keeps the romantic model of intimacy culturally relevant, despite the emergence of a newer model of intimacy that sees love very differently. Swidler's findings at least partially contradict the idea of a wholesale transformation of intimacy, as well as the idea that marriage has lost much of its influence as a cultural model for intimate relationships.

Other studies have also challenged Giddens's ideas about the nature and extent of change occurring in intimate relationships. A 2002 study by Neil Gross and Solon Simmons used data from a national survey of American adults to test Giddens's predictions about the effects of "pure relationships" on their participants. They found support for some of the positive effects described by Giddens: people in pure relationships appear to have a greater sense of autonomy and higher relationship satisfaction. But the survey results did not support the idea that pure relationships lead to higher levels of anxiety and addiction. A 2004 British interview study of members of transnational families (that is, people with one or more close family members living in another country) found that people often strike a balance between individualistic approaches to marriage and attention to the marriage values of their home countries, families and religions. Study authors Carol Smart and Beccy Shipman conclude that Giddens's theory of a radical transformation of intimacy overlooks the rich diversity of cultural values and practices that exists even in highly modernized Western nations. And sociologist Lynn Jamieson has critiqued Giddens's theory for ignoring the vast body of feminist research that documents ongoing gender inequalities, such as in housework, even among heterosexual couples who consider their relationships to be highly egalitarian.

In his recent book *The Marriage-Go-Round,* even Cherlin acknowledges the fact that the deinstitutionalization of marriage has not gone as far in the U.S. as in many other Western countries. Americans have established a pattern of high marriage and remarriage rates, frequent divorce and separation, and more short-lived cohabitations, relative to other comparable countries. The end result is what Cherlin calls a "carousel of intimate partnerships," leading American adults, and any children they have, to face more transition and upheaval in their personal lives. Cherlin concludes that this unique American pattern results from the embrace of two contradictory cultural ideals: marriage and individualism.

The differing importance placed on marriage is obvious in the realm of electoral politics, for example. The current leaders of France and Italy, President Nicolas Sarkozy and Prime Minister Silvio Berlusconi, have weathered divorces and allegations of extramarital affairs without any discernible effect on their political viability. In the U.S., by contrast, the revelations of extramarital dalliances by South Carolina governor Mark Sanford and former North Carolina senator John Edwards were widely viewed as destroying their prospects as future presidential candidates.

Broader Horizons

Mainstream media paints a picture of different generations holding substantially different attitudes toward intimacy. In some ways, young people's attitudes toward relationships today are quite similar to the attitudes of their parents. A 2001 study by sociologist Arland Thornton and survey researcher Linda Young-DeMarco compares the attitudes of high school students from the late 1970s to the late 1990s. They find strong support for marriage among all students across the two-decade period. The percentage of female students who rated "having a good marriage and family life" extremely important was roughly 80% throughout this time period, while for males, it hovered around 70%.

Some studies track changes in young people's specific expectations regarding intimate partnerships. For example, a study by psychologist David Buss and colleagues examined college students' preferences for mate characteristics over a period of several decades. They found that both male and female students rank mutual love and attraction as more important today than in earlier decades. Changing gender roles also translated into changes in mate preferences across the decades, with women's financial prospects becoming more important to men and men's ambition and industriousness becoming less important to women. Overall, differences in the qualities men and women are looking for in a mate declined in the second half of the 20th century, suggesting that being male or female has become a less important factor in determining what young people look for in intimate partnerships.

We compared the relationship attitudes and values of lesbian/gay, bisexual, and heterosexual 18–28 year olds in a recent study published in the *Journal of Marriage and Family*. Notably, people in all of these groups were highly likely to consider love, faithfulness, and lifelong commitment as extremely important values in an intimate relationship. Romantic love seems to be widely embraced by most young adults, regardless of sexual orientation, which contests stereotypes and contrary reports that sexual minorities have radically different aspirations for intimacy. Yet, we also found modest differences that indicate that straight women are especially enthusiastic about these relationship attributes. They are more likely to rate faithfulness and lifelong commitment as extremely important compared to straight men and sexual minorities. Our findings are similar to other studies that consistently show that while both men and women highly value love, affection, and lifelong marriage, women assign greater value to these attributes than men.

Sociologist Michael Rosenfeld argues in *The Age of Independence* that both same-sex relationships and interracial relationships have become more common and visible in the last few decades in large part because of the same social phenomenon: young people today are less constrained by the watchful eyes and wishes of their parents. Unmarried young adults are much less likely to be living with their parents than in generations past, giving them more freedom to make less traditional life choices. And making unconventional choices along one dimension may make people more willing to make unconventional choices along other dimensions. Thus, while people's aspirations for romantic love may not be changing substantially, partner choice may be changing over time as taboos surrounding a broader range of relationships erode. In our study, we find that sexual-minority young adults report being more willing to date someone of a different race or enter into less financially secure relationships than heterosexual young adults, lending support to Rosenfeld's claim.

Weighing Our Options

If the ideas of today's young adults are any indication, Americans still place a high value on traditional, romantic love ideals for their relationships, including the ideal of lifelong marriage. Yet, all evidence suggests that many of us do not follow through.

In 2004, sociologist Paul Amato outlined the typical positions on whether that shift matters. The *marital decline position* argues that changes in intimacy are a significant cause for concern. From this perspective, the current decline in lifelong marriage and the corresponding increase in single-parent and disrupted families are a key culprit in other social ills like poverty, delinquency, and poor academic performance among children. This is because stable marriages promote a culture in which people accept responsibility for others, and families watch over their own to protect against falling prey to social ills. In short, marriage helps keep our societal house in order.

The *marital resilience perspective,* in contrast, contends that changes in family life have actually strengthened the quality of intimate relationships, including marriages. From this perspective, in the past many people stayed in bad marriages because of strong social norms and legal obstacles to exit. Today, however, no-fault divorce provides an opportunity to correct past mistakes and try again at happiness with new partners. This is a triumph for individual freedom of choice and opportunities for equality within intimate relationships.

Perhaps today's intimacy norms dictate more individualism and a corresponding reduction in the responsibility we take for those we love or loved. Maybe we are better for it because we have more freedom of choice—after all, freedom is one of America's most cherished values. Americans in general seem willing to live with mixed feelings on the new norms for intimacy. Most of us value the commitment and security of a lifelong partner, but we also want the option of exit (tellingly, almost half of people who marry use this option).

Some evidence does suggest, though, that the "carousel of intimate relationships" may be taking its toll. Sociologists Mary Elizabeth Hughes and Linda Waite recently compared the health of middle-aged Americans who were married once and still with their partner to those who were never married, those who were married then divorced and remarried, and those who were married, divorced, and not remarried. They found that those who experienced divorce reported more chronic conditions, mobility limitations, and depression years later, and remarriage boosted health some (particularly mental health), but not to the level of those who never divorced in the first place. Those who divorced and did not remarry had the worst health, even after accounting for many factors that may make one more likely both to have poor health and to divorce. Having loved and lost appears to have lasting consequences.

Academic and policy debates, as well as conversations among friends and neighbors, often hinge not on adults, but on what's best for children. A fair amount of research suggests that kids are more likely to avoid most social ills and develop into competent, successful adults if they are raised by two happily and continuously married parents. But marital *happiness* is key. A number of studies have found that frequently quarrelling parents who stay married aren't doing their kids many favors. Children of these types of marriages have an elevated risk of emotional and behavioral problems. But with the notable exception of parents in high-conflict marriages, most children who are raised by caring parents—one or two of them, married or not—end up just fine. Further, if our social policies provided greater support to all varieties of families, not just those characterized by lifelong heterosexual marriage, we might erase the association between growing up with happily married parents and children's well-being. More family supports, such as childcare subsidies, might translate into happily-ever-after for most kids regardless of family form.

Finally, the new rules of relationships have societal implications that go well beyond family life. If social order is substantially buttressed by traditional marriage, and a new model of intimacy is weakening the norm of lifelong, heterosexual marriage, logic suggests that we're eroding social cohesion and stability. If we think this is a threat, it seems a few policy adjustments could help to promote social order. For example, if marriage has the senefits of status, institutional support, and legitimacy, granting the right to marry to same-sex couples should bolster their relationships, making them more stable and long-lasting. Therefore, same-sex marriage would bring some Americans into the marital fold, benefiting the adults and children in these families and society more generally.

In the meantime, there'd still be legions of those who already have access to the rights and protections of marriage, and either chose to divorce or never marry at all. Without reinforcing marriage as the ideal family form, some question whether healthy, well-functioning societies can be maintained. Evidence from other Western nations does suggest that different models of intimacy are compatible with societal well-being, but they also show that social policy must be aligned with the types of relationships that individuals choose to form. Many comparable countries have lower marriage rates and higher cohabitation rates than the U.S.

Those that extend significant legal protection and recognition to non-marital relationships seem to do as well as, or sometimes better than, the U.S. on key measures of social and familial well-being. For example, Swedish children who live with only one parent do better, on average, than American children in the same circumstance, possibly because of Sweden's pro-family policies including long periods of paid maternity and sick leave and government-subsidized, high-quality childcare. Since all Swedes are eligible for these family supports, the differences in care received by children across family types are minimized.

In the end, current research suggests a paradox. Most people, including young adults, say things to researchers that suggest they hold fast to the ideal of an exclusive, lifelong intimate partnership, most commonly a marriage. Yet often people behave in ways more aligned with the "pure relationship" Giddens argues is the ascendant model of intimacy. Perhaps it's harder than ever for people to live out their aspirations in the area of intimacy. Or perhaps we are indeed in the midst of a transition to a brave new world of intimacy, and people's willingness or ability to articulate new relationship values has not yet caught up with their behavior.

CHALLENGE QUESTIONS

Do Adults Need to Place More Value on Marriage?

1. Wilcox and colleagues suggest that increased rates of cohabitation are now more of a threat to marriage than high divorce rates. Do you agree? What might be the relationship between cohabitation and divorce?
2. Despite a significant and well-intentioned push toward marriage from people promoting family values, a majority of voters in recent elections within the United States have rejected the idea of allowing homosexual couples the right to legal marriage. If marriage is good for adults, should we not allow all adults the opportunity to marry? Or would that change the nature of marriage to such a degree that it would no longer maintain its traditional value?
3. If alternatives to marriage such as cohabitation become the norm rather than the exception, would it still be considered problematic?
4. Several of the conclusions drawn by Wilcox relate the importance of marriage to children's well-being, though Hull, Meier, and Ortyl note that unhappy marriages are not necessarily good for kids. Should the promotion of marriage be central to promoting children's well-being, or might there be more effective alternatives for helping children?
5. What do you make of Hull, Meier, and Ortyl's point that "if our social policies provided greater support to all varieties of families, not just those characterized by lifelong hetero-sexual marriage, we might erase the association between growing up with happily married parents and children's well-being." Might the benefits of marriage come because it is the institution most supported by society, rather than because of anything particular to marriage itself?

Is There Common Ground?

The evidence that marriage does, on average, associate with good outcomes for adults, children, and communities has accumulated in recent years to the point of guiding social policy. The phenomenon was described by one 2003 *New Yorker* article as "The Marriage Cure," describing ways marriage is promoted as a cure-all for social and personal ills. Yet, as Kathleen E. Hull, Ann Meier, and Timothy Ortyl point out, the very institutional value we ascribe to marriage may reinforce its advantages and preclude other viable relationship types. Efforts to exclude same-sex couples from legal marriage are only one example of this process. So although both sides of this issue are aware of the data showing marriage to associate with positive markers of healthy adult development, they differ in how to interpret that data. Is it the case that contemporary adults do not fully recognize the positives of a good marriage? Or do most adults understand that a good marriage is only positive when it puts people in a position to earn society's recognition?

Suggested Readings

P.R. Amato, A Booth, D.R. Johnson, and S.J. Rogers, *Alone Together: How Marriage in America is Changing* (Harvard University Press 2007)

A.J. Cherlin, *The Marriage-Go-Round: The State of Marriage and the Family in America Today* (Alfred A. Knopf 2009)

R.D. Conger, K.J. Conger, and M.J. Martin, "Socioeconomic Status, Family Processes, and Individual Development," *Journal of Marriage and Family* (June 2010)

S. Coontz, *Marriage, a History: From Obedience to Intimacy or How Love Conquered Marriage* (Viking 2005)

D.T. Lichter and Z. Qian, "Serial Cohabitation and the Marital Life Course," *Journal of Marriage and Family* (November 2008)

C. Osborne and S. McLanahan, "Partnership Instability and Child Well-Being," *Journal of Marriage and Family* (November 2007)

G.I. Roisman, E. Clausell, A. Holland, K. Fortuna, and C. Elieff, "Adult Romantic Relationships as Contexts of Human Development: A Multimethod Comparison of Same-Sex Couples with Opposite-Sex Dating, Engaged, and Married Dyads," *Developmental Psychology* (January 2008)

J. Stacey, *Unhitched: Love, Marriage, and Family Values from West Hollywood to Western China* (NYU Press 2011)

L. Waite and M. Gallagher, *The Case for Marriage: Why Married People are Happier, Healthier, and Better off Financially* (Doubleday 2000)

ISSUE 16

Is Parenthood a Detriment to Well-Being?

YES: **Robin W. Simon**, from "The Joys of Parenthood, Reconsidered," *Contexts* (vol. 7, no. 2, Spring 2008)

NO: **Bryan Caplan**, from "The Breeders' Cup," *The Wall Street Journal—The Saturday Essay* (June 19, 2010)

Learning Outcomes

As you read the issue, focus on the following points:

1. Despite folk wisdom extolling the "joys of parenthood," researchers consistently find that parents are less happy than childless adults.

2. One of the main challenges of contemporary parenthood is the financial and emotional investment assumed necessary to raise successful children.

3. Despite reporting lower levels of emotional well-being, parents do report a greater sense of purpose in life and most are glad that they had children.

4. It may be that parenthood can be a joyful part of adult development if people would recognize that extensive stress around parenting is often unnecessary.

ISSUE SUMMARY

YES: Researcher Robin W. Simon finds that although adults willingly believe in the "joys of parenthood," research consistently suggests that having children results in decreases in many different measures of well-being.

NO: Economist Bryan Caplan acknowledges that research finds some association between becoming a parent and being unhappy, but argues that the magnitude of that finding is small and barely applies after parents already have one child. He also suggests that the reason some parents seem unhappy is because they put unnecessary pressure on themselves.

As editor of this Taking Sides book, I became interested in the relationship between parenthood and healthy adult development a few years ago when several provocative articles reported that parenthood associates with decreased psychological well-being. That immediately struck me as a controversial claim, and a fascinating issue to address. I simply assumed it would be easy to find vociferous empirical arguments arguing for the "joy of parenthood." But what I found surprised me. There were many anecdotal stories from parents talking about how their children make their lives better. And there were scholars theorizing about why adults want to become parents. But I could not find a single data-driven argument suggesting that parents were happier than the childless. Could millions of parents be wrong?

According to an overwhelming preponderance of data, most contemporary parents are wrong. When large representative surveys compare the well-being of parents and the childless, parents report being less happy. This effect is particularly striking when surveying daily emotional states by asking adults to report their feelings at any given time on any particular day. As Robin W. Simon notes in the YES article, her research finds that "parents residing with minor children report significantly less frequent positive feelings (calm, contentment) but significantly more frequent negative feelings (fear, anxiety, worry, anger) than adults not living with young children. We further found that full-nest parents don't report more frequent feelings of happiness, excitement, joy, and pride than adults not residing with dependent offspring." Additionally, while some have hoped this effect was limited to the day-to-day stress of raising children but not the fact of having children, the evidence that parents are happier once their children leave home has only limited support.

In the NO article, Bryan Caplan acknowledges the consistency of finding parents less happy than the childless, but points out that commentators rarely mention the small magnitude of that difference. Becoming a parent, Caplan finds, has a much smaller statistical effect on well-being than something like being single rather than married. Further, when parents are asked about what Caplan calls "customer satisfaction" the vast majority report they are glad they had children and would do so again if they had to do it over. Caplan also interprets twin studies undertaken by behavioral geneticists as demonstrating that stressing out about parenting does not do anyone any good—he thinks children are going to turn out how they turn out regardless of how much effort parents put in.

With the claim that intensive parenting efforts do not make much difference Caplan is delving into a broader developmental question about nature and nurture, though he does so from his perspective as an academic economist. His is a rational cost-benefit analysis, but it is unclear whether most adults approach parenthood using a purely rational approach. Adults may recognize logically that spending excessive amounts of time and energy on children probably does not do much good—it is as likely to stress out parents as it is to enrich children. But that logical recognition is often overwhelmed by emotional exuberance—parents want to do everything they can for their children, just in case it makes a difference.

Parenthood has probably not always been so emotionally overwhelming. Both authors allude to the fact that in previous generations adults thought of children more like discrete economic assets that could help with labor around the homestead or take on the family farm. According to social historian Viviana Zelizer, that thinking has gradually shifted to the point where children are now thought of as "economically useless but emotionally priceless." In other words, to justify a potentially irrational investment in children we think of their value in purely emotional terms. Unhappy, stressed out parents keep pushing themselves to do more for their children because they *feel* as though they can never do enough.

Many adults do, of course, recognize that massive economic and emotional investments in children can pose challenges to adult development. In fact, this recognition may be one reason for the declining fertility rates cited by Caplan: contemporary adults are having fewer children than previous generations, partially because many have come to think of child-rearing as arduous. Yet, most adults do still have children (as Simon notes, "sooner or later about 80 percent of the adult population has biological children"). Even if it is not good for adult well-being, it would make sense that our predisposition is to want to procreate. As evolutionary psychologists have pointed out, if everyone thought of going childless as the rational decision that would not be very good for the species. But surprisingly few scholars are willing to argue that having children is demonstrably good for individual adults.

YES

Robin W. Simon

The Joys of Parenthood, Reconsidered

Hallmark stores stock baby cards filled with happy wishes for new parents, acknowledging and celebrating their long-awaited and precious bundle of joy. Too bad their selection doesn't include cards that recognize the negative emotions that often accompany parenthood.

Perhaps they should. Sociologists find that as a group, parents in the United States experience depression and emotional distress more often than their childless adult counterparts. Parents of young children report far more depression, emotional distress, and other negative emotions than non-parents, and parents of grown children have no better well-being than adults who never had children.

That last finding contradicts the conventional wisdom that empty-nest parents derive all the emotional rewards of parenthood because they're done with the financially and psychologically taxing aspects of raising young kids.

These research findings, of course, fly in the face of our cultural dogma that proclaims it impossible for people to achieve an emotionally fulfilling and healthy life unless they become parents. And that's a problem, because the vast majority of American men and women eventually have children, yet conditions in our society make it nearly impossible for them to reap all the emotional benefits of doing so.

The Greatest Gift Life Has to Offer

Americans harbor a widespread, deeply held belief that no adult can be happy without becoming a parent. Parenthood, we think, is pivotal for developing and maintaining emotional well-being, and children are an essential ingredient for a life filled with positive emotions like happiness, joy, excitement, contentment, satisfaction, and pride. Even more than marriage and employment, our culture promotes the idea that parenthood provides a sense of purpose and meaning in life, which are essential for good mental health.

As a result, we encourage men and women to have children in a variety of subtle and not so subtle ways. Then, we congratulate them when they become parents with baby showers, flowers, balloons, and cigars. These and other cultural celebrations of the transition to parenthood reflect, reinforce, and perpetuate Americans' beliefs that there's no better guarantee of achieving an emotionally fulfilling and healthy life than having children.

From *Contexts*, Spring 2008, pp. 41–45. Copyright © 2008 by the American Sociological Association. Reprinted by permission of the University of California Press via the Copyright Clearance Center.

And most fall right in step. The vast majority of men and women in the United States become parents either through birth, adoption, or marriage. The 20th century witnessed important changes in the timing of parenthood (men and women are now deferring it until they're older, compared to previous generations), yet demographers have found that sooner or later about 80 percent of the adult population has biological children. Nothing indicates a decline in the near future as cohorts of young adults who are currently childless are still in their childbearing years.

These cultural beliefs about the importance of parenthood for achieving a happy and emotionally healthy adulthood extend to the way we respond to adults who either can't or choose not to have children. Because our culture equates childlessness with feelings of sadness, loneliness, emptiness, purposelessness, and meaninglessness—particularly as men and women approach the golden years, when the emotional rewards of parenthood are assumed to be at their peak—we feel sorry for and pity childless adults. We assume it's difficult, if not impossible, for them to have an emotionally fulfilling life without offspring. We also assume that those who are voluntarily child-free are selfish, unhappy, and will regret their decision after it's too late.

In her 1995 book on childlessness and the pursuit of happiness, Elaine Tyler May writes that in light of our cultural idealization of children, many reproductively challenged Americans subject themselves to expensive and invasive medical procedures in order to procreate. Heterosexual women and lesbians are increasingly conceiving offspring through *in vitro* fertilization, while heterosexual couples and gay men often turn to adoption and sometimes surrogacy to become parents. Culturally, we encourage those who can't have biological children to adopt—an idea buttressed by the highly publicized recent overseas adoptions among the Hollywood elite. There are no reliable estimates of the percentage of conceptions through artificial insemination or surrogacy, but between 2 percent and 4 percent of adults in the United States adopt children at some point in their lives.

Only in recent years have the media provided an alternative to the idealized portrayal of parenthood that has dominated the cultural landscape since the 1950s—a period marked by a strong, positive outlook on having children. Television shows like *Roseanne* and films like *Parenthood* that appeared in the 1980s debunked the overly romanticized conceptions of parenthood that had loomed large in our culture, portraying parents of young children as exhausted, frustrated, and at their wits end. Some recent films like *Meet the Parents* and television shows like *Everyone Loves Raymond* and *Brothers and Sisters* also depict strained relationships between empty-nest parents and their adult children.

But we're not deterred. These darker, though perhaps more realistic, portrayals of parenthood notwithstanding, most of us still adhere to the cultural belief that there's no better guarantee of a happy, healthy, and emotionally rich and rewarding life than having children, who are presumed to be "worth" the financial and psychological costs associated with raising them. Although most people today would probably agree that parenthood is often challenging, sometimes difficult, and involves continual self-sacrifice, periodic disaster, and occasional heartache—particularly when children enter the tumultuous adolescent years—our culture continues to promote the idea that the emotional rewards associated with parenthood far outweigh the personal costs.

Numbers Show Otherwise

Contrary to all of this, sociological research based on national surveys of American adults finds an association between parenthood and depression, emotional distress, and other negative emotions. While studies indicate parents derive more purpose, more meaning, and greater satisfaction from life than non-parents, they also reveal parents experience lower levels of emotional well-being, less frequent positive emotions, and more frequent negative emotions than their childless peers. Sara McLanahan and Julia Adams first summarized the evidence on parental status differences in mental health 20 years ago, but similar findings are evident in more recent research.

For example, a recent study I conducted with Ranae J. Evenson based on the National Survey of Families and Households—which includes a nationally representative sample of more than 10,000 adults in the United States—revealed that parents report significantly more symptoms of depression (feelings of sadness, loneliness, restlessness, and fear) than nonparents their own age. Several other studies based on different national surveys of adults also indicate that parents currently raising children are significantly more depressed and emotionally distressed than childless adults. Many others have found that living with minor children is associated with significantly lower levels of psychological well-being. The details of these studies can be found in a 2005 *Journal of Health and Social Behavior* article I wrote with Evenson, as well as McLanahan and Adam's 1987 *Annual Review of Sociology* article.

Additionally, Leda Nath and I studied Americans' everyday emotional experiences as reported on the General Social Survey, a nationally representative sample of more than 1,400 adults. It revealed that parents residing with minor children report significantly less frequent positive feelings (calm, contentment) but significantly more frequent negative feelings (fear, anxiety, worry, anger) than adults not living with young children. We further found that full-nest parents don't report more frequent feelings of happiness, excitement, joy, and pride than adults not residing with dependent offspring. Based on another national survey, Catherine E. Ross and Marieke Van Willigen also found that parents with young children in the home are angrier than adults not living with kids.

Conventional wisdom tells us the emotional rewards of having children are fewest during the "full-nest" stage and greatest during the "empty-nest" stage of parenthood. Free of the onerous financial and psychological responsibilities associated with raising young offspring, empty-nest parents are ostensibly able to focus on the love, friendship, companionship, emotional support, and all sorts of assistance they receive from their adult children. Indeed, Debra Umberson's research on parent-adult child interaction in the United States indicates that most parents have frequent contact with their non-resident adult children, often speaking with them at least once a week.

However, studies based on recent national surveys indicate that empty-nest parents report similar levels of well-being as childless adults their own age. As a matter of fact, Evenson and I found *no* group of parents that reports significantly greater emotional well-being than people who never had children. This goes for married parents, cohabiting parents, single parents, noncustodial parents, and stepparents, as well as for fathers versus mothers, despite the fact that epidemiological research documents women's less frequent positive emotions, more frequent negative emotions, and higher levels of depression and emotional distress than men in general.

It's important to emphasize that while parents aren't any emotionally better off than their childless counterparts, parents' other social statuses—particularly their marital, employment, and socioeconomic status—influence the association between parenthood and mental health.

For example, research finds that single parents report higher levels of depression and emotional distress than married and cohabiting parents. Unemployment exacerbates the negative emotional effects of parenthood involving young children, particularly for men. Parents with lower levels of education and household income also experience higher levels of depression and emotional distress than their more advantaged peers. And, not surprisingly, parents who enjoy satisfying relationships with their children report greater emotional well-being than parents who have unsatisfying relationships with their offspring.

But, while these social characteristics influence or moderate the association between parenthood and mental health, little evidence exists that parenthood actually improves adults' emotional well-being. In fact, most evidence seems to point to the contrary.

The Stresses of Parenthood

Why doesn't parenthood have the positive emotional effects on adults that our cultural beliefs suggest? The answer to this question lies in the social conditions in which Americans today parent—they're far from ideal for allowing them to reap the full emotional benefits of having children. Parents are exposed to a number of different stressors that cancel out and often exceed the emotional rewards of having children. Making matters worse, parents and others perceive this stress as a private matter and reflective of their inability to cope with the "normal" demands of having children.

In their research examining change in the association between parenthood and psychological well-being from the 1950s to the 1970s, McLanahan and Adams found parenthood was perceived as more stressful and was more closely associated with emotional distress in the 1970s than in the 1950s. Much of this trend was due to changes in the employment and marital status of parents, they said.

A significant source of parental stress stems from the extraordinarily high financial cost of raising a child to adulthood these days. Even the basics such as food, clothing, and (for those who have it) healthcare are expensive, not to mention extracurricular activities parents feel compelled to provide their kids. Although the figures vary depending on parents' household income, the U.S. Department of Agriculture estimates families spend anywhere from $134,370 to $269,520 raising a child from birth through age 17. These figures don't include the astronomical cost of a college education; the College Board reports tuition alone is presently more than $20,000 at state universities, more than $80,000 at private universities, and continues to rise by an average of 6 percent to 7 percent each year.

Indeed, the increasing cost of raising kids is one factor that contributed to the large number of mothers who joined the labor force in the second half of the 20th century. Demographers estimate 70 percent of children in the United States are currently being raised in households in which all adults work outside the home. However, as Jennifer Glass and others point out, there's a fundamental incompatibility between employment and raising children, which makes juggling parenthood and paid work highly stressful.

Arlie Hochschild was the first to document that the lack of flexible work schedules, high-quality and affordable child care for preschool-aged children, and after-school care for elementary-aged children all contribute to stress from what's now commonly referred to as the "second shift" for employed parents, particularly employed mothers, who leave their jobs at 5 o'clock only to start another job caring for children at home. However, there are few policies or programs to alleviate the stress. In the end, our collective response to "stressed out" employed parents is that they need to become better organized.

Although financial stress and the stress of the second shift subside as children age and become independent, the majority of parents continue to be involved in their adult offspring's lives and worry about them. Among other things, parents worry about their grown children's financial well-being, their social relationships, their happiness, and both their mental and physical health. These observations have led sociologists to conclude that parenthood is the quintessential job that never ends.

Parents also shoulder the daunting responsibility for the development and well-being of another person, and our culture places high expectations on them for the way children "turn out." Irrespective of their children's age, we question parents' childrearing skills when they have problems. In fact, the way children turn out seems to be the only measure our culture offers for assessing whether men and women are "good" parents.

Alice S. Rossi has argued that unlike other societies, Americans receive relatively little preparation for parenthood and most parents raise their children in relative social isolation with little assistance from extended family members, friends, neighbors, and the larger community. At the same time, parents alone are accountable for raising children to be moral, responsible, intelligent, happy, healthy, and well-adjusted adults, and this awesome responsibility doesn't end when children are grown.

Shifting the Reward-Cost Analysis

Children provide parents with a sense of immortality, an important social identity, and emotional connections to extended family members and people in their communities. Children fulfill some basic human desires—including having someone to love and nurture, carrying on family traditions, and allowing us to become grandparents. Watching children grow and develop is enjoyable and parents feel comforted by the perception that they won't be alone to fend for themselves in old age. The parent-child relationship is perhaps the most important and enduring social bond in the lives of individuals, which is probably why parents derive more purpose and meaning in life than adults who never had children.

At the same time, the emotional benefits of having children are often overshadowed by the onerous demands and stressors associated with the role. Although experienced by mothers and fathers at a deeply personal level, the stressfulness of contemporary parenthood is firmly rooted in the social conditions in which people parent as well as our current social, economic, and cultural institutions.

In America we lack institutional supports that would help ease the social and economic burdens—and subsequent stressfulness and emotional disadvantages—associated with parenthood. Instituting better tax credits, developing more and better day care and after school options, as well as offering flexible work schedules for employed mothers and fathers would go far toward alleviating some of the stress for parents raising children.

However, providing these forms of assistance is only part of the solution, since parents whose children are grown don't report higher levels of emotional well-being than childless adults their own age. Affordable health care would insure individuals' basic health needs are met and would, therefore, lessen this lingering source of stress for all parents—irrespective of their children's age. Although there are no existing studies that systematically compare the mental health of parents and childless adults in other countries, it's likely that parents residing in societies with family-friendly and other social welfare policies enjoy better mental health than parents in the United States.

Of equal importance is the need to take stock of and reevaluate existing cultural beliefs that children improve the emotional health and well-being of adults. These cultural beliefs—and our expectations that children guarantee a life filled with happiness, joy, excitement, contentment, satisfaction, and pride—are an additional, though hidden, source of stress for all parents. Indeed, the feelings of depression, emotional distress, and other negative emotions parents experience on a daily basis may cause them to question what they're doing wrong. These negative emotions may also lead parents with children of all ages, especially mothers, to perceive themselves as inadequate since their feelings aren't consistent with our cultural ideal.

To this end, reducing the enormous and unrealistic cultural expectations we have for parenthood is as important as greater cultural recognition of the unrelenting challenges and difficulties associated with having children of all ages. Although there's no guarantee these changes would drastically improve the emotional lives of American mothers and fathers, at least they would help minimize the emotional costs and maximize the emotional benefits of parenthood in the United States today.

NO

The Breeders' Cup

Amid the Father's Day festivities, many of us are privately asking a Scroogely question: "Having kids—what's in it for me?" An economic perspective on happiness, nature and nurture provides an answer: Parents' sacrifice is much smaller than it looks, and much larger than it has to be.

Most of us believe that kids used to be a valuable economic asset. They worked the farm, and supported you in retirement. In the modern world, the story goes, the economic benefits of having kids seem to have faded away. While parents today make massive personal and financial sacrifices, children barely reciprocate. When they're young, kids monopolize the remote and complain about the food, but do little to help around the house; when you're old, kids forget to return your calls and ignore your advice, but take it for granted that you'll continue to pay your own bills.

Many conclude that if you value your happiness and spending money, the only way to win the modern parenting game is not to play. Low fertility looks like a sign that we've finally grasped the winning strategy. In almost all developed nations, the total fertility rate—the number of children the average woman can expect to have in her lifetime—is well below the replacement rate of 2.1 children. (The U.S. is a bit of an outlier, with a rate just around replacement.) Empirical happiness research seems to validate this pessimism about parenting: All else equal, people with kids are indeed less happy than people without.

While the popular and the academic cases against kids have a kernel of truth, both lack perspective. By historical standards, modern parents get a remarkably good deal. When economist Ted Bergstrom of the University of California, Santa Barbara reviewed the anthropological evidence, he found that in traditional societies, kids don't pay. Among hunter-gatherers, children consume more calories than they produce, and grandparents produce more calories than they consume virtually until the day they die. Agricultural societies are much the same. Only in recent decades did people start living long enough to collect much of a "pension" from their kids. While big financial transfers from children to their parents remain rare, only in the modern world can retirees expect to enjoy two decades of their descendents' company and in-kind assistance.

It's also true that modern parents are less happy than their childless counterparts. But happiness researchers rarely emphasize how small the happiness gap is. Suppose you take the National Opinion Research Center's canonical

General Social Survey, and compare Americans with the same age, marital status and church attendance. (These controls are vital, because older, married and church-going people have more happiness and more kids). Then every additional child makes parents just 1.3 percentage points less likely to be "very happy." In contrast, the estimated happiness boost of marriage is about 18 percentage points; couples probably have fewer highs after they wed, but the security and companionship more than compensate. In the data, the people to pity are singles, not parents.

A closer look at the General Social Survey also reveals that child No. 1 does almost all the damage. Otherwise identical people with one child instead of none are 5.6 percentage points less likely to be very happy. Beyond that, additional children are almost a happiness free lunch. Each child after the first reduces your probability of being very happy by a mere .6 percentage points.

Happiness researchers also neglect a plausible competing measure of kids' impact on parents' lives: customer satisfaction. If you want to know whether consumers are getting a good deal, it's worth asking, "If you had to do it over again, would you make the same decision?" The only high-quality study of parents' satisfaction dates back to a nation-wide survey of about 1,400 parents by the Research Analysis Corp. in 1976, but its results were stark: When asked, "If you had it to do over again, would you or would you not have children?" 91% of parents said yes, and only 7% expressed buyer's remorse.

You might think that everyone rationalizes whatever decision they happened to make, but a 2003 Gallup poll found that wasn't true. When asked, "If you had to do it over again, how many children would you have, or would you not have any at all?" 24% of childless adults over the age of 40 wanted to be child-free the second time around, and only 5% more were undecided. While you could protest that childlessness isn't always a choice, it's also true that many pregnancies are unplanned. Bad luck should depress the customer satisfaction of both groups, but parenthood wins hands down.

The main problem with parenting pessimists, though, is that they assume there's no acceptable way to make parenting less work and more fun. Parents may feel like their pressure, encouragement, money and time are all that stands between their kids and failure. But decades' worth of twin and adoption research says the opposite: Parents have a lot more room to safely maneuver than they realize, because the long-run effects of parenting on children's outcomes are much smaller than they look.

Think about everything parents want for their children. The traits most parents hope for show family resemblance: If you're healthy, smart, happy, educated, rich, righteous or appreciative, the same tends to be true for your parents, siblings and children. Of course, it's difficult to tell nature from nurture. To disentangle the two, researchers known as behavioral geneticists have focused on two kinds of families: those with twins, and those that adopt. If identical twins show a stronger resemblance than fraternal twins, the reason is probably nature. If adoptees show any resemblance to the families that raised them, the reason is probably nurture.

Parents try to instill healthy habits that last a lifetime. But the two best behavioral genetic studies of life expectancy—one of 6,000 Danish twins born between 1870 and 1900, the other of 9,000 Swedish twins born between 1886 and 1925—found zero effect of upbringing. Twin studies of height, weight and even teeth reach similar conclusions. This doesn't mean that diet, exercise and tooth-brushing don't matter—just that parental pressure to eat right, exercise and brush your teeth after meals fails to win children's hearts and minds.

Parents also strive to turn their children into smart and happy adults, but behavioral geneticists find little or no evidence that their effort pays off. In research including hundreds of twins who were raised apart, identical twins turn out to be much more alike in intelligence and happiness than fraternal twins, but twins raised together are barely more alike than twins raised apart. In fact, pioneering research by University of Minnesota psychologist David Lykken found that twins raised apart were more alike in happiness than twins raised together. Maybe it's just a fluke, but it suggests that growing up together inspires people to differentiate themselves; if he's the happy one, I'll be the malcontent.

Parents use many tactics to influence their kids' schooling and future income. Some we admire: reading to kids, helping them with homework, praising hard work. Others we resent: fancy tutors, legacy admissions, nepotism. According to the research, however, these tactics barely work. Dartmouth economist Bruce Sacerdote studied about 1,200 families that adopted disadvantaged Korean children. The families spanned a broad range; they only needed incomes 25% above the poverty level to be eligible to adopt. Nevertheless, family income and neighborhood income had zero effect on adoptees' ultimate success in school and work.

Other aspects of family environment mattered in the Korean adoptee study, but not much. If a mother had one extra year of education, her adoptee typically finished five more weeks of school, and was two percentage points more likely to graduate from college—but didn't earn more money. If an adoptee was raised with one extra sibling, he typically finished six fewer weeks of school, was three percentage points less likely to graduate from college, and earned 4% less. Studies of Swedish adoptees, and American, Australian and Swedish twins say about the same.

Behavioral geneticists also find that the effect of upbringing on morals is quite superficial. Parents have a strong effect on which religion and political party their kids identify with, but little on their adult behavior or outlook. Some, but not all, twin and adoption studies find that parents have a modest effect on tobacco, alcohol and drug use, juvenile delinquency, and when daughters (but not sons) start having sex. The most meaningful fruit of parenting, however, is simply appreciation—the way your children perceive and remember you. When 1,400 older Swedish twins were asked to describe their parents, identical twins' answers were only slightly more similar than fraternal twins,' and twins raised together gave much more similar answers than twins raised apart. If you create a loving and harmonious home for your children, they'll probably remember it for as long as they live.

Critics often attack behavioral genetics with a reductio ad absurdum: "If it doesn't matter how you raise your kids, why not lock them in a closet?" The answer is that twin and adoption studies measure the effect of parenting styles that people frequently use. Locking kids in closets fortunately isn't one of them. It's also important to remember that most studies focus on kids' long-run outcomes. Parents often change their kids in the short-run, but as kids grow up, their parents' influence wears off.

Many find behavioral genetics depressing, but it's great news for parents and potential parents. If you think that your kids' future rests in your hands, you'll probably make many painful "investments"—and feel guilty that you didn't do more. Once you realize that your kids' future largely rests in their own hands, you can give yourself a guilt-free break.

If you enjoy reading with your children, wonderful. But if you skip the nightly book, you're not stunting their intelligence, ruining their chances for college or dooming them to a dead-end job. The same goes for the other dilemmas that weigh on parents' consciences. Watching television, playing sports, eating vegetables, living in the right neighborhood: Your choices have little effect on your kids' development, so it's OK to relax. In fact, relaxing is better for the whole family. Riding your kids "for their own good" rarely pays off, and it may hurt how your children feel about you.

Once parents stop overcharging themselves for every child, the next logical step is straight out of Econ 101: Buy more. When you raise your children the easy way, another child is more likely to pass the cost-benefit test. This doesn't mean you should copy the Duggars with their 19 children; when prices fall, Econ 101 says "Buy more," not "Buy dozens." But whatever your priorities, the science of nature and nurture tilts the scales in favor of fertility.

As you weigh your options, don't forget that the costs of kids are front-loaded, and the benefits are back-loaded. Babies are a lot of work even if you're easy on yourself. But the older kids get, the more independent they become; eventually, you'll want them to find time for you. So when weighing whether to have another child, you shouldn't base your decision on how you feel after a few days—or months—of sleepless nights with a new baby. Focus on the big picture, consider the ideal number of children to have when you're 30, 40, 60, and 80, and strike a happy medium. Remember: The more kids you have, the more grandkids you can expect. As an old saying goes, "If I had known grandchildren were this much fun I would have had them first."

Father's Day is a time to reflect on whether you want to be a parent—or want to be a parent again. If you simply don't like kids, research has little to say to you. If however you're interested in kids, but scared of the sacrifices, research has two big lessons. First, parents' sacrifice is much smaller than it looks, and childless and single is far inferior to married with children. Second, parents' sacrifice is much larger than it has to be. Twin and adoption research shows that you don't have to go the extra mile to prepare your kids for the future. Instead of trying to mold your children into perfect adults, you can safely kick back, relax and enjoy your journey together—and seriously consider adding another passenger.

CHALLENGE QUESTIONS

Is Parenthood a Detriment to Well-Being?

1. Does the research demonstrating that parents are less happy than childless adults surprise you? Why does conventional wisdom usually portray parenthood as the font of joy?
2. Are fertility rates (the average number of children per person) going down because people recognize parenting is increasingly challenging? What are other reasons for the declining fertility rate?
3. Simon presents research showing that parenthood has not always associated with less happiness. What has changed historically that seems to make parenting less fun than it used to be?
4. Caplan suggests that adults would be a lot happier if they put less effort into parenting, and recognized that kids will develop in their own way. Why is this advice so hard for parents to accept? What makes contemporary parenting so stressful?

Is There Common Ground?

The selections for this issue fundamentally agree on the point that may be the most surprising to those who have not studied the issue before: data consistently shows parents to be less happy than childless adults. Robin W. Simon and Bryan Caplan do differ in whether they think that data is particularly meaningful, but they agree that there seems to be a significant psychological cost to becoming a parent. Yet many adults persist in thinking of parenthood as a joy. Is this a masochistic trend in the adult psyche? A trick played by our genes to ensure the survival of the species? A market driven illusion designed to replenish the workforce and line the pockets of baby clothiers? Or is it possible that parenting can actually constitute one of the joys of adulthood, if not for the many other pressures of modern life that draw adult attention? Simon and Caplan would likely agree with this last possibility: becoming a parent does not have to make adults less happy. So why does data suggest that it usually does?

Suggested Readings

B. Caplan, *Selfish Reasons to Have More Kids: Why Being a Great Parent Is Less Work and More Fun Than You Think* (Basic Books 2011)

A. Claxton and M. Perry-Jenkins, "No Fun Anymore: Leisure and Marital Quality Across the Transition to Parenthood," *Journal of Marriage and Family* (February 2008)

J. Dew and W. Bradford Wilcox, "If Momma Ain't Happy: Explaining Declines in Marital Satisfaction Among New Mothers," *Journal of Marriage and Family* (February 2011)

R.J. Evenson and R.W. Simon, "Clarifying the Relationship Bewteen Parenthood and Depression," *Journal of Health and Social Behavior* (December 2005)

S. Lyubomirsky and J.K. Boehm, "Human Motives, Happiness, and the Puzzle of Parenthood," *Perspectives on Psychology Science* (May 2010)

K.M. Nomaguchi and M.A. Milkie, "Costs and Rewards of Children: The Effects of Becoming a Parent on Adults' Lives," *Journal of Marriage and the Family* (May 2003)

J. Senior, "All Joy and No Fun: Why Parents Hate Parenting," *New York Magazine* (July 4, 2010)

V.A. Zelizer, *Pricing the Priceless Child: The Changing Social Value of Children* (Basic Books 1985)

Internet References . . .

National Institute on Aging

The National Institute on Aging Web site offers health and research information related primarily to the science of later adulthood.

http://www.nia.nih.gov/

AARP

The AARP is a nonprofit organization organized to help "people 50 and over improve the quality of their lives," and offers related research information on its Web site.

http://www.aarp.org/research/

The Urban Institute

The Web site for the Urban Institute provides research based information related to retirement and contemporary society.

http://www.urban.org/retirement_policy/

Trinity University

An academic's site with references to information about "social gerontology" or the study of sociological aspects of old age.

http://www.trinity.edu/~mkearl/geron.html

Alzheimer's Association

At this Alzheimer's Association Web site there is a wide-range of information about Alzheimer's Disease and related dementias (including "Mild Cognitive Impairment").

http://www.alz.org/alzheimers_disease.asp

Snenscence.info

A Web site with links to information about research into mostly biological aspects of aging.

http://www.senescence.info/

The American Geriatric Society Foundation for Health in Aging

The American Geriatric Society Foundation for Health in Aging works to connect aging research and practice.

http://www.healthinaging.org/

The SENS Foundation

The SENS Foundation focuses on "Strategies for Engineered Negligible Senescence" and has been a prominent advocate for anti-aging science."

http://sens.org/

The Gerontological Society of America

The Gerontological Society of America is an "interdisciplinary organization devoted to research, education, and practice in the field of aging."

http://www.geron.org/

Later Adulthood

*T*he central question for thinking about later adulthood, gener-ally defined as the period of life after retirement age, is whether it is an inevitable period of decline or merely a period of adaptation. Although we often think of old age as a time of deterioration, research suggests that most people in this stage actually adjust to the challenges of aging reasonably well. Yet, there are unquestionable challenges, including changing social roles, the eventual decline of cognitive functioning, and the inevitability of death. The issues in this section consider each of these challenges in turn, while broadly addressing the nature of old age as a time of continuing development.

- Is More Civic Engagement Among Older Adults Necessarily Better?
- Is "Mild Cognitive Impairment" Too Similar to Normal Aging to be a Relevant Concept?
- Should We Try to "Cure" Old Age?

ISSUE 17

Is More Civic Engagement Among Older Adults Necessarily Better?

YES: Sheila R. Zedlewski and Barbara A. Butrica, from "Are We Taking Full Advantage of Older Adults' Potential?" *Perspectives on Productive Aging* (Number 9, December 2007)

NO: Marty Martinson, from "Opportunities or Obligations? Civic Engagement and Older Adults," *Generations* (Winter 2006–2007)

Learning Outcomes

As you read the issue, focus on the following points:

1. While civic engagement through work and volunteering has documented benefits to individuals and communities, people often think about it simply as an individual choice without recognizing the structural forces that shape the nature of old age.

2. By suggesting that civic engagement makes life meaningful for older adults, the implication is that without such engagement old age is meaningless—ignoring viable roles with less direct economic value such as caregiving and political activism.

3. Although the economy may benefit from older adults staying engaged in work and volunteering, that same fact may oblige people to burdensome work or negative stigmas for those unable to stay productive.

4. Governments and public institutions can look to older adults for ongoing contributions, but there is a risk that will come at the expense of contributing to their well-being.

ISSUE SUMMARY

YES: Urban Institute researchers Sheila R. Zedlewski and Barbara A. Butrica, writing as part of a broader project to investigate the changing nature of retirement, argue that promoting civic engagement is good for both individuals and society.

NO: Critical gerontologist Marty Martinson acknowledges that promoting civic engagement in old age can be useful, but suggests that it also serves to shift attention away from broader social problems and responsibilities toward individuals who may or may not benefit from conventional civic engagement.

The American population and the world population are both aging. People are living longer, and spending more time in the stage generally described as old age. With more people living longer and longer there has been increasing interest in the field of "gerontology," which is defined as "the comprehensive study of aging and the problems of the aged" (according to the Merriam-Webster Dictionary). This definition points out the traditional emphasis in gerontology on problems, deriving from a general assumption that old age is a period of inevitable decline. In response to this assumption, many gerontologists have tried to address ways that old age can be re-conceptualized in more optimistic terms. One such effort has involved promoting older adults as a resource toward the civic good. But it turns out that overly optimistic conceptions of old age may have as many problems as overly pessimistic ones.

In work that some scholars describe as the "new gerontology" attention has been devoted toward focusing less on fixing the problems of old age and more on promoting "successful aging." One of the tenants of "successful aging" is to emphasize the importance of staying active and engaged during older adulthood. While this emphasis may seem uncontroversial, critical gerontologists have pointed out that not all people have the option of staying active in old age. Critical scholars suggest that emphasizing activity as the basis for "successful aging" risks promoting a "new ageism" that discriminates against people who have been confronted by significant challenges through their lives.

Nevertheless, many organizations and public policy efforts have taken up the call of the "new gerontology" to promote ways that older adults can and should stay active. The selection from Zedlewski and Butrica is one example, deriving from a project by the Urban Institute to promote "productive aging." In their review of research and literature about ways that civic engagement during older adulthood might influence well-being, they find only positive effects—there is, for example, a clear correlation between good health and being engaged with activities such as work and volunteering.

But scholars know that correlation does not necessarily equal causation, and Marty Martinson points out that the relationship between active civic engagement in old age and well-being may be due to social forces rather than individual choices. Martinson defines civic engagement "broadly to include not only formal volunteering, but also things like political activism, caregiving, and community organizing," yet she notes that much public policy takes civic engagement to focus only on volunteerism in service of institutional goals. Acknowledging that civic engagement can have some benefits, Martinson raises questions about whether more is always better and whether older adults are just being expected to offer free labor. These questions are well worth considering for our aging society and for the study of life-span development—should old age just be about continuing adult-like productivity, or does the nature of older adulthood offer something different?

POINT

- Staying engaged with work and volunteering in old age has significant benefits for both individuals and communities.

- There are many capable older adults who could be more involved than they currently are, and many would benefit economically.

- Civic engagement offers a sense of purpose, social status, and better health by encouraging social interactions and access to resources.

- With changing economic climates, there are likely to be more opportunities for non-physically demanding jobs and for non-profit volunteer work.

COUNTERPOINT

- While civic engagement among older adults has some value, people too often think about it simply as an individual choice without recognizing the structural forces that shape the nature of old age.

- By suggesting that civic engagement makes life meaningful for older adults, the implication is that without such engagement old age is meaningless—ignoring viable roles with less direct economic value such as caregiving and political activism.

- Promoting civic engagement in old age may end up obliging people to burdensome work at all ages, and may promote negative stigmas for people who are unable to stay productive.

- Emphasizing volunteer civic engagement can serve to diminish the responsibility of governments and institutions for addressing social problems.

YES

Sheila R. Zedlewski and
Barbara A. Butrica

Are We Taking Full Advantage of Older Adults' Potential?

Staying engaged in work and formal volunteer activities at older ages significantly benefits the health and well-being of the volunteers themselves, the organizations that count on them, the people served by those organizations, and the economy. Yet, numerous studies show many older adults, especially those in low-income groups, sit out these opportunities. Why isn't completely clear. Do some older Americans simply prefer to relax and spend time with family, friends, and hobbies after long and sometimes stressful years on the job? Do such personal challenges as poor physical or mental health or limited skills keep them from connecting? Or are opportunities scarce or out of sync with older adults' preferences?

The answers to these questions have broad and pressing policy implications. In 2008, the oldest baby boomers will start turning 62—the age at which many people retire. Since this cohort is 76 million people strong, the societal and economic payoffs for encouraging boomers to stay engaged could be enormous.

Using data from the 2004 Health and Retirement Study, we estimate the potential for increasing engagement among adults 55 and older. We define engagement as working for pay or volunteering for an organization, and summarize the literature that documents the key benefits of engagement at older ages. We then examine engagement rates among older adults and the characteristics that distinguish the engaged from the unengaged, highlighting income differences. We then estimate which and how many unengaged older adults would most likely benefit from increased engagement opportunities. Finally, we ask how well demand for older workers and volunteers is likely to mesh with supply.

We find enormous potential for increasing the number of engaged older Americans. More than 10 million healthy older adults with no caregiving responsibilities, including 3.6 million low-income individuals, are now on the sidelines. Over half of these able seniors are under age 75, and 9 out of 10 have worked before. And recent surveys indicate that this larger group is interested in both paid work and volunteer opportunities. Given this untapped potential, shortages of volunteers and workers should prompt employers and nonprofits to court this talent. That said, public policies that boost engagement among interested low-income seniors—who have the most to gain—may also be needed to ensure broad participation.

From *Perspectives on Productive Aging,* December 2007, pp. 1–6. Copyright © 2007 by The Urban Institute. Reprinted by permission.

The Payoff to Engagement

Research increasingly documents how engagement in work and formal volunteer activities benefits the participants, the recipients of volunteer services, and the economy. Those who regularly work or volunteer enjoy better health and live longer, thanks to stimulating environments and a sense of purpose. Recipients of volunteer services, especially children, benefit from interactions with older adults. In addition, older adults' volunteer activities are what make many nonprofits viable. And older Americans' work and volunteering boost economic vitality.

Engagement Improves Health Status

A raft of recent studies documents the benefits of formal volunteer activities on older adults' health. . . . Using multiple data sources and methods, 10 studies published since 1999 document the significant positive associations between volunteer activity and decreased mortality and depression, improved health and strength, greater happiness, and enhanced cognitive ability.

Research on work also tends to find positive effects. Calvo . . . shows that paid work at older ages reduces morbidity and improves health. Following a sample of early retirees for 30 years, Tsai and coauthors . . . find that this group had higher morbidity rates than workers who retired later. In the same vein, Dhaval, Rashad, and Spasojevic . . . find that complete retirement (defined in most such studies as withdrawal from paid work) takes a toll on physical and mental health. In contrast, Charles . . . finds that retirement improves mental health, while Bound and Waidmann . . . find that retiring has little effect on health either way. Gallo and coauthors . . . show that involuntary job loss at older ages decreases well-being.

Investigations of why engagement improves health and mortality generally point to increased cognitive activity, exposure to stimulating environments, and social interactions. . . . Enhanced social status . . . and greater access to social, psychological, and material resources can also play a role. . . . Some activities help older adults develop knowledge and skills that boost their self-images and mental outlooks. . . . Greenfield and Marks . . . document that formal volunteering helps older adults mitigate the loss of a sense of purpose.

Engagement Provides Social and Economic Benefits

Children, in particular, benefit from older adults' engagement, especially in educational activities. . . . The evaluation of the Family Friends program found that volunteer home visitors age 55 and older significantly reduced hospitalization rates among chronically ill and disabled children and improved the overall well-being of parents and families. . . . When adolescents with behavioral problems or struggles in school were linked with older mentors in the Across Ages program, they showed improved class attendance, more positive attitudes toward school, and reductions in substance use. . . . More generally, Wheeler, Gorey, and Greenblatt . . . reviewed 37 studies across a variety of program models and found that 85 percent of the individuals served by older adults showed significantly improved results.

Nonprofits increasingly rely on volunteers, a significant portion of whom are older adults. Over 6 in 10 nonprofits report working with volunteers between the ages of 65 and 74. . . . Volunteers who manage or deliver social services allow nonprofits to save money and get more done, extending the reach of their staff and stabilizing their resources. . . .

Finally, both paid work and formal volunteer activities benefit the economy. Johnson and Schaner . . . value formal volunteering activities among older adults at $44.3 billion in 2002. Paid work also increases the retirement security of older adults. Even a few additional years can significantly boost retirement income, especially among lower-paid workers. . . .

Today's Engagement Patterns

More than half of adults age 55 and older formally engaged in paid or volunteer work in 2004 (table 1). About 2 in 5 worked for pay and 1 in 3 volunteered for organizations. Compared with higher-income older adults, considerably smaller shares of low-income older adults worked for pay

Table 1

Activities of Adults Ages 55 and Older in 2004, by Income Level and Engagement Status (percent)

	Total	Low Income	Higher Income
Type of formal engagement			
Any	57	33	65*
Work	39	15	46*
Volunteering	34	23	37*
Type of informal engagement			
Any	67	55	71*
Informally volunteering	52	38	57*
Providing care	39	32	41*
Population (000s)	63,952	16,307	47,645

Source: Authors' estimates from the 2004 Health and Retirement Study.

Note: The universe is respondents ages 55 and older in 2004.

*Mean value for the low-income group is significantly different from the comparable mean value for the higher-income group at the 10 percent level or better. Results are based on a total, unweighted sample size of 15,871.

(15 percent versus 46 percent) or volunteered for organizations (23 percent compared with 37 percent). In 2004, two-thirds of older adults also volunteered informally by helping their neighbors or caring for a family member. Higher-income older adults informally volunteered more often than their low-income counterparts.

How older adults spend their time may reflect differences in their personal traits and job experiences (table 2). Engaged older adults tend to be younger, healthier, and better educated than same-age adults who choose not to work or volunteer. For example, more than half of engaged older adults are under age 65, in very good to excellent health, and have some education beyond high school. Nearly two-fifths have managerial or professional experience. In contrast, only 1 in 4 of the unengaged report being very healthy, 3 in 10 have more than a high school degree, and 1 in 5 has managerial experience.

Race and ethnic differences between the engaged and the unengaged are relatively small, though statistically significant. Also, there is little urban/rural difference between the engaged and the unengaged, countering some worries that older adults in rural areas have fewer chances for work or volunteer activities. Access to transportation does differ significantly between the two groups; 92 percent of engaged adults own a vehicle, compared with 77 percent of the unengaged.

What Is the Potential?

A large share of older adults continues to work or volunteer, but many more still don't. Adults with the lowest rate of participation tend to have lower incomes, less education, and more physically demanding jobs. Getting this group to stay engaged requires both a strong demand for older workers and volunteers and a large supply of willing and able individuals. Fortunately, the evidence is positive for both supply and demand.

Demand Is Strong

Toossi . . . at the Bureau of Labor Statistics projects a 15 million–person increase in the labor force between 2004 and 2014. Adults age 55 and older will account for 11 million, or 73 percent, of this increase. Additionally, Johnson, Mermin, and Resseger . . . show a more favorable job climate for older workers, as the physical demands of most U.S. jobs decline. Yet, as the authors point out, older adults, particularly those with limited education who worked in physically demanding jobs, may need job training to update their skills.

Nonprofit organizations will likely need more workers and volunteers, owing to the government's increasing reliance on nonprofits to deliver public services. Tierney . . . expects nonprofits will grow because of projections of large future donations and wealth transfers. Between 2002 and 2004, the nonprofit paid and volunteer workforce grew by 5.3 percent, compared with an overall employment decline of 0.2 percent. . . . The bulk of nonprofit opportunities are in human services and, more particularly, in health services. Also,

Table 2

Characteristics of Adults Ages 55 and Older in 2004, by Formal Engagement Status (percent)

	Total	Engaged	Unengaged
Age			
55–64	45	59	27*
65–74	29	26	32*
75	26	15	40*
Health status			
Fair/poor	28	17	42*
Good	31	31	32
Excellent/very good	41	52	26*
Depressed			
Yes	13	8	20*
No	79	86	71*
Race/ethnicity			
White, non-Hispanic	83	85	80*
Black, non-Hispanic	9	8	10*
Hispanic	6	5	8*
Other race	2	2	3
Educational attainment			
High school or less	56	46	71*
More than high school	44	54	29*
Occupation of longest job			
Manager, professional	31	38	21*
Sales, clerical, service	36	37	36
Operator, craftsperson	28	24	33*
Never worked	5	1	10*
Urban/rural			
Urban	47	47	47
Suburban	21	21	22*

Continued

Table 2 (Continued)

Characteristics of Adults Ages 55 and Older in 2004, by Formal Engagement Status (percent)

	Total	Engaged	Unengaged
Rural	32	32	32
Own a vehicle			
Yes	86	92	77*
No	14	8	23*
Family income			
Low income	25	15	40*
Higher income	75	85	60*
Population (000s)	63,952	36,449	27,503

Source: Authors' estimates from the 2004 Health and Retirement Study.

Notes: The universe is respondents ages 55 and older in 2004. Engaged is defined as working or formally volunteering. Occupation is based on those with nonmissing values.

*Mean value for the engaged is significantly different from the comparable mean value for the unengaged at the 10 percent level or better. Results are based on a total, unweighted sample size of 15,871.

nonprofits are experiencing shortages in executive skills. As the nonprofit sector grows and seasoned executives retire, these shortages are expected to worsen. . . .

Supply Is Ample

Older adults want to work and volunteer, according to recent surveys. . . . Boomers say they plan to work well into their 60s and 70s. . . . Some will continue working because of a growing insecurity about retirement income, including changes to the Social Security retirement age, the decline in employer-sponsored pensions, and the erosion in retiree health benefits. The desire to continue working is also a desire to stay involved; most older adults say they plan to work longer because their work interests them, not out of economic necessity. . . .

More than half of adults age 55 and older who do not volunteer indicate some interest in volunteering now or in the future. . . . Surveys document boomers' strong interest in the nonprofit sector. . . . One survey by VolunteerMatch . . . found that white-collar workers and women were most likely to express interest in volunteer opportunities. Many potential volunteers said they want to work on causes that matter to them (56 percent) and to use their skills (35 percent); convenience (43 percent) and flexible scheduling (46 percent) were also deemed important.

We expect that the older adults most willing and able to stay engaged are healthy and free of caregiving responsibilities. Out of 27.5 million unengaged older adults, 8.7 million report good health and 7.2 million report excellent health (table 3). Also, 18.4 million of the unengaged have no family caregiving responsibilities. All told, 10.3 million unengaged older adults had good or better health and no caregiving responsibilities in 2004, including 3.6 million low-income persons. These adults could be targeted for new engagement opportunities.

More than half of the most able unengaged older adults are relatively young (age 55 to 74), including 44 percent of the low-income group and 55 percent of the higher-income group. About 1 in 3 have more than a high school degree, but the share drops to 1 in 5 for those in the low-income group. Many adults with more than a high school education have managerial or professional experience (3.6 million, or 17 percent of the entire unengaged group); skills often sought by nonprofits. In contrast, most of those with only a high school education had careers in services (such as sales or clerical work) or as operators and craftspeople. Only 9.4 percent of the most able unengaged adults had never worked, including 7.5 percent of those in the low-education group and 1.9 percent of those in the high-education group.

Potential workers and volunteers are a geographically diverse group, with nearly half living in urban areas. Table 3 also shows the percent of older adults volunteering informally, as a potential indicator of their propensity to enjoy formal volunteer positions. About 4 out of 10 older adults, including 35 percent of those with low incomes and 41 percent of those with higher incomes, report helping their neighbors and friends.

The number and profile of healthy, unengaged older adults with no current caregiving responsibilities demonstrate ample opportunity for engaging greater numbers of older adults. Many have sales and clerical experience, skill sets that will grow in demand with the rise of service occupations and non-profit agencies. Others who worked in more physically demanding jobs, such as craftspeople or machine operators, may need job training outside their fields to find more opportunities to work and volunteer.

Discussion and Next Steps

More than 10 million healthy older adults without caregiving responsibilities do not engage in paid work or formal volunteering. More than half of these able adults are under age 75, and more than 9 out of 10 have some paid work experience. Recent surveys show that many of these individuals would enjoy a paid work or volunteer position. Low-income individuals—3.6 million strong—would especially benefit from the additional dividend of extra income from paid work.

Opportunities for older boomers seeking volunteer or paid work are ample, but policy interventions are needed to engage a larger share of those with limited education and work experience not well matched to high-growth job and volunteer opportunities. Particularly needed is more funding for training programs that target low-income older adults and broader communication networks that connect older adults to available volunteer and work

Table 3

Demographic Characteristics of Unengaged Adults
Ages 55 and Older, 2004

	All Unengaged (000s)	Most Able: Good to Excellent Health and Without Caregiving Responsibilities		
		All	Low Income	Higher Income
Population (000s)	27,503	10,337	3,561	6,775
Total (Percent)		100.0	100.0	100.0
Age				
55–64	7,535	19.2	17.8	20.0
65–74	8,868	31.8	26.5	34.6
75	11,101	48.9	55.7	45.4
High school or less				
Manager, professional	1,683	8.2	7.5	8.6
Sales, clerical, service	6,654	27.4	31.1	25.4
Operator, craftsman	7,100	24.3	29.8	21.4
Never worked	1,997	7.5	12.5	4.8
More than high school				
Manager, professional	3,631	17.0	6.1	22.7
Sales, clerical, service	2,330	9.2	6.8	10.5
Operator, craftsman	1,043	4.6	3.7	5.1
Never worked	367	1.9	2.5	1.6
Urban/rural				
Urban	12,826	47.9	41.0	51.6
Suburban	5,995	21.8	21.2	22.1
Rural	8,682	30.3	37.9	26.3
Informally volunteer				
No	17,551	60.9	65.0	58.8
Yes	9,952	39.1	35.0	41.2

Table 3 (Continued)

Demographic Characteristics of Unengaged Adults
Ages 55 and Older, 2004

	All Unengaged (000s)	Most Able: Good to Excellent Health and Without Caregiving Responsibilities		
		All	Low Income	Higher Income
Characteristics used to identify most able Health status				
Fair/poor	11,596	0.0	0.0	0.0
Good	8,699	56.0	61.2	53.2
Excellent/very good	7,208	44.1	38.8	46.8
Provide care				
No	18,429	100.0	100.0	100.0
Yes	9,074	0.0	0.0	0.0
Family income				
Low income	10,866	34.5	100.0	0.0
Higher income	16,637	65.6	0.0	1.6

Source: Authors' estimates from the 2004 Health and Retirement Study.

Note: The universe is respondents ages 55 and older in 2004. Unengaged is defined as not working or formally volunteering. Occupation is based on those with nonmissing values. The sample size for the total unengaged population is 7,560.

opportunities. Public-sponsored outreach to older adults on the advantages of engagement while receiving Social Security benefits is also needed.

Policymakers must understand the payoffs of keeping older adults engaged. Longer careers increase retirement incomes, generate greater tax revenue, and reduce net Social Security payouts. Increased volunteerism improves physical and mental health, potentially reduces public health care costs, and benefits those receiving the services older adults provide. Investments in training older adults for new work and volunteer opportunities will have large personal, community, and national economic rewards. . . .

Marty Martinson

 **NO**

Opportunities or Obligations? Civic Engagement and Older Adults

Last spring, Meredith Minkler and I presented our critical perspective on the promotion of civic engagement and older adults at the Joint Conference of the American Society on Aging and the National Council on Aging. With all the current enthusiasm and support for civic engagement initiatives among gerontologists, academics, and others working with or in behalf of older adults, I was surprised, pleased, and a bit curious that almost all the chairs in our presentation room were filled. Preparing for an audience that would not necessarily agree with our position, Meredith joked with the group about how we were grateful that the conference organizers had given us a room with two exit doors behind the podium, in case we needed to make a quick escape. I similarly began the presentation with a quote from Maggie Kuhn . . . who, as the founder of the Gray Panthers, encouraged others to "Stand before the people you fear and speak the truth, even if your voice shakes." . . . While I was not truly fearful of the audience, evoking Kuhn's words was a way to acknowledge our contrarian perspective and of inviting the group to contemplate our questions about the promotion of late-life civic engagement. I hoped to broaden the discussion, which had thus far remained fairly limited in its scope.

Our concerns and critique resonated with many, including those who, like Meredith and me, are deeply involved in programs that support volunteerism among older adults. It is with their inspiration, and a desire to keep these critical questions on the table while the promotion of civic engagement moves ahead, that I write this essay.

My goal here is not in any way to disparage civic engagement (which I define broadly to include not only formal volunteering, but also things like political activism, caregiving, and community organizing) for and by older adults. I firmly believe in the value of such activity, be it on the individual, community, or policy level. Rather, my intent here is to look more closely at the context in which this promotion of civic engagement has emerged and how the discourse around it affects and reflects meanings being constructed and experienced about aging.

I use a critical approach to unpack some of the assumptions embedded in the civic engagement movement that have thus far been taken for granted. As the critical gerontologists Carroll Estes, Simon Biggs, and Chris Phillipson . . .

From *Generations*, Winter 2006–2007, pp. 59–65. Copyright © 2007 by American Society on Aging. Reprinted by permission.

write, "a critical approach, then, sees 'common sense' about age as a starting point, not as an answer in itself." . . .

In the case of civic engagement, if it is "common sense" that such engagement is good for older adults and for society, it is important that we ask how that came to be and who decided it is true. From there, we can explore other important questions: For example, What assumptions are being made in the promotion of civic engagement about the roles older adults might or should play in society? What expectations are being created for older adults and internalized by them? What happens to those who cannot or do not fulfill these roles and expectations, who are they likely to be, and will they experience adverse consequences because they do not fit into these roles? What types of civic engagement are being promoted and what types are being played down? And finally, who is served by the promotion of these types of civic engagement?

This article is a follow-up to previous work in which Meredith Minkler and I, as "loving critics," used a critical gerontology framework to explore the political and economic context in which the new emphasis on civic engagement is situated, the roles older adults are being encouraged to play as community volunteers within that context, and the possible exclusionary effect on older adults who do not play these roles. . . .

In this article, I again use a critical gerontology approach, with its overlapping perspectives from political economy and from the humanities, to more closely examine the potential impact of this burgeoning movement on images and perceptions of aging and of what it means to grow old. As gerontologists, we must consider the possible consequences of the current framing and promotion of late-life civic engagement in order to best develop and support civic opportunities for those older adults who take a civic-engagement path, while also supporting and honoring other experiences of aging.

Framework of Critical Gerontology

Using a critical gerontology approach allows us to explore the ways in which political, economic, and social structures affect the aging processes of the diverse population. Estes, Biggs, and Phillipson . . . have described this critical framework as "one diat goes beyond everyday appearances and the unreflective acceptance of established positions. It examines the structural inequalities that shape the everyday experience of growing old." . . . In order to move beyond the individual focus of traditional gerontology, critical gerontology considers "the critical role of social policy and social institutions in structuring and restructuring the life course and the meanings of old age." . . . This is not to say that the aging individual is without agency, but rather that structural forces affect how people see and experience themselves as aging beings as they internalize, wrestle with, and integrate these forces and ideologies into a sense of self and others. In considering the civic engagement initiatives of the national gerontological associations as well as those emerging from the 2005 White House Conference on Aging, this critical gerontology framework allows us to understand the ways in which these social policies and programs are situated within a specific political, economic, and socio-historical context and how the policies and programs both shape and are shaped by meanings ascribed to aging through the opportunities they create, the messages they promote, and the alternatives they ignore.

Politics of Retrenchment

Useful insights regarding how the emerging discourse on civic engagement and older Americans contributes to particular meanings of aging can be gained by using two interrelated paths of critical gerontology: a political-economy approach, which identifies how socio-structural factors influence aging . . . , and a humanities-based one, which explores aging and old age on a relational and personal level, from the inside out. . . . As examined in previous work . . . , the political economy lens reveals how the current push for civic engagement and volunteerism among older Americans is situated within the politics of retrenchment that began in earnest in the Reagan years and have since been a central feature of American political and economic life. With the introduction of the anti-welfare-state agenda of the Reagan administration, which included major cutbacks in federal spending on social programs and services, came a particular framing of the value of volunteerism in the United States. President George H. W Bush's 1989 inaugural address spoke volumes about how responsibility for managing budgetary shortfalls—and their disastrous social consequences—would henceforth be shifted to the American people and away from the government:

> My friends, we have work to do. There are the homeless, lost and roaming. There are the children who have nothing, no love, no normalcy. There are those who cannot free themselves of enslavement to whatever addiction—drugs, welfare, the demoralization that rules the slums. The old solution, the old way, was to think that public money alone could end these problems. But we have learned that is not so . . . We have more will than wallet; but will is what we need. . . . We will turn to the only resource we have that in times of need always grows—the goodness and the courage of the American people. . . .

This presidential speech exemplifies a politically conservative, individualistic view of volunteerism that places the responsibility for solving social problems on the shoulders of American volunteers while government retreats. The diminished federal funding for social services and public programs that has been a hallmark of political life beginning in the 1980s and continuing through today, has placed increasingly greater responsibilities on already deficit-ridden states and municipalities, which often then turn to individuals, families, and volunteerism to help take up the slack. George H. W. Bush put forth a call for a certain type of civic engagement—volunteerism in service and social programs serving the country's most vulnerable residents—while simultaneously reducing or eliminating federal funds for those services and programs.

Now in the new millennium, older adults are being called upon to embrace civic engagement as a meaningful and beneficial activity. Given that many older adults are among the most vulnerable Americans affected by years of budget cuts, what does it mean to be asking them to fill these gaps?

Emergence of Active, Successful, and Productive Aging Models

Along with cuts in social programs, increased privatization of services, and a growing emphasis on individual responsibility, a contentious discourse has emerged regarding the consequences of the rapidly aging U.S. population for society. The "apocalyptic demography" scenario . . ., embraced by the media, many policy makers, and others for the past three decades, presents the aging of America as a foreboding economic and social catastrophe, with precious resources being engulfed by burdensome and greedy older adults and their skyrocketing health-care costs. . . .

Gerontologists, including researchers and practitioners, have moved quickly to counter these negative images with the presentation of "active aging," "successful aging," and "productive aging" models. These models highlight involvement, mobility, and productivity as means for older people to maintain independence and thus prove the value and worthiness of the older adult population to the larger society. In turn, a number of critical gerontologists have joined the discourse by presenting eloquent critiques of these models. . . . Such critiques assert that in their well-intended attempts to present alternative scenarios to the negative images of older adults, proponents of the active, successful, and productive aging models have shaped cultural norms of aging that are limited, exclusive, and even oppressive.

For example, Stephen Katz unpacks the "gerontological nexus connecting activity, health, and successful aging" in Western societies . . . by examining the ways in which neoliberal policies, emphasizing individual responsibility amid declining government programs and services for the most vulnerable populations (many of whom are older adults), have created "market-driven programs to 'empower' older individuals to be active to avoid the stigma and risks of dependency." . . . In doing so, he asserts, "positive agendas based on activity and mobility can downplay traditionally crucial values such as wisdom and disengagement by translating the latter into 'problems' of inactivity and dependency." . . .

Estes, Biggs, and Phillipson . . . further point out how active, successful, and productive aging models, created with the good intention of countering negative stereotypes, actually serve to maintain the inequities of the status quo by providing homogenized models of aging that emphasize individual responsibility while ignoring structural inequities that affect people's life-course experiences and their likelihood of fitting into these glorified ways of being old.

Estes and her colleagues assert that the productive aging scenario in particular, with its ideal of aging constructed "through the lens of economic usefulness" . . ., presents an especially troubling model as it links individualistic solutions to the very market economy that has penalized and discriminated against older adults and other vulnerable groups. Furthermore, the productive ideal is culturally irrelevant or inappropriate for some subpopulations and leaves out other ways of aging that exist outside this mainstream notion of productivity.

These concerns are echoed by Martha Holstein . . ., who identifies the particularly "troubling implications" of the productive aging scenario for women who have traditionally carried the unacknowledged burden of caregiving responsibilities throughout their lives. By suggesting that old age must involve continued productivity, women are further burdened with expectations to continue in this role throughout their lives. In addition, Holstein asserts, the emphasis on productivity may "impose negative value on those who are not productive in the traditional sense or who do not maintain youthful vigor and independence. It can also intensify the prejudice that already marks social attitudes toward the elderly who have physical and mental impairments." . . .

Making a similar point in their critique of the concept of successful aging within gerontology, Holstein and Minkler . . . describe how such models ignore socio-cultural and environmental influences on the life course that create opportunities for some and limitations for others. In viewing aging processes through such an individualistic lens, proponents of successful aging may perpetuate a kind of victim-blaming for those older adults who do not age "successfully." As Holstein and Minkler assert:

> By suggesting that the great majority of those elders in wheelchairs could indeed have been on cross-country skis had they but made the right choices and practiced the right behaviors can burden rather than liberate older people . . . [C]oncepts such as successful aging are marked by important and unacknowledged class, race and gender concerns that result in further marginalizing the already marginalized . . .

Civic Engagement as Another Permutation

Civic engagement is being presented as yet another strategy for promoting health among older adults while countering images of decline and loss and addressing societal anxieties about "greedy geezers" . . . and a shrinking workforce. As such, the strategy raises questions and concerns similar to those expressed about the active, successful, and productive aging models. Proponents of civic engagement have described older adults as "a growing yet largely untapped civic resource for responding to community needs through both paid and unpaid work." . . . They have asserted that this resource of aging Americans can address the desperate need to fill the gaps in services left underfunded by government while also helping to address labor shortages anticipated with the mass retirement of baby boomers. Furthermore, civic engagement initiatives are put forth as providing "opportunities for greater fulfillment and purpose in later years." . . .

Calling upon older (and younger) Americans to be involved in their communities, and suggesting that such involvement can be meaningful both in individual and community terms, is certainly justifiable. However, the unintended consequences of framing a desirable old age within the boundaries of civic engagement are troubling. Given that civic engagement among older adults has primarily been put into practice as volunteerism . . ., what we are seeing is the placement of volunteer activity within the productive aging paradigm as a means of justifying older adults' existence, addressing society's ills, and shaping meanings of old age through "productive" roles. Civic engagement, in the form of volunteerism, is presented as a way of attaining validity in a society that values productivity and individualism over other ways of being and relating. Any lifestyle outside of that productive paradigm is unwittingly discouraged and therefore read as undesirable. Civic engagement is also promoted as a means of finding purpose and meaning in the later years—with the promoters defining that purpose in very specific ways. While attempting to counter ageist stereotypes, this promotion of civic engagement thus framed may serve to further enforce such stereotypes by inadvertently suggesting that without productive activity, older adults have no purpose.

In his critical examination of the social policies and public discourse promoting volunteerism in the U.K., the U.S., and other Western societies, the writer Simon Biggs . . . describes how these policies force older adults to struggle with placing themselves within or outside of restrictive definitions of aging. He asserts, "For older people, a narrative is emerging of social value through work or near-work situations. If you are active, volunteering and mentoring are identified as legitimized fields of social inclusion." . . . Less visible activities such as caregiving and activities like political activism, which Biggs called delegitimized, are absent from this civic engagement agenda: "This story of late life development . . . has little place for dissident or alternative pathways for self and social development other than through work." . . .

Civic Engagement as One Path of Many

Any promotion of civic engagement must be developed with thoughtful attention to the audience—who it speaks to and who it doesn't. As with promotion of the active and productive aging models, which, perhaps inadvertently, creates a kind of outsider or deviant status for those who do not fit the model, proponents of civic engagement must recognize that not all older adults can or will choose a civic engagement path. As the political analysts Ramakrishnan and Baldassare have aptly noted, "although civic engagement may involve acts of individual choice, these choices are often structured by various social, economic, and institutional factors." . . .

Thus, poverty, education, cultural norms, mental or physical disabilities, family obligations, and other factors will influence whether or not an older adult engages in volunteerism. Elevating civic engagement as an ideal for aging may further marginalize those people who, for any number of reasons, are not civically engaged and thus do not reflect that ideal.

In addition, as efforts are made to expand opportunities for civic engagement for those who do choose such a path, the realm of activities visibly encompassed by this term must also be expanded beyond traditional notions of volunteerism in the service or private sector.

Political activism, for example, is another type of activity that has dramatic public consequences and therefore ought to be embraced in the realm of civic engagement. I was pleased to see political engagement included in the working definition of civic engagement for this issue of *Generations,* especially given that political activism has been largely ignored in civic engagement promotions to date. The danger in promoting service volunteerism as the only type of desirable civic involvement and ignoring the value of political participation is that doing so may reinforce a trend among the citizenry to shy away from political involvement and replace efforts to create systemic change upstream with one-on-one efforts downstream. . . .

Such community service is of course valuable, but localized efforts will not address the societal ills that many civic engagement proponents suggest they will. As Theiss-Morse and Hibbing . . . assert, "Volunteering in a soup kitchen will help hungry individuals in a town but will do nothing to address broader problems of homelessness and poverty." . . . We would all be at much greater risk of losing an essential safety net for our increasingly diverse aging population were it not for the thousands of older Americans who have worked tirelessly as political activists to defend the preservation of Social Security. And it is notable that they have done so even though recently proposed changes will not have any effect on their own generation's benefits. Such civic engagement efforts that directly address the structural inequities of our society must be celebrated and supported for the scale of their public consequences, especially for society's most vulnerable groups.

Finally, the option of not being involved in civic engagement as an older adult must be honored. As Biggs notes, "There is an astonishing absence of diversity in policies that assume that everyone from a white male in his fifties to a black woman in her nineties has the same personal and social priorities." . . . We as gerontologists can learn far more about aging and be better advocates for older adults by recognizing the multiple ways in which people experience late life—be they active, inactive, dependent, independent, civically engaged or not. David Lynch's stunning 1999 movie, *The Straight Story,* presents another model: Alvin Straight, a 73-year-old farmer (played by the 79-year-old Richard Farnsworth) who travels on a lawn mower from Iowa to Wisconsin to visit his estranged brother, who has fallen ill. As we watch Alvin's slow journey, we discover how much more he sees from his decelerated vantage point. When a younger woman speeding past him at seventy-five miles per hour hits a deer (her fifth deer murder that week), Alvin stops to roast the deer and then honors it by placing its antlers on the front of his cross-country lawn mower. Later, when his vehicle breaks down along the road, he simply sits there quietly rather than immediately jumping up and trying to fix it. After some time, and with encouragement from a passing gray-haired tractor driver, he turns the key again and the lawn mower starts up.

Lessons on the advantages of moving slowly, and of aging outside the mainstream of a productive, active, competitive market economy, are found in the faces of Alvin Straight and of many other aging Americans. Let us not assume that aging looks just one way, that all baby boomers are alike, or that older adults need some packaged program in order to find purpose and meaning in their lives. Rather, let us honor the many ways in which people age, recognize and seek to address inequities faced by those who have been particularly marginalized throughout the life course, and celebrate community involvement in all its manifestations without asserting such involvement as the ideal way of growing old. . . .

CHALLENGE QUESTIONS

Is More Civic Engagement Among Older Adults Necessarily Better?

1. This issue has significant public policy implications in that retirement is often guided by legal guidelines; what is the role of developmental research in shaping public policy agendas relevant to old age?
2. Zedlewski and Butrica note that more "higher-income" adults stay engaged in old age, and argue that low-income older adults constitute a missed opportunity. Why might this class difference exist, and what are alternative explanations for its consequences?
3. Though Martinson is specifically addressing old age, how might her critique of volunteerism as a trend that addresses immediate needs at the expense of deeper structural problems apply at other stages of the life-span?
4. Why do we mandate a specific retirement age when there is so much individual variation in people's capabilities during old age? How might developmental perspectives contribute to thinking about the appropriate time to retire?

Suggested Readings

M. Martinson and M. Minkler, "Civic Engagement and Older Adults: A Critical Perspective," *The Gerontologist* (June 2006)

R.B. Hudson, "Aging in a Public Space: The Roles and Functions of Civic Engagement," *Generations* (Winter 2006–2007)

J.W. Rowe and R.L. Kahn, *Successful Aging* (Pantheon, 1998)

M.B. Holstein and M. Minkler, "Self, Society, and the 'New Gerontology'," *The Gerontologist* (December 2003)

J. Birren, K. Schaie, *Handbook of the Psychology of Aging* (Academic Press, 2005)

M.R. Gillick, *The Denial of Aging—Perpetual Youth, Eternal Life and Other Dangerous Fantasies* (Harvard University Press 2006)

P. Baltes, J. Smith, "New Frontiers in the Future of Aging: From Successful Aging of the Young Old to the Dilemmas of the Fourth Age," *Gerontology* (March/April, 2003)

G.E. Vaillant, *Aging Well: Surprising Guideposts to a Happier Life from the Landmark Harvard Study of Adult Development* (Little, Brown, 2002)

ISSUE 18

Is "Mild Cognitive Impairment" Too Similar to Normal Aging to be a Relevant Concept?

YES: Janice E. Graham and Karen Ritchie, from "Mild Cognitive Impairment: Ethical Considerations for Nosological Flexibility in Human Kinds," in *Philosophy, Psychiatry, & Psychology* (March 2006)

NO: Ronald C. Petersen, from "Mild Cognitive Impairment Is Relevant," in *Philosophy, Psychiatry, & Psychology* (March 2006)

Learning Outcomes

As you read the issue, focus on the following points:

1. There is no definitive biomedical test for Alzheimer's disease, dementia, or mild cognitive impairment (MCI)—leading to a blurry line between the disorders and normal aging.
2. Like many maladies of old age, the diagnosis of MCI may be helpful to health care professionals but it also risks being driven by marketing and pharmaceutical concerns.
3. While diagnosing MCI is complicated and while it should not be confused with a "purely biological" disorder, it does offer some hope of early intervention for the types of cognitive decline that can become full dementia.

ISSUE SUMMARY

YES: Philosophers Janice E. Graham and Karen Ritchie raise concerns that rigidly defining Mild Cognitive Impairment (MCI) as a disorder associated with aging artificially creates the harmful impression that the conditions of old age are merely biomedical problems.

NO: Medical doctor and researcher Ronald C. Petersen has been a prominent proponent of defining MCI as an intermediate stage between normal aging and Alzheimer's disease. In this selection he counters Graham and Ritchie by emphasizing the usefulness of MCI as a diagnosis.

Among the sometimes scary aspects of growing old is the prospect of cognitive decline—the gradual loss of intellectual functioning. Studying cognitive and intellectual changes over the life-span has thus been an important area for researchers learning about old age. Over decades of study a general picture has emerged with some consistency. We know, for example, that dramatic cognitive decline is not an inevitable fact of aging, although in some ways our intellectual functioning does inevitably change with time. We also know that not all cognitive and intellectual functioning reacts to aging in the same way.

But we also know that many older adults do experience some degree of cognitive impairment, and that extreme forms such as Alzheimer's disease are a very real problem for our aging population. Alzheimer's disease is the most common type of dementia, which is a general category of enduring cognitive problems that most often occurs during older adulthood. Most forms of dementia, including Alzheimer's disease, are impossible to cure and difficult to diagnose. Despite much attention from researchers and practitioners, there is no single diagnostic test that conclusively defines types of dementia. As such, some scholars worry that focusing on the biomedical aspects of dementia create a misleading sense that there is a clear distinction between it and normal aging.

Janice E. Graham and Karen Ritchie are among the concerned scholars. When they promote "nosological flexibility," they are referring specifically to nosology as the medical science responsible for classifying diseases. Though such classification may seem to be a simple matter of putting physical symptoms together with labels and definitions, in fact it can be a complex process of interpreting biological and social realities. Graham and Ritchie point out that the relatively new diagnosis of Mild Cognitive Impairment (MCI) offers a challenging example of these complexities. From their perspective, MCI is too similar to normal aging and too poorly understood to merit a distinct diagnosis. In fact, by presenting MCI as an established disorder, Graham and Ritchie are concerned that older adults may be misled by pharmaceutical concerns and doctors towards the conclusion that slight degrees of memory loss or minor deficits in information processing indicate the start of a devastating illness.

Ronald C. Petersen, a medical doctor and researcher at the Mayo Clinic in Minnesota, is more focused on using the diagnosis of MCI to help make progress against more intractable problems such as Alzheimer's. Petersen is often credited with defining MCI as a disorder, and thus has a vested stake in this controversy. But he also makes the quite reasonable claim that simply because a disorder is complex does not mean it is not a disorder. Throughout the life-span, from childhood behavioral problems to adult struggles with mental health, developmental characteristics regularly tread a fine line between "normal" and "abnormal." As such, thinking about MCI as either a part of or deviation from "normal aging" also provides a valuable opportunity to think through what exactly is "normal" in older adulthood.

POINT

- The concept of MCI as a clear disorder is not true to the reality that age-related cognitive decline comes in many diverse forms; MCI in some cases may be early stage dementia, but it is impossible to be sure.
- There is a risk of MCI as a diagnosis being driven more by marketing and the pharmaceutical industry than by actual processes of aging.
- There are few benefits to defining MCI as a clinical disorder, but the costs negatively label people even when they may be simply experiencing normal aging.
- Labeling MCI creates a false sense that it is a "purely biological" disorder requiring medical and pharmaceutical attention rather than social investment.

COUNTERPOINT

- The construct of MCI is actually flexible enough to account for a variety of causes and consequences, and while defining MCI it has been important to make clear distinctions between normal and abnormal aging processes.
- Despite claims that the pharmaceutical industry drives the definition of MCI, most research on the condition has originated in non-profit settings.
- Focusing on MCI before it becomes full Alzheimer's disease or dementia may allow for early intervention that can prevent cognitive decline during old age.
- Just because treating conditions such as MCI is complicated does not mean we avoid characterizing and diagnosing those conditions.

YES

**Janice E. Graham and
Karen Ritchie**

Mild Cognitive Impairment: Ethical Considerations for Nosological Flexibility in Human Kinds

. . . **T**his paper examines mild cognitive impairment (MCI), an emerging classification that does not meet all the criteria for dementia, and explores the advantage of allowing nosological flexibility between normal and pathologic definitions associated with aging-related modifications in cognitive performance. We frame the origins of the concept of MCI, and the problems with the premature application of criteria, within a nosological phenomenon: the drive to define a heterogeneous condition as a reified disease entity works against both scientific discovery and human compassion. Who "calls" MCI, and for what reasons? What reliability and validity does this designation have?

The social and ethical implications of identifying and treating those speculated to have an early form of inevitable dementia, a kind of disorder more remarkable for its variability than its predictability . . . , demands attention. Any diagnostic decision is based on anecdotal evidence of improvement or decline, and/or measurements calculated from scientifically standardized instruments. No matter what the source, these everyday and scientific explanatory models serve particular purposes and interests. When potential treatments become available, we must be sure that the market does not determine nosology. We need to examine the possibility that MCI is principally an entity defined to create a market for a product of unknown value.

The micromoral social worlds where decision making takes place contain vulnerable individuals and groups . . . , but the worlds of leading researchers driven by their colleagues' results, and busy clinicians dependent on pharmaceutical representatives, are also laden with opinion and belief. Diagnostic evidence may come from scientific research, a clinician's anticipation of treatment success, or a sufferer's hopes and fears. Research-clinicians, though trying to relieve suffering, may be contributing to premature and speculative hype.

Origins of the Mild Cognitive Impairment Concept

Chronic cognitive deficits, in the absence of neurodegenerative disorder, have been documented since Aristotle as an inevitable feature of the aging process. Such deficits are commonly associated with difficulties in the performance of

From *Philosophy, Psychiatry & Psychology,* March 2006, pp. 31–41. Copyright © 2006 by Johns Hopkins University Press. Reprinted by permission.

daily activities. Clinical interest in such conditions has mainly centered on differentiating them from potentially treatable disorders such as depression, metabolic disorders, and toxic reactions and also from early stage neurodegeneration. These subclinical cognitive symptoms are principally distinguished from neurodegenerative disorders such as Alzheimer's disease (AD) by their far slower progression, and by their milder impact on daily performance, and linguistic and visuospatial functions. Nevertheless, recent research into the nature and long-term prognosis of aging-related modifications in cognitive performance has begun to question the extent to which these changes may be considered normal. This questioning is refected in the evolution of a nosology for these subclinical alterations.

In keeping with the notion that mild cognitive deficits are a common feature of aging, early definitions were based on the comparative performance of young and elderly cohorts on a limited number of cognitive tests. Recognizing particular clinical populations using these concepts began with Kral's . . . concept of benign senescent forgetfulness. Later, Crook et al. . . . defined *age-associated memory impairment* (AAMI) as changes in subjective complaints of memory loss in elderly persons measured by a decrement of at least one standard deviation on a formal memory test in comparison with means established for young adults. Blackford and La Rue . . . refined the excessive inclusiveness of Crook's criteria. They defined their concept of "late-life forgetfulness" as performance between one and two standard deviations below the mean on at least fifty percent of a battery of at least four tests. Flicker, Ferris, and Reisberg . . . grappled with the normal–dementia divide. Levy et al. . . . introduced *aging-associated cognitive decline,* a concept that stipulated that the deficit should be defined in reference to norms for the elderly and not for young adults. This point signaled a subtle conceptual shift: MCI patients are still judged as normal, but they are now to be compared to an "optimum" level of functioning.

Subclinical cognitive deficit in the elderly had become a clinical entity even in the absence of any specific therapeutic management. Recognition by the major international classifications of disease—of subclinical cognitive deterioration linked to the normal aging process—began with the appearance in DSM-IV (American Psychiatric Association [APA] . . .) of *age-related cognitive decline* (ARCD). It refers to an objective decline in cognitive functioning caused by the physiologic process of aging for which no clinical criteria or cognitive testing procedures are specified. Subsequent attempts to operationalize ARCD using data from two general population studies in France and the United States have concluded that the concept has little value either in predicting clinical outcomes or in identifying comparable populations for research purposes.

As research into the causes of dementia and cerebrovascular disease began to shed new light on the etiology of aging-related neuronal decline, it became evident that many of the physiologic abnormalities seen in these pathologies were also present to a lesser extent in subjects identified as having a normal aging-related cognitive disorder. Consequently, elderly persons with subclinical cognitive deficits have become the subject of neurologic and geriatric research that seeks to discover whether cognitive deficits of this type may be caused by treatable pathologic processes. Alternative concepts have subsequently appeared in the literature linking cognitive disorder to various forms of underlying pathology. As an example of this research, the tenth revision of the *International Classification of Diseases* . . . lists *mild cognitive disorder* (MCD). MCD refers to disorders of memory, learning, and concentration, often accompanied by mental fatigue, which must be demonstrated by formal neuropsychological testing and attributable to cerebral disease or damage, or systemic physical disease known to cause dysfunction. MCD is secondary to physical illness or impairment, excluding dementia, amnesic syndrome, concussion, or postencephalitic syndrome. The concept of MCD, which was principally developed to describe the cognitive consequences of autoimmune deficiency syndrome, but was then expanded to include other disorders in which cognitive change is secondary to another disease process, and is applicable to all ages, not just the elderly. In practice, attempts to apply MCD criteria to population studies of elderly persons suggest it to be of limited value in this context; it has doubtful validity as a nosological entity for this age group. . . . The DSM IV . . . has proposed a similar entity, namely, *mild neurocognitive disorder* (MNCD), which encompasses not only memory and learning difficulties, but also perceptual–motor, linguistic, and central executive functions. Although the concepts proposed by the two international classifications—MCD and MNCD—do not provide sufficient working guidelines for application in a research context, they do give formal recognition to subclinical cognitive disorder as a pathologic state requiring treatment and as a source of handicap, and are thus likely to be important within a legal context.

A provisional classification, in this case meant specifically for elderly populations, is *cognitive impairment—no dementia* (CIND). CIND was developed within the context of the Canadian Study of Health and Aging (CSHA) with an epidemiologic view to research rather than clinical treatment. It is defined by reference to neuropsychological testing and clinical examination. . . . As with MCD and MNCD, persons with CIND are considered to have cognitive impairment attributable to an underlying physical disorder, but they may also have "circumscribed memory impairment," a modifed form of AAMI that accords with Blackford and LaRue's revisions. . . . CIND encompasses a wider range of underlying etiologies such as delirium, substance abuse, and psychiatric illness. MCD, MNCD, and CIND are constructs that have been developed principally for research. They consider cognitive disorder in the elderly as heterogeneous and not necessarily progressive. Their treatment should be determined by the nature of the underlying primary systemic disease. Operational concepts intended for research afford them an heuristic utility unconstrained by the clinical need to relieve symptoms. The first long-term prospective studies of subclinical cognitive disorders suggested that they are not benign, with many neurologists arguing that they are principally, if not exclusively, early stage dementia. These studies mark a complete turn around in the conceptualization of mild aging-related cognitive deficits: whereas in the 1990s, dementia was generally considered to constitute an upward extension of a "normal" process of progressive aging-related cognitive deterioration, subclinical cognitive deficit was now conceptualized as a downward extension of dementia.

In 1997, Petersen et al. proposed diagnostic criteria for a new category, MCI, defined as complaints of defective memory and demonstration of abnormal memory functioning for age, with normal general cognitive functioning and conserved ability to perform activities of daily living. Importantly, MCI was considered to be a prodrome of AD. Neurologists accepted MCI in theory; a period of early cognitive disability in which intellectual difficulties did not yet reach formal diagnostic levels for dementia was self-evident. But MCI criteria were difficult to apply in practice; too much depended on individual clinical judgment and ability to differentiate MCI at one point in time from cohort effects and low intelligence. A later study refined the initial definition by referring to memory impairment beyond that expected for both age and education level. . . . An alternative approach has been to simply define MCI in terms of early stage dementia.

Problems with the Application of Mild Cognitive Impairment Criteria

The identification of subjects for research and treatment for MCI has been problematic owing to the lack of a working definition based on designated cognitive tests and other clinical measures. The result has been that population prevalence, the clinical features of subjects identified with MCI, and their clinical outcomes, vary widely between studies and even within studies where there has been longitudinal follow-up. . . . It is also unclear whether MCI should include any form of cognitive change or whether it should be confined exclusively to isolated memory impairment as initially defined. Although there is some evidence that a purely amnesic syndrome may exist . . . , it appears in only a very small proportion (six percent) of elderly persons with cognitive deficit when the full range of cognitive functions are examined.

An MCI consensus group meeting in Chicago . . . concluded that subjects with MCI should be considered to have a condition that is different from normal aging and is likely to progress to AD at an accelerated rate; however, they may also progress to another form of dementia or improve. This group thus proposed subtypes of MCI according to type of cognitive deficit and clinical outcome distinguishing MCI amnestic (MCI with pronounced memory impairment progressing to AD), MCI multiple domain (slight impairment across several cognitive domains leading to AD, vascular dementia, or stabilizing in the case of normal brain aging changes), and MCI single non-memory domain (significant impairment in a cognitive domain other than memory leading to AD or another form of dementia). It has subsequently been suggested that MCI be further subdivided according to the suspected etiology of the cognitive impairment in keeping with international classifications of dementing disorders: for example, MCI-AD, MCI-LBD, MCI-FTD, and so on. However, this proposal is complicated by more recent neuroradiologic and post-mortem research that suggests the borderline between the principal forms of dementia (AD, vascular, Lewy body, and frontotemporal) is problematical and calls for a revision of dementia nosology. . . .

Although early identification of memory and language disorders might well mark individuals likely to manifest AD . . ., other forms of dysfunction are also likely to signal early pathologies worthy of clinical observation. To date, evidence supports the prognostic irrelevance of MCI subcategories in identifying specific entities predictive of dementia. . . . Some individuals diagnosed with early cognitive impairment in CSHA did not progress to dementia, and others were diagnosed five years later as having no cognitive impairment. A longitudinal study of a general population sample with subclinical cognitive deficits has demonstrated multiple patterns of cognitive change with variable clinical outcomes including depression, and cardiovascular and respiratory disorders, as well as dementia. . . . Current criteria for MCI pick up all these causes. Should researchers only be focusing on cases at risk of evolving toward AD? Even if we could do these studies based on the identification of MCI in general practice (and it is here that subjects will be principally presenting if a treatment is ever available), results suggest that current criteria have poor predictive validity for dementia in this setting and, applying theoretical criteria for the establishment of a formal diagnostic category, that MCI cannot be considered to be a separate clinical entity. . . .

Mapping Nosologies to Flexible Concepts

Although the recognition of MCI as a pathology marks an early step toward the recognition of nondementia cognitive disorder as an important clinical problem with a potential for treatment, it does not yet meet the criteria for a formal nosological entity. . . . Useful conceptual taxonomies should be able to accommodate more flexible kinds. Clinical research on MCI focuses narrowly on forms that lead to AD, the specter of which drives researchers, policymakers, and the public . . . to identify research subjects earlier. The expansion of the potentially affected population coincidentally provides a potential pharmaceutical market of from one quarter to one half of the population over sixty-five.

Ian Hacking's writing on natural and human kinds and his concept of "dynamic nominalism" can inform this discussion. The concept shows how new objects can be introduced into the world; these facts and categories are both socially created and real. Hacking describes the effects of this phenomenon,

> People classified in a certain way tend to conform to or grow into the ways that they are described; but they also evolve in their own ways, so that the classifications and descriptions have to be constantly revised. . . .

How might Hacking's looping of cause and effect, the way observation and identification changes the subject under study, affect those subjects who are identified early? Furthermore, how might those who escape this surveillance fare? How can the diagnosis of MCI be sustained when it has such poor predictive validity? Case identification remains a key issue in MCI as it did in dementia. . . . Accommodating the effects of education continues to require special screening and diagnostic criteria. Cognitive decline in both the normal and CIND groups is associated with older age, lower MMSE, and education, and increased functional impairment at baseline. . . . Concern about missed cases in MCI research outweighs concern about including individuals who are not cognitively impaired (false positives).

Dynamic nominalism stresses how much the act of classifying people changes both the classifier and the subject of classification. . . . Abnormal must predicate normal as a deviation from it, yet some absolute state of normal is itself simply constructed from an averaging of the cases selected. This paradox prompted Schneider to differentiate disease from abnormal variations in the early half of the last century, and both Canguilhem . . . and Foucault . . . to challenge the presumed stability of normal health. Recently, Davis has creatively employed the paradox to address the dynamic flexibility of health as a "plurality of possibilities and potential transitions to new norms." . . . New norms represent flexible adaptation to a new environment. Flexibility as a marker for health can be usefully compared to frailty, a benign accumulation of comorbidities and progressing severity. . . . But the progression from healthy flexibility to frailty is neither linear nor inevitable; it is less a paradigmatic dualism of incommensurable biological and social factors than a balancing board with often undetectable weights dropped on and off and interacting synergistically and antagonistically with one another. . . .

Although individuals do age, and they do become subject to pathologic processes marked by inadaptability and disease, evidence suggests that there is considerable deviation in cognitive impairment within and among individuals. In contrast to Davis's view . . . that dementia "tolerates no deviation" different processes may well play varying roles; cognitive degeneration is neither inevitable nor "natural" and it remains subject to interpretation, for example, by ascertainment bias. An individual identified as having MCI might embody behavioral symptoms that are a response to the diagnosis itself. These characteristics, in turn, are associated with progressive decline (i.e., agitation, irritation, depression, apathy). Moreover, the worried well may turn to self-monitoring, evaluating, discussing, and further data gathering. The act of identifying provides a comfortable prompt category and repository for information. What would be normal in the unhailed . . ., serves to reinforce pathology. Researchers, clinicians, patient advocates, or pharmaceutical companies can then mobilize these new human kinds to exert influence on policy decisions. . . .

MCI, like the dementias that it is presumed to precede, is a heterogeneous condition with no certain biomarker or known etiology. At this stage, MCI still incorporates multiple patterns of pathologic, cognitive, behavioral, and functional criteria. Useful conceptual nosologies should be able to accommodate a plurality of causal explanations as they consolidate research operational definitions with empirical evidence to build new models to explore etiologies. Although suggesting causal subtypes of MCI, Petersen's . . . focus on Alzheimer's disease constrains his "MCI" to a specific ontological passage, and should perhaps more accurately be identified as "mild AD." As noted, clinical research is focused on forms of MCI that lead to AD. Practical kinds offer a way out of this etiologically constrained box. They accommodate dimensional approaches and combine theoretical and empirical evidence to help us understand cognitive impairment and cognitive decline within a complex matrix of social and biological determinants of health. . . .

Technical, Social, and Corporate Relationships

The pathologic process of neurodegeneration is situated in sociodegeneration, or what Davis . . . refers to as *socioneurologic degeneration*. The quality of disintegrating relationships defies a simple normative–pathologic dualism. These relationships only have meaning, can only be defined in historically contextualized complex exchanges of shared memories and experiences, social interactions that are situated, embodied expressions of agency. . . . The persistence in viewing cognitive impairment as a purely biological process, as a natural kind that sits in contrast to some ideal normal healthy state, lacks internal validity—the complex heterogeneities of a variable sociodegenerative process incorporate redundancies, synergies, and antagonisms of intricately woven biocultures. . . . For Canguilhem . . . , pathology was a product of the clinical encounter, the therapeutic intervention between a doctor and patient. If only recognized upon the clinician's diagnosis, then pathology or disease have no relevance or meaning beyond that clinical encounter. Over half a century ago, Kurt Schneider suggested that suffering be a criterion for pathology. . . . Is the diagnosis of MCI cause for more suffering?

Treatments for cognitive impairment show only modest benefits in individuals with dementia . . . and, therefore, have given rise to a need to show efficacy through new clinically meaningful treatment outcomes. Clinicians are using qualitative methods to ground their judgments in refined operational definitions and criteria that evoke patient and caregiver perceptions, meaningfulness, and hope for symptomatic relief in anticipation of a progressive decline in memory, thought, and action. Tests such as the MMSE and ADAS-Cog are cognitive scales with an emphasis on logical and linguistic dimensions. These standardized packages categorically reify some evoked pathology . . . in a person who then too easily becomes a Clinical Dementia Rating Scale 2, MMSE 15, ADAS-Cog 47; these categories contribute little insight into personhood or identity. The real, clinically meaningful markers are localized in actions and relationships . . .—working, doing housework, canning fruit with a daughter, washing oneself in front of a mirror, walking the dog along a worn mnemonic path. Such everyday activities received scant attention before their affectual qualities were realized to mark a potential "treatment success" whose documentation as "clinically meaningful" might further the treatment's sales. This clinical turn places patient desires and expectations at the top of clinical management and treatment goals and it is an important and worthy movement; nevertheless, we need to reflect on the reasons for it and who profits from it.

We are now in the midst of a quiet revolution, as the desires and responses of the patient as subject, if not quite participant, are brought into focus. At the heart of the issue remains measurement. Formerly, the hold of quantitative psychometric and biometric gatekeepers, there is a growing body of research that measures qualitative everyday events and the values that individuals attach in the context of their socioneurodegeneration. Efforts to assess these measures are continuing. . . . But with earlier ascertainment of subtle cognitive impairments and the availability of questionable techniques to link individual responder subtypes to therapies . . . comes a responsibility.

The 1990s saw a turn away from a command and control regulatory apparatus. The U.S. Food and Drug Administration, concerned that pharmaceutical companies might not be rigorous enough in their testing procedures when it set out standardized criteria for measuring efficacy . . ., adopted partnerships with sponsor companies and now relies almost exclusively on company data to show efficacy and safety. There is a pressure to get products to the market faster. Rather than relying on objective psychometric measures of efficacy, as was outlined by the committee in 1990, there are increasing calls to adopt more clinically meaningful outcomes . . . that necessarily require a different approach to measurement. Research-clinicians and industry now ask what the quantitative data actually mean in everyday life. They look to patient expectations to measure success. Whether the rush to market has an effect on the methods and findings of these studies and whether data are subject to equally rigorous critical appraisals requires further analysis. New operational definitions require evidence that stand up to standards of accountability, reliability, and validity; consensus decisions to adopt these methods must be subject to scrutiny.

But what happens when new operational criteria and methods are proposed that equate treatment improvement to maintenance or "staying the same"? A common sense argument is constructed that accepts no further decline as a positive finding for an elderly person. Clinicians elicit narrative meaning from their patients; the existing assessment tools that cannot establish efficacy for a treatment get replaced by patient testimonials; panels of scientists agree that no decline is improvement. They form consensus committees, publish practice guidelines, set international standards, and authorize this paradox. Moreover, the emotionally resonant influence of personal testimonies from sufferers is used as evidence. A constellation of signs, symptoms, and social and technical relations are being mapped based on patient and caregiver hopes and fears, not the least of which is the concern about affordable access to their only hope. The noise from these heterogeneous sociotechnical relations creates accounts that cannot make sense. . . . Pharmaceutical grammar (in the form of hopes and fears and treatment success) feeds clinician desires to assist the sufferer who wants access to anything that might possibly work. If treatment effect is to be used to identify the category boundaries for practical kinds, but operational definitions for response continue to be diluted to maintenance, they may well mimic the variable states found in untreated Alzheimer's patients. . . . A vulnerable incipient disease population can be created by excessively loose inclusion criteria. . . .

Although the pharmaceutical industry may be pushing the treatment of MCI at a pace that is detrimental to clinical validity, it must be acknowledged that it is fulfilling its role as a market provider. It has played an important role, responding rapidly to changing social attitudes toward aging and a demand for increasing intervention to improve quality of life in the elderly, in the face of a lagging public health policy that has, for too long, neglected psychogeriatrics. Although it has promoted these causes to their shareholders gain, it is clearly the role of the clinicians implicated in industrial research, and not the industry itself, to ensure that the clinical limits of trial outcomes are adequately discussed.

Despite poor clinical predictive validity, MCI has market appeal to an anxious public. Personal testimonies of modest results risks exaggerating the efficacy of treatments, but it also overlooks the fact that many people do not respond to treatment. In identifying subgroups who may be more prone to treatment effects than others, researchers could underestimate the true potential of a therapy by averaging results across heterogeneous patient subgroups. Although MCI cannot be considered a formal nosological entity (it is rather a heterogeneous syndrome in which dementia is "nested"), it is being treated as though it were and may thus risk being used as a diagnosis in a legal sense—as such it could be evoked in damages, to exclude persons from responsibilities and services (notably elderly care admission) or employment. On the other hand, we have to be careful—MCI is important socially: we are no longer saying that cognitive decline is just normal aging, which the elderly have to tolerate (thus also underlying common attitudes to the elderly as incompetent), but that they should be investigated as practical kinds. Various treatments that might be detected using more flexible nosologies, which allow researchers and clinicians to understand more practical kinds better, might be actively sought. The cholinesterase inhibitors may be only one approach among many provided we are clearer about who we are giving them to and why. . . .

Ronald C. Petersen

NO

Mild Cognitive Impairment Is Relevant

Graham and Ritchie ... have contributed a scholarly document that implores us to reexamine nosological categories and certain diagnostic outcomes. They have chosen mild cognitive impairment (MCI) as the target of their scrutiny and have raised several interesting issues. I would like to comment on their approach and suggest that MCI is a useful clinical entity that does serve a practical function and hopefully will lead to a better quality of life for aging persons.

There are several clarifications concerning the construct of MCI that need to be emphasized. Graham and Ritchie have asserted that all persons with MCI eventually evolve to Alzheimer's disease (AD) and have claimed that this is the inevitable outcome of the disorder. Although it is true that many of the early studies on MCI focused on the amnestic subtype as a precursor to AD ..., subsequent work has expanded the construct to include prodromal forms of other disorders. ... As such, the construct of MCI has become flexible in recent years to account for alternative types of intermediate cognitive impairment.

The authors state that MCI addresses those individuals speculated to have an inevitable dementia. Certainly, we do not presume that dementia is inevitable in the aging process; rather, we posit that if certain criteria are fulfilled in persons who are aging, the likelihood of a person progressing to a certain type of dementia is quite high. As such, this is an important precondition about which to learn, because interventional strategies may be available.

Graham and Ritchie argue that some cognitive changes with aging are "normal" and trying to classify these individuals as "abnormal" is performing a disservice to much of the aging population. We draw an important distinction between the cognitive changes of normal aging, as they are recognized to exist, and what we feel constitutes the pathologic changes of MCI. We believe that the abnormal cognitive function found in MCI has a high probability of progressing to a greater degree of cognitive dysfunction in a relatively short period of time and these behavioral changes are accompanied by pathologic brain changes that are manifested on magnetic resonance imaging scans, positron emission tomography scans, cerebrospinal fuid biomarkers, and autopsy studies. ... This type of progression is in contradistinction to other individuals who are experiencing cognitive changes of normal aging. These individuals do not progress rapidly to greater degrees of impairment and autopsy studies reveal that their brains do not harbor the pathologic changes found in the MCI population. . . .

The cognitive and behavioral changes accompanying persons with MCI are devastating and cannot be ascribed to "senility" or "He is just getting old." It is a mistake to imply that by labeling people with a condition such as MCI we are doing them a disservice. Most of these individuals are seeking medical attention for their perceived difficulties. Consequently, addressing these concerns and educating the individuals on the implications of their symptoms are important services. Although we may not have adequate therapies at present, this does not imply that we should ignore the symptoms.

We cannot treat many conditions at present, yet we do not avoid the opportunity to characterize the condition and make a diagnosis. Even if this were part of the aging process, this does not mean that we should ignore the disability and refuse to treat it. Most individuals develop an inflexibility of their optical lenses as they age, yet corrective lenses of one type or another are believed to be extremely beneficial at alleviating this disability associated with the aging phenomenon. No one would argue that it is inappropriate to treat this condition because it is "just a part of aging."

It should be noted that I have stressed the situation in which individuals are seeking medical attention for their cognitive concerns. It is quite a different situation if an investigator were proactively to enroll a subject in, for example, an epidemiologic study and then label subjects as having some type of disorder such as MCI. In this instance, the individual subject is not seeking attention for any medical concerns and consequently it is inappropriate to intrude proactively on their daily activities and put a research label on them. This is particularly important while MCI is still evolving with regard to its refinement, and as such has not been completely delineated. However, in the clinical situation whereby an individual is seeking medical attention, the responsibility of the evaluating clinician is quite different.

Graham and Ritchie strongly imply that the entire research and clinical enterprise in MCI is driven by the pharmaceutical industry. Statements such as ". . . the possibility that MCI is principally an entity defined to create a market for a product of unknown value . . ." . . . are false and an inappropriate indictment of the research community. Virtually all of the MCI research that has emanated from the Mayo Clinic has been supported by the National Institute on Aging (NIA). Similarly, most of the major longitudinal studies on which these data are based—the Religious Order Study, the Cache County Study, the Cardiovascular Health Study, and the Monongahela Valley Epidemiologic Study—are all federally funded. These investigators do not have ties to the pharmaceutical industry. Furthermore, the MCI criteria currently in place have been adopted by federally funded agencies to promote research such as the NIA-sponsored Alzheimer's Disease Centers research program and the NIA-supported Alzheimer's Disease Neuroimaging Initiative. . . . To imply that this work is driven by pharmaceutical interests to create a market for marginally effective products is a distortion of the intents of the academic community.

Our work in Rochester, Minnesota, grew out of a longitudinal study on aging and dementia in which we observed individuals who exhibited cognitive concerns and impaired performance through a longitudinal follow-up study. We appreciated that these individuals progressed more rapidly to dementia and particularly AD than would be expected solely on the basis of aging. This observation led us to codify the criteria for these subjects and perform a longitudinal observational study. After many years of scrutiny, it became apparent that these individuals were progressing more rapidly than would be expected on the basis of age, and that this condition likely was the clinical precursor of dementia. There was no influence from the pharmaceutical industry in the design, execution, analysis, or reporting of these data. Yet, Graham and Ritchie would assert that the entire MCI research enterprise was spawned by the pharmaceutical industry.

This is not to say that the pharmaceutical industry has not appreciated this line of research as a marketing opportunity, and partnerships have developed between federally funded grants and industry, for example, the Alzheimer's Disease Cooperative Study, in an attempt to develop treatments for this condition. As such, with appropriate oversight and scrutiny, the public is likely to benefit from a combination of resources of these two partners. Having said that, when the Alzheimer's Disease Cooperative Study reported its MCI treatment trial involving donepezil and vitamin E, the final analysis, interpretation, and reporting of the data were under the auspices of the Alzheimer's Disease Cooperative Study without pharmaceutical company authorship. . . . Strict guidelines were in place in the Alzheimer's Disease Cooperative Study restricting the key investigators from having collaborative relationships with sponsoring pharmaceutical companies. Consequently, these assertions are false and distracting from the essential discussion.

Claiming that MCI research is the product of the pharmaceutical industry would be tantamount to saying that the diagnosis, cognitive impairment—no dementia (CIND) from the Canadian Study of Health and Aging was motivated by the development of a market for the pharmaceutical industry. CIND has not been the study of clinical trials because the overall concept lacks the specificity required to test certain pharmaceutical interventions. However, some Canadian researchers have defined subcategories of CIND that are virtually identical to the subtypes of MCI, and hence have demonstrated the utility and similarity of these two constructs. . . .

Graham and Ritchie claim that the identification of MCI subtypes for research and treatment has been problematic. That is, in part, true. However, with increasing attention and education of clinicians, these subjects are being recognized at an increasing rate. The threshold for detection of a meaningful cognitive impairment is shifting toward lesser degrees of impairment, and subjects are being recognized at earlier stages. A significant number of people with full-blown dementia still go unrecognized in general practice, and this problem would be magnified as one considers milder degrees of impairment. Yet, the threshold is moving and many individuals in general clinical practice are now becoming aware of more subtle forms of impairment and national organizations such as the American Academy of Neurology have recommended that clinicians identify these individuals because they are at increased risk of progressing to dementia. . . . With increased refinement of the criteria including subtypes and etiologies, a great deal of the variability among the studies in the literature can be avoided.

An issue raised by Graham and Ritchie concerns the worry that the act of classifying might alter the classifier and the subject of the classification. This is a relevant and valid; since both the classifier and the classified are probably changed by the process. However, one can look at this issue from a positive as well as a negative perspective. That is, as noted, as clinicians become more aware of the subtleties involved in identifying early impairment, they may refine their own techniques for classification. In a similar fashion, the process of classifiying may well have an impact on the subjects of that classification system. Investigators have a moral responsibility for monitoring the labels they place on individuals and this needs to be respected. On the one hand, some individuals appreciate the classification of concerns about their own symptoms, although we must be concerned that labeling people with a condition that is still under refinement may be problematic. We need to caution people about the uncertainties involved in the classification system and indicate the research that is underway. Nevertheless, if this is done in a responsible fashion, this should not dissuade the clinician from exploring new constructs that may be of potential benefit to their patients.

Finally, Graham and Ritchie claim that conceptual nosologies should accommodate a plurality of causal explanations. The authors criticize MCI as a heterogeneous condition as if that were a detrimental quality. They claim that the depiction of MCI is driven only by a treatment focus. Once again, this appears to be an oversimplification of the issues. MCI is by definition heterogeneous because in its broadest sense, it is a precursor to a variety of dementing illnesses. If dementia is characterized by a loss of cognitive capacity of a sufficient degree to impair daily function, then by definition, there must be multiple causes. As we know, from many of the diagnostic manuals, dementia is the first step in a multilayered process of arriving at an ultimate diagnosis. Once the diagnosis of dementia is made, then the clinician must decide the etiology of that dementing syndrome, for example, degenerative, vascular, metabolic, or traumatic. After that determination is made, then a specific diagnosis can be entertained, such as AD, frontotemporal dementia, dementia with Lewy bodies, or vascular dementia.

In a similar vein, if many of these conditions have a prodromal state (e.g., MCI), then MCI should have multiple causations as well. Therefore, the most recent iteration of the MCI diagnostic process includes a specification of a particular subtype based on clinical features such as amnestic or nonamnestic and single or multiple domains. This type of clinical classification leads the process in the direction of diagnostic specificity. However, stopping at this stage produces variability in the longitudinal outcomes of the various clinical subtypes. That is, if a study only classifies the subjects syndromically, then one would expect variable outcomes owing to the multitude of etiologies that could produce the clinical syndrome. Therefore, when an epidemiologic study claims that the syndrome of MCI is "unstable" because some subjects get better and some get worse, this is what one would expect. This is not a problem with the MCI entity itself. Some persons with a memory impairment caused by an evolving degenerative condition will likely get worse; others with the same clinical syndrome caused by depression or medication would be expected to improve once the offending cause has been eliminated. This is not an indictment of the construct of MCI; rather, this variable outcome is to be expected if the consideration of an etiology of the syndrome is not considered. This would be analogous to someone making the diagnosis of dementia and then claiming that dementia is unstable because all of the cases do not ultimately turn out to be AD. Dementia can have multiple etiologies in a similar fashion to the broad syndromic definition of MCI. Therefore, after the designation of the clinical syndrome is made, the clinician must assess the likely etiology. If an amnestic MCI subtype is determined and the likely cause is believed to be cerebral degeneration, then and only then can the specificity of amnestic MCI leading to AD be determined.

All this is to say that MCI does accommodate a plurality of causal explanations and the result and heterogeneity of the construct is a positive attribute. When MCI diagnostic algorithms are utilized to their fullest extent, they do exhibit the appropriate sensitivity and specificity to make the construct a useful clinical tool.

In closing, it is probably quite obvious that I am not a philosopher. The arguments of Graham and Ritchie are forceful and well expressed. Ultimately, I must classify myself as a pragmatist. I believe we can contest these issues interminably, probably to little avail. It is my contention that data will ultimately settle the issues. Prospectively designed longitudinal studies employing the most recent iteration of the diagnostic schemes and tools for MCI will determine the ultimate utility of the construct. Finally, I would contend that although academic exchanges are useful to clarify the issues, the final determination regarding the viability of the construct will be made by the clinicians and patients themselves. If clinicians find the construct of MCI useful, predictive, and helpful with patients, and if patients similarly find the construct explanatory and useful in communicating with each other and with their physicians, then the construct will prevail. At the very least, the construct of MCI has spawned a great deal of interest, debate, and research and that in and of itself is likely useful. . . .

CHALLENGE QUESTIONS

Is "Mild Cognitive Impairment" Too Similar to Normal Aging to be a Relevant Concept?

1. What are the relative advantages and disadvantages to "creating" disorders associated with the declines of aging before fully understanding their cause and treatment?
2. At present there are few treatments for cognitive decline, and no "cures" for Alzheimer's disease. How might this create a contentious situation for pharmaceutical companies and doctors working with older adults?
3. Graham and Ritchie identify MCI as part of a broader problem where complex changes with age are defined as exclusively bio-medical concerns. What other changes and characteristics might also fit as part of this problem?
4. Petersen claims that he is more of a pragmatist than a philosopher, and argues that MCI is a pragmatic diagnosis. What are the relative advantages and disadvantages to approaching the study of older adulthood as a pragmatist?
5. These selections are primarily concerned with the way professionals define and think about MCI. How might those considerations relate to the actual experience of older adults confronting cognitive impairment?

Suggested Readings

R.C. Petersen and D.S. Knopman, "MCI is a clinically useful concept," *International Psychogeriatrics* (September 2006)

P.J. Visser and H. Brodaty, "MCI is not a clinically useful concept," *International Psychogeriatrics* (September 2006)

R.C. Petersen, *Mild Cognitive Impairment: Aging to Alzheimer's Disease* (Oxford University Press, 2003)

P.J. Whitehouse and D. George, *The Myth of Alzheimers: What You Aren't Being Told About Today's Most Dreaded Diagnosis* (St. Martin's Press, 2008)

S. Artero and K. Ritchie, "The Detection of Mild Cognitive Impairment in the General Practice Setting," *Aging and Mental Health* (Issue 4, 2003)

D.H. Davis, "Dementia: Sociological and Philosophical Constructions," *Social Science & Medicine* (January 2004)

J.C. Hughes, "Views of the Person with Dementia," *Journal of Medical Ethics* (April 2001)

K. Schaie, *Developmental Influences on Adult Intelligence: The Seattle Longitudinal Study* (Oxford University Press, 2005)

A. Kramer and S. Willis, "Enhancing the Cognitive Vitality of Older Adults," *Current Directions in Psychological Science* (October 2002)

ISSUE 19

Should We Try to "Cure" Old Age?

YES: **Michael J. Rae et al.**, from "The Demographic and Biomedical Case for Late-Life Interventions in Aging," in *Science Translational Medicine* (vol. 2, no. 40, July 14, 2010)

NO: **Robin Holliday,** from "The Extreme Arrogance of Anti-Aging Medicine," in *Biogerontology* (vol. 10, no. 2, April 2009)

Learning Outcomes

As you read the issue, focus on the following points:

1. Many Western societies have had great success extending the lifespan, but that success has coincided with an aging population that often requires costly care.
2. Today's longer lifespans are largely a result of improvements in standard health care, particularly in combating illness and disease, but little science has addressed the aging process directly.
3. Antiaging science had some preliminary success with techniques such as calorie restriction and is investing hope in more direct "regenerative therapies," though to this point there are few scientifically supported techniques that can definitely slow or reverse aging.
4. People have invested hopes in a "fountain of youth" for thousands of years, and it has long been important to distinguish hopeful marketing from genuine scientific progress.

ISSUE SUMMARY

YES: Michael J. Rae was lead author on an article presenting the position a group of prominent antiaging scholars. They promote more funding and support for what they consider promising research directions towards slowing or even curing aging.

NO: Molecular biologist Robin Holliday takes a skeptical view of antiaging science, coming away from his own work on cellular aging with a respect for the necessary inevitability of old age.

Why do we have to get old? Though often asked as a rhetorical question by those frustrated with the realities of aging, this question is surprisingly difficult to answer. There is no obvious or necessary reason that the human body and mind has to deteriorate, nor is there a perfect logic to the current limit of the human lifespan (which is often taken to be in the 110-year range—though at least one individual has lived to 122). In fact, we all know that the lifespan of different animals varies considerably such that we regularly refer to abstract things such as "dog years." So if there is no obvious or necessary limit to the lifespan, why not try to extend it?

The logic and appeal of antiaging and life-extension certainly has an enduring appeal. Tales of a "fountain of youth" have appeared at least since ancient Greece, and the modern media is full of schemes for longer life from cryogenic chambers to ozone therapy that offer hope despite little scientific support. Science has, however, offered some legitimate promise and life expectancy has increased dramatically through recent centuries. In the United States, for example, life expectancy went from 49.2 years in 1900 to 77.5 years in 2003 according to data from the National Center for Health Statistics. In other words, improvements in health care and decreases in environmental risks have added almost 30 years to the average lifespan in only 100 years time. At that rate of change, by the turn of the next century the average life span for Americans will well exceed 100 years. But is it reasonable to expect such rapid change will continue? And is it a good thing if it does?

The fact that people are living longer already poses significant social challenges to many nations who have to support longer years of retirement at a time when decreasing fertility rates in the West make for fewer workers. An aging population stresses health care systems, financial systems, and community capacity. But since asking people to live shorter lives is obviously not an option, countering the debilitating effects of aging may be a more pragmatic alternative.

Michael J. Rae and a large group of colleagues prominent in antiaging science certainly think countering the effects of aging would be good policy. They point out that most of what science has contributed to the increase in life expectancy to this point is based on "conventional, disease-centered medical innovation." That is to say that the field of medicine has effectively managed to decrease the toll of communicable diseases such as small pox and to manage chronic illness such as heart disease. But Rae and colleagues think that model can only go so far. Instead in the YES selection, which was written as an advocacy statement by a large panel of scholars, they propose large-scale investment in a newer "antiaging" science that would use a variety of techniques to "directly target-age related changes themselves." In this vision of things, we would not just respond to illness as a threat but also proactively deter the cellular and metabolic changes of aging. They acknowledge this would require significant scientific advances, but think there are grounds for optimism.

For scientists such as Robin Holliday, however, advocating an antiaging science is more arrogance than optimism. In fact, as an example of arrogance Holliday cites a quote from one of Rae's colleagues and coauthors Aubrey de

Grey: "I think that the first person to live to be 1,000 may today be 60 years old." To Holliday this belief in antiaging is neither good science nor wise policy. From a scientific perspective it denies millions of years of evolutionary adaptations setting the limits of human functioning. From a policy perspective it plays into the schemes of marketers and hucksters who have long preyed on the dream of effortless immortality.

With these criticisms in mind, it is worth noting that whatever success antiaging science has found to date has not been anything approaching effortless. Rae and colleagues, for example, note that calorie restriction diets have shown some promise in extending the lifespan (though most of the research has been on animal, rather than human, models). These antiaging diets, however, usually recommend cutting food consumption by at least a third—which seems unlikely amidst a growing obesity epidemic. Even Rae and colleagues point out that calorie restriction would only have significant effects on the lifespan if begun at an early age, when the challenges of aging are often of least concern. They nevertheless conclude that going beyond calorie restriction to other forms of "regenerative therapies" is worth the effort because, despite the challenges, "a policy of aging as usual will lead to enormous humanitarian, social, and financial costs." The question here is whether efforts to "cure" aging have the potential to ameliorate those costs, or whether the end of the lifespan will always carry a heavy toll?

YES

Michael J. Rae et al.

The Demographic and Biomedical Case for Late-Life Interventions in Aging

Introduction

Age is the greatest risk factor for most major chronic diseases in the industrialized world and to an increasing degree in the developing world. After adolescent development, functionality declines progressively with age, and mortality rates increase exponentially, doubling roughly every 7 to 8 years after puberty. This exponentiality manifests as a progressive, roughly synchronous rise in the incidence of disease, disability, and death from chronic diseases beginning after midlife and suggests a causal—rather than a casual—relationship.

The physiological basis of these phenomena lies in the progressive lifelong accumulation of deleterious changes in the structure of the body at the molecular, cellular, and tissue levels. These changes (aging damage) arise primarily as damaging side effects of normal metabolism, aggravated by environmental toxins and unhealthy lifestyle. Aging damage contributes to pathology either directly (by impairing the function of specific biomolecules) or indirectly [by eliciting cellular or systemic responses that generally serve near-term protective functions but ultimately are deleterious]. As damage accumulates, organisms suffer progressively diminished functionality, homeostasis, and plasticity, reducing the capacity to survive and recover from environmental challenge. These changes both contribute etiopathologically to specific age-related diseases and increase the organism's vulnerability to other insults that contribute to them, leading to increasing morbidity and mortality.

The surprising conclusion from the past two decades of research on biological aging is that aging is plastic: Within a species, maximum life span is not fixed but can be increased by dietary manipulation [particularly calorie restriction (CR)] or genetic manipulation [particularly dampened insulin/insulin-like growth factor–1 signaling (IIS)]. These interventions generally reduce the generation, enhance the repair, and/or increase the tolerance of the molecular and cellular damage of aging. Although our ability to assess "health span" in model organisms remains incomplete, these interventions generally preserve "youthful" functionality in regard to tested parameters and reduce the incidence of age-related disease.

There have long been calls for greater efforts to translate this research into clinical interventions to expand the healthy, productive period of human life. By targeting the aging damage that is responsible for the age-related rise in disease vulnerability, such interventions would reduce the incidence of most, if not all, age-related diseases in unison, by modulating the underlying biology that drives them all, rather than treating each in isolation, as in conventional medicine. To date, however, investments in such research by the National Institutes of Health (NIH) and its international equivalents have been disproportionately low relative to their potential return; for example, the NIH $28 billion budget allocates <0.1%—perhaps as little as $10 million—to research on biological aging. Contrast this allocation with the costs of medical care for today's aged, such as the current Medicare budget of $430 billion, and with projected outlays many times that number to treat future increases in the diseases of aging.

Calls for an intensive agenda of research on the biology of aging have particular salience today because of two converging trends: one demographic and one scientific. Demographically, we are entering a period of unprecedented global aging, as the ratio of retired elderly to younger workers increases dramatically within the next decades in both developing and industrialized nations. Age-related disease and disability greatly increase medical costs, even when adjusted for survivorship, and are major determinants of the decline in productivity and labor force participation after midlife. Thus, the results of biological aging are both a rise in social costs and a decrease in a national workforce's ability to produce the goods and services necessary to meet those costs. The costs of global aging to individuals and societies are therefore high and are projected to inflate into an unprecedented economic and social challenge in coming decades.

Scientifically, this phenomenon coincides with the first robust reports of effective interventions into the biological aging of mammals that are already in late middle age when treatment begins. In 2004, CR was first shown to extend life span in mice as old as 19 months, which is broadly equivalent to the current average age of postwar "baby boomers." And 2009 saw the first demonstration of pharmacological intervention into the biological aging of similar-aged mice, with preliminary evidence of delays in cancer incidence and other changes in gross pathology.

Intervention in the degenerative aging process need only lead to a simple delay in the appearance of age-related disability and rising medical costs in order to alleviate the projected social costs and challenge of global demographic aging. This alone would increase the ratio between productive workers of all ages and the dependent frail elderly, simultaneously expanding the resources available to bear the costs of supporting a subpopulation of frail elderly and reducing the relative size of that subpopulation during the critical period of demographic transition. The benefit to be gained from intervention in biological aging would be even greater, however, if it were able to not only delay the onset but reduce the absolute ultimate burden of age-related disease. Preliminary evidence from animal models of retarded age-related degeneration [for example,] and the identification of human subpopulations characterized by extreme survivorship with surprisingly little morbidity (possibly indicative of a phenotype of slow biological aging) suggest that such intervention might have this even more beneficial effect. Whether it would actually do so, however, is uncertain.

Preliminary glimpses of the benefit to be anticipated from therapeutics targeting the underlying degenerative aging process can be gleaned from two studies performed a quarter-century apart. Recently, Manton et al. demonstrated that, by improving the health of older adults, investment in conventional medical technology in the late 20th century buffered projected declines in labor force productivity and thereby contributed significantly to economic growth. Such investment thereby constrained the growth of health care costs as a share of gross domestic product, effectively paying for itself; the authors provide analysis to suggest that ongoing investments can be projected to continue to do so. Economic modeling performed independently in the 1980s indicated that even greater economic benefits can be expected from interventions that successfully slow the rate of biological aging. But this analysis is probably an underestimate, because it preceded and does not factor in the rapid rise in dependency ratios that lies ahead today, the alleviation of which represents a significant part of the benefits now projected to be realized by expanding investment in even conventional medical technology. Incorporating this new demographic challenge into the analysis of the economic impact of interventions targeting the underlying degenerative aging process would clearly substantially amplify the benefits to be expected.

In light of these convergent scientific and demographic phenomena, we advocate an intensive, dedicated, and focused R&D agenda by developed and rapidly developing nations globally, to devise interventions to restore and maintain the health and functionality of humans in late middle age and older.

Research Roadmap

Our consensus is that a realistic path toward this goal exists, by targeting age-associated changes that, based on existing research, are known or thought to be important primary components of human age-related degeneration and thus drivers of vulnerability to age-related disease. Here we outline such an agenda, focusing on targets that are likely to be biomedically tractable, even later in life, and would make efficient use of intellectual, capital, and temporal resources.

We propose a global biological aging research agenda focused on the detailed understanding of the following overlapping core age changes and developing therapies for decelerating, arresting, and reversing them: (i) the loss of proliferative homeostasis, (ii) neurodegeneration, (iii) somatic mutations in both nuclear and mitochondrial DNA, (iv) nonadaptive alterations in gene expression, (v) immunosenescence, (vi) nonadaptive inflammation, and (vii) alterations of the extracellular milieu. See the supporting online material (SOM) for brief elucidation.

To ameliorate age-related changes, we identify three broad modes of intervention that should be exploited in addition to ongoing conventional, disease-centered medical innovation: (i) reduction in exposure to environmental toxins and amelioration of other risk factors through improved public health; (ii) modulation of metabolic pathways contributing to age-related changes; and (iii) a more broadly conceived regenerative medicine, to embrace the repair, removal, or replacement of existing aging damage or its decoupling from its pathological sequelae.

Public Health and Medical Advancements

There remains substantial room to improve healthy life expectancy through improvements in public health and lifestyles, medical control of disease risk factors, and traditional disease-oriented medicine. However, we note their limitations in the late-middle-aged cohorts in whom intervention is most urgent. These improvements are most effective when applied relatively early in life, especially during development; in later life, the effect of environmental influences declines. In fact, age-related changes lead to paradoxical relationships between disease risk factors and outcomes in the elderly: The relationship between well-established risk factors—such as overweight, hypertension, and hyperinsulinemia—and adverse outcomes often declines in magnitude or even reverses relative to their relationship in younger people. The causes and implications of these changes are often unclear. Some may be the result of "reverse causation," in which the causal relationship between two closely associated phenomena is mistakenly taken to be the reverse of what it actually is; for example, mild overweight in older adults is associated with longer life expectancy, which may not indicate a protective effect of excess weight but rather that thinness in older adults is often the result of medical conditions that themselves cause weight loss (such as cancer, chronic obstructive pulmonary disease, or depression) or of the cachexia (wasting syndrome) and sarcopenia (the loss of muscle mass, strength, and function) of aging. But others may represent genuine age-related changes in the causal relationship between a risk factor, its underlying metabolic basis, and clinical disease. This uncertainty creates potential for unintentional worsening of patient health through mismanagement of the risk factor. Improvements in public health and conventional medicine will therefore contribute primarily to the future health of currently young people rather than people already in late middle age and beyond.

Modulation of the Metabolic Determinants of the Aging Damage

Interventions that mimic the modulation of metabolic pathways influencing the rate at which aging damage accumulates in model organisms—such as pharmacological mimetics of CR and down-regulation of IIS—have thus far received more attention than alternative routes to postponing human age-related degeneration. This avenue is undoubtedly promising, but we note possible limitations. Many of these promising interventions have been demonstrated in model organisms with simpler signaling systems than those of humans; the inbred laboratory strains of model species that have dominated research to date may create experimental artifacts; and whereas life-span extension is readily quantitated, effects on age-related functional decline (reduced health span) are difficult to assess and characterization is limited. Accordingly, the benefits of even faithfully translated interventions in the health and functionality of aging humans remain uncertain.

Additionally, the modulation of metabolic pathways typically imposes substantial side effects in model organisms, such as impaired immunity, low bone mass, vulnerability to cold, and lower fertility. Rapamycin, a likely CR mimetic because its inhibitory effects on a nutrient-sensing pathway parallel those of CR and several longevity mutations, was recently shown to extend life span in mice when first administered late in life. This drug is an immuno-suppressant, induces hyperlipidemia in humans (which would only modestly affect mouse life span, because wild-type mice are not susceptible to athero-sclerosis), and might interfere with normal brain function—none of which were assessed in the recent report.

Finally, even if interventions that favorably modulate the metabolic origins of aging damage can be fully translated to humans and any deleterious side effects mitigated, there remains the progressively reduced efficacy of such interventions the later in life they are initiated. These interventions decelerate age-related decline but cannot arrest or reverse its course. Thus, even assuming full human translatability, a rough extrapolation from results to date suggests that a CR mimetic might extend human life expectancy by 25 years beyond the 85-year life expectancy that would otherwise result from "aging as usual" if begun at weaning but only 9.3 years if begun at age 54.

Regenerative Therapies

A third mode of intervention in the degenerative aging process is to directly target age-related changes themselves, rather than their environmental and metabolic determinants. This is the goal of regenerative medicine, a term often limited to cell therapy and tissue engineering: replacing lost cells and tissues with versions that are new and structurally youthful to restore function. We propose to broaden its scope to include conceptually similar interventions targeting other age-related changes.

Where they are possible, regenerative therapies would have the advantage of being effective even after youthful functionality has been lost. This feature also implies simpler and more rapid clinical testing, because any effects will necessarily be more immediate and direct. Regenerative therapies are thus especially attractive because they have effects even when initiated late in life, when the body has already accumulated extensive age-related changes.

Regenerative therapies, too, would have limitations. Their effects would necessarily be segmental, specifically affecting changes linked to the particular damage that a given therapy repairs. Further, it is unclear whether such therapies could be developed to address all age-related changes, although proofs of concept exist and other potential interventions can be foreseen from existing developments.

It is possible that therapies of different types might be used complementarily. Whereas regenerative therapies are segmental, metabolic interventions (especially CR) are highly pleiotropic, decelerating many, if not all, degenerative aging processes. The two approaches could thus be synergistic, with metabolic interventions decelerating age-related degeneration systemically and regenerative therapies used to restore functionality in particular tissues more fully. If regenerative therapies strengthen the weakest links in the chain of age-related changes decelerated by metabolic modulation, a disproportionate increase in healthy life span might result.

Policy Priorities

Funding

Recognizing the potential of this research agenda to avert enormous economic, social, and human costs, we advocate that substantial new investments be made by governments, while engaging and facilitating the participation of the biomedical industry. A previous proposal that included one of us (R.N.B.) as an author suggested that the United States invest $3 billion annually (<1% of the current Medicare budget) in a broadly similar agenda; we suggest that this funding level is inadequate to deliver interventions in time to avert demographic crisis. We therefore urge a larger investment, targeted specifically to late-life interventions, matched by other developed and developing nations in proportion to the means and demographic urgency of each.

Regulatory Changes

Because they would reverse existing age-related changes, the effects of regenerative therapies may be so rapid as to be amenable to direct testing for their effects on specific diseases in time frames similar to those of conventional medicines, allowing their evaluation in clinical trials within existing regulatory frameworks. However, new regulatory structures will also need to be developed for the unique features of this class of medicines, especially for interventions targeting modulation of the metabolic determinants of the rate of accumulation of aging damage, whose effects will be more global and will emerge more gradually.

Regulatory agencies such as the U.S. Food and Drug Administration (FDA) should be charged with developing new guidelines for testing interventions that do not necessarily target a single specific disease but that retard, arrest, or reverse the structural degeneration and loss of functionality associated with aging. Preliminary meetings exploring a subset of such issues have occurred between geriatricians and FDA officials; they will need to be expanded into interdisciplinary working bodies drawing in experts in the basic biology of aging (particularly experimentalists with extensive experience in lifelong interventional studies in mammals) and translational medicine. The ability of an agent to extend life span and health span in mammalian models, based on evidence of a broad spectrum of health effects in rodent models with robust historical controls, should be evaluated as sufficient preclinical evidence of efficacy for clinical trials.

For human testing, new surrogate outcomes will need to be designed that would offer evidence for parallel effects without necessitating a measurement of life span, such as the panels of nonspecific deficits used in cohort frailty studies, reducing the acceleration of total mortality rate over the course of 8 years, and the cautious use of metabolic changes observed in animal models that are thought to be mechanistically important to the observed deceleration of the rate of biological aging.

We also advocate that regulatory agencies charge interdisciplinary panels with identifying age-related dysfunctions that are sufficiently well character- ized to merit consideration as new licensable therapeutic indications (that is, medical conditions for which regulatory bodies will approve effective thera- pies for marketing). A pressing example is sarcopenia, which occurs even in master athletes and in which loss of mass is only one relatively reversible ele- ment. Sarcopenia is a major contributor to age-related frailty and adverse out- comes, ranging from loss of activities of daily living to institutionalization, fracture risk, and increased mortality. It is estimated to cost the United States $18.5 billion ($11.8 billion to $26.2 billion) per year (~$1.5% of total health care expenditures) in direct medical costs alone. Exercise and supplemen- tal energy and protein consumption can increase muscle mass to a limited extent but do not address the degradation of myocyte and neuromuscular unit structure. Beyond this, clinicians can at best resort to non–evidence-based off- label use of medications, risky and minimally effective hormone therapies, or unregulated, putatively ergogenic dietary supplements. Yet because sarcopenia is not a licensable indication, no incentive exists to develop therapies specifi- cally targeting it. New treatments targeting determinants of sarcopenia other than loss of muscle mass could greatly benefit the health and functionality of older adults, and expert panels should explore this and other causes of age- related disability as possible new licensable indications.

We also advocate efforts to include more people over the age of 65 in clinical trials. Older adults are the largest consumers of prescription medica- tions and have the highest prevalence of the diseases for which many drugs are indicated. Yet they are sorely underrepresented in clinical trials and are often perversely excluded from trials precisely because of their burden of other age-related disease. For example, an analysis of 3470 community-living older adults with possible or probable Alzheimer's disease (AD) found that >90% would be precluded from participation in either of two trials for cholinesterase inhibitors, the main drug class approved to treat AD symptoms. Extrapola- tion of the results of trials performed in younger adults into older patients is fraught with potential artifacts because there are substantial differences in drug pharmacokinetics and in the range and severity of adverse reactions, because of primary and secondary age-related changes.

This exclusion of older people is a major problem in conventional medi- cine testing and will almost preclude the testing of agents whose purpose is to retard, delay, or reverse age-related changes in late life. In addition to imple- menting comprehensive reforms to address weaknesses in the existing system (proposals from the American Geriatrics Society and the American Association for Geriatric Psychiatry merit consideration), we advocate that trials of therapeutics specifically targeting biological aging or new indications for age-related diseases should be required to undergo testing in persons 50 years old and above, with significant representation of people over 65, beginning no later than in phase II trials.

Conclusions and Beginnings

We therefore advocate the development and implementation of all three forms of intervention in age-related degeneration discussed above, but with emphasis on metabolic and regenerative interventions, and on the most aggressive schedule possible, bearing in mind the urgency of the demographic challenge before us. We cannot be certain of success. Nor can the full range of social impacts, positive and negative, of a dramatic increase in healthy human life span be known with certainty in advance.

One obvious and quantifiable challenge that would result from a rapid decline in late-life mortality would be upward pressure on global population. Contrary to what is widely assumed, however, the net effect should be relatively minor. Because the effect on global population of adding each additional entire human life span (and one future parent) to the world is greater than the effect of adding some fraction of a life span onto each extant life, the effect of birth rates on population growth is much greater than the effect of late-life death rates. Without intervention in biological aging, the emerging global shift into subreplacement fertility is likely to lead to the stabilization and later ongoing shrinkage of world population at ~9 billion in the 2050–2070 range. Demographic modeling in the contemporary Swedish population of the effect of a reduction in the rate of acceleration of mortality of the same magnitude (50%) as is required to achieve our proposal finds that population would continue to decline over the next century. In fact, even a much more radical intervention into age-related mortality than we envision, in which the rate of age-related mortality is arrested at the equivalent level of today's 50-year-olds, would result in a surprisingly low increase of 35% in global population over the critical 50-year period of concern for global demographic aging. And of course, fertility rates themselves can be the subject of policy decisions, both directly and indirectly.

But it should also be emphasized that the social challenge posed by over-population is not determined by sheer numbers but by a variety of factors within the sphere of public policy, such as the efficiency of resource use and the equity of resource distribution, as well as the rate of economic growth. Moreover, the predictable early expansion of productive capacity resulting from intervention in biological aging will increase the resource pool available to meet the population and other challenges to which such intervention may contribute and with which it will interact.

This and other potential impacts of intervention in the degenerative aging process must be the subject of open, early, and serious public dialogue; in our view, such challenges should be met under the broad approach called the "vigilance principle:" that action should be taken for the greater social good based on current knowledge, acknowledging uncertainty surrounding its possible future ramifications (positive and negative), and monitoring such consequences actively. The resilience and adaptability exhibited by human cultures throughout history should be recognized and engaged, with more specific policy-based remedies applied judiciously in cases in which organic social response proves insufficient to mitigate specific deleterious effects that actually (rather than hypothetically) emerge.

In the case of late-life intervention in human age-related degeneration, what we can be certain of today is that a policy of aging as usual will lead to enormous humanitarian, social, and financial costs. Efforts to avert that scenario are unequivocally merited, even if those efforts are costly and their success and full consequences uncertain. To realize any chance of success, the drive to tackle biological aging head-on must begin now.

Robin Holliday

 **NO**

The Extreme Arrogance of Anti-Aging Medicine

Introduction

In recent years a new branch of medicine has appeared and become extremely influential. This proposes that ways and means can be found to intervene in the process or processes of aging, with the specific aim of extending the human lifespan. Although this anti-aging movement is relatively new, it already makes very strong claims that it will succeed. For examples, Klatz (1996) wrote in the forward to the book *Advances in Anti-Aging Medicine:* "within the next 50 years or so, assuming an individual can avoid becoming the victim of major trauma or homicide, it is entirely possible that he or she will be able to live virtually for ever." One part of the anti-aging movement has adopted the slogan SENS, for Strategically Engineered Negligible Senescence. The main protagonist is Aubrey de Grey, who has said: "I think that the first person to live to 1,000 may today be 60 years old." (de Grey 2004). Both these statements, and many others that have been published (see Olshansky et al. 2004; de Grey 2006), clearly demonstrate that the anti-aging movement does not just have modest aims, but extraordinarily ambitious ones. The protagonists of anti-aging medicine are not by any means a homogeneous group. There are those whose main aim is to create a multi-million industry by promoting existing products that are claimed to bypass or reverse aging. There are those who believe that new research will in the near future uncover powerful interventions in the processes of aging. Also, there are those who have more modest claims about interventions.

The search for the fountain of youth, the elixir of life or their equivalents, is not at all new. Throughout history all manner of proposals have been made for lengthening the life span, or achieving immortality of the body. None of these could be said to have a rational or scientific basis, and they need not be reviewed here. The anti-aging movement is distinct from all the earlier proposals in that it claims to be supported by scientific investigation. It is stating, in effect, that scientific or medical research will result in the discovery of interventions in the aging process. It is based entirely on the view that this research will be successful. This has been an essential component of its influence so far: by adopting the label of scientific respectability it has been able to infiltrate the media, and thereby take its message to the general public. The financial interests are enormous, as it is not difficult to see that any marketed treatment which claims to delay the natural lifespan, will be eagerly sought and paid for by a gullible public. In fact, it is often hard to distinguish those in the anti-aging movement whose aim is to generate commercial profit, and those who genuinely believe that its research will be successful.

A great deal is now known about biological aging. Several scientists in the field came to realize at the end of the twentieth century, that the biological reasons for the ubiquity of aging in the animal kingdom was now well understood. Three books with positive titles were published: *How and Why We Age* by Hayflick (1994, 1996); *Understanding Aging* by Holliday (1995), and *Why We Age,* by Austad (1997). The books were written independently and are by no means the same, but their major conclusions are very similar, namely, that the large number of studies of aging in the twentieth century (both experimental and theoretical) have finally provided the explanation of the very widespread existence of aging in almost all animals. In other words, aging is no longer a mystery or some unsolved problem of biology.

In this article I will expose the scientific ignorance of all those that believe that millions of years of evolution can be readily bypassed by advances in medicine or biotechnology in the near future. Previously, a wide-ranging assessment of the claims of the anti-aging movement was published under the title "Position statement on aging" (Olshansky et al. 2002). This was supported by 51 established scientists in the field. Also, the specific claims of SENS have previously been critically reviewed by a large group of biogerontologists (Warner et al. 2005).

In discussing the opinions of the anti-aging medicine protagonists, it is important to distinguish arrogance from visionary prediction. For example, it would not be arrogant to predict the development of an implanted artificial heart entirely composed of non-living mechanical and structural components. It would be arrogant to maintain that in the future a normal human heart could function for 1,000 years. A dictionary definition of arrogance is: "Having or revealing an exaggerated sense of one's own importance or abilities."

Aging and Human Pathology

The assertion of arrogance is based on two sources of information about aging. The first is the full medical documentation of what actually happens to people as they age. The second is our understanding of the evolutionary origins of those anatomical and physiological characteristics of animals and man that inevitably lead to aging. In this section, I summarise and discuss the pathological changes that accompany aging.

The effects of aging are evident to everyone. They include greying and whitening of the hair, the wrinkling of the skin, the loss of accommodation (lens focussing) of the eye, and the loss of muscular strength and physical stamina. In addition, there are commonly, but not invariably, altered posture and reduced stature; imbalance; loss of memory; incontinence; deafness; and reduced visual acuity. Even without medical investigation, it is evident that aging affects many different components of the body. The changes in the body that occur internally are largely within province of medical investigation.

From them, one can add to the list of age-associated changes which lead to one pathology or another. These include hardening of the arteries and increased blood pressure; increased probability of cerebrovascular disease; the increased likelihood of renal failure, dementia, cancer, type 11 diabetes, osteoporosis, osteoarthritis, blindness from cataracts or retinopathy; and a decline in immunological functions. These are only some of the better known pathological changes, and there are many others less well known, but documented in any comprehensive textbook of pathology.

It is sometimes said that these pathologies are independent of natural aging, and one argument used is that if someone dies of a specific cause, such as a heart attack, many of the changes just mentioned may be insignificant. In such case, the death certificate may cite a specific cause of death. Nevertheless, any clinician—and especially a geriatrician—knows very well that if one pathology in an old person is successfully treated, another is likely to develop, and so on. In other words, there is a degree of synchrony, but by no means exact synchrony, in the appearance of age-associated pathologies. The fundamental point is that the external changes that quickly reveal to any observer the approximate age of an individual, are accompanied by internal changes that effect almost every organ system. Without doubt there are a multiplicity of changes in molecules, cells, tissues, and organs when senescence sets in. Aging is multicausal.

How has the medical establishment responded to this complex situation? It has produced specialists who become experts in one particular field. If one scrutinises the whole field of biomedicine, one sees that that broadly speaking there are two classes of individuals. First, there are those whose remit is to diagnose and then treat a particular disease, according to the best available medical practice. Second, there are those who are carrying out research to improve both diagnosis and treatment, or to develop preventative measures.

This can be illustrated by the example of the age-associated cancers known as carcinomas. Diagnosis may be in several stages: suspicion, the removal of tissue (a biopsy) for examination by an appropriate pathologist, and the use of X-rays and scanning devices. The examination of all the results is by an oncologist, who also advises the patient on the treatments recommended, and then the decision on how best to proceed. That is one part of the medical involvement. The other part is ongoing research on cancer, carried on in specialised institutes around the world or in other laboratories, commonly by teams of clinical and non-clinical scientists. It involves the most advanced procedures of cell biology, molecular biology and biotechnology. There are many journals devoted entirely to publishing the results of ongoing cancer research. The research may provide improvements in diagnosis and treatment; it may involve a search for the "magic bullet" which will target malignant cells in the body; it may involve the analysis of the steps involved in the change from a normal cell to a cancer cell. There are huge congresses devoted entirely to the problem of cancer, which are attended by specialists in this particular disease. That is only one fraction of biomedical research. There is similar specialisation in dementias and Alzheimer's disease, in coronary disease, in haematology, in endocrinology, in renal disease, in osteoporosis and osteoarthritis, in immunology, in vision and hearing, and much else, all related in one way or another to the better understanding and treatment of all the age-associated diseases that exist. The number of scientists and clinicians involved is enormous, and the total expense world-wide is phenomenal. Those who study aging itself often complain that in comparison to the amount spent on age-associated diseases, that spent on aging research is miniscule. That is true, nevertheless, in a world of specialisation, biomedical research scientists become expert and knowledgeable in only a tiny fraction of one aging process, that is, in one age-related disease. To put it another way, to understand the whole set of events that occur during aging, one has to abandon specialisation and take a broad view of all the changes that occur during aging. This is, in effect, an impossible task. The best that a biogerontologist can do is to be aware of the complexity of the changes occurring during aging, and if possible to persuade the clinical specialist to take note of the fundamental causes of aging. In this way better understanding and earlier diagnosis could be achieved.

With regard to anti-aging medicine, the arrogance lies in the fact that the movement claims that it can do better, in a short space of time, than all the combined biomedical research on age-associated pathologies. They maintain that they will soon eliminate cardiovascular disease, dementias, cancer, and all the other deleterious events that have been mentioned. They will, in effect, abolish all those changes that occur during aging and which limit lifespan. This is what they claim, and they are also claiming that they will achieve much more than all those research scientists around the world who are devoting themselves to one part of the whole set of those biological changes that are documented in thousands of specialist journals and books.

The Evolutionary Origins of Aging

To understand aging, one must understand its evolutionary origins. Apart from a few primitive animals such as coelenterates, all animals are characterised by somatic aging. As Weissman first pointed out, the germ cells must be potentially immortal if a species is to survive, but the soma survives for only a finite length of time. Since simple animals such as nematodes have a clearly defined lifespan, it is not surprising that all those taxonomic groups which exhibit greater complexity in their body structures also exhibit aging. There is no mystery in the fact that all animals age. Animals must survive to reproduce, but it is counterproductive to invest in the maintenance of the body, or soma, after reproduction. The reasons for a life history strategy that includes aging have been discussed at length (e.g. Kirkwood and Holliday 1979; Holliday 1995; Kirkwood and Austad 2000).

Nematodes and also many insects have adult bodies made up of post-mitotic cells, and all of these are quite short-lived. I have argued elsewhere that any non-dividing cell cannot be expected to survive indefinitely (Holliday 1995), and I will return to this crucial fact later on. All vertebrates exhibit aging, but some have argued that large reptiles and fish which keep growing during their adult life do not age in the same way as vertebrates with adult bodies of constant size. That may well be so, but these large animals have not been studied in any depth. I do not think anyone would claim that they survive indefinitely, but they may well have gradual senescence (Finch 1990).

Warm blooded mammals and birds have clearly defined lifespans, and with regard to the claims made by the anti-aging movement, we can confine discussion to the aging of humans. The general anatomy of the body is entirely derived from our evolutionary forebears. There are a series of organ structures that change during senescence and aging. The heart is a very efficient pump, but it consists largely of non-dividing cells, with very limited replacement. The major arteries undergo a large number of changes, including the loss of elasticity of their walls and accumulation of plaques and lesions on the inner endothelium. There have been an enormous number of studies of the pathological changes that occur during the aging of the human vascular system. All these demonstrate that the anatomical design is not compatible with indefinite survival. It is the design that would be predicted from its evolutionary origins.

The same applies to the structure and anatomy of the human brain. There are vast numbers of interconnecting neurons, which are post-mitotic cells. Most experts believe that brain function, including memory, are based on specific neuronal circuits, which can survive for many decades. There may be disagreement about the number of cells in the brain that can divide, but there is no disagreement about the importance of non-dividing neurons. Many studies of the damaged brain show that it has very limited powers of repair and regeneration. There are many other components of the body that clearly have finite lifespan, including the lens and retina of the eye, collagen and elastin which become cross linked, or otherwise altered, the structure of bone joints, progressive changes in skin, and so on. All these features of the mammalian body are the result of many millions of years of evolution.

So how would one set about changing the body so that it can last as long as the claims made by protagonists of anti-aging medicine? One would have to completely change the anatomy and physiology of body components just mentioned. For example, to construct an immortal vascular system one would need two hearts and two sets of the major arteries. Then one could shut one down for complete repair, whilst the other continued its function. Normal life depends on the continual function of the brain. Within a living brain, how could one replace huge numbers of neurons that are gradually accumulating defects? How could one preserve the knowledge, experience and memory of a lifetime? The point is well made by considering what would be necessary for an eye transplant. All the thousands and thousands of axons which extend from the retina to the optic tectum in the brain, would have to be severed and replaced, but in such a way that the specificity of all the connections is perfectly maintained.

The human body is made up of dividing cells, and also non-dividing cells that have to "last a life time." It is certainly worth noting that the survival of the non-dividing cells in organisms such as a fruit-fly or a nematode is measured in days, and the non-dividing cells of a human being is measured in decades, which is indeed a huge difference. Yet to believe that non-dividing cells could live for a hundred decades or more is totally unrealistic. Cells can die from many causes: a dominant lethal mutation, loss of the active X chromosome, the accumulation of defective mitochondria, the precipitation of insoluble protein aggregates, the loss of essential membrane receptors, and so on. How could one possibly prevent not one, but all these changes?

The anti-aging movement is arrogant because it maintains that it can reverse what has evolved over millions of years. And it claims that it can do this by tinkering around the edges of vital functions: a few new stem cells here, some new molecules there, perhaps a transplant from self-tissue grown in the laboratory, activation of telomerase, and so on. de Grey (2006) lists "seven deadly things," which need to be reversed to prevent senescence, backed up by just three references (all his own). Is this real or imagined science? There is not much doubt that it is the latter, and demonstrates unequivocally that there is very little understanding of the realities of aging and senescence. In fact, the proposals made are largely based on a combination of ignorance and wish-fulfillment.

Modulating the Expectation of Life

The discovery of pathogenic bacteria and viruses, the introduction of good hygiene, the development of vaccines, the discovery of antibiotics have been some of the major contributors to the dramatic increase in human expectation of life in the last 100 years or so. To this can be added the gradual improvements in the treatments of disease and general health care, which have lead to even greater life expectancy. Some have said that there have been no successful interventions in aging itself, but this is not true. Elevated cholesterol increases the probability of heart failure, and this has lead to the development of treatments that reduce the level of cholesterol in the blood. Similarly, high blood pressure can cause a stroke, so there are now ways and means of reducing high blood pressure. The beneficial affects of aspirin in reducing the likelihood of blood clot formation are well known. The huge investment by the pharmaceutical industries, and the ongoing advances in biomedical research on age-associated diseases provide many other examples of successful health care of aged individuals. All these treatments lead to populations of longer lived individuals. It is quite another thing to believe that the current expectation of life in developed countries can be multiplied several times. At least we will be saved from discussion of all those social and demographic issues which would arise if the predictions of Dr Klatz and Dr de Grey and their supporters had any scientific or medical basis.

Conclusions

Over the centuries there has been much written about the possibility of human immortality or extreme longevity. This was done when very little was known about the biology of aging: speculations about life-extension gained the authors some notoriety, and sometimes some serious attention. The situation is quite different today; there is a vast amount of information about aging and age-associated disease, and the biological reasons for the evolution of aging have become apparent. There is now every reason to believe that the maximum survival time of human beings is determined by the evolved anatomical and physiological design of their bodies.

The views put about by those in the anti-aging movement are overbearingly arrogant, first, because they claim that they can be much more successful than the thousands of biomedical scientists who carry out research on age-associated diseases, and second, because they claim they can reverse millions of years of evolution in a very short space of time. Their predictions have little relationship to medicine and science. They are no more than a somewhat curious mixture of pseudo-science and wish-fulfillment. This mixture is manna to the media, and the gullibility of the public means that a huge and profitable industry of "anti-aging" potions and products has been generated. Regrettably, the futuristic scenarios that have been widely publicised also generate financial support for the further expansion and influence of the anti-aging movement.

CHALLENGE QUESTIONS

Should We Try to "Cure" Old Age?

1. Why is an aging population considered a social problem for many Western countries? Wouldn't a longer lifespan simply magnify that problem, or would living longer be a boon to national prospects?
2. Rae and colleagues promote large increases in funding, particularly from governments, for antiaging research and technology. Does that seem like a worthy investment? How would you feel about your tax dollars going to antiaging research?
3. What if antiaging medicine succeeds? Rae and colleagues note that it is impossible to know in advance "the full range of social impacts, positive and negative, of a dramatic increase in healthy human life span." What would you hypothesize to be the positive and negative impacts?
4. Holliday notes that "it is often hard to distinguish those in the antiaging movement whose aim is to generate commercial profit, and those who genuinely believe that its research will be successful." What might help us to make that distinction? How can we evaluate what constitutes real scientific progress in the area rather than ambitious marketing?
5. Why are people so eager to live longer? What is so hard about accepting the limits of the human lifespan?

Is There Common Ground?

The debate around antiaging science really involves two distinct questions: Is it possible to "cure" aging, and is it a good idea. These particular readings touch on both questions, but focus primarily on whether antiaging medicine is possible. Because Holliday thinks it is not, he does not much bother with the question of whether it would be a good idea—though it is clear he is negative on that as well. Ultimately, however, both sides are making different interpretations of scientific knowledge about aging. In doing so, both sides are actually subtly validating the value of scientific work to understand the aging process. As such, even if we cannot (or should not) cure aging, it is interesting to think about the outer limits of what we might learn about the aging process. We might even add a third question to the debate around antiaging science: what can we learn about the lifespan itself?

Suggested Readings

S. Arrison, *100 Plus: How the Coming Age of Longevity Will Change Everythings, From Careers and Relationships to Family and Faith* (Basic Books 2011)

A.V. Everitt, S.I.S. Rattan, D.G. Couteur, and R. Cabo (Eds.), *Calorie Restriction, Aging, and Longevity* (Springer 2010)

J.R. Fishman, R.H. Binstock, and M.A. Lambrix, "Anti-Aging Science: The Emergence, Maintenance, and Enhancement of a Discipline," *Journal of Aging Studies* (December 2008)

A. de Grey and M. Rae, *Ending Aging: The Rejuvenation Breakthroughs That Could Reverse Human Aging in Our Lifetime* (St. Martin's Press 2007)

R. Holliday, *Aging: The Paradox of Life—Why We Age* (Springer 2007)

J. Weiner, *Long for This World: The Strange Science of Immortality* (Ecco 2010)

I. Zs.-Nagy, "Is Consensus in Anti-Aging Medical Intervention an Elusive Expectation or a Realistic Goal?" *Archives of Gerontology and Geriatrics* (May–June 2009)

Contributors to This Volume

EDITOR

ANDREW M. GUEST is a developmental psychologist and faculty member in the department of social and behavioral sciences at the University of Portland. He has research experience investigating development in impoverished communities, studying culture in relation to social development during middle childhood, and evaluating the influence of extracurricular activities during adolescence. He also has experience working with programs focused on enhancing lifespan development for disadvantaged populations in the United States, Malawi, Mexico, and Angola. He received a B.A. from Kenyon College in psychology, an M.S. from Miami University in sports studies, and a M.A. and Ph.D. from the University of Chicago's Committee on Human Development.

AUTHORS

CRAIG A. ANDERSON is a Distinguished Professor of Liberal Arts and Sciences in the Department of Psychology at Iowa State University and author of the book *Violent Video Game Effects on Children and Adolescents.*

JEFFREY JENSEN ARNETT is a research professor in the department of psychology at Clark University. He has done extensive scholarly work on the concept of "emerging adulthood" as a lifespan stage between adolescence and adulthood, including publishing a book titled *Emerging Adulthood: The Winding Road from the Late Teens Through the Twenties.*

JULIE E. ARTIS is a faculty member in the sociology department at DePaul University. She studies motherhood, family, and law.

EUGENE BERESIN is professor of psychiatry at Harvard Medical School, director of the Child and Adolescent Psychiatry Residency Training Program at Massachusetts General Hospital, and director of the Center for Mental Health and Media at Massachusetts General Hospital/Harvard Medical School.

PHYLLIDA BROWN is a writer based in the UK who has specialized in science journalism.

BARBARA A. BUTRICA is a labor economist and Senior Research Associate at The Urban Institute who has done a great deal of research about retirement-related issues.

BRYAN CAPLAN is a professor of economics at George Mason University, a blogger at EconLog, and author of the book "Selfish Reasons to Have More Kids."

PHILIPPE CHASSY is a psychologist who has done research on cognition at institutions including the University of Toulouse and University Hospital Tuebingen.

THE CHILD & ADOLESCENT BIPOLAR FOUNDATION is a nonprofit mental health advocacy organization that works to improve "the lives of families raising children and teens living with bipolar disorder and related conditions."

AMY CHUA is a professor at Yale Law School and author of *Day of Empire, World on Fire: How Exporting Free Market Democracy Breeds Ethnic Hatred and Global Instability,* and *Battle Hymn of the Tiger Mother.*

TIM CLYDESDALE is a professor of sociology at the College of New Jersey and author of the book *The First Year Out: Understanding American Teens After High School.*

EDWARD T. COKELY was a postdoctoral research fellow at the Max Planck Institute for Human Development in Berlin, and now directs the Decision Science and Decision Engineering Laboratory as a faculty member in psychology at Michigan Tech University.

M. BRENT DONNELLAN is a faculty member in the Department of Psychology at Michigan State University. His research focuses on social and personality factors associated with transitions across the lifespan.

JACQUELYNNE S. ECCLES is the McKeachie-Pintrich Distinguished University Professor of Psychology and Education at the University of Michigan. She is a national expert on adolescent development, and a past president of the Society for Research on Adolescence.

PAUL EHRLICH is the Bing Professor of Population Studies in the department of Biological Sciences at Stanford University. He is an expert in population and natural resource issues, and is a prominent voice in concerns about global overpopulation.

LISE ELIOT is a neuroscientist at the Chicago Medical School of Rosalind Franklin University and author of the book *Pink Brain, Blue Brain: How Small Differences Grow Into Troublesome Gaps—And What We Can Do About It.*

K. ANDERS ERICSSON is the Conradi Eminent Scholar of Psychology at Florida State University, a Fellow of the American Psychological Association, and served as coeditor of *The Cambridge Handbook of Expertise and Expert Performance.*

MARCUS FELDMAN is a professor of biological sciences at Stanford University, with primary research focusing on the interaction of biological and cultural evolution.

JOSHUA D. FOSTER is a social psychologist and faculty member at the University of South Alabama. His research focuses on the self, personality, and relationships.

HOWARD GARDNER is professor of cognition and education at the Harvard Graduate School of Education and founder of *Project Zero*, a research group to aid development of personalized curriculum designed for multiple intelligences (the theory Gardner is most known for). Winner of numerous honors in the fields of education and psychology, Garner is also author of more than 20 books.

FERNAND GOBET is professor of cognitive psychology and director of the Centre for the Study of Expertise at Brunel University, West London. He has published extensively on the psychology of expertise, language acquisition, and computational modeling.

JANICE E. GRAHAM is a medical anthropologist and Canada Research Chair in Bioethics at Dalhousie University in Halifax Nova Scotia. Her work takes an interdisciplinary approach to cultural, technical, and moral issues as related to health.

MICHAEL GURIAN an author of multiple books about gender and learning, is the founder of the Gurian Institute, which identifies its mission as "helping boys and girls reach their full potential by providing professional development that increases student achievement, teacher effectiveness, and parent involvement."

ELIZABETH HAMEL is associate director, public opinion and survey research for the Kaiser Family Foundation.

ANGEL L. HARRIS is on the faculty of Princeton University in the Department of Sociology. His research focuses on academic inequality.

JUDITH RICH HARRIS has psychology degrees from Brandeis and Harvard Universities and has authored several textbooks in developmental psychology, most notably *The Child and Infant and Child*. She writes extensively about child environments, parenting, and the nature-versus-nurture question.

LEO B. HENDRY is a professor of psychology at the University of Glamorgan in Cardiff, Wales, where he is also a founding member of the Lifespan Research Centre. He has done extensive research and writing about lifespan development in diverse international contexts.

ROBIN HOLLIDAY is molecular biologist, a fellow of the Australian Academy of Science, and the author of books including *Understanding Aging* and *Why We Age*.

KATHLEEN E. HULL is a faculty member in the department of sociology at the University of Minnesota, and author of *Same-Sex Marriage: The Cultural Politics of Love and Law*.

THE KAISER FAMILY FOUNDATION is a nonprofit foundation, which describes itself as "a non-partisan source of facts, information, and analysis for policymakers, the media, the health care community, and the public."

STUART L. KAPLAN is a practicing child psychiatrist with over 40 years of experience treating children, adolescents, and their families. He is a clinical professor of psychiatry in the Penn State College of Medicine and has been the director of Child and Adolescent Psychiatry and Director of Child Psychiatry Training at university medical schools.

KELLEY KING is a school administrator and staff member of the Gurian Institute, which identifies its mission as "helping boys and girls reach their full potential by providing professional development that increases student achievement, teacher effectiveness, and parent involvement."

MARION KLOEP is a professor in psychology and codirector of the Centre for Lifespan Research at the University of Glamorgan in Cardiff, Wales. Her main research interests are in adolescence, but she also investigates adulthood and old age.

LAWRENCE KUTNER is a cofounder of the Center for Mental Health and Media at Massachusetts General Hospital/Harvard Medical School, and executive director of the Jack Kent Cooke Foundation. He is also coauthor of the book "Grand Theft Childhood: The Surprising Truth About Violent Video Games and What Parents Can Do."

JOSEPH L. MAHONEY is a developmental psychologist and faculty member in the Department of Education at the University of California, Irvine. He was formerly on the psychology faculty at Yale, and edited the book *Organized Activities as Contexts of Development*.

MICHAEL MALES is a senior researcher for the Center on Juvenile and Criminal Justice and the online information service YouthFacts.org. He has also worked widely with youth and community programs, and taught sociology at the University of California.

GARY F. MARCUS is the director of the NYU Center for Child Language, and a Professor of Psychology at New York University. His books include *Kluge, The Birth of the Mind, The Algebraic Mind,* and *The Norton Psychology Reader.*

MARTY MARTINSON is a public health scholar and critical gerontologist examining the ethics and ideals of aging as they may exclude or devalue certain groups of older adults.

ANN MEIER is a faculty member in the department of sociology at the University of Minnesota who studies the form, character, and consequences of adolescent relationships.

JULIA MOSKIN is a writer and journalist for *The New York Times* who writes primarily about food and dining.

CHERYL K. OLSON is a cofounder of the Center for Mental Health and Media at Massachusetts General Hospital/Harvard Medical School. She is also coauthor of the book *Grand Theft Childhood: The Surprising Truth About Violent Video Games and What Parents Can Do.*

TIMOTHY ORTYL is in the department of sociology at the University of Minnesota and studies gender, sexuality, and nontraditional families.

RONALD C. PETERSEN is a medical doctor, researcher, and Director of the Mayo Clinic's Alzheimer's Disease Research Center. His scholarly work focuses on aging, mild cognitive impairment, dementia, Alzheimer's Disease, and neuroimaging.

MICHAEL J. PRIETULA is a professor at the Goizueta Business School at Emory University and has been a research scholar at the Institute for Human and Machine Cognition.

MICHAEL J. RAE is a researcher and science writer at the SENS ("Strategies for Engineered Negligible Senescence") Foundation, where he serves as a research assistant to prominent antiaging scientist Dr. Aubrey de Grey.

VICTORIA RIDEOUT is a vice president for media and public education at the Kaiser Family Foundation, where she directs the Program for the Study of Entertainment Media and Health.

KAREN RITCHIE is a neuropsychologist and epidemiologist. She is currently a Research Director with the French National Institute of Medical Health and Medical Research.

MICHAEL ROBB is the Early Learning Environment Program Manager at the Fred Rogers Center at Saint Vincent College. He studies the media and children's development, having previously worked in the television industry doing educational outreach for children's programming.

RICHARD W. ROBINS is a Professor of Psychology at the University of California, Davis. His research explores self and other perceptions.

ALVIN ROSENFELD graduated from Harvard Medical School and works in private practice doing child and adult psychiatry. He is also an associate psychiatrist at Massachusetts General Hospital and serves on the Board of Governors for Harvard Medical School's Center for Mental Health and Media.

MARKELLA RUTHERFORD is a faculty member in sociology at Wellesley College. She is the author of the book *Adult Supervision Required: Private Freedom and Public Constraints for Parents and Children*.

ROBIN W. SIMON is a faculty member in the sociology department at Florida State University. Among other research topics, she examines the relationship between gender, anger, and distressing emotions among adults.

LAURENCE STEINBERG the Distinguished University Professor and Laura H. Carnell Professor of Psychology at Temple University. He is a prodigious scholar of adolescence and author of several hundred articles along with the leading college textbook on adolescent development.

KATHY STEVENS is the executive director of the Gurian Institute, which identifies its mission as "helping boys and girls reach their full potential by providing professional development that increases student achievement, teacher effectiveness, and parent involvement."

KALI H. TRZESNIEWSKI is a faculty member in the Department of Psychology and director of the Life Span Development Lab at University of Western Ontario.

JEAN TWENGE is a faculty member in the department of psychology at San Diego State University. Her recent book, coauthored with W. Keith Campbell, is titled *The Narcissism Epidemic: Living in the Age of Entitlement*.

THE U.S. DEPARTMENT OF HEALTH AND HUMAN SERVICES (HHS) is the U.S. government's principal agency for protecting the health of all Americans and providing essential human services, especially for those who are least able to help themselves. Within HHS, the Surgeon General serves as America's Doctor by providing Americans the best scientific information available on how to improve their health and reduce the risk of illness and injury.

ELLEN WARTELLA is Sheik Hamad bin Khalifa Al-Thani Professor of Communication, Professor of Psychology and Professor of Human Development and Social Policy at Northwestern University. Formerly a Distinguished Professor of Psychology at the University of California, Riverside, she has researched and written widely about children and media, and serves on the Board of Trustees of Sesame Workshop among other national groups.

W. BRADFORD WILCOX is a faculty member in sociology and director of the National Marriage Project at the University of Virginia. He chaired a team of family scholars to produce the third edition of *Why Marriage Matters: Thirty Conclusions from the Social Sciences*.

DIANE WINSTON holds the Knight Chair in Media and Religion in the Annenberg School for Communication, University of Southern California and is the author of several books on American religion.

SHEILA R. ZEDLEWSKI Directed of The Urban Institute's Income and Benefits Policy Center for 20 years, and has been involved with research projects related to retirement policy.